Music in American Life

*A list of books in the series appears
at the end of this volume.*

The Stonemans

The Stonemans

An Appalachian Family and the Music That Shaped Their Lives

Ivan M. Tribe

University of Illinois Press
Urbana and Chicago

Publication of this book was supported in part by a
grant from the University of Rio Grande.

© 1993 by the Board of Trustees of the University of Illinois
Manufactured in the United States of America
1 2 3 4 5 C P 5 4 3 2 1

This book is printed on acid-free paper.

Library of Congress Cataloging-in-Publication Data

Tribe, Ivan M.
    The Stonemans : an Appalachian family and the music that shaped
their lives / Ivan M. Tribe.
        p.   cm. — (Music in American life)
    Includes bibliographical references and index.
    Discography: p.
    ISBN 0-252-01978-4 (alk. paper).—ISBN 0-252-06308-2
(pbk : alk. paper)
    1. Stoneman Family (Musical group) 2. Stoneman, Ernest V.
3. Country musicians—United States—Biography.   I. Title.
II.   Series.
ML421.S8T7 1993
781.642'092'2—dc20
[B]

                                                            92-22232
                                                                 CIP
                                                                  MN

To

Pattie Inez "Patsy" Stoneman Murphy

Her labors of love for her family
made it possible

Prayers and Pinto Beans

You could hear the music comin' from our house most any time,
With a fiddle tune ringing loud and clear;
The neighbors would be sittin' round the porch to see the sights,
But through it all you could hear our mama's prayers.

Music in our lives has meant so much to us,
It always helped to get us through it seems;
But I guess the most important part of all the things we had,
Were mama's prayers and daddy's pinto beans.

When times were gettin' hard and things were goin' bad,
We always called upon the ones we knew;
Mama fed our souls with the Bible and her prayers,
Then pinto beans and music saw us through.

We helped our daddy feed us with the music that we played,
And each of us tried to do our share;
But I think the things that helped us most and got us where we are,
Were the direct results of hearin' mama's prayers.

From the first I can remember till the time they passed away,
Mom and Dad were always by our side;
And I guess the most remembered things that went into our lives,
Were the prayers and pinto beans that they supplied.

—Patsy Stoneman
Used by permission of
Silverhill Music, BMI

Contents

Illustrations follow pages 74 and 164

Preface

My first acquaintance with the name Ernest Stoneman took place more than a quarter-century ago. At that point in my life, my musical interests had begun returning to those fascinating sounds I had listened to in my preadolescent pre–social conscious days that everyone called "hillbilly." Being of a history-minded nature, I learned that a whole generation of such musicians thrived before Ernest Tubb, Hank Snow, Roy Rogers, and Hank Williams. Magazine articles often spoke of Jimmie Rodgers, and I recalled Uncle Dave Macon in his last days on the Opry, as well as folks like Lew Childre and the McGee Brothers. We had two or three records of Vernon Dalhart around the house, but I soon came to realize they were just the tip of the iceberg. Remembering the Uncle Josh record my grandmother had brought me many years before, I went out to her farm home to inquire if she still had any old discs. She came up with about twenty or so old 78s, mostly on the Silvertone, Challenge, and Victor labels. There were more Uncle Josh discs and several by Vernon Dalhart, a Georgia Yellow Hammers, and one by Ernest Stoneman of "The Poor Tramp"/"Fate of Talmadge Osborne." As I played them the latter quickly became my favorite, and I wondered who this man was who sang such a crisp, clear vocal accompanied by his own guitar. Within a few months I read an article on the Autoharp in the *New York Folklore Quarterly* and read the now famous "Hillbilly Issue" of *The Journal of American Folklore*. Both contained brief mentions of Stoneman. About the same time, I went to Cincinnati with my cousin and another friend and we visited Jimmie Skinner's record store. I could easily have bought every disc in the place, but I only had about ten dollars. My cousin wanted "Orange Blossom Special" so I bought it on a 45 by the Stanley Brothers and two fairly new Starday albums by Ernest Stoneman and the Stoneman Family. The backliner provided a brief biography which proved fascinating and managed to raise more questions than it answered.

In the early part of 1967, I was walking through my parents' home (I had recently married but did not yet own a TV) on a Saturday afternoon when the Stonemans suddenly appeared on the television screen. A few minutes later "Pop," as they called him, began singing "The Poor Tramp" and my own father, who almost never sang, joined in on the chorus. I explained to him that the old man on the screen was the same guy who sang on the record some forty years earlier, but it certainly did not excite him nearly as much as it did me. By this time I had bought tapes of 78s from people like Robert Nobley and David Freeman and hoped someday that the Stoneman Family might play in our neighborhood. But they didn't, and Pop Stoneman passed away in 1968 without my having had the opportunity to see him. I finally got to see the rest of the Stoneman Family at a bluegrass festival at New Tripoli, Pennsylvania, on August 9, 1970. While impressed by Donna's sweetness and beauty, Roni's banjo and comedy, and Patsy's reverence for her father, I wasn't captivated all that much by most of the material they performed. I bought one of their picture books. Other than that my main recollection of the event was of an elderly man who hobbled up to Donna while she stood behind their record table, stuck his face about three inches from her nose, and said, "You know, I reckon you're just about the prettiest little thing I ever did see." Donna smiled and said, "Thank you."

That fall I went to the other end of the state to work on a doctorate in history. As the years went by, I attended festivals and began to write some pieces for *Bluegrass Unlimited* about musicians who seemed significant but underrepresented in terms of printed material on their careers. I also contributed a couple of pieces to *Old Time Music* and a pair of more scholarly essays to the *J E M F Quarterly*. Shortly after going to Toledo, I met John Morris, who had started a record company and began to do some old-time reissues. Through the research and work on the aforementioned publications I had become acquainted with music researchers

such as Norm Cohen, Archie Green, Doug Green, Pete Kuykendall, Bill Malone, Charles Wolfe, and the other folks at *Bluegrass
Unlimited*. I saw the Stonemans a couple more times during the
seventies, but as they were not total unknowns there seemed little
that I could add to their story. In 1977 I did an article for the West
Virginia folklife journal, *Goldenseal*, which after the success of
Charles Wolfe's monograph *Tennessee Strings* became the foundation for a similar book on West Virginia music and musicians
called *Mountaineer Jamboree*. About the time I finished the rough
draft for that volume, I learned that the Stonemans were going to
play at a 1982 Labor Day weekend festival in Milton, West Virginia. A few months earlier I'd heard that Donna was coming
back with the family. Her return, I thought, would make a good
piece for *Bluegrass Unlimited*, and Pete Kuykendall concurred. The
result of that weekend appeared as "The Return of Donna Stoneman: First Lady of the Mandolin" in June 1983. More significantly,
it proved the beginning of a close friendship with the Stonemans,
particularly Donna and Patsy. The latter—I soon learned—was
the "mortar" who held the bricks of the Stoneman edifice together. Or at least she had occupied this role since "Daddy" died
in 1968.

Charles Wolfe suggested that I seriously consider a book-length
Stoneman biography. Patsy had entertained some earlier hopes
that a mass-market volume with the appeal of *Coal Miner's Daughter* might be possible and had amassed a sizable collection of papers with this goal in mind. By the spring of 1985 she decided that
a more scholarly approach might be preferable and I agreed to
work on it. The result has taken longer than either of us planned
and sometimes has been tedious and often interrupted by work
commitments at the University of Rio Grande. Nonetheless, I
greatly value the friendship and trust that Patsy, Donna, and the
others placed in me. I also appreciate the freedom they gave me as
I put their lives together. The Stoneman story provides an in-
depth look at a single family's experience through nearly seven
decades of country music history in both prosperity and hard
times. It does more, however, by showing something of the tra-
vails of Appalachian people in their struggle to adjust to the
changes wrought by industrialization, urbanization, migration,
and the vicissitudes of life in general.

Others who helped in various ways deserve a word of appreciation. I hope no one has been omitted, but if so it is unintentional. All the living Stonemans and their spouses, except for John and Billy, and including the now-deceased Dean, either volunteered or contributed information when requested. Former in-laws who contributed information include Richard Adams, Bill Bassin, Bob Bean, the late Eugene Cox, Cecile Howard, and Bill Zimmerman. Former Stoneman musical associates Jack Clement, Peter "Zeke" Dawson, and David Dougherty each spent several hours with me, and Ed Ferris contributed his memories of the Blue Grass Champs and of his work as bassist with the Patsy Stoneman show. Scholars and collectors to whom I am indebted include Joe Bussard, Norm Cohen, David Crisp, David Freeman, Archie Green, Kaw Hendricks, Leon Kagarise, Pete Kuykendall, Kip Lornell, Frank Mare, the late Guthrie Meade, John Morris, W. K. McNeil, Eddie Nesbitt, Robert Nobley, Kinney Rorrer, Neil Rosenberg, Richard Spottswood, Eugene Wiggins, and Charles K. Wolfe. One of my undergraduate advisees, Billy Joe Adkins, introduced me to his father, Doug Adkins, who had been a regular patron at the Ozarks in D.C. when the Blue Grass Champs played there. Oscar Hall and Bobby Patterson helped out in the Galax area and introduced me to Rosa Cox. Glenn Stoneman provided material on his father, George Stoneman, and Kent Stoneman helped unweave some of the still-unraveled Stoneman genealogy. Stella Stoneman Rutledge supplied a cousin's perspective. The late Kahle Brewer and his wife, Edna, provided details about their musical association with Ernest Stoneman, as did Walter Couch of North Wilkesboro, North Carolina. The entire manuscript benefited from careful readings by the aforementioned Drs. Cohen and Wiggins, who made many useful suggestions for improvement of the text.

Loyal Jones and the Berea College Appalachian Studies Fellowship program provided some financial support. The National Endowment for the Humanities gave me an opportunity to study "The Family in History" with Professor Maris Vinovskis at the University of Michigan. Bill Shurk at the Popular Culture Music Library at Bowling Green State University opened his facilities to me. Bob Pinson, Ronnie Pugh, and John Rumble at the Country Music Foundation Library and Media Center, the staff of the

Galax, Virginia, Public Library, and the staff at the courthouses in Hillsville and Independence, Virginia, all extended the proper courtesies. In addition to all the other help they provided, Patsy and Murph helped me stretch my budget on more than one occasion by putting their spare bedroom at my disposal, along with a place at their table.

Closer to home, Dr. Paul Hayes, president of the University of Rio Grande, provided his encouragement, warning—correctly as events evolved—that biography was more difficult than narrative history. He also helped with financial support. Vice-presidents Ray Boggs and Clyde Evans gave encouragement, as did secretary Debbie McGuire of the School of Liberal Arts and faculty colleagues Linda Bauer, Marcella Biro-Barton, and Donna Dixon. Former students Mrs. Lori Billings and Mrs. Donna Thompson always sustained my spirits with their heart and humor. The latter's grandmother, Mrs. Margaret Pasquale, a Stoneman fan of some years' standing, reported regularly on Roni's appearances on TNN and "Hee Haw," pointing out some current developments that would otherwise have escaped my attention. Neil and Marie Dickson and Lester and Ruth Young helped in a variety of ways, Mrs. Karen Starkey put the entire manuscript on computer disc, and Dr. Judith McCulloh of the University of Illinois Press kept pressing me onward. Rich and Kelly Griffith helped with proofreading on the final copy. On the homefront, nephew B. R. Robinson and Deanna Tribe were there too. They have all earned my gratitude. But again, those to whom I am most indebted are Donna, Patsy, and Veronica Stoneman, together with John Murphy, Jr. More than anyone else, their caring made it possible.

Cast of Characters

Ernest Van Stoneman (1893–1968)   Country music pioneer and family head.

Hattie Frost Stoneman (1900–1976)   His wife; also a musician.

His Children

Eddie Lewis Stoneman (b. 1920)   Oldest son; played banjo, fiddle, and electric guitar; married *Katherine Copeland* (d. 1987).

Irma Grace Stoneman (b. 1921)   Eldest daughter; married (1) *Jack Jewell* (divorced); married (2) *George Jewell* (divorced); married (3) *James Dugan* (deceased).

John Catron Stoneman (b. 1923)   Second son; seldom played music; married *Bonnie Deeta Yeary.*

Pattie Inez "Patsy" Stoneman (b. 1925)   Principal leader of musical group after father's death; plays guitar and Autoharp. Married (1) *Charles Streeks* (divorced); married (2) *R. H. Cain* (divorced); married (3) *Donald Dixon* (widowed); married (4) *John J. Murphy, Jr.*

Joseph William Stoneman (1926–90)   Vocalist, guitarist, and banjo picker. Disabled World War II veteran. Married *Barbara Brooks.*

Anna (or Annie) Juanita Stoneman (1927–32)   Died young.

Jack Monroe Stoneman (1929–92)   Bass player; married (1) *Jean Todd James* (divorced); married (2) *Nola Story* (divorced).

Gene Austin Stoneman (b. 1930)   Guitarist and vocalist; married *Peggy Edelen.*

Dean Clark Stoneman (1930–89)   Mandolinist; married *Faye Casper.*

Calvin Scott Stoneman (1932–73)   Superb fiddler and proficient on other instruments; teacher of others; married (1) *Cecile Phipps* (divorced); married (2) *Paula Brogan* (divorced); married (3) *Ann ???* (divorced); married (4) *Mary Madison.*

Donna Laverne Stoneman (b. 1934)   Mandolinist and evangelist; married *Robert Bean* (divorced). Bean managed group until 1977.

Oscar James Stoneman (b. 1937)   Bass player and vocalist; married (1) *Peggy Brain,* Dobroist (divorced); married (2) *Mary Grubb Urich.*

Rita (or Reta) Vivian Stoneman (1937–37)   Died young.

Veronica Loretta "Roni" Stoneman (b. 1938)   Banjoist, vocalist, and comedian; married (1) *Eugene Cox* (divorced and deceased); married (2) *George Hemrick* (divorced); married (3) *Richard Adams* (divorced); married (4) *William Zimmerman* (divorced); married (5) *Larry Corya* (divorced).

Van Haden Stoneman (b. 1940)   Guitarist, banjoist, and vocalist; married *Helen Alvey.* Sons *Van, Jr.,* and *Randy* also in music.

His Ancestors

James Stoneman (1735–1829)   First Stoneman to settle in Blue Ridge, either descended from a kidnapped indentured servant or one himself. Married *Sarah Freeman* (1751–1844).

"Quaker" John Stoneman (1792–1874)   Son of James; prosperous Blue Ridge farmer; disowned sons; married *Elizabeth Hickman* (1792–1886).

Martin Stoneman (1812–83)   Son of Quaker John; known for big appetite; married *Eliza Lundy* (1820–1900).

Elisha Stoneman (1849–1934)   Son of Martin and father of Ernest; married (1) *Lauretta Montgomery* (1851–88); married (2) *Rebecca*

Bowers (1868–96), mother of *Ernest, Ingram Boyd* (1894–1973), and *Talmer* (1896–1916); married (3) *Susan Bowers Wells* (1880–19??); legally separated 1913.

Stephen Drake Stoneman (1861–1944)   Brother of Elisha and uncle of Ernest. Married *Lydia Bowers;* father of *Emory Burton* (1881–1956) fiddler, *George W.* (1882–1966) banjoist, *Bertha (Hawks)* (1886–1983), *Myrtle (Hawks)* (1894–1986), all close to Ernest as playmates, musical associates, and song sources.

His In-laws

John William "Bill" Frost (1866–1952)   Father of Hattie and an old-time fiddler and instrument maker; married (2) *Martha Ann "Pattie" Melton*, a descendant of *Greenbury "Green" Leonard*, legendary nineteenth-century Grayson and Carroll County fiddler.

Bolen Frost (1907–67)   Brother-in-law of Ernest and brother of Hattie; old-time banjo picker.

Irma Frost (1907–64)   Twin of Bolen; known as "Aunt Jack" to Stoneman children; musical associate of Ernest; died in tragic kitchen fire.

Alex "Uncle Eck" Dunford (1878–1953)   Old-time fiddler, guitarist, vocalist, and storyteller; kin to Frosts through marriage to *Callie Frost* (1889–1921). Musical associate of Ernest and after his departure from Galax of the Ward Family.

His Musical Associates

Lee Kahle Brewer (1904–89)   Fiddler with Dixie Mountaineers from 1926 to 1928; wife *Edna* (b. 1907) also a singer with group.

Herbert and *Earl Sweet*   Fiddler and banjoist from near Damascus, Virginia; recorded with Ernest in 1928.

Frank (1888–1945) and *Oscar Jenkins*   Fiddle-banjo father-son team from Dobson, North Carolina. With Ernest in 1929 and sometimes thereafter for several years.

Tom Leonard and *Walter Mooney* (1876–1965) Vocalists with Dixie Mountaineers.

Iver Edwards Musician with Stoneman group at Bristol in 1927.

Willie Stoneman (1907–67) Vocalist with Stoneman group in 1928; son of George Stoneman by first wife.

Fields and *Sampson Ward* Members of Galax's musical Ward Family. Did a record session with Ernest in 1929 as Grayson County Railsplitters.

Emmett Lundy (1864–19??) Fiddler in 1925.

Joseph Samuels New York studio fiddler in one session.

His Children's Musical Associates

Billy Barton (*a.k.a. Johnny Grimes*) Songwriter and musician for whom Donna and Jimmy worked as band members, 1954–55; later produced their Gulf Reef Records and secured guest spot on the Opry in 1962.

Jimmy Case Early guitar player with Blue Grass Champs; later a booking agent in Nashville.

Porter Church (b. 1934) Banjo picker with Blue Grass Champs, Patsy Stoneman, Red Allen, and others.

Don Owens (d. 1963) Deejay and emcee of Stoneman TV shows in Washington; produced their Blue Ridge disc; killed in auto crash.

Lew Childre (*a.k.a. Lew Houston*) Dobro player for Blue Grass Champs; reportedly killed in auto crash.

Jerry Monday Dobro player, drummer, and vocalist with Stonemans in Nashville, 1966–68 and 1971.

Cathy Manzer Songwriter and musician with Stonemans, 1971–72; also a musical partner of Donna in late 1970s.

Jack Clement (b. 1932) Manager and record producer for Stonemans, 1964–70.

Buck White Mandolinist with Stonemans, 1973.

David Dougherty   Banjo player with Stonemans, 1972–77.

Johnny Bellar   Dobro player with Stonemans, 1973–84.

Eddie Mueller   Banjo player with Stonemans, 1977–81.

Chuck Holcomb   Banjo player with Stonemans, 1981–84.

Noboru Moreshige   Fiddler with Stonemans, 1973–74.

Mitch Fuston   Fiddler with Stonemans, 1981.

Roland White   Mandolinist with Stonemans off and on in late 1970s; also an associate with Scott in the Kentucky Colonels; member of several name bluegrass bands.

1

Galax

August 1985

If Nashville is the contemporary country-music capital, the old-time mountain string bands and vocalists that perhaps comprise its principal component have their center in Galax, Virginia. Located in the mountainous southwestern portion of the Old Dominion, Galax spends most of the year as a relatively sedate industrial and commercial town of some seven thousand five hundred inhabitants. Each year during the second week of August, however, its size mushrooms. Hundreds of musicians and thousands of fans gather in Felts Park for the annual Old Fiddler's Convention sponsored by the local Moose Lodge. As 1985 would be the fiftieth year of the event, it constituted an especially significant milestone.

Another thing made the 1985 convention unusual, too. Ordinarily only amateurs and semiprofessionals competing on stage for prize money and recognition entertained there, but, for 1985 the arrangements committee contracted with the Nashville-based Stoneman Family to pick and sing. This act—although perhaps not publicized as well as it could have been—represented something of a tribute to the man who, some six decades earlier, had done the most to put Galax on the musical map. While he neither created the Galax sound nor apparently went to more than one of its fiddler's conventions, the late Ernest "Pop" Stoneman had in a sense been as much the father of Galax's musical eminence as he had been the father of the five (and on a few numbers, eight) musicians who made up the Stoneman Family.

The Stonemans open the show on Wednesday evening. The audience numbers several hundred and increases steadily during the group's fifty-minute performance. Accustomed to working with electric pickups on their instruments and using their own sound system, the band is a little uneasy, but still thoroughly accomplished and professional. They begin with the western-style song "Cimmaron" from 1942, which gives them an opportunity to display their vocal harmonies and a sampling of their instrumental specialities. Roni, by far the best-known Stoneman in the 1980s because of regular television exposure on "Hee Haw," takes a banjo break and breaks into the broad grin showing the wide space between her front teeth. This summer is the first time since early 1971 that Roni has worked regularly with the family group, and they are obviously quite pleased, although occasionally caught off guard by her quick wit and sharp tongue.[1]

One by one, the other Stonemans receive an opportunity to share a little of the spotlight. Donna, the petite and attractive mandolin picker, smiles as sweetly as ever and dances with a grace and enthusiasm, holding the electric pickup cord of her mandolin (that goes nowhere on this occasion) out of the way of her flashing feet. She, too, has spent some time away from the group and while she has been back with them for more than three years, it is the first time many fans have seen her in action since her return. Because she is radiating a spirit of wholesomeness and eternal youth, it seems hard to believe that Donna has been singing and dancing on stage longer than most people would guess she has been alive. On the second song of the set, bass-fiddle player Jimmy Stoneman takes the vocal lead. His song, "The Poor Tramp Has to Live," was a popular number for Ernest back in 1927. Shy by nature and seemingly uncomfortable off stage—a situation probably caused in part by life-long health problems—Jimmy appears at ease only when playing the bass or contributing his vocals, both of which he renders with class and distinction.

Coming to the forefront more slowly than the others are the two who have in many ways been the mainstays of the group. Van, the youngest Stoneman in age but not in appearance, plays both rhythm and lead guitar (depending on the song), with occasional switches to clawhammer banjo, sings much of the lead, and does the yeoman's share of the emcee work. Van packs considerable physical weight and sports a full beard that obscures his relative youthfulness. Although often overshadowed on stage by his more colorful sisters, his musical role in the group is one that is hard to overstate. Finally, there is Patsy Stoneman, who above all the others bears the torch of tradition in the band. Offstage, Patsy is the backbone and spokeswoman of the group, the leader, the one to whom the others look for guidance, support, and advice. Onstage, she plays rhythm guitar, does Autoharp numbers, and contributes some featured vocals. As one becomes acquainted with Patsy Stoneman, one comes to admire her tremendously. She is a survivor who has borne an unduly heavy share of personal and professional burdens; and while a touch of bitterness shows through, she generally faces the world with a cheerful countenance that is in itself remarkable.

After "The Poor Tramp," the show moves along briskly. Van introduces Donna, who showcases her mandolin composition "The Girl from Galax," recorded back in 1962. Donna explains that the title is a reference to "Mommy," Hattie Frost Stoneman, a country-music pioneer of considerable renown in her own right. Her number reveals a high degree of both originality and talent, which shows why she has become known as the "First Lady of Mandolin" and once was called the "best in the world" by no less a picker than the late Jethro Burns. While Roni takes a banjo break, Donna dances with customary fervor before her fingers resume their dexterity on the neck of her Gibson F5. Roni then takes center stage for several minutes. Her slightly risqué comedy grabs the attention of the entire audience, "When you're hot, you're hot; when you're not, you can't give it away!" The crowd roars with laughter, and Donna Stoneman, who does evangelistic work and ministers the Gospel as often as possible, looks a little embarrassed. Roni then goes into a rousing version of "Foggy Mountain Breakdown" while Donna goes into some of her faster dance steps. The two sisters then do "Theme from Deliverance," followed by Roni, illustrating her vocal talents on an old bluegrass favorite, "Ruby, Are You Mad at Your Man."

As Roni retires from center stage, Patsy dons her Autoharp to sing "The Whip-poor-will Song," one of the old numbers that Pop's musical associate Uncle Eck Dunford recorded with him in 1927. She then picks out her dad's instrumental favorite, "Stoney's Waltz," which, she points out, is anything but a waltz. Van takes a clawhammer banjo in hand and Donna temporarily switches to rhythm guitar. The Stonemans then perform their arrangement of "The Sinking of the Titanic," a ballad that provided Pop with his original hit record some six decades earlier. The newer styling has a little more gusto and somewhat less of the sense of dour tragedy, but it stands as creditable old-time music. Patsy then brings out her Jew's harp and she and Van exchange leads on an instrumental rendition of "Little Liza Jane." The gospel song of the set is a well-executed version of the Paul Buskirk–Willie Nelson standard "Family Bible," with Donna playing some excellent mandolin solos. For a closing number, "Jimmy's Thing" is a bass-fiddle feature instrumental that also lets Donna, Roni, and Van get in some fine breaks. The audience is warm and receptive throughout but does not go wild. A Galax audience is there to listen and does so; it is not there to engage in hand clapping, sing-alongs, or to make a lot of noise. It is a throng of sober adults with their emotions under control. After all, encores are not really part of the way things are done in Galax. Since most performers are also contestants, one expects you to do your thing and make way for whoever is next.

A better indication of the Stoneman reception than applause meters could be gained by watching the enthusiasm of those who gather and patiently wait for autographs or to buy cassettes, pictures, albums, T-shirts, or caps. Van's son and Roni's husband are there to help with the distribution of material, and many fans add that they are distant cousins from the area. The Galax vicinity still contains numerous souls bearing such surnames as Frost, Melton, Lineberry, Lundy, and, of course, Stoneman. One couple recalls being in grade school at Pine Ridge with the oldest Stoneman boy, Eddie, now sixty-five and down from his Forestville, Maryland, home to watch his younger siblings in action and later join them on stage for a number. Some wish to see close up for themselves whether Roni is really as homely as her "Hee Haw" characterization, "Ida Lee Nagger" (they tend to think she is not), or whether Donna is as beautiful as they recalled her as being (they tend to think that she is indeed). Others wish to share religious experiences with Donna. She autographs one-page tracts printed on both sides, having a separate one for children, and generally remains near, but somewhat apart, from the more commercial aspects of post–stage show activity.

After an hour or so, the crowding fans thin out somewhat, although Roni and Donna are still attracting them. A couple wearing a pair of outrageous caps bearing the respective captions "Old Fart" and "Old Fart's Wife" happen along. Roni, ever the ham, dons the latter cap and dashes off to the sidelines to clog a bit as the fiddling on stage provides appropriate instrumentation. Donna again seems somewhat embarrassed by this display of worldliness and possibly engages in a brief silent prayer that might go something like, "Lord, I love my sister with all my heart, but I do wish she'd stop this." A few minutes later, they engage in a few words as Roni complains about having to autograph so many tracts. Still later, Roni, fearful that she has hurt Donna's feelings, takes up a collection to help pay for printing the tracts (Donna never asks for money to support her evangelistic endeavors); it nets seventeen dollars. Needless to say, family harmony returns quickly. When sufficient darkness has set in, the Stonemans prepare to do their brief second appearance. Preceded by a twelve-minute audio-slide presentation giving the historical background on Pop and the family's musical heritage, they perform a couple of quick numbers, "Black Mountain Rag" and "Orange Blossom Special." Roni promises that she will even sign autographs on Donna's tracts. When a pair of children later approach her with tracts in hand, she temporarily feigns insanity and screams, but does sign the papers. Later she offers her chair to older brother Dean, whose health is not too good and who looks tired. Dean, ever the gentleman, tells Roni to keep her seat. Finally, Roni, always the master of psychology, gets Dean to sit down. She tells him that if he does not take her chair, she will start cussing him out in front of everyone and embarrass Donna. An hour or so later, the Stonemans do their final brief performance of the evening. This time the extended family group consisting of oldest brother Eddie and the Stoneman twins—Dean and Gene—join them. Eddie fiddles a respectable version of "Old Joe Clark" and Dean sings his favorite, "Mule Skinner Blues." Joking now about their poverty-stricken childhood, Roni tells about the time she fell into the outhouse and contends that on another occasion when Van was small, he swallowed a dime and that she followed him for three days with a stick. She then closes with the bluegrass banjo favorite "Dear Old Dixie." Somewhat ironically, a fellow near the stage who had yelled a resounding "no" when the emcee asked if the crowd wanted to hear a few more Stoneman numbers, applauds and cheers throughout the three-song set.

The next day, the Stonemans occupy themselves with a variety of activities involving kinfolk or old friends. Unfortunately, there are more of these than there are hours in the day and Patsy worries about hurting the feelings of some of them. Furthermore, newsmen from WDBJ-TV Roanoke are scheduled for interviews at 2:30 P.M. Roni takes daughter Barbara and husband Bill to show them the homeplace of their maternal grandparents, where they had numerous summer visits as children, and also the house where their parents had lived prior to their personal financial collapse in 1931–32. They also visit a few more relatives along the way.

Eddie, Patsy, and Donna participate in an all-too-brief nostalgic trip into the Stoneman past. Kahle Brewer and his wife, Edna, the last surviving members of the classic Stoneman string band of the 1926–28 period reside some four miles from Galax. Brewer was one of the great string-band fiddlers of the era, and next to Ernest Stoneman himself, the key figure in the band. Edna went to Bristol with them for a Victor recording session and helped sing on the chorus of several sacred songs. Only Eddie, eight years old when Brewer left the band, has direct recollections of Kahle and remembers sitting at his feet during practice sessions. Patsy was an infant at the time and Donna wasn't born until some years later, but they all knew who Kahle Brewer was and the role he played in the Stonemans' musical development. Kahle brags about what a great fiddler Grandpa Frost was and Eddie agrees, adding Kahle Brewer to the list. Edna is a bit disappointed that Roni isn't there. Since the Brewers see Roni on television weekly, she is the visual link between the Stoneman past and present. Nonetheless, Edna and Donna hit it off well together. The quintet poses for some pictures and the Stonemans unsuccessfully try to coax Kahle to strike a few licks on his fiddle, Donna even going so far as to play a little herself. The visit is indeed memorable, but the

Stonemans have to get back to Galax for the television interview. Sadly, they all wave good-bye.

Back in Galax, the TV newsmen gather in the parking lot of the Midtowner Motel. Roni dons her Ida Lee Nagger costume, which consists of a battered old housecoat and a wig with rags tied on it. She picks up a doll baby, suddenly jumps in front of the cameras, caresses the doll, and yells, "I told Laverne to be careful; that I was a desirable womern!" Patsy gives a short résumé of the Stoneman musical heritage and chats with the announcer. Meanwhile, a host of kinfolk have again gathered to say howdy, most notably ninety-one-year-old Myrtle Stoneman Hawks. This remarkable lady is a first cousin of Ernest and anonymously appears in one of the most noted photographs in the annals of old-time music. She is the young girl in front row center on the cover of *The New Lost City Ramblers Song Book*. Unfortunately, her mind has retreated backwards to about 1930 and she rambles back in time, talking about Uncle Elisha and her brother and her sister-in-law Lilly somewhat incoherently. Patsy and Donna give their best regards and chat with her daughters. Donna privately expresses some dismay that no real honor has been bestowed on "Daddy," either by the city of Galax or the convention officials. Couldn't they name a street after him or erect signs at the city limits proclaiming this as the original home of Ernest "Pop" Stoneman, she inquires?

Patsy urges patience, but deep down, all the Stonemans know that Galax has been represented by a two-sided situation in their life. On one hand Galax was the ancestral home whence both their genetic and musical roots sprouted. It was the locale of their revered grandparents' farm and the burial place of many ancestors and kinfolk, including two sisters who died in childhood. On the other hand, Galax was also the place that had treated Ernest Stoneman so royally as a hometown hero and had extended liberal financial credit when he was a recording star in 1926, 1927, and 1928. But when the bottom dropped out in the Great Depression, some of these "fair-weather friends" became nasty creditors, repossessed many of his material properties—including his home—and literally tossed him, his wife, and nine kids into the street during 1931 and 1932. Ernest and Hattie Stoneman paid a heavy price for overextended finances, and Ernest's humorous look at hard times recorded in 1925, "All I Got's Gone," became an ironic portent. Not surprisingly, he left Galax and decided to take his chances in the Washington, D.C., area. He seldom returned. He brought the wife and kids to visit her parents and perhaps visit briefly with his own kin. In 1956, he and one of his groups, the Little Pebbles, won the band contest at the convention and a decade later he and Hattie had tombstones erected for the children who had died in the thirties. However, he requested that he not be buried there. The bitter memories of 1932 left a "wound that time could not erase." Perhaps if he had lived until 1985, when the Stonemans were better received, his feelings would have changed. Who knows?

By six o'clock the Stonemans are back in Felts Park to do their second day of performing. Backstage, Roni makes jokes about herself and fellow banjo picker Raymond Fairchild not seeing eye to eye (both have a visual problem). Fortunately, the sound quality is better than it was the first night. They open with "Mule Skinner Blues" and go on through their set, repeating some numbers from Wednesday but doing some different ones, too, including the perennial favorite, "Rocky Top," Roni's partly recomposed (to a Galax setting) "Old Dogs, Children, and Watermelon Wine," and Donna's inspired rendition of the old Martha Carson spiritual "Satisfied." Although not part of their show as such, young Van Stoneman, Jr., is honored by being chosen to sing the national anthem just before a new round of contestants takes the stage.

Life goes on for the Stonemans and so, too, does the Galax Old Fiddler's Convention. On Friday the Stonemans returned to North Carolina, where they continued a summerlong engagement at the Cherokee Entertainment Center. Later that month they made an appearance in Arkansas and returned to their Nashville base. After two more days of competition, the fiftieth convention was history and the cleanup process was followed by the beginning of new planning for the 1986 event at Galax. Somewhere, one might hope, the spirits of Ernest, Hattie, and George Stoneman, together with those of Uncle Eck Dunford, Iver Edwards, Joe Hampton, Bolen and Irma Frost, Tommy Jarrell, Frank and Oscar Jenkins, Green Leonard, Emmett Lundy, Crockett and Wade Ward, and the other deceased creators of the Galax sound, smiled and approved of the proceedings. The hundreds of competitors—210 in old-time fiddle alone and a grand total of 1,285 contestants—together with the continuing professional careers of the Stoneman Family, represent the legacy of these Appalachian musicians from the hills of Carroll, Grayson, and Surrey counties to American and indeed world culture.

2

Prelude to Country Music Pioneerdom

1893–1924

The rugged hills of Grayson and Carroll counties, Virginia, may not have been the most fertile ground for farming. They may not have produced any better folk musicians than many other areas, either. But since the 1920s these two Blue Ridge areas must have delivered one of the highest yields per acre for Anglo-Celtic-American music makers than any other comparable section of the rural United States. Furthermore, many of these musicians—fiddlers, banjoists, guitarists, and vocalists—exhibited a high quality of talent. One might ask the question, just how did it happen?

Like other parts of Appalachia, the settlers who populated Grayson and Carroll came from a mixture of English, German, and Scotch-Irish backgrounds. Most of them practiced subsistence agriculture as a means of earning a living. Although slavery had become quite common in sections not many miles eastward, there were few slaves and even fewer slaveholders in the Blue Ridge. While some social stratification developed in the area, the society remained a relatively egalitarian one through the nineteenth century and persisted that way into the twentieth. Those who held higher-quality land would likely be considered most affluent. The locality also remained quite rural, as no town in the area could claim as many as three hundred people until after 1900. As with other pioneer and rural cultures, the populace tended to devise its own entertainment.

The Virginia legislature created Grayson County in 1793. This political unit stretched along the northern and southern slopes of the Blue Ridge adjacent to the North Carolina border. The northern and western sides were drained by the New River, a stream which ran a crooked course through many deep valleys and gorges until it eventually helped form the Kanawha River a few miles east of present day Charleston, West Virginia. Those who settled Grayson County in the early years included people who had come from farther east in the Virginia and Carolina Piedmont region. Folks who located there had also moved southward from such middle colonies as Pennsylvania and New Jersey. Several of these families brought their Quaker religious beliefs, while others would be attracted to various forms of the frontier Baptist and Methodist faiths. Still others would remain unchurched.

One of the early arrivals in Grayson County bore the name James Stoneman. This hardy individual had been born, possibly in Pennsylvania, on June 17, 1735, the son of John and Elizabeth Markham Stoneman.[1] According to unsubstantiated oral tradition, the first of the family to arrive in America, Joshua Stoneman, had been kidnapped and transported to the colonies as an indentured servant about 1659. Prior to this traumatic event, the youth had lived in a small village along the Thames River about twelve miles from London. James was presumably a grandson (or perhaps great-grandson) of this "colonist in bondage." More recent Stoneman genealogists hold that James Stoneman himself was their revered indentured ancestor.[2]

Although no documentation can be found linking a Stoneman ancestor to the kidnapped-indentured-servant tale, there is a ring of truth to it. For one thing, the story has been handed down through several lines of descendants. For another, the practice apparently flourished in the middle and later seventeenth century, and many colonists came from indentured-servant backgrounds, voluntary and otherwise. In 1662, the mayor of Bristol, England, charged "some are children and apprentices run away from their parents and masters" while at other times "unwary and credulous persons have been tempted on board [ships] by menstealers." Whether these servants constituted the "riffraff" of Great Britain, being largely "rogues, whores, vagabonds, cheats and rabble of all descriptions, raked from the gutter and kicked out of the country," as one historian described them, or predominantly "the middling classes: farmers and skilled workers, the productive groups in England's working population," as another scholar termed the unfortunates, depends in part upon one's viewpoint. Certainly for a youth whose opportunity in Britain tended to be limited, transportation to the colonies—if one survived—could provide some potential for advancement.[3]

If Joshua Stoneman was indeed transported to the colonies as early as 1659, the chances are that he would have been taken to either Virginia or Maryland, where he would have been put to work on a tobacco plantation. After four or five years, his indenture would have been terminated and he would have become a free person. Sometime after 1681, either he or his son migrated northward into Pennsylvania. If Stoneman's transporting and indenture took place a generation after 1659, he may also have been taken to a tobacco colony or he may have been taken directly to Pennsylvania or possibly to New Jersey.[4]

Whatever the migrations of his father or grandfather may have been, James Stoneman moved south. The next documented event following his birth took place some thirty-two years later when he exchanged marriage vows with a sixteen-year-old Quaker girl named Sarah Freeman. Her parents, John and Hannah Freeman, were Pennsylvanians who had moved to North Carolina sometime after Sarah's birth. James and Sarah's nuptials took place on December 25, 1767, in what was then Orange County but would be within the borders of present-day Alamance County, North Carolina. Since James Stoneman did not adhere to the Quaker faith, Sarah's local meeting dismissed her from the church rolls in 1772. The early years of James and Sarah's marriage coincided with that period of domestic discontent and social unrest in their section of North Carolina known as the Regulator movement. These disturbances eventually culminated in a pitched battle between the rebellious Regulators and the militia of Royal Governor William Tryon at Alamance in 1771. James Stoneman served in the militia from May 1 to June 29, 1771, and may have been involved in the battle. Later he moved northward into Caswell County and then returned to Orange. Then, in the early 1790s, the family moved west and north a few miles into Virginia.[5]

By the time Sarah Stoneman gave birth to her youngest child on January 29, 1792, she had been received back into the Quaker faith at a Friends meeting in Surrey County, North Carolina. This political unit is immediately south of Grayson County and shares a cultural heritage similar to that of neighboring locales in the Virginia Blue Ridge. James and Sarah's family by then consisted of seven children, ranging from newborn John (the only male Stoneman of that generation actually born a Quaker) to older children who were grown. The young John, who would always be known as "Quaker John," would endure some eight decades of the rugged Blue Ridge farm life.[6]

In 1794, James Stoneman acquired title to 100 acres of land on Elkhorn Creek near "Chisel Knob" in Grayson County (now Carroll County). Elkhorn Creek flowed into Crooked Creek, which is a tributary of the New River. In subsequent years James would acquire title to an additional 165 acres of land. The area would be a few miles south of the modern town of Galax (which did not exist until 1903). In 1813, James made his will, leaving most of his land to the youngest son, John S. Stoneman. His "beloved wife Sarah" was to receive "one bay horse and saddle that she now rides, two cows, all my stock of hogs and sheep . . . and . . . full privilege to live in the house we now live in during her natural life." The other children received less. James Stoneman, Jr., and three married daughters were each bequeathed one dollar, while eldest son Joshua Stoneman (1772–1840) was to get "ten cents and not a penny more." Although this inequitable distribution suggests a degree of estrangement, it seems more likely that some children had already received aid, as Joshua had been deeded land by his father in 1808 and John would subsequently receive acreage in 1819. The Stonemans ranked among the early settlers of Grayson County, which had only 3,912 residents in 1800. A majority of these early settlers tended to possess more wealth in land than in other material possessions. An 1815 tax list shows that James Stoneman owned three horses and eight head of cattle. He lived to the ripe old age of ninety-four, dying on June 29, 1829. His widow, Sarah, survived him until April 14, 1844.[7]

Quaker John Stoneman lived almost as long as his father. He married Elizabeth Hickman while in his later teens. John had several sons and a daughter named Rachel. As the sons grew to adulthood, they seemingly strayed from Quakerism and one by one were all legally disowned by their father. The two elder sons,

Martin and William, lost favor in 1836, followed by Lewis in 1838, Milton in 1839, and finally the youngest, Newel, in 1852. Whatever his relationship with his children, Quaker John prospered on his Blue Ridge farm and by the time he reached the age of sixty-eight, he and Elizabeth owned real and personal property valued at $6,800. John Stoneman lived until April 24, 1874, and Elizabeth survived him until April 1886, when she died at the advanced age of ninety-four. In an age when the rigors of hard work and child-bearing took a heavy toll, Stoneman men and the women they married proved themselves atypically durable. In 1914, a Grayson County historian, commenting about the family generally, wrote, "We find them solid and fine. They are as their name indicates 'Stone Men.' "[8]

Among the first two generations of Stonemans in Grayson County, Quaker John's oldest brother, the aforementioned Joshua, seems to have made the largest impact. Admitted into the Quaker faith at the same time his mother was received back at the Surrey County meeting, young Joshua had somewhere learned the skills of a physician and "was for a long time the only doctor in this country." Although he had a son, it was his daughters who followed in their father's occupational footsteps, being "well posted in vegetable medicines, and very useful and attentive in sickness." The elder daughter, Elizabeth, "had her horse and saddle bags always ready, and travelled all over this country at night or in daytime," while another daughter, Mary, "would go to attend the sick whenever called."[9]

Perhaps because Quaker John's sons had been disowned, and also probably because of the increasing scarcity of premium quality land in the rugged mountain areas of southwest Virginia, none of them did as well in the economic sphere as their father. Three of the boys—William, Lewis, and Newel—remained in the area around Piper's Gap, nearer the old family homeplace, which eventually went to the daughter Rachel and her husband. Two other sons, Martin and Milton, moved several miles northward to the community of Iron Ridge. According to family tradition, these two prospered even less than the others. Martin D. Stoneman, the oldest son, born in 1812, married Eliza J. Lundy and sired a family of twelve children.[10]

Like Martin's Grandmother Freeman's people, the Lundys came from a Pennsylvania Quaker background. Eliza's grandfather, Amos Lundy, Sr., had been born at Maiden Creek, Pennsylvania, on June 7, 1743. With his wife, Ann Collins, he came to Grayson County and reared a large family, including Eliza's father, Amos, Jr. Like the Stonemans, the Lundy family eventually produced numerous musicians to enrich the local cultural heritage of their section of the Blue Ridge. No oral recollections survived, however, of Martin Stoneman's possessing any musical talent. Decades after his death people did remember him, mostly for his big appetite.[11]

Martin Stoneman must have been a big man physically as well as being what one would term a big eater. According to one anecdote, he walked through his yard and saw a bushel basket of apples someone had placed there. He sat down and proceeded to eat every single one. He then went on about his daily tasks, and some of his family became worried that he might have gotten sick. One went to see if he was all right and found him sitting on a tree limb eating wild grapes. One almost has to assume that the limb must have been a sturdy piece of timber. Oral tradition also has it that Martin Stoneman's zest for food caused his death, although accounts of the incident vary. One story has it that he fell down from a haystack and was so full of food that he burst, while another has it that he burst internally while pulling fence posts after overeating. Either way, so went the moral of the story, his appetite had proved fatal. As late as the 1920s, children who overindulged in food were warned to beware the fate of Martin Stoneman.[12]

Meanwhile, back in 1842, when Martin Stoneman was just getting his family started, the Commonwealth of Virginia divided Grayson County by detaching roughly the eastern half and creating from it the new Carroll County. The hamlet of Hillsville became the seat of government for the new county, while that for Grayson was shifted west from what had been centrally located Oldtown to Independence. Many of the Stonemans would henceforth be residents of Carroll County while others would continue to live in Grayson. The population of both counties remained totally rural, with their residents widely scattered. In 1840, Grayson County had 9,087 inhabitants, while the 1850 returns showed

5,909 in Carroll and 6,677 in Grayson. This increase of 27.8 percent compares with state and national increases of 8.4 and 26.4 percent, respectively. These same census returns convey some notion of the Stoneman family's place within the society of mid-nineteenth-century Carroll County. Martin possessed land valued at $500, which was equal to or a little better than that of many of his neighbors and relatives. For example, William Henckler and David Hanks owned land worth $250 and $125, respectively, while the somewhat more distant William Davis and James Wilkenson held property priced at $400 and $1,500. Among Martin's brothers, Milton's holdings were valued at $300, while William's amounted to only $200. A third brother, Lewis, possessed somewhat more means, holding $1,000 worth of real estate. However, this meant but little in such an age, for Lewis would soon die, leaving his despondent widow, Huldah Hanks, with seven small children.[13]

A somewhat broader analysis of the census returns for Carroll County suggests a similar finding relative to Martin Stoneman's place in local society. Of 988 households in the county, some 326, or nearly a third, owned no land at all. Another 377, or 38 percent, owned real estate worth less than that of Martin Stoneman. Nearly a quarter of the householders, 232, held title to land valued at more than that of Martin Stoneman, while some 53 (or nearly 5.4 percent) owned land valued at about the same amount. By contrast, the two wealthiest men in the county (according to land value), Sam Bowman and John Blair, each possessed acreage priced at $10,000. However, that Blair owned ten slaves compared to Bowman's three suggests that Blair probably enjoyed greater overall affluence.[14]

Subsequent decades saw Martin Stoneman's economic standing fluctuating somewhat, but generally in a downward direction. By 1860, Eliza had given birth to ten children, but Martin had lost his real property and reported only $162 worth of personal property. By 1870 his economic condition had improved somewhat because three older children had left home and only two new births had occurred. He now reported $875 in real, and $346 in personal property. Thereafter his fortunes declined again, for when Martin Stoneman died in 1883, the value of his entire estate was only $12.[15]

During the decade between the aforementioned census enumerations, the Blue Ridge, Virginia, and the entire nation experienced the trauma of secession and civil war. In the early weeks of 1861, delegates from throughout the Old Dominion debated the secession question in a specially called convention. Former county court clerk and Hillsville storekeeper Fielden Hale represented Carroll County. He initially opposed Virginia's departure from the Union, but after the fall of Fort Sumter and Lincoln's call for volunteers, his sentiments changed and on the final vote he stood with the 85–55 majority. Unionist sentiment remained particulary strong in some parts of the Appalachian South, and opinions, sometimes even within families, became sharply divided. In the mountainous portions of Confederate states and adjacent border zones of slave states that remained within the Union, a vicious type of guerrilla warfare prevailed, pitting neighbor against neighbor, and produced hatreds that endured for decades. Grayson and Carroll counties, however, seem to have escaped much of the strife and bitterness that characterized some mountain areas. Unlike secession-convention delegate Fielden Hale, who served as a captain in the Confederate army and subsequently lost much of his modest fortune, many residents seem to have given little more than lukewarm support to the Southern cause. The numerous Quakers, who manifested coolness to both slavery and war, perhaps helped to moderate the local situation. Some residents joined the Confederate army, but on the whole the local populace exhibited little willingness to martyr itself for the Lost Cause.[16]

Stoneman recollections of the Civil War tend to be scanty. Patsy Stoneman recalls that the Civil War was something heard about only in school. Unlike the oral tradition about the indentured-servant ancestor or the degree of pride that both Patsy and Donna recall in their father's saying that "no Stoneman ever owned a man" in reference to slaveholding, there were no family tales whatsoever about the war for Southern independence. A family genealogist and distant cousin, Kent Stoneman, adds that although some Stonemans served in the Confederate army, they "do not seem to have been very good soldiers" and may have been reluctant or even unwilling conscripts.[17]

Although Martin Stoneman fathered a dozen children, only two are of central concern in this narrative. The first, Elisha C.

Stoneman, was born in October 1849 (the fifth child), and the second, Stephen Drake Stoneman, was born on April 4, 1861 (the eleventh child). By 1870, Elisha was the oldest of Martin and Eliza's children who remained at home. No doubt he had already made the acquaintance of a neighboring family. Joshua Montgomery, a forty-one-year-old "house carpenter" and his wife, Penelope, had several children, the eldest being a seventeen-year-old daughter, Lauretta. Romance blossomed between the two and on July 23, 1871, Elisha and Lauretta said their marriage vows. Almost no information has survived in oral tradition concerning this union except that one child, possibly a son, died in infancy. Lauretta Stoneman died on July 7, 1888. Some close ties persisted among the families, however, as Elisha's younger brother Garland married Lauretta's younger sister Elizabeth.[18]

A widower at a relatively early age, Elisha Stoneman took a second bride on July 16, 1891. Rebecca Bowers, some nineteen years Elisha's junior, had been born on January 7, 1868. The Bowers family had lived in the region almost as long as the Stonemans. Rebecca's great-grandparents, George Bowers and Sarah Short, had been married in Grayson County in 1809. George Bowers held a 175-acre tract along Chestnut Creek somewhat to the north and east of the original Stoneman grant. The family came from German forebears, having migrated to Botetourt County (a rather huge frontier domain at the time), during the eighteenth century. The 1850 census reveals that George held farmland valued at $350, while Rebecca's grandparents, William and Rebecca Porter Bowers, held only a small $75 tract. Daniel Bowers, father of Elisha's new bride, was only four years older than his new son-in-law. The family, although of somewhat less means than the Stonemans, nonetheless ranked as an old and respected clan in their community and of generally similar status. Also, some ties of kinship already existed between the two families, since Elisha's younger brother Drake Stoneman had married Rebecca's cousin Lydia Bowers. At the time of their marriage on May 27, 1880, Drake was only a few weeks past his nineteenth birthday; the somewhat older Lydia was nearly twenty-one.[19]

The marriage of Elisha Stoneman and Rebecca Bowers seems to have been a happy but tragic union. At least the next generation, somewhat couched in the culture of Victorian sentimentalism, pronounced it so. The couple's first child, a boy, died at birth on April 24, 1892. The birth of the first surviving son, Ernest Van Stoneman, took place on May 25, 1893, and that of the second son, Ingram Boyd, on November 13, 1894. The last son, Talmer E. Stoneman, was born on December 18, 1896, the same day his mother died. Widowed a second time, Elisha Stoneman now had three young children to rear alone. Since he was both a farmer living on Iron Ridge about a mile from Monarat Post Office and a lay Baptist preacher at nearby Hickory Flats, one can hardly be surprised that his grandchildren could later recall him as being an elderly octogenarian almost totally devoid of humor. The thirty-seven years that he survived his second wife's death also contained numerous unpleasant developments that would further contribute to his pessimism and depression.[20]

How Elisha Stoneman fared during the years immediately after Rebecca's death cannot be ascertained today, but somehow he and the children survived. As an old song credited to another Virginia mountain family aptly states, "motherless children have a hard time when mother's dead." However, the situation, while difficult, could hardly be described as uncommon. Many women still died in childbirth, particularly in regions where medical knowledge remained somewhat primitive. Often, numerous female kinfolk in the large extended families on both sides tended to be close at hand. The person who seems to have filled the main role of surrogate mother for the three young Stoneman boys was Uncle Drake's oldest daughter, Bertha. Seven years older than Ernest and a decade older than baby Talmer, Bertha later told Ingram's daughter Stella that the boys "stayed with her quite a bit . . . because Elisha had a hard time trying to take care of them and . . . she felt sorry for the . . . young boys. Elisha was a very strict or stern father and was rough on them."[21]

After more than seven years as a widower, Elisha Stoneman married a third time. This bride—already his sister-in-law—Susan Bowers Wells, was a widow with two small daughters. At the time of their marriage on May 12, 1904, Susan was twenty-four and Elisha Stoneman only five months shy of his fifty-fifth birthday. Whether Ernest's later characterization of his stepmother as a "trollop" reflects an accurate description or evidence of a generation gap, one certainly existed. On August 20, 1913,

"Elisha and Susan Stoneman . . . being unable to live together in peace and harmony and desiring to settle their property rights and differences between them without litigation," agreed to a legal separation. What happened to Susan Stoneman after that is not known. Ernest, who apparently had little use for his stepmother, once saying he "could never understand how two sisters could be so different," did possess considerable affection for his two stepsisters. Daughter Roni has a vague recollection of his describing their final parting and the little girls' boarding a train and waving good-bye to him. One cannot help but note the parallels with the lyrics of Victorian sentimentalism that may have conditioned Ernest's sad feelings at this point. Still, being twenty years old and fully grown at the time, Ernest must have felt some remorse to have tears come to his eyes when telling of the event a half-century afterward.[22]

Patsy Stoneman today assesses her father's childhood as being generally an unhappy one. Although one cannot disagree with that evaluation, there is some evidence that, at least in retrospect, Ernest Stoneman's youth did have its pleasant moments. A few months before his death, the Stoneman television announcer, Bob Jennings, asked "Pop" (as he was known by then) what, in his estimation, constituted "the good old days." Almost without hesitation, Ernest spoke of the years of his youth spent in a little mountain cabin back on Iron Ridge with his father and brothers. He nostalgically talked of going to the one-room school, hunting rabbits and wild honeysuckle, going to the creek, fishing, paddling around in the river, and the all-around "happy days of childhood." No doubt he had tried to forget the less-memorable aspects of those years, such as the early death of his mother, the unpleasant stepmother, an excessively stern father, and the poverty that plagued not only his childhood but most of his adult life as well. Still, it also seems likely that Ernest had less awareness of these problems, which filled his younger days with so much of the bitterness of life and so little of the sweetness, than we have today. In the final analysis, one must conclude that much of his childhood had to be rather similar to that of other contemporaries maturing in the various rural communities of the Blue Ridge.[23]

Among the prominent contemporaries of Ernest Stoneman in the Iron Ridge community, his neighbors and cousins in the

Drake Stoneman family occupy a significant position. Although a dozen years younger than Elisha, Drake Stoneman's older children were roughly a dozen years older than Elisha's children. Emory Burton Stoneman, born on February 25, 1881, and George W. Stoneman, born on December 26, 1882, had considerable influence on Ernest and Boyd, particularly as they began to take an interest in music and musical instruments. Quite possibly the next boy, Lawrence, did too, but since he died in 1900 at the age of fifteen, his role is difficult to measure. Bertha Stoneman, born on September 8, 1886, became something of a mother substitute and Drake's youngest daughter, Myrtle, born on June 8, 1894, played a key role as childhood playmate and likely sister substitute. Bertha and Myrtle subsequently married brothers, Yancey and Conley Hawks, respectively, and lived near Woodlawn, Virginia. It apparently grieved Ernest a great deal in his later days that he had little opportunity to visit these cousins, whom he held in high regard. We have previously noted how Myrtle Hawks had such high regard for Ernest that she came to visit his children at the Galax Old Fiddler's Convention in 1985 at the age of ninety-one and with her own memory quite cloudy (it was only a year before her death). Oddly enough, neither Ernest nor his family seemed to have held much affection for Uncle Drake, whom they recalled as being about as cantankerous as Elisha but without being nearly as old or senile. Their main recollection of their dad's uncle was that he generally went around threatening to take anyone who disagreed with him to court. But his children, especially musical associate George and childhood playmate Myrtle, had to rank among the most congenial folks one could have for kin.[24]

Another cousin, Steven Landreth, also provided a refuge of sorts for young Ernest. Landreth made instruments, including fiddles and cellos. His daughter Rosa, who became an Autoharp player and folk singer of some renown herself in later years, remembered Ernest and her dad going to the forest for hours at a time searching for the right wood to use in a fiddle or other instrument. She further stated that such incidents took place not only while she lived at home as a child, but also later on in the 1920s after she had grown up and married.[25]

Two particular aspects of life in the Virginia Blue Ridge during Ernest Stoneman's youth deserve careful attention. The first concerns the social and cultural sphere; the second concerns the economy and the changes that it would undergo during the time when Ernest was coming of age. Unfortunately, during his lifetime Ernest said precious little about the social and cultural conditions that would have a major bearing upon his life. Luckily, his cousins, who, unlike Ernest, left too little of their musical heritage on record, did preserve considerable commentary on the musical life of nineteenth-century Grayson and Carroll counties.

The scattered rural communities of the Blue Ridge managed to break the monotony of work with a variety of home-created entertainment. The country dance held a special attraction, and neighbors would gather from a wide area to participate. Since larger public buildings seldom existed, neighbors simply gathered at some farm home. A couple of rooms would be cleared of furniture and a fiddle player, perhaps standing in a doorway between the two rooms, would provide music for two rooms of dancers. From an 1824 description of such an event in (West) Virginia and an 1835 affair in Georgia, accounts of country dances abound in travel accounts and autobiographies. Historian Bill Malone calls "the rural house party one of the great seedbeds of country music."[26]

The rural house party flourished in the southwestern Virginia Blue Ridge with as much intensity, if not more, than elsewhere in the Appalachian region. One mountain fiddler in particular who gained an extraordinary reputation for skill and repertory, Green (or Greenbury) Leonard, born about 1810, remained prominent in the memory of a later generation of musicians for more than a half-century after his death. Virtually no documentation of Leonard's life exists except for an 1833 marriage record and he probably died sometime after 1892. According to oral tradition, Leonard made his first fiddle from a gourd, sometimes became intoxicated, and became a semicripple in later life after breaking his leg when he fell at a dance where he had imbibed excessively. He took considerable pride in his wide knowledge of tunes and in his playing skill. Leonard gloried in the fact that no other fiddlers could "catch his tunes" (that is, learn his material) until in old age Emmet W. Lundy, a cousin of Elisha and Drake Stoneman, managed to "catch" a few of them. As Lundy later explained, Green Leonard "liked his dram and enjoyed his fiddlin' and was said to be the best fiddler in these mountains. . . . In his last days, he told me I was the only one that tracked him down and he wanted me to learn some old pieces before he died. He didn't want them to be buried, and [read *but* for *and*] live after he was gone, but I never did get to learn them all. . . . The tears come in his eyes."

Lundy added that most of Leonard's fiddles probably were homemade and that he himself had made his first fiddle out of a canteen his older brother had carried in the Civil War by adding a neck to it and using horsehair for strings. He recalled that the instrument sounded pretty good, but keeping it tuned proved challenging. "It kept me half the time tuning instead of playing," the elderly fiddler told John and Elizabeth Lomax in 1941.[27]

Burton Stoneman recalled the social activity that flourished in the community during his childhood days. Explaining the conditions to Mrs. Lomax, he said:

> We'd go to places, gatherin's, have a good time, all play music, people'd all go home, everybody'd be satisfied, friendly. . . . I recollect you'd go to a party, and they'd bring it [whiskey] in a bucket with a dipper in it, set it on a table. People'd come in with their music—banjo and fiddle—that was mostly all they had in that day and time. I never seen a guitar till I was up about twelve years old, I reckon. Just a fiddle and banjo was all we had and you could take a drink of whiskey. A man could go and tend to his business and you never did see nobody drunk. Nobody was drunk at all. And when the thing was all over with, they'd dance, they'd fiddle, they'd dance, everybody'd go peaceable . . . go home; never have no disturbance at all in them days when I was a small boy.[28]

Dances also could serve as the culminating event for a community work experience. Burton recalled that folks would take part in "log rollin's, brush pilin's, burnin's, [and] grubbin's," then, when the work had ended, "at night, they have'em a dance." Fiddle music could be heard in the one-room public district schools, particularly—at the time of spring "closing," when something of a festive spirit prevailed. Emmet Lundy recalled one such incident (probably in the early 1880s) at Hampton Settlement when he and a cousin, Fields Lundy, dropped by:

An old fellow by the name of Avery Jones was teachin' the school and we carried our violins over. . . . They wanted us to play some, and this old log house, the floor wasn't nailed down and my cousin had on brogan shoes. He could pat his foot awful heavy and he got pattin' his foot. Directly the scholars got at it, and the house was in a rock. This old feller, Avery Jones, was a Methodist preacher, and he had a mighty savage look and he looked all around. He says "there's no harm in the fiddle, but it puts the devil in the foot and I want this pattin' stopped around here." Well, after that the kids they did stop, but Fields patted the harder and it wasn't long till it was in a rock again. Directly the old preacher got to grinnin' and looked around but he didn't say nothin'.

The school incident not only gives some idea of the appeal fiddle music had for young and old alike, but also contains a hint of the dislike that prevailed among some religious groups for fiddle music. Some church congregations frowned on dancing and because of the association of the fiddle with dancing, it became known in some circles as "the devil's box." George Stoneman once heard another preacher refer to the banjo as "the devil's circuit rider." While conceding that anything could be abused or used in the wrong manner, both Lundy and Stoneman, faithful members of the Primitive Baptist and Holiness churches, respectively, saw no harm in playing or listening to good string music.[29]

Throughout the nineteenth century, agriculture, mostly of the subsistence variety, dominated the economy of Grayson and Carroll counties. Folks grew corn to feed themselves and their livestock and converted some of the corn into whiskey for local use and occasional sale, which local authorities seemed to tolerate within certain limits. They supplemented the corn crop with a variety of garden vegetables, especially potatoes and turnips, which could be preserved for use throughout the winter. Local farmers kept cows for dairy purposes and sometimes for beef, but hogs tended to be the preferred animal for meat. Boys and men still hunted wild game to supplement their diets. When certain varieties of wild berries, nuts, and roots were in season, girls and women assisted in gathering these seasonal delicacies. Food production and gathering occupied much of the average family's time, and food preservation ranked high in significance as well.

The canning, pickling, and drying of fruits, vegetables, and meat required a great deal of labor. Children learned to help with all of these processes as soon as they became old enough. Since much of the soil was not especially fertile and the topography did not always favor high productivity, farming generally required the efforts of most family members to ensure a sufficient food supply.[30]

By and large, only small amounts of cash and coin passed through the hands of the typical mountaineer farmer. Some bartering of goods took place among neighbors and even at the local store. One might, on occasion, sell some livestock, tobacco, or corn liquor for money. At other times, one could hire out his own—or his children's—labor to some more affluent neighbor for cash wages, but such opportunities did not always exist. Since the population of the mountain regions continued to increase throughout the nineteenth century, more and more people tended to be crowded onto increasingly submarginal farmland. The standard of living may actually have declined in the latter half of the 1800s as agricultural technology failed to keep pace with population growth.[31]

People in the Blue Ridge found themselves with two possible solutions to this dilemma. Some chose to leave their mountain homes to seek a livelihood elsewhere, for there were a few opportunities for employment within a one-hundred-mile radius of Grayson and Carroll counties. The coalfields of southern West Virginia began to boom in the closing years of the century, and some folks chose to go there.[32] Ernest Stoneman's brother Ingram chose this route, working for decades in the coal mines of McDowell County. The youngest brother, Talmer, also went to work in the bituminous veins but died in a mine accident on April 23, 1916, at Elbert, West Virginia. Elisha brought the boy's remains back to Iron Ridge and had a fine headstone placed over his grave. The incident no doubt contributed to the aging father's "constant sorrow." Although Ingram continued to toil in the mines, Ernest tended to shy away from them, especially after Talmer's death. However, he did go to the coalfields in later years, but to do other forms of labor, chiefly carpenter work.[33]

Another option in seeking outside employment was to move east to the Piedmont and obtain employment in a cotton mill. The textile industry in the South expanded vigorously during this period as many thousands of poor white sharecroppers and tenant farmers, including some from the mountains, moved into mill work. Low wages plagued the workers, but many found it preferable to the declining state of marginal farming on poor soil and steep hillsides. Most probably found the regimentation of industrial life more difficult than the pay scale.[34] Many of the early figures in country music moved into the textile mills at an early age. Ernest Stoneman, however, had only minimal work experience in the cotton factories and in his case it did not involve much change of residence because in 1902 the Industrial Revolution made a belated appearance in his locale.[35]

The last quarter of the nineteenth century witnessed the "discovery of Appalachia" by three groups of outsiders with divergent interests. Local-color writers, whose pens poured forth with fashionable magazine pieces bearing such titles as "A Strange Land and a Peculiar People," made up the first wave of explorers. Close on their heels came the "home missionaries," who aspired to convey the values and virtues of the urban middle class to the native mountaineers, whose "quaint folkways" seemed an anachronism. The third group—the one that ultimately had the biggest, albeit unevenly spread, effect—saw some of the mountain areas as "a magnificent field for capitalists." They sought to transform the Appalachian economy by introducing the virtues of the Industrial Revolution. More often than not, this meant extending railroad lines into mountain valleys, followed by extraction of the timber and coal resources. Just such activity had created the employment opportunities that attracted young men from the Blue Ridge to southern West Virginia. Grayson and Carroll counties lacked coal resources, but the coal- and freight-oriented Norfolk and Western Railroad extended a branch line along the New River to the Carroll-Grayson border. Although this track hardly resulted in turning the area into an industrial center, it did bring moderate changes that must have seemed relatively dynamic to the people who lived along that part of New River and the adjacent Blue Ridge.[36]

Two new towns mushroomed in the opening years of the twentieth century along the Grayson-Carroll county line. The first surge of modernization occurred in 1900 when Washington Weaving Corporation of Winston-Salem, North Carolina, announced plans for construction of a textile mill on the New River. The town of Fries, named for a corporate official, developed around the mill, which must have seemed like a monstrous building to the natives of that portion of the New River Valley. Over the next few years, the mill was enlarged.[37] In November 1902, cornerstones were laid for a new public school to accommodate five hundred children and a Methodist Episcopal church that could seat eight hundred persons.[38] Since most folks in that neighborhood had never before seen any schools larger than the rural one-room variety or churches that occupied much more space, the festive celebration that accompanied the cornerstone ceremony must have been an impressive one. The immediate effect of these events on the Stonemans of Iron Ridge cannot be ascertained, but in his last years, Patsy Stoneman recalled driving Ernest to Fries. They stopped on a hill overlooking the valley town and he told her that he had helped work on the mill's construction as a boy and that it was probably there that he became an apprentice carpenter, picking up the labor skills that would be his principal means of livelihood for some forty years. It seems probable that he also worked in Fries as a mill hand for brief periods as well.[39] Washington Weaving Corporation soon became Fries Textile Company, and the mill continued operations until the late 1980s. Because the work force has become more mobile in recent decades, the town has declined somewhat from its peak population of two thousand two hundred in the 1920s, but the mill, with nine hundred workers in 1983, remained the largest employer in Grayson County.[40]

The second new town, Galax, sprang up somewhat later than Fries and a few miles to the south where the rail line terminated. Local speculators organized a land company and laid out a new townsite. According to tradition, excessively muddy streets characterized the town in its early years. One apocryphal tale told of a man walking down Main Street and seeing a gentleman's hat lying in the mud. He picked up the hat and somewhat surprisingly found a live human head underneath in mud up to the chin. The finder asked the man if he needed help. The man in the mud replied, "Oh, I'm all right, I'm on horseback." Incorporated in 1906, Galax eventually outgrew its reputation as an urban mudhole and in 1954 gained status as an independent city. By the early 1920s, the town had become a center for wood processing and furniture manufacturing. Later, textile mills were located there as well, and Galax became the metropolis (albeit a small one) for the Grayson-Carroll region. Folklorists came to refer to the music of the three-county area (which also includes Surrey County, North Carolina) as the "Galax Sound," probably because the town was the site of what eventually became the nations' most famous fiddler's convention. The Galax Sound, however, dates back earlier than the convention, which began in 1935, or even the 1903 founding of Galax.[41]

The roots of the Galax Sound go back to the aforementioned generation of Green Leonard. The next generation, best typified (or at least documented) by Emmet Lundy, took the music into the twentieth century. The third generation of Galax musicians, led by Ernest Stoneman and a host of associates, made at least some portion of the entire nation, and indeed the world, aware of that sound. Later generations, both within and without the Galax area, continue to maintain and modify the music, for it would be false to assume that the region's musical traditions, while perhaps distinct, have ever been static and unchanging.

The rural society in which Ernest Stoneman and his cousins advanced from childhood through youth changed, although in retrospect it may seem remarkably stable compared to the 1980s. For one thing, the quality of musical instruments changed rapidly; the experiences of George Stoneman and his banjo illustrate the trends quite well. In 1941, Mrs. Elizabeth Lomax, representing the Library of Congress, directed a detailed inquiry to George about the banjos he had owned. He explained that as a small child, "my father made me a little banjo out of a half-gallon cup—tin cup. And he put a little kind of a neck in it about two feet long, I reckon. He took a black spool of thread strings—sewin' thread—and made some strings to put the pick on out of [sic]. That's how I learned to pick the banjo."

Within a year or so, George Stoneman had mastered this crude banjo. At that point a neighbor in the community, "Bill Frost[,] made us a banjo. We got him to make us a kind of a home-made banjo. . . . He killed a cat and tanned its hide and stretched its hide over the banjo and made a banjo of it. . . . [The rest of the instrument] was made out of a piece of maple—a round hoop— and then the neck was made out of maple, it was made with a plane, I imagine, a knife, a draw-knife, something like that."

The aspiring young banjoist soon saw an opportunity to obtain an even better instrument: "My father got contracted for some houses over near Max Meadows [in neighboring Wythe County] and there's a lad over there had a banjo and he wanted to sell it. We got our father to buy it for us . . . and we thought we had all the banjo there was because it was a store-made banjo. . . . It didn't have no resonator, it wasn't no fine banjo like this [his current instrument, he was then holding]. . . . It had twelve brackets on it."

Back in Green Leonard's heyday and during Emmet Lundy's youth, most musical instruments were made in the community. Some, like those made from gourds or fashioned from army canteens, tended to be relatively crude, but some could be finely crafted and relatively high-quality instruments. Fiddles and banjos predominated at this time, with the guitar being rather scarce before the 1890s. Through most of the nineteenth century the guitar had primarily been a middle-class urban parlor piece (like the piano, only cheaper, simpler, and smaller). Some folklorists associate the introduction of the guitar in rural and mountain homes as being a phenomenon linked to the presence of mail-order catalogs and services that developed in the closing decade of the century. In addition to guitars, other manufactured musical instruments began to enter mountain farmsteads, including the Autoharp, harmonica, and mandolin. Musical devotees in the Blue Ridge soon acquired a proficiency with them that equaled their skills on the older and more traditional banjo and fiddle.[42]

George Stoneman discussed the people from whom he had learned to play the banjo (folks also recall that George played excellent guitar as well). Musical influences came from within his family to some degree. He mentioned that relatives on both sides of the family played music to some extent, but the Bowers side played more. Later generations of Stonemans would contend that the family inherited more of their musical skills from the Bowers connection. George specifically credited two of his mother's kin, Joe and Allen Bowers. He gave even more credit to "Mr. Sid Frost's boys," Sid Frost, Jr., Tom Frost, and the aforementioned John William "Bill" Frost. The latter not only could make handcrafted banjos but is remembered today as having been one of the better Galax fiddlers of his day. Some kinship connections existed between the Frost and Bowers families, and in 1918 young Ernest Stoneman would marry Bill Frost's daughter.

When Ernest Stoneman discussed his musical influences in later years, his remarks bore considerable similarity to George's, the main exception being his mention of paternal cousins, which meant George and Burton. These, he recalled, played fiddle, banjo, guitar, and mandolin. He added that his father did sing some—primarily church songs—and that his mother did, too, but he had no recollection of hearing her sing. Ernest said he spent a lot of time at his uncle's house and that all of his uncle's children were older except one (Myrtle). They sang and played instruments, and Ernest wondered if he could do it. When his uncle ordered a small five-bar Autoharp about eighteen inches long from Montgomery Ward, Ernest became infatuated with it and determined to play. As he remembered, his first tune, "Old Molly Hare," a favorite with children, had been learned from his grandmother. He thought this took place about 1903 when he was ten years old. Although, he never specified which grandmother, one might assume it was Mrs. Bowers, since Eliza Lundy Stoneman had passed away in 1900.[43]

After this modest beginning, Ernest began to develop some proficiency on other instruments. He next obtained "a little peanut-banjer" about twenty inches long with a seven-inch head. He "traded for it." Folks in the Blue Ridge habitually swapped such items as watches, guns, and musical instruments. The youngster worked on mastering the tune "Cripple Creek," which he recalled his stepmother singing around the house. From banjo, Ernest went on to learn other instruments. As he told Bob Jennings in 1967, "I'd try everything—Jew's harp, harmonica, banjer, fiddle, . . . I wore out a wheelbarrow load of harmonicas trying to learn to play them." He failed to mention the guitar, which he may not have learned to play until a later date. During his career, Stoneman recorded most frequently with harmonica, guitar, and Autoharp and quite sparingly on banjo. Vocal leads, however, became his strong point.[44]

The songs Ernest Stoneman learned and performed from his youth onward reflected his cultural heritage. Some of the lyrics came from folk origins, such as the aforementioned "Old Molly Hare" and "Cripple Creek." A few of the old ballads had British origins, and a few were derived from Afro-American tradition. However, the larger number had been composed either in the last half of the nineteenth century or, as was the case with a few, in the early years of the twentieth. A goodly number tended to be religious songs, but the ones Ernest came to favor most often were Tin Pan Alley lyrics from the 1880–1900 era. Songs that reflected Victorian sentimental themes—parted lovers, dying sweethearts, and heart-tugging tragedy items—appeared early in his repertoire and remained there. Certainly these numbers, which had poured from the pens of Northern, urban, market-minded songwriters like Charles K. Harris, Gussie L. Davis, James Thornton, Harry Von Tilzer, and Andrew Sterling, found favor with rural, Southern, and mountain audiences, who took them to their hearts and claimed them for their own long after they had passed from the memories of those for whom they had been created. Such songs as "The Girl in Sunny Tennessee," "When the Roses Bloom Again," "Katie Kline," and "My Only Sweetheart" (later known as "Somebody's Waiting for Me") became part of Ernest Stoneman's cultural baggage early in life and remained with him. During his early days he sang quite a few older popular comedy and minstrel songs as well, but they did not seem to have the enduring power that the sentimental lyrics held. He also came to favor tragic-event songs dealing with train wrecks and other catastrophes and eventually composed a few himself, but how much of this reflected his natural inclinations and how much reflected his increasing awareness that such ballads could have potential market value is—after the fact—difficult to determine. We cannot go back to 1923 and obtain a representative sample of the type of numbers he might have sung to entertain family or friends.[45]

Ernest Stoneman's formal education was limited. He attended a one-room district school long enough to go through what we might today call the seventh grade. School terms in the rural South at the beginning of the twentieth century tended to be rather short, even when measured by the standards of the rural North or Midwest. A "year" of schooling in Carroll County was probably no more than six months, possibly even less. Nonetheless, Ernest continued to accumulate a stock of knowledge all through his life and possessed a storehouse of geographical facts that enabled him to be a successful quiz-show contestant.[46]

Soon after leaving school "to go to work," Ernest Stoneman met the girl who would become the one human love interest of his life. A few months before his death, he related that he "met her on a Decoration Day at a Quaker Cemetery." From a modern-day viewpoint, this might seem like an unlikely spot for romance, but in Carroll County in 1913 it probably did not appear unusual. In retrospect, one can only wonder why they had not met any earlier, because the young lady in question, Hattie Frost, was the oldest daughter of Bill Frost, who had been at the very least a sometime musical associate of Burton and George Stoneman for a decade or more. In fact, Bill Frost, Myrtle Stoneman, and Burton Stoneman all posed for a photograph together that seems unlikely to have been taken later than 1908–9. What seems probable is that Ernest had been around Hattie earlier but had not really paid much attention to her. By May 1913, however, Ernest had just turned twenty, and Hattie, born on September 28, 1900, was approaching thirteen. In the prevailing fashion of backwoods courtship, Ernest asked her if he could walk her home. Hattie replied— according to the same ritualistic custom—that she would have to ask her paw. Either she didn't want to go or Bill Frost opposed the idea. At any rate, Ernest made small talk with a Frost cousin, and someone else walked Hattie home.[47]

From this modest beginning there ensued a courtship that lasted until the fall of 1918. Ernest's favorite recollection of the affair was in telling that he walked five miles each way, twice weekly, to visit the Frost homestead. He contended that he must have walked a total of some five thousand six hundred miles (which by simple arithmetic suggests that he must have missed a few regular visits). Bill Frost played a fine old-time fiddle, and Hattie had already learned to accompany him on banjo. Later Hattie learned to be a competent fiddler herself, and Ernest would back her on banjo or guitar. She also learned to play a soft accompaniment behind his vocalizing, a talent that she would eventually exhibit in both recording studios and stage shows.[48] Daughter Patsy later wrote: "Mom always said that Pop was not in love with her alone, that one of her attractions was the fact that Grandpa was a fine fiddler and banjo player and had taught her. Since music always seemed to hold a big part of Dad's heart, maybe she was right."[49]

Hattie's family had been in the Blue Ridge even longer than the Stonemans. John Frost (1756–1834), a native of Morris County, New Jersey, had fought at Brandywine and Germantown and had survived Valley Forge. With his wife, Mary, whom he married in 1786, he came to Chestnut Creek in 1789, reared eleven children, and farmed until his death. In 1836 the "family fell upon hard times" and lost the farm, but one of the sons later managed to buy part of it back.[50] John William Frost, born on May 7, 1866, experienced an early marriage and one of the region's rare divorces before marrying Martha Ann Melton on December 22, 1898. Hattie was the couple's first child. In 1907 they had twins, a boy named Bolen and a girl christened Irma Lee, which completed their family.[51] Martha Frost, whom everyone called Pattie, was descended from the famed pioneer fiddler Green Leonard. The Frosts, whom virtually everyone described as a very congenial pair, enjoyed fifty-three years of marital happiness—the last forty-five in a platonic relationship—until Bill died in 1952. The Stoneman girls all considered them as the ideal grandparents, especially when compared to what few memories they retained of the stern and humorless Elisha Stoneman.[52]

Ernest and Hattie's long courtship eventually culminated with their marriage in November 1918. One can speculate that they chose that particular time because Hattie had just turned eighteen, or perhaps it was because the war in Europe was about to end, making it unlikely that Ernest would be called into military service. The children contend that Ernest literally had to fight several suitors for Hattie's favor, since she, being a petite and attractive blonde, had attracted a number of male admirers. Ernest recalled that he proposed several times before she "finally said yes." He also remembered that he and a neighbor who owned a Model T Ford journeyed to Independence to obtain the license (which the county-court clerk neglected to record in the marriage book) and that it rained all the way there and all the way back. The couple's wedding on November 10, 1918, took place at the rather spacious brick Methodist Church in Galax. A photograph survives of the newlyweds, Ernest looking somewhat too serious and uncomfortable in an uncharacteristic suit and the more confident Hattie looking every bit the "pretty . . . proud, vain lady" that her niece later characterized her as being.[53]

After the ceremony, Ernest and Hattie went to the place of one of his cousins on Iron Ridge. By that time he owned his own horse and either "rented or borrowed a buggy" in which he could transport his bride. The couple then moved in with the aging Elisha. The family patriarch had expressed opposition to the match because of alleged "bad blood" in the Melton family. Hattie, however, soon won her father-in-law over by pitching in and carrying her share of the work in their crude cabin home. At the time, Ernest had regular work as a carpenter helping to build an addition to the cotton mill in Fries. In the following months the couple made the necessary adjustments to married life and no doubt made plans to establish their own residence.[54]

Unlike some young men, Ernest Stoneman never seemed to have any problems with settling down to a more peaceful lifestyle. Patsy says Hattie made him promise that he would never touch alcohol or tobacco before she would consent to matrimony. Although Ernest as a young bachelor had taken a drink from the jug now and then, eldest daughter Grace recalled that after his marriage "Dad never drank, smoked or used cuss words."[55]

On June 30, 1920, Hattie gave birth to her first child, named Eddie Lewis Stoneman. Obviously not writing from memory, he says, "I weighed in at 3 lbs. and was a very delicate baby [and, one might safely add, several weeks premature]. Eddie managed to survive, however, and fourteen months later, on August 29, 1921, a second child, Irma Grace, named for Hattie's younger sister, arrived in the Stoneman household. There was a longer lapse of time (during which Hattie may have miscarried) before the birth of another live child. John Catron Stoneman was born on August 20, 1923, adding a second boy to a young but rapidly growing family.[56]

At the age of thirty, Ernest Van Stoneman had survived a difficult but not unusually unpleasant childhood in the semi-isolated Virginia Blue Ridge. He lived in a community where folks endured in rather close proximity with the land and a rather complex family-kin network. Although cash tended to be scarce in the mountains, Ernest had attained a fairly varied degree of work experience as a farmhand, textile-mill hand, coal miner, and, most significantly, carpenter. The latter would be an advantage because he also had an attractive young wife and a growing family to support. Although he probably was not fully aware of it at the time, he had had several years of immersion in a cultural heritage of music. Within the next year he began to realize that this music had a commercial potential greater than picking up an extra dollar or a basket of turnips that one might receive for entertaining at a local gatherin' or a neighborhood dance.

The remaining years of the 1920s would be dynamic ones for Ernest Stoneman, his family, and his musical associates. The musical skills they had picked up from childhood onward, mostly for home and local amusement, would take them to locales quite different from their mountain homeland. These would be places—like New York, Chicago, and Philadelphia—that folks in Carroll County had heard about but most had never seen. By means of phonograph discs and cylinders, his voice would be heard throughout much of the rural South and Midwest; indeed, a few folks scattered all over the world would hear him. Historians have differing opinions about the third decade of the present century. While some have labeled it the "Roaring Twenties," others have seen it as the time of the "nervous generation," when people anxiously tried to adjust to their changing society by looking for ways to reaffirm old values. Oddly enough, their role in those events served as a cultural reinforcement to people seeking links with past traditions. To be sure, this Stoneman version of "roaring" hardly resembled that of the characters in the F. Scott Fitzgerald novels, yet, like much of American society through those years, the close of the decade would see Ernest Stoneman's family near the brink of disaster.

3

The Golden Years
1924–29

The summer of 1924 found Ernest Stoneman doing carpenter work in Bluefield, West Virginia. Although not very different culturally from Carroll County, the town served as an urban marketing center for the relatively prosperous Pocahontas Coal Field of southern West Virginia and adjacent parts of the Old Dominion. Hattie and the three children remained at home near Galax. Ernest went back to see them whenever he had a free day or two. Such practices had become the norm, and still remain that, for numerous workers in the building trades; you go where steady work at reasonable wages flourishes and you remain at home when things tend to be a bit slow. For some now forgotten reason, Ernest passed by Warwick Furniture Company and heard a familiar sound. In those days, phonographs were marketed by furniture dealers, and local retailers often played recordings to attract attention. The music and vocal featured the kind of sound that folks in Grayson and Carroll County had been playing as local entertainment for years. Hitherto the sounds that emanated from phonograph horns had been the kind of music that city folks considered currently popular.[1]

Stoneman got a second surprise a few minutes later when he found that the singer was none other than Henry Whitter, a man he had known from his cotton-mill days at Fries. Whitter, a mill hand whose background did not differ substantially from his own, had gone to New York on his personal initiative the year before and made some test recordings for General Phonograph Company. It appears that company officials probably allowed him to do this as a form of what might be called a polite brush-off. In essence, give him an audition and we'll probably never hear any more about it. Whitter's recordings apparently lay on the shelf, semiforgotten, for several months. In the meantime, another company official, Ralph Peer, had accidentally stumbled onto a new market. While in Atlanta that spring to scout and record Afro-American talent, Peer had been contacted by a local distributor named Polk Brockman. The latter suggested the company capture some sounds on disc by one John Carson, a rural-style fiddler with a considerable following among the local working class. Brockman believed there was a large audience for Fiddlin' John's brand of entertainment. As radio broadcasts had become increasingly common, record sales had hit a slump in the past couple of years that had been only partly redeemed by the discovery of the "race" market (which meant black music for black audiences). Peer decided to take a chance, and somewhat surprisingly, Carson's disc of "The Old Hen Cackled and the Rooster's Going to Crow"/ "The Little Old Log Cabin in the Lane" (OKeh 4890) became a hit in the South and seemingly enjoyed decent sales in other areas as well. The company requested that Carson make some additional recordings. Someone recalled the Virginia mountaineer with the quaint nasal twang who accompanied himself on guitar and harmonica, and Henry Whitter found his music in demand. Peer brought him back to New York and induced him to record nine numbers. Other companies began to search for practitioners of the so-called old-time tunes.[2]

Whitter's initial disc release, "The Wreck on the Southern Old 97"/ "Lonesome Road Blues" (OKeh 40015), found a favorable audience. The market for such music must have been considerable indeed for, as Bill Malone wrote, "Whitter was a good harmonica player . . . , a passable guitarist, but a mediocre singer at best." This latter characteristic led the generally modest Ernest Stoneman to declare to Hattie when he went home for the Fourth of July, "I know that I can outsing Henry Whitter any time—if I couldn't, I'd quit." Hattie replied, "Why don't you go and make one?" Ernest seemingly had the idea on his mind already because he had built a wire rack to hold his harmonica and he believed that Autoharp strumming would make a rather novel musical backup for his vocal. Continuing to do carpenter work in Bluefield, he began to practice on his own and with a few fiddle, banjo, and guitar players. Recalling that a decade earlier a neighbor named Albert Leonard had obtained an Edison home recorder, upon which he had made a little soft cylinder cut out of a harmonica tune, Ernest did not think the process could be much different in New York. He wrote two companies—Columbia, whose initial old-time tunes by Riley Puckett and Gid Tanner may have been released by that time, and General, whose OKeh label had been the vehicle for the Carson and Whitter successes—that he hoped also would be interested in what he had to offer.[3]

The Columbia people scheduled him for a September 1 audition and General told him to come whenever it was convenient. By the end of August, Ernest had put aside forty-seven dollars in savings, which likely represented about two weeks of his earnings. He purchased a train ticket to New York, and although he had never been there before (or to any other big city for that matter), he reported that he "had no trouble." Keeping his appointment at Columbia, Stoneman evidently made a positive impression because the people there offered him a flat fee of a hundred dollars for some eighteen or twenty songs but preferred a guitar to the Autoharp. In later years he recalled giving them a rather tense answer, "I may see you next Christmas and I may never see you," as he walked out. In retrospect, since he had no offer yet from Peer at OKeh, he more than likely adopted a wait-and-see attitude. After all, the Columbia offer seems insulting only in light of Ernest's later success with Ralph Peer.[4]

The next day, Stoneman went to the offices of Ralph Peer, where he performed four or five numbers. Peer must have liked what he heard and made an offer both more and less promising: fifty dollars for two songs and sixty for train fare and hotel expenses. The actual recording, however, would have to be delayed until the recording equipment and engineers returned from Atlanta. John Carson had his second session there on August 27, and a variety of other musicians, both black and white, also had been recorded there. By Ernest's recollection, he returned to the studio on Thursday, September 4 (company ledgers indicated Friday September 5), and placed two songs on the soft-wax masters.[5]

The two songs Ernest chose for his initial effort as a recording artist illustrated both a degree of influence and some innovation on the precedent set by Henry Whitter. The first number, "The Face That Never Returned," had the same tune as the Whitter lyric about the wreck of Old 97. It told the story of two lovers who parted and the man never returned. Folklorists have collected it under such varying titles as "The Parted Lover" and "The Man Who Never Returned." Henry Clay Work, a popular songwriter of the 1860s who had composed such memorable titles as "Kingdom Coming" (also known as "The Year of Jubilo"), about the end of slavery, and the still-heard-today "Grandfather's Clock," wrote a number called "The Ship That Never Returned." The tune lent itself very well to other lyrics, as the Whitter performance indicated.[6]

Since Henry Whitter achieved success with a song about a train wreck, Stoneman chose a song about a shipwreck. The railroad accident commemorated in Whitter's song had been a memorable event only in the area around Danville, Virginia. The disaster in the Stoneman memorial had captured the imagination of the entire Western world back in 1912. At the appropriate moment, he strummed his Autoharp and began to sing:

> It was on Monday morning, just about one o'clock,
> That the great Titanic, began to reel and rock,
> Then the people began to cry, saying Lord, I'm going to die,
> It was sad when that great ship went down.
> It was sad when that great ship went down,
> It was sad when that great ship went down,
> Husbands and wives, little children lost their lives,
> It was sad when that great ship went down.

Two more verses and the repeating chorus followed, but that song became the one that the current and future generations would link with the name Ernest V. Stoneman.[7]

Following the session, Ernest returned to his carpentry work in Bluefield to await public reaction to his efforts of bettering Henry Whitter. About a month later he received a package and a letter from Ralph Peer. A later listening had convinced company executives that Ernest had sung competently but excessively fast. Reviewing the enclosed test pressings convinced him that the judgment of Peer and his associates was correct. Ernest then wrote Peer, suggesting: " 'I'd like to do this record over again and do it right. If you let me do two more numbers, I'll pay my own way up there and back. You pay me for the two [new] numbers . . . and I'll do that one free again.' So I paid my way up there and back . . . fifty-seven dollars it cost me, I had seven dollars to come out my own pocket and he give me fifty dollars for the next two numbers." Stoneman made his return engagement to New York on January 8, 1925, recutting the first two songs and adding a pair of humorous lyrics, "Me and My Wife" and "Freckled Face Mary Jane," numbers he had learned from a friend, Joe Hopkins, who would soon start a career of his own as member of a recording group.[8]

General Phonograph released the record a few weeks later as OKeh 40288. The side labeled "The Titanic" attracted the most attention. Sometime in April, OKeh released the second disc. Early sales convinced Peer that Stoneman had considerable commercial potential, so he sent him a five-year contract (apparently this was a contract with Peer rather than with General because when Peer switched to the Victor Talking Machine Company the following year, he virtually took Stoneman along). On May 27, he brought Ernest back to New York to record eight more songs.[9]

Since "The Titanic" became the song most associated with Ernest Stoneman, some discussion concerning the lyric, tune, and recording appears to be in order. In 1967, Ernest told Bob Jennings that he obtained the words from a poem in a newspaper. The ship sank on April 12, 1912. Stoneman understood that a man in Maine wrote the poem and he (Stoneman) himself had "put the tune to it." Sometime earlier, in September 1966, Ernest explained in some detail to Minnesota record collector Willard Johnson that he and daughter Donna once did some checking on the copyright and identified the man in Maine as E. V. Body. Apparently, Ernest did not know that "E. V. Body," was a pseudonym for early hillbilly songwriter Carson Robison, who used the name when copyrighting public domain–type material. One can question the assumption that when Ernest said he "put the tune to it," he meant that he had set down and composed a musical score as such. A more likely situation would be that he used some existing tune that seemed to fit the rhyme and meter, much as those folk had done, albeit more consciously, who put "The Wreck of the Old 97" to the tune of "The Ship That Never Returned." Some have suggested that the tune derived from an old hymn entitled "How Firm a Foundation," but comparison of two tunes to which this lyric has been sung suggests that the two are unrelated (however, some other Titanic ballad may fit). A final observation might be relevant to the lyrics. Unless poets intend for their efforts to become songs, they do not normally put in a chorus. It may well be that Stoneman composed the chorus by simply repeating the last line of the first verse and adding a line about the husbands, wives, and little children. Whatever the origin of the song, the version that has become the standard one is that which he recorded for OKeh in January 1925.[10]

An equally complex situation has developed concerning the sales of OKeh 40288. Somewhere in the last sixty years the tradition has developed that the record sold a million or more copies. Perhaps it did. A recent standard work by Joseph Murrells entitled *Million Selling Records: From the 1900s to the 1980s* credits the work accordingly. However, in his preface, Murrells points out that no record company ever acknowledged that a disc had sold that many records until Victor presented Glenn Miller a gold record in 1942. The first such award to a country artist went to Elton Britt in 1944. Since 1958, these awards have been certified by the Recording Industry Association of America (RIAA). Record companies have not generally made such information public knowledge. No actual sales figures or pressing numbers have been found for releases on the OKeh label. Sales figures have come to light for some record labels in recent years, most notably those in the Columbia 15,000-D series and both the Victor 40,000 and 23,500 series. These numbers, together with sales figures that Victor Talking Machine Company produced in court in a 1931 lawsuit involving authorship of "The Wreck of Old 97" and fragmentary sales sheets from Starr Piano Company's recording division, have led to the development of what one might call a "revisionist or conservative school of thought" regarding record sales. Based on fairly substantial evidence, one could easily conclude that most reports of record sales have been exaggerated in the past.

The number of phonographs in the twenties was not all that large. Victor material generally sold better than Columbia releases, and Columbia releases sold better than those of the remaining firms. The only country record (if you call it country) to sell a million copies, "The Prisoner's Song"/"The Wreck of the Old 97" (Victor 19427), did not go over the magic amount by much. Claims that other artists have had million sellers, based on these assumptions, do not hold water. These include arguments that have been advanced for such legendary figures as Jimmie Rodgers, the Carter Family, Fiddlin' John Carson, and the Skillet Lickers. The evidence favoring a more conservative estimate of record sales remains a persuasive one. Researcher Joel Whitburn's efforts to reconstruct popular-music charts for the 1920s led him to suggest that "The Titanic" would have entered the charts in mid-May and remained there for ten weeks, eventually reaching the No. 3 position. It would seem more proper, in the final analysis, to say that Ernest Stoneman's OKeh recording of "The Titanic" constituted the first documentation of a most important ballad, that it chalked up impressive sales, and most significant of all, that it launched the career of one of the key figures in the early years of country music.[11]

Ralph Peer called Ernest back to New York, where on May 27, 1925, he recorded eight more numbers for release on OKeh. This followed something of the precedent set earlier for both Carson and Whitter. After initially doing only two sides for a single release and waiting until it had met with some success, Peer got them into the studio and cut sufficient material for periodic releases over the next several months. By this time, other musicians from the Galax-Fries area had found their way to New York and made "graphophone" discs. In July 1924, Henry Whitter had taken John Rector and James Sutphin with him to act as a backup band, calling them Whitter's Virginia Breakdowners. Rector and some additional musicians believed, like Stoneman, that they could assemble a better group. After an initial rebuff from Victor, the band, consisting of Rector, Tony Alderman, Joe Hopkins, and Joe's brother Al, who served as leader, recorded under Peer's supervision in New York on January 15, 1925, only a week after Stoneman appeared to redo his first session. Also in that month, Kelly Harrell, another Fries textile worker, made his debut as a vocalist on the Victor label. Although he had not yet acquired a band for his sessions, Ernest did take a fiddler to New York with him. The senior ranking Galax-area bow wielder, Emmet Lundy, played on two of the eight numbers, albeit with unsatisfactory results.[12]

The songs put on wax at this session indicated the broadening of Stoneman's repertoire. "Uncle Sam and the Kaiser" came from World War I and reflected both humor and pride in America. Henry Whitter also recorded the song. Coupled with a piece of comic nonsense that poked gentle humor at Irish ethnics, entitled "Dixie Parody" because it used the tune of the well-known Southern anthem, these numbers became the last from the session to be released. The first release featured a pair of sentimental pieces that became standard in old-time music. "Jack and Joe" (sometimes titled "Give My Love to Nell") came from the pen of William B. Gray in 1894. Numerous early-day recording artists seized upon this lyric, including Riley Puckett and Blind David Miller, among others. In many respects it typifies the Victorian sentimental lyrics that country folk, both singers and their audiences, took to heart and made traditional. The same can be said for its coupling, "The Lightning Express." This old sentimental combination of the railroad–pitiful child theme had been written in 1898 by the songwriting team of J. Fred Helf and E. P. Moran. Ernest Thompson, a blind ballad singer for Columbia, recorded the song the previous year, and it appears likely that Peer wanted the number in his catalog in both a twelve- and ten-inch version (Fiddlin' John Carson covered it for the former series in August 1924). A second release featuring sentimental fare coupled "Sinful to Flirt" with "The Dying Girl's Farewell." The former became an oft-recorded hillbilly ballad whose origins have not yet been traced (a 1940 version by the Carter Family called it "He Took a White Rose from Her Hair"), while the latter obscure ballad has been attributed to J. D. Patton. This could be either a now forgotten Gilded Age composer or someone around Galax who was Hattie's kin (she had a cousin named Jenny Patton). The final two items, both instrumentals with Lundy, deserved a better fate. Lundy played a fine old-time fiddle, but it couldn't be heard very well on the recording. Between the inadequate acoustical process of recording in those days and Ernest's being too close to the microphone, Lundy's contribution could barely be heard. Stoneman's harmonica was too loud, and Lundy, unfortunately, lost interest in recording and never tried again.[13]

When Stoneman received his five-year contract with Peer, it called for increasing his payment to fifty dollars per song, in essence doubling his salary. Whether he got this increase before or after his session of May 27 is not clear. Certainly by the time he did his next session in Asheville, North Carolina, Ernest did receive the higher fee. He probably needed it because Hattie had given birth to their fourth child, a girl named Pattie Inez (first name for Grandma Frost's nickname and middle name for Ralph Peer's secretary), on May 27, the day he and Emmet Lundy made their disc. By the time Peer had set up the portable sound equipment in the Carolina mountain city, OKeh apparently had decided to begin its "Old Time Tunes" series and resolved to search out talent from a broader area than Atlanta and Galax. Although the series was not actually inaugurated until October of that year, all Stoneman releases appeared in the new 45,000 series except for a pair of long ballads that came out on a twelve-inch disc. Of West Virginia origin, "Wreck on the C. & O." chronicled a memorable train wreck that occurred in 1890 near Hinton, West Virginia, in which a young railroad engineer lost his life. Ernest reported that he had learned this song from a newly released scholarly folksong collection. After years of research, West Virginia University English Professor John Harrington Cox had just had his book *Folk-Songs of the South* published. A Stoneman fan from Louisville, Kentucky, had sent him a copy of the newly released work, along with some large yellow tomatoes, which gives some idea of the down-home style of respect country fans had, from the very beginning, for their musical favorites. The other side of the disc, "John Hardy," a ballad about a black gambler, also reputedly came from the Cox book, except that Ernest's text differed considerably from those Cox printed. Other tunes recorded at the Asheville session included an early version of the new Carson Robison composition "Blue Ridge Mountain Blues" and a humorous lyric about a young fellow whose lady friend spent more money than he could afford. Stoneman titled it "The Fancy Ball," but in later generations it is usually known as "When I Had But Fifty Cents." Finally he did a cover of one of Uncle Dave Macon's recent Vocalion re-

leases called "All I've Got's Gone." According to Macon, his in-
spiration came from a phrase he heard a friend use back in 1902,
although he must have added some verses at a later date. Although humorous in tone, it would become a song that Ernest
would record twice more in the coming years, and also one that
virtually described his own financial collapse in the forthcoming
Great Depression.[14]

Since recording sessions occupied only a few days of Ernest
Stoneman's life in the mid-twenties, it might be relevant to discuss what else he did with his time. Although he had increasingly
come to view music as a lucrative source of income, Ernest continued to work at the carpenter's trade. Once he learned that he
could make as much money for singing a single song into a record
horn as he could for working a week and more with the hammer
and saw, it would seem likely that he didn't work quite so fer-
vently as a carpenter. Making records, of course, did not constitute a full-time occupation, unless one could do things the way
that Vernon Dalhart (real name Marion Slaughter) did on a regular basis around the studios in New York. Ernest, while contracted
to Peer, eventually tried his hand at this, with mixed results. Another possibility would be to organize a group and play live shows
throughout the countryside. Henry Whitter did this to a degree,
and Ernest also tried his hand at it. Country schoolhouses were
potential sites. Herman Williams, who later became the historian
of the Galax Old Fiddler's Convention, recalled such a show from
his days as an Iron Ridge country schoolteacher: "Ernest with two
of his cousins, George . . . and . . . Burton, played one night for
the school. Admission was 25 cents and 10 cents and the proceeds
were a little less than $10.00 of which the school got $5.00 and the
Stoneman boys $1.50 each."[15]

The point to this is that in most mountain areas of Appalachia,
communication and transportation had not yet advanced to the
point where one could make much money from personal-
appearance concerts. A little handbill advertising "a musical program" by the Carter Family has been seen by thousands of readers
of the books and album covers on which it has appeared, and a
less publicized one of similar vintage also exists for G. B. Grayson
and Henry Whitter. The chances are, however, that the number of
folks who have seen the reproduction of that Carter brochure

would vastly outnumber the crowd that saw the family's "musical program at Roseland Theater." Ernest Stoneman and various associated musicians undoubtedly played quite a few shows through the area surrounding Galax, and their earnings probably did not average much more than those at the Iron Ridge event described by Williams. Fiddler Kahle Brewer, who played on several of Ernest's record sessions in 1926, 1927, and 1928, recalled working at dances and on schoolhouse programs with Stoneman (and other recording artists from the area as well), but they seem to have been no more than local events.[16]

A few country artists of the 1920s, most notably Jimmie Rodgers, Al Hopkins and the Hill Billies, and the Blue Ridge Ramblers of H. M. Barnes, managed sometimes to obtain bookings on vaudeville theater circuits, which unquestionably yielded more income. Charlie Poole, a banjo picker from the North Carolina Piedmont who began recording for Columbia in 1925, sometimes toured extensively through the coalfields of southern West Virginia, where a little more cash circulated and the populace tended to be more concentrated. There is no evidence that Ernest Stoneman ever attempted touring in this area. In March 1968, Stoneman told Poole's biographer, Kinney Rorrer, that he once worked for a few days, probably in the spring of 1924, with Poole, fiddler Posey Rorer, and a flimflam preacher known as the Reverend Holner. They staged a few fiddling contests in some mountain towns of southwest Virginia, but the itinerant evangelist skipped out with the money in Tazewell and the musicians never received their share. Apparently, Ernest Stoneman thought of himself primarily as a recording artist and carpenter through most of the decade, as opposed to a stage performer.[17]

The year 1926 would see Ernest more than double his recording activity. He began in April with another session in Asheville. His eight sides featured some of his more unusual material. For instance, "The Religious Critic" poked gentle fun at religious hypocrites (it would later appear on record by other artists under the better known title "S-A-V-E-D"). The reverse side, "When My Wife Will Return to Me," told of a man whose wife had left him and would return only under extremely remote circumstances. Originally written as a comic song in 1889 by Charles D. Vann, the Stoneman version later was covered on better-selling labels by

Kelly Harrell and Charlie Poole. The song emerged again in western-swing style in 1947 with Bob Wills and the Texas Playboys. Ernest also did a cover of Poole's best-selling Columbia side (102,000 copies), "Don't Let Your Deal Go Down," on which he played guitar rather than the Autoharp, which had been his main instrument up to that time. In fact, from that time onward, the guitar became his main instrument for recording.[18]

Ernest's songs at the second Asheville session included his first effort at a cowboy ballad, "The Texas Ranger," a lyric he had learned from Bertha and Myrtle Hawks. He did renditions of three pieces of Victorian sentimental fare that would become standard in old-time country music: "Sweet Kitty Wells" (1860), "In the Shadow of the Pine" (1895), and that sad lament containing echoes of the Social Gospel, "The Orphan Girl," who dies of starvation and freezing "at the rich man's door / but her soul had fled to a home above / where there's room and bread for the poor." Perhaps most unusual of all, Stoneman sang another song of the same era, "Asleep at the Switch" (1897), in which a Horatio Alger–like heroine, "brave . . . Nell," prevented a train wreck, saved the family of the railroad president, redeemed her dead father's reputation, and received a handsome cash reward, all in thirty-two lines.[19]

Not long after this experience, Ernest endeavored, as he put it, to "follow Dalhart" by making contact with other companies to seek recording agreements. On May 2, 1926, he wrote to Thomas A. Edison, Incorporated, the original inventor, manufacturer, and still purveyor of "Blue Amberol Cylinders," as well as "Diamond Discs." The manager of the recording division, W. T. Miller, responded favorably to Stoneman's proposal, stating simply that "we will accept your proposition of making 10 selections for us for $75.00 each, plus $60.00 allowed for carfare." Edison had little old-time material in its catalog except for some Dalhart masters, but Miller optimistically said, "We will try them out and see if we can work up some business with them." Ernest went to New York some six weeks later, cutting the ten masters over a three day period in June. He did the entire session by himself, playing harmonica and guitar. Edison had considerably better equipment than OKeh, and as a result Stoneman's vocal quality sounds considerably better than on his earlier sessions. New cuts of previously recorded OKeh masters, "Wreck on the C. & O."/ "Sinking of the Titanic" took up one of the records, while another one consisted of remakes of a current Victor cowboy hit, "When the Work's All Done This Fall"/ "Bad Companions," that was doing well for Texan Carl T. Sprague. Stoneman recorded two traditional Appalachian ballads, "John Henry" and "Wild Bill Jones," that had not yet (but would eventually) become standard fare on recorded discs. Two more lyrics that would become standards were the minstrel-derived "Watermelon Hanging on the Vine" and the sentimental weeper "Bury Me beneath the Willow," which the Carter Family chose to cover at their first trip into a studio some fourteen months later. Another seldom-recorded number was "My Little German Home across the Sea," a nearly forgotten song from 1877. Finally, Ernest recorded a song that he seemingly obtained from a local preacher named Carper and subsequently recut for three additional companies. Entitled "The Old Hickory Cane," it must have been one of his favorites (or one the other companies wanted badly), perhaps because its vivid image of a stern father at a rural fireside using his cane as a symbol of authority must have reminded him of seventy-seven-year-old Elisha, still living in his log cabin and doing a little preaching and farming on his fifty-one acres of harsh land at Iron Ridge.[20]

By now, with his coming home with seven hundred fifty dollars in hand from New York, Ernest and Hattie must have begun to exhibit a degree of confidence and prosperity that not many natives of the Carroll County Blue Ridge could possess. At the age of thirty-three and in only four days of work for the recording companies, he had grossed more cash than most families in that locality earned in a year. Besides, his photograph—cradling his Autoharp and flanked by guitar, banjo, and brand-new discs— could be found in an OKeh catalog of Old Time Tunes that went out to record retailers in an area extending from at least Maryland to Texas and perhaps even farther. With the background removed, this same photo shared the cover of said catalog with Henry Whitter, Fiddlin' John Carson, Roba Stanley, and the Andrew Jenkins Family. Hattie had four lively children and would soon give birth to a fifth, Joseph William Stoneman, on November 4, 1926. About this time, the children began to have recollections of "hired girls," sometimes as many as five "at one time, something unheard of" in that area. Ernest felt sufficiently confident to have a printed letterhead reading "ERNEST V. STONEMAN OF THE BLUE RIDGE MTS. ARTIST FOR EDISON, AND OKEH RECORDS, R.D. 1, GALAX, VA." Since high morale prevailed at many levels of society in those days, the man whom Edison subtitled "the Blue Ridge Mountaineer" on his widely marketed discs and cylinders had reason to feel confident about his present and future.[21]

In August, Ernest went to New York to record a session for OKeh. Although Hattie accompanied him, she did no recording at this time for General Phonograph. The first four masters cut for that label did, however, have an extra musician. Joe Samuels, who did violin work around the New York studios, played a tasteful style behind Ernest's first four vocals. These included a cover of the other side of the already-covered Charlie Poole hit "May I Sleep in Your Barn Tonight Mister?" a sentimental tale of a wandering hobo in search of his son, wife, and the stranger who had seduced her while staying in their home as a boarder. Stoneman also waxed an old love song entitled "Are You Angry with Me, Darling?" His most interesting numbers with Samuels (dubbed "Fiddler Joe" on record), consisted of two songs from the early twentieth century about Indian maidens, "Silver Bell" and "My Pretty Snow Dear [sic]." Percy Wenrich, a Joplin, Missouri, tunesmith, had moderate success with these songs. At the dawn of the century, Kerry Mills, another popular songwriter, enjoyed tremendous acclaim with "Red Wing," a song about a lonely Indian girl. A wave of similar songs hit the market, including "Fallen Leaf," the somewhat tongue-in-cheek "Pretty Little Indian Napanee," and the two songs by Wenrich and his collaborators. With only his guitar and harmonica, Stoneman recorded four more numbers, including a cover of his earlier "The Old Hickory Cane," a cover of another Uncle Dave Macon comic lyric about the most dismal eatery in old-time-song imagery, "The Old Go Hungry Hash House," and an early Victorian lyric about a lovely girl, "Katie Kline," who lived in a pastoral setting. His most unusual song, "He's Going to Have a Hot Time By and By," undoubtedly derived from the minstrel stage. It told in all the racial stereotypes common to that day of how a nouveau riche Afro-American had been living an excessively worldly life and in his last days had begun to worry about his status in the afterlife.[22]

Following this paid session for the General Phonograph Corporation, Ernest visited the office of the Starr Piano Company's
Gennett Recording Division. A much smaller company based
primarily in Richmond, Indiana, it paid only royalties and not the
flat fee that OKeh and Edison provided. Although he later said
that he went into the studios with some reluctance, he figured
that since he had already been paid for the OKeh recordings, he
had nothing to lose. He recorded six numbers in Gennett's New
York studio under the direction of Gordon Soule on August 28,
1926. In a manner similar to that which Joe Samuels had used a
few days earlier, Hattie played fiddle behind Ernest's vocals. Four
of the songs duplicated his just-completed OKeh masters, but two
were new numbers. One, "The Girl I Left in Sunny Tennessee,"
covered Charlie Poole's Columbia cut of the previous year in a
somewhat different arrangement. The song, derived from a Tin
Pan Alley piece that Harry Breasted wrote in 1899, became a
country standard. The second one, "Barney McCoy," was a more
obscure piece of sentimentality. Written in 1881, it concerned a
pair of young Irish lovers threatened by separation when the male
chose to emigrate to America and the girl had to choose between
losing her lover or leaving her family behind. This represented
Hattie's first effort at recording, but it would not be her last visit.[23]

Back in Galax, Ernest began to put a band together in order to
get a fuller sound on his recordings. Although both Carson and
Whitter had recorded with larger groups as early as 1924, as had
the Hill Billies from early 1925, the more complete string-band
sound consisted of a lead fiddle with rhythm backing that included banjo and guitar and came into its own after the initial success of Charlie Poole and his North Carolina Ramblers on the rival
Columbia label beginning in late July 1925. String bands sounded
even better when recorded with the new electrical process to
which most companies had been switching during 1926. Further
development took place when Ralph Peer, hitherto recording director for OKeh, transferred his employment to Victor Talking Machine Company, the largest and most successful firm in the
business. Ernest Stoneman definitely had a place in Peer's plans.

Whether the idea to record with a string band originated with
Peer or with Stoneman cannot be determined at this point. We
know only that Stoneman took an extended group to Camden,

New Jersey, that September when he went there to begin his first business experience with Victor. Peer and Stoneman's initial plan seemed to consist of recording several sacred songs and perhaps a fiddle tune or two. Stoneman took five additional musicians to Camden. His wife's nineteen-year-old sister, Irma Frost, would play parlor organ, while Hattie and a pair of neighbors, Walter Mooney and Tom Leonard, contributed vocal choruses on the sacred numbers. The most important new figure, Lee Kahle Brewer, played fiddle and also helped on the sacred vocals. Brewer, born near Fries on June 12, 1904, had been playing the fiddle since the age of eight and had absorbed much of the style of Joe Hampton, another legendary old-time fiddler of the region. Brewer also recalls learning from Emmet Lundy, Isom Rector, and Charlie Higgins, all respected musicians from the generation that preceded his own. He had been acquainted with Stoneman for three or four years prior to their recording experiences and would play a key role in Ernest's sound for the next two years.

At the beginning of the session, Peer told Stoneman he wanted the group to recut six fiddle band tunes the Powers Family had recorded for Victor eighteen months earlier, before the company switched from the acoustical recording process to the electrical. Although unprepared for this twist of events, Ernest informed Peer that he needed a banjo player and sent for Irma's twin brother, Bolen Frost. The youngster had never been away from home before but arrived in Philadelphia by train the next day. In his haste to catch the train in Radford, Frost had left his banjo at home. Stoneman sent Peer to get a banjo and a set of metal strings. Having already cut seven sacred numbers on the twenty-first of September, Peer expected the group to have the Powers tunes rehearsed and ready by the twenty-fourth.

The band apparently disturbed some of the hotel customers with their noise and loud foot patting, but Stoneman had the hotel people get carpets for the floors, which helped deaden the sound enough to solve the problem. By the twenty-fourth, Ernest had the Dixie Mountaineers in form and they waxed the six numbers in two takes on each one. Original Victor files suggest that "Virginia Sorebacks" may have been the name initially given to the band, but by the time of release it had become Dixie Mountaineers. At times Ernest also used the name Blue Ridge Corn

Shuckers for his group, but Dixie Mountaineers seems to have been the preferred sobriquet.

The Powers recuts were all standard old-time tunes: "Cripple Creek," "Sourwood Mountain," "Ida Red," "Old Joe Clark," "Sugar in the Gourd," and Carson's original hit "Little Old Log Cabin in the Lane." The ten sacred numbers all received a good mountain-sound treatment, with "Going Down the Valley" and "Hallelujah Side" perhaps being the most outstanding. In addition, Brewer performed on two fine fiddle tunes, the obscure "West Virginia Highway" (known as "Ebenezer" in West Virginia), which he learned from his mentor Joe Hampton, and "Peek-a-boo Waltz," which his mother had picked out on the guitar (some years later, Uncle Dave Macon recorded this 1881 pop tune with vocals). As a finale, Stoneman, Brewer, and Frost returned to the studio on the twenty-fifth and did a remake of the Macon vocal "All Go Hungry Hash House" with fiddle and banjo. In all, the Dixie Mountaineers had made a promising start as Victor's premier country artists.[24]

Ernest did not record again until late January 1927, when he went to New York waxing sessions for Edison, Gennett, and OKeh. Kahle Brewer and Bolen Frost accompanied him as musicians. The threesome did three fine instrumentals for Edison, "Once I Had a Fortune," "The Long Eared Mule," and "Hop Light Ladies." Since Stoneman did not play harmonica, the recordings really gave Brewer the chance to be heard on fiddle as only "West Virginia Highway" had earlier provided. Others featured string bands with vocals, such as the sentimental "Two Little Orphans," the sacred "Tell My Mother I Will Meet Her," and the old James Bland minstrel favorite "Hand Me Down My Walking Cane." He also recut "Kitty Wells" with full band and did the Appalachian rendition of "Red River Valley," retitled "Bright Sherman Valley," with string-band backing. However, he cut his own particular rendition of "We Courted in the Rain," a cover version of Dock Walsh's arrangement on Columbia with only his own guitar and harmonica. The Dixie Mountaineers closed their Edison sessions, which they had spread out over four days, by doing "Bully of the Town," primarily as an instrumental refrain.

In between the trips to the Edison studios, Stoneman, Brewer, and Frost made two visits to the OKeh office, where they took the name Ernest V. Stoneman Trio. Although they recorded a total of nine masters on two different days, only four sides were released at the time. This may have been because most of these numbers were already available (or soon would be by Stoneman on other labels). The exception to this, "The Wreck of the Old 97," had not been recorded before by Stoneman, but other versions of the song by other artists were readily available (including two on OKeh by Whitter and Harrell), so perhaps General Phonograph decided to let all of them remain in the vaults. Those tunes the company did release had not previously been recorded for other firms. They included Whitter's other early release, "Lonesome Road Blues," "Round Town Girls," and the old sentimental favorite that Gussie L. Davis and W. H. Windom had first hit big with in 1886, "The Fatal Wedding." The final song, "The Fate of Talmadge Osborne," probably comprised the first actual lyrics that Stoneman himself had composed for a phonograph record. A tragic-event song, it briefly told the story of a young Grayson County native who had been killed while attempting to jump a freight train, possibly in the vicinity of Keystone, West Virginia. The lyrics contain some interesting social commentary about the fate of those "walking on the company's right-of-way" and its reference to the "Johnson Law," a West Virginia court decision that exempted corporations from liability to those who trespassed on their private property (in essence the companies were liable only for paying passengers and employees). Although a fine ballad in the tradition of "The Wreck of the Old 97" and "The Death of Floyd Collins," it had considerably less impact (he did it twice more for both Edison and Victor) and seems not to have entered the realm of tradition.[25]

A week after the OKeh visit, apparently still in New York, the three musicians went to the Gennett studios. Kahle Brewer apparently became disgruntled about the pay situation with Gennett and refused to do the entire session. Either the system of royalties did not appeal to him or perhaps he thought that Ernest would get all or too much of the money. However, his name did appear on some of the releases as fiddler, which indicates that he relented, at least partly. In a 1964 interview Stoneman suggested that Hattie filled in for the rest of the session, but she seems not to have been present at the February session, whereas Brewer had not been present at the one during the previous August. It appears that in 1964, Ernest was somewhat confused concerning the two times he recorded for Gennett in New York.[26]

Stoneman recorded four numbers at the February 5 Gennett visit that he had not done previously. "Kenny Wagner's Surrender," a song that dealt with the recent exploits of a Tennessee-Mississippi outlaw, had been a 1926 composition of Georgia songwriter Andrew Jenkins that Vernon Dalhart had also put on record. "Sweet Bunch of Violets" came to Ernest by way of cousins Bertha and Myrtle but probably constitutes one of the more obscure post–Civil War sentimental pieces. In brief, it tells a tale of a slain soldier whose comrade takes "a bunch of withered violets" his lover had given him before he went away to battle. The friend returns to deliver the deceased's symbol of loyalty just after she has wed "another with gold." In the better-known "When the Roses Bloom Again" (1901), the dying soldier bids his comrade to take his body (whether dead or still clinging to life) to the place where he and his lover had arranged to meet. "The Poor Tramp Has to Live" probably was the single most important song Ernest recorded that day. The lyric originated about 1880 when a man named Billy Kearney wrote a song that he called "The Tramp." Someone in the next forty-five years recomposed the song, making the tramp into a disabled former railroader. A 1926 version by Walter Morris on Columbia attracted little attention, but Ernest's rendition for Gennett (and a little later for Victor) did pretty well, thanks to its sales through Sears, Roebuck, and Company labels; royalty statements for only two quarterly periods show sales of 11,525 copies.[27]

During this trip to New York, Ernest, Kahle, and Bolen had one of their first experiences with the darker side of big-city life. They entered a bank to get their Edison check cashed. Carrying their musical instrument cases with them, Ernest went up to a teller's window while the others waited in the rear. Suddenly the police appeared and asked for their identification. It seemed that a neighboring bank had been robbed a few days earlier by a gang of criminals who hid their weapons in guitar, fiddle, and banjo cases. Bank officials and police apologized for the inconvenience, but one suspects that the Virginia mountaineers hesitated somewhat before taking instruments into New York City banks again.[28]

Ernest returned to New York in May, with Hattie coming along. During this stay, they recorded for five different companies over a period of at least eleven days. The two did four numbers for Edison on May 10, with Hattie fiddling behind Ernest's vocal, guitar, and harmonica. However, only one of these masters was not previously recorded by Stoneman; that song, "Pass Around the Bottle," was the only one Edison chose not to release. Two days later the couple made their last appearance at the OKeh studio, recording a pair of songs. The first, "The Road to Washington," was Ernest's version of Charlie Poole's "White House Blues," a lyric which looked rather lightly at the assassination of William McKinley and Teddy Roosevelt's ascension to the presidency. The second number, "The Mountaineer's Courtship," consisted of a dialogue between a relatively naïve mountain girl and a middle-aged widower with six children. A later version featured Irma Frost in the girl's part and additional comments of an editorial nature by Eck Dunford. "The Mountaineer's Courtship" remained a Stoneman favorite for the next forty years. Ernest eventually developed it into a little dramatic skit with daughters Patsy and eventually Roni taking the female part. Although Stoneman never explained his departure from General Phonograph, one cannot avoid noting a link between it and Peer's earlier move to Victor.

A week later, Ernest cut four solo sides for Victor. He had cut three of them earlier that year for other firms, and while these new versions probably outsold their competitors, only the fourth master was a new song. Apparently a man in Georgia named Rosco Balance sent Ernest an old poem about a lonely girl pining away for a lover who had not yet fulfilled his promise to return. The words probably came from an old Victorian poem—likely cut from a newspaper or magazine—and, as with "The Titanic," Stoneman put the tune to it. Entitled "Till the Snowflakes Fall Again," it was coupled with "The Old Hickory Cane" and became one of his more popular Victor releases. He did two more songs for Victor a couple of days later, only one of which was released. Kelly Harrell, the other southwest Virginia vocalist for Victor, composed an event song about the disastrous Mississippi River flood that had occurred only a few weeks before. Exactly why Peer chose Stoneman, rather than Harrell, to record the song cannot be determined, but Peer coupled it with another new event song about the flight of Charles Lindbergh recorded by Atlanta based journalist-musician Ernest Rogers. Stoneman recorded yet another flood lyric that day called "Joe Hoover's Mississippi Flood Song," which was never released. A common story is that Stoneman learned a flood song from a black janitor in the Victor building, and it is probably this latter number that Stoneman learned from the custodian rather than the Harrell lyric, which definitely does not follow the pattern of Afro-American folksong.[29]

In between these sessions, Peer arranged for Ernest Stoneman to do some additional work for two other firms. First he did four songs for the Plaza Music Company, which released material on such labels as Banner, Domino, and Oriole. He had already done all the songs before for other companies, which might be why Peer cooperated. As events developed, Plaza released the version of "Pass Around the Bottle," although the Plaza master featured only Ernest with vocal, guitar, and harmonica. A few days later, again with Peer making the arrangements, Stoneman did four additional numbers for Cameo Record Corporation, a division of the Scranton Button Company, which released records on such additional labels as Lincoln, Perfect, and Romeo (later that year it merged with the old French firm of Pathé as well). As with Plaza, the songs had all been recorded earlier for other companies.

During the May trip to New York, Ernest also discussed with Peer the auditioning of other potential talent in the vicinity of Galax. At this point, Peer probably began making plans to hold several days of session work at some Appalachian location in the manner of the two OKeh sessions conducted earlier in Atlanta and Asheville. Stoneman took the viewpoint that many fine musicians could not be persuaded to come to New York but would come to a location nearer their mountain homes. Peer himself would meet Ernest in Galax and the two would look over some possible artists there. The actual recording would be done at a somewhat later date in the city of Bristol, Tennessee-Virginia. Numerous musicians lived in the vicinity of Galax, but undoubtedly dozens more lived in the adjacent mountain regions of neighboring states. Having had experience in the aforementioned cities, Ralph Peer probably did not have much trouble being persuaded.[30]

Ernest Stoneman went home and made plans for Peer's visit in mid-July. Although not quite six at the time, Grace Stoneman remembered that when Ralph Peer came to visit, he brought his secretary-wife with him. She especially recalled that "Dad and everyone would get real excited and busy when he was coming." Ernest rented a room in a Galax hotel and they listened to several mountain performers. However, Peer chose only two to go to Bristol: Iver Edwards and Alex Dunford. Edwards sang and played harmonica and ukulele. Grace remembered that he was a young fellow, slightly crippled, and that he subsequently worked some with Ernest's band. The other discovery, Dunford, proved to be an exceptional personality.[31]

Alex Dunford was born in Carroll County about 1878. People remember him as seeming better educated than the average person around Galax. He could quote Shakespeare and Burns with what appeared to be authority to those of more limited schooling. Some folks also thought he was what mountain people politely called a "woods colt" or "base born" (that is, illegitimate). He picked up the skills of photography and in 1908 married young Callie Frost, a distant kin of Hattie. His wife died an early death in 1921, and by all accounts, Dunford, usually called Uncle Eck, was quite lonely. He played an excellent fiddle and an equally fine guitar, but his unusual speaking voice made him a natural for certain types of songs and monologues. He spoke with a deliberate drawl that was most uncommon in Grayson and Carroll counties. Some folks called it an Irish brogue, but it bore little resemblance to what most people would call an Irish accent. Others believed it was "put on," but he apparently talked that way all the time. More likely it was some archaic manner of speaking that he had picked up from someone in his youth. Whatever else you could say about the way he talked, it certainly made Uncle Eck Dunford an authentic Blue Ridge original.[32]

About July 21, Ralph and Inez Peer, having bid farewell temporarily to Ernest and Hattie Stoneman, arrived in Bristol and met two engineers who had brought the proper equipment. They leased the Taylor-Christian Building on the Tennessee side of State Street. Since a great deal of mythology in the annals of country music has evolved as a result of the Bristol sessions, some discussion of it seems relevant at this point.

The most ridiculous tale that sprang from the Bristol events is that virtually no country music existed on record before that time. Actually, of course, country music had been recorded on phonograph discs since 1922 and with considerable enthusiasm since the 1923 successes of Carson and Whitter. Victor had its initial experience with Eck Robertson in 1922, and while it paid little attention to that, it took a lively interest from the time Vernon Dalhart became a prosperous artist. Prior to Bristol, Victor had material by Kelly Harrell, the Powers Family of Dungannon, Virginia, and Alf Taylor's Gospel Quartet in its catalog in addition to the aforementioned Robertson, Dalhart, and, most obviously, Ernest Stoneman and the Dixie Mountaineers.

While Peer hoped to discover new talent at Bristol, he already planned to make use of that which he already had, as a news story in the *Bristol Herald-Courier* for July 24, 1927, makes clear: "Mountain singers and entertainers will be the talent used for record making in Bristol. Several well-known native record makers will come to Bristol this week to record. Mr. Peer has spent some time selecting the best native talent. The mountain of 'hill billy' records of this type have become more popular and are in great demand all over the country at this time. They are practically all made in the south."[33] The article went on to explain how "the mountains of East Tennessee and Southwest Virginia" constituted the major repository of preserved "pre-war melodies and old mountaineer songs." The "well-known native record makers" could of course refer to no one but Ernest Stoneman and those musicians, like Kahle Brewer and associates, who had already worked for Victor, since Kelly Harrell and the other experienced artists did not appear (although they may have been scheduled).[34]

Besides the news feature, that issue of the *Herald-Courier* also carried an advertisement for Victrolas from the local dealer, Clark-Jones-Sheeley Company, containing this insert: "The Victor Co. will have a recording machine in Bristol for 10 days beginning Monday to record records—Inquire at our Store."[35]

On Monday the sessions began with the work of Peer supervising—as country-music historian Charles K. Wolfe terms him— his " 'star' performer, Ernest V. Stoneman, and company." The "company" included most of those who had been with Ernest at Camden in September, plus Dunford, Edwards, and Edna Brewer, the young wife of fiddler Kahle Brewer. Their first song, a new arrangement of "The Dying Girl's Farewell," featuring Ernest's lead vocal and guitar augmented by the choral voices of the Brewers and Mooney, would have a historic significance as the first country song ever recorded in the state of Tennessee.

Following this sacred song, Ernest and the Dixie Mountaineers recorded nine more numbers that day, only two of which were of secular nature. The gospel lyrics included a recut of "Tell Mother I Will Meet Her" that he and Hattie had done two months earlier for Edison, and the others were all different. The two most outstanding were probably Elisha Hoffman's "Are You Washed in the Blood of the Lamb" and "I Am Sweeping through the Gates," an 1876 hymn by John Parker and Philip Phillips. Nearly all these songs featured Ernest doing the lead vocal and guitar rhythm while Irma Frost's portable organ and the fiddles of Brewer and Dunford rounded out the instrumentation. Kahle Brewer also sang on the chorus, as did Edna Brewer, Hattie Stoneman, Tom Leonard, Walter Mooney, and Irma Frost. The other songs included "I Know My Name Is There," "No More Goodbyes," "The Resurrection," and "I Am Resolved."

The rearranged version of "The Mountaineer's Courtship," featuring Ernest, Irma, and Uncle Eck, was probably the definitive version of this fine skit. Irma would sing "How long do you think you'll court me . . . My dear old Nicholas boy?" while Ernest would reply with "I expect I'll court you all night . . . If the weather is warm." Then Uncle Eck would comment in a droll deadpan voice, "He can't sit up all night long." At the end Dunford said in the same wry style, "You can go home now Parson, it's all off." The other secular lyric featured Ernest and Irma by themselves in a rendition of an old British ballad of the sea, "Midnight on the Stormy Deep." Except for tiny fragments of this tune that appeared on a Billy Jones–Ernest Hare novelty disc called "Twisting the Dials," it lay unreleased in the Victor vaults for sixty years and finally appeared on a historic anthology of songs commemorating the historic Bristol session of 1927.[36]

Peer and the Victor engineers spent most of the following day with a group of religious singers from the Barbourville, Kentucky, area, Ernest Phipps and his Holiness Quartet. Becoming somewhat worried because little of the anticipated native talent had appeared, Peer recalled in 1953: "I then appealed to the editor of a local paper. . . . He thought that I had a good idea and ran half a column on his front page." This feature, in the *Bristol News-Bulletin*, not only brought Ralph Peer his new talent discoveries, it provided the best contemporary description of Ernest Stoneman and his musical associates in action:

> This morning Ernest Stoneman and company from near Galax Virginia, were the performers and they played and sang into the microphone a favorite in Grayson County . . . namely, "Love My Lulu Bell." Eck Dunford was the principal singer while a matron, 26 years of age, and the mother of five children, joined in for a couple of stanzas. Lulu Bell is nothing like the production witnessed on the New York stage during the past year. It is a plaintive mountain song, expressing wonder over what the singer will do when his money runs out. The synchronizing is perfect: Ernest Stoneman playing the guitar, the young matron the violin and a young mountaineer the banjo and mouth harp. Bodies swaying, feet beating a perfect rhythm, it is calculated to go over big when offered to the public. . . .
>
> Probably a number, with which the citizens of this city and territory are better acquainted, is entitled "Skip to Ma Lou My Darling" by the same quartette. It has been one of the favorites of every country dance held in this section for half a century, vying with "Cripple Creek" "Old Dan Tucker," "Sourwood Mountain," and other square dance numbers. This morning the management gave the number, following a rendition by the quartette, back over the record and it is a palpable hit. "Yonder She Comes, How Do You Do," and the ladies were honored all; "You've Got Money, and I Have Too," as the rights and lefts were exchanged; "All Around the House and the Pig Pen Too," as the birds flew into the cage and out again; "Pretty as a Red Bird—Prettier Too," as the ladies do, and the gents you know— Through the entire gamut of the figures came trooping out of memory's hall and were re-enacted again as in the halcyon days of yore.
>
> The quartette costs the Victor Company close to $200 per day—Stoneman receiving $100, and each of his assistants $25. Stoneman is regarded as one of the finest banjoists [*sic*] in the country, his numbers selling rapidly. He is a carpenter and song leader at Galax. He received from the company $3,600 last year as his share of the proceeds on his records.[37]

The song which the Bristol reporter identifies as "I Love My Lulu Bell," appears in the Victor files and on record as "What Will I Do, for My Money's All Gone?" and the musicians are, of course, Ernest and Hattie Stoneman, Dunford, and Iver Edwards. Before the journalist arrived, Dunford, with Ernest's help, recorded a vocal number entitled "The Whip-poor-will Song" and after the reporter's departure a recut of "Barney McCoy" that featured Uncle Eck on the singing. Finally the entire Stoneman entourage got together and performed their first rural drama skit, which they called "Old Time Corn Shuckin' Party." This undoubtedly constituted the Victor response to the popularity of the genre Columbia had initiated a few months earlier with the Skillet Lickers, which included such fare as "A Fiddler's Convention in Georgia" and the especially popular "A Corn Likker Still in Georgia" (it eventually ran for fourteen parts).[38]

After the finale, the Stoneman musicians returned to the Galax area. In retrospect, their visit to Bristol marked the zenith of their career as old-time-music recording artists. The scheduling of the sessions at Bristol and the coverage in local newspapers of Stoneman's activities there convey some notion of the prestige and esteem that he enjoyed at the time, particularly in the eyes of Ralph Peer. Somewhat ironically, later developments at Bristol would set in motion events that eventually led to a decline in Stoneman's prestige and probably damaged his later career.

Peer and the Victor engineers remained in Bristol for several more days, auditioning and recording country talent. A few of these probably had been scheduled by Peer, especially Blind Alfred Reed and perhaps the Johnson Brothers, but some of the others would change the primary thrust of country music. Two acts recorded in Bristol in early August became the premier country talents of the pre–World War II era: the Carter Family and Jimmie Rodgers. Rodgers, especially in the short run, would have considerable influence, for within a year the major focus of country stylings would shift from a string band with vocals to a blues-influenced singer-yodeler with varied instrumental backing. Put another way, the styles previously typified by musicians like John Carson, Henry Whitter, Charlie Poole, Riley Puckett, and Ernest Stoneman would increasingly be "out," while those typified by Jimmie Rodgers, Gene Autry, and Jimmie Davis would increasingly be "in." The change would not occur overnight, but by 1929 it was more obvious.[39]

However, in August 1927, no one realized what was about to happen, certainly not Ralph Peer, who had cut only two Rodgers masters as opposed to six by the Carters and sixteen by the Stoneman group. Back in Galax, Ernest Stoneman made continued plans for his recording career and some personal plans as well. On July 11, Edison's W. T. Miller had written him again concerning another session. Miller specifically inquired about six titles, two of which Stoneman had already waxed for Victor. Ernest took the Dixie Mountaineers to New York in September and cut six numbers, including four Miller had requested. The Edison engineers fouled up the session, and officials chose not to release any of the material, although they paid the musicians anyway—presumably their customary fee of seventy-five dollars per song. Ernest's notes indicate that he also planned to do additional work "for Banner" (Plaza) during that trip, but the session never materialized.[40]

A significant development that did occur on the September 1927 visit to New York came on September 13 when Ernest, Bolen Frost, and Uncle Eck Dunford made their debut on live radio. At 8:30 P.M. the threesome appeared on WGBS, owned by the Gimbel department store, and rendered five numbers, "Silver Bell," "Pretty Snow Deer," "The Unlucky Road to Washington," "Hand Me Down My Walking Cane," and "When the Roses Bloom Again." Two evenings later, on Thursday, September 15, they appeared at 8:40 P.M. and did four more songs, "Midnight on the Stormy Deep," "There'll Come a Time," "Going Down the Valley," and "He Was Nailed to the Cross for Me." This may have been the initial instance of native Appalachian musicians appearing on radio in New York City. Ernest made these arrangements on his own, recalling in 1967 that he had called a Mr. King at WGBS from his hotel room and received the reply "Come on down" from the station official.[41]

Back in Galax, the Stonemans also kept busy. On September 19, Ernest purchased, for the sum of seven hundred dollars, a 2.21-acre tract of real estate from F. B. and Vergie Leonard. Primarily using his own skills, he constructed a comfortable frame home for Hattie, the children, and himself. Hattie gave birth to another daughter, Anna Juanita, whom they usually called "Nita." Although hardly large or spacious by most standards, the home contained more space than most rural Blue Ridge dwellings—three rooms seems to have been more typical, with smaller ones not uncommon. It had modern conveniences that were still beyond the reach of most rural families. Grace recalls "a Delco motor in the celler which gave us electricity for the curling irons, washing machine, ironing, etc." Patsy remembers that "we had a telephone . . . the kind you cranked," and as for furnishings, "a big dining room table with white table clothes and a big Buffet that had two doors in the bottom where the table clothes and things were kept."[42]

Other forms of conspicuous consumption graced the Stoneman household. Hattie in particular, who had already been somewhat spoiled by her parents, enjoyed many of the things associated with modern living. Grace remembers: "Mom had two pair of curling irons, one to curl with and one that waved the hair. Wavy hair was the thing in those days. I use to watch her as she would dress to get ready for a trip and think how pretty she was with the White Fox Fur around her neck."[43] Some people no doubt thought Hattie may well have gone to extremes in her preoccupation with appearance. Cousin Stella recalls one such instance:

> Daddy took me to visit Ernest sometimes alone—because I would beg to go with him. This one time, we got to Ernest['s house] late one night. Hattie was sick and Ernest was getting ready to go after the doctor. Daddy took Ernest and told me to stay with Hattie. She was in bed. She asked me to bring her a box or case from another room. I did, and sat down in a chair and watched her as she fixed her hair—then put make up on. Eye make up and all. I had never seen anyone use that and it fascinated me. I remember every little bit—she stopped and seemed to be hurting—but so young I didn't understand. Anyway, she was finished with the case. The doctor came; I was shown to the bedroom to sleep. Next morning someone woke me up to go look at the little baby the doctor brought last night. One thing for sure Hattie got her make up on and looked pretty for the event.[44]

While the Stonemans may have got caught up in the prosperity of the twenties, they had not abandoned the more admirable characteristics of neighborliness and generosity associated with mountain people. At a time when their annual income may have reached $5,000, that of the average Virginia factory worker in 1925 was only $944. For many, if not most, families in the Blue Ridge, income was probably less. Patsy says, "Things were good for us and Mommie and Daddy shared. Mommies pretty clothes were used by the hired girls and Daddy kept signing notes and loaning money." On the latter, she elaborated, "It seemed that Daddy had a lot of friends. Any time they needed someone to sign notes or borrow money, they were there."[45]

Except for a little more affluence than the average Appalachian family, most other things associated with the Stoneman children's early years seems to have been much closer to the normal. To quote Patsy's recollections again: "And there was always the 'Big Rock' as we kids called it, for us to play on, and the side of the mountain to climb. One time Mom told Grace and Eddie to take me along and watch out for me. I can tell you that they were not too pleased about it, and got even by picking wild strawberries for me and putting rabbit pills between them and fed them to me. Mommie sure had a fit when she found out about it, but I still love strawberries." As for the Big Rock, she remembered that it "stayed one of our favorite places for many years. It was said that Indians had used it to camp around and [for] cooking. You see, there was a place in the middle of it that looked sorta scooped out, so maybe that was what it was. But no matter, it was an Indian rock to us and it gave us many hours of pleasure."[46]

Grace recalls other joyful incidents, such as visits from their father's relatively worldly brother, "Uncle Ingram," who presented a contrast to the "straight" Ernest: "Uncle Ingram drank, gambled, and did all kinds [of things] that was exciting to us kids. He would bring one of his fighting roosters or a pet groundhog along with his carload of children and wife, and sometimes stay a week or more. We sure had a good time, but I don't think that Mom, Dad or Granny had too good a time though but us kids weren't worried about that."[47] Ingram's daughter Stella equally recalled those visits, albeit from a slightly different perspective: "To me, Ernest was the greatest. He wasn't strict—or stern—seemed so gentle compared to my Daddy and so good to me, always. I've heard him lay my Daddy out for driving while he was drunk with my mother & us kids in the car. . . . I thought Ernest was so great because he didn't drink and remember when we would be there—he would prepare the meals along with Hattie's sister Erma [*sic*]. . . . Daddy was so rough on me and Ernest seemed to have so much patience with his kids. I looked at him as being so different."[48] Grace adds that Ingram also possessed considerable musical abilities because he "could play the Autoharp about as well as anyone I ever heard, but his interest didn't go to such things." She concludes that "he was a coal miner . . . and he and his wife Lilly had . . . 9 children." Stella also presents the strong side of Ingram, pointing out that although he may have drank and gambled while being "a pool shark" and addicted to "game roosters and . . . cock fights . . . [he] never missed a day [of] work . . . always owned a car . . . and was very proud of his family."[49]

The children's maternal grandparents lived on adjacent land and in fact sold Hattie an additional acre in October 1929. They were a source of considerable joy to Ernest's growing family, as were Irma and Bolen Frost. By contrast, the elderly Elisha Stoneman "lived at least 5 miles from us in a little place called Iron Ridge, and he would walk to visit us with his walking cane. He was a old time Baptist Minister (part time), and it seemed to us kids that everything was a sin. . . . His favorite word was 'SIREE.' He said idle words was a sin. . . . He wasn't anything like Moms dad. He wasn't a 'fun' Grandpa, but I'm sure he meant well."[50] Grace and Patsy further recall that they and their brothers indulged in little pranks that must have contributed to Elisha's attitude. In one instance they tied window weights to the near octogenarian's arms while he snoozed in a chair. The old man awoke with such mutterings as "SIREE! Siree! These children! Siree! Siree!" Stella remembers that the old man had kindly moments, too, such as when he took her with him to the little general store on Iron Ridge in "an ox drawn wagon to get his feed and what else he'd buy there, and always buy me a stick of candy or a big round ball of hard candy." Her recollections of "riding with him on that wagon" as being a real "treat to me" revealed a degree of positivism that Ernest's children never saw in Elisha Stoneman. Stella recalls his service as a minister at Hickory Flats, "preaching and singing—one song I heard him sing a lot was 'Just Over in the Glory Land.' " At times, however, Elisha could display the cantankerous side that Ernest's children always saw. Stella remembered: "One time I followed him to the out house, which I remember very well was to the back of the house. He locked the door on me and would not let me in. I kicked the door and cried, 'Granny let me in!' (Back then I called him granny). I remember him saying, 'I ain't your granny—your granny's in W.Va.' "[51]

In retrospect, one can contrast the Stoneman grandparents' ages as well as their differing personalities. It seems likely that Grace, Patsy, and the others were too young to realize that Grandfather Stoneman was seventeen years older than Grandfather Frost. It also appears likely that the elder Stoneman had also reached a state of senility by the latter 1920s. Whatever the children may have recalled, there is no doubt that Ernest enjoyed an amiable relationship with his father, probably to Elisha's personal detriment, as later events would show.

In late October 1927, Ernest Stoneman would have his final recording session in what would become his peak year as a "graphophone" artist. However, in this instance his role would be subordinate to that of his friend and associate Uncle Eck Dunford. Taking advantage of the latter's unique voice, Peer arranged for him to do four humorous monologues in the style that Cal Stewart had made famous back in the early years of the century with his creation of a mythical bucolic New Englander known as "Uncle Josh." Ernest remembered several practice sessions with Dunford at his little cabin on Ballard Branch, where the droll-voiced mountaineer labored to get the word inflections and timing the way he wanted it. Stoneman confined his role to picking a quiet banjo behind Dunford's four stories. Recorded in Atlanta on October 11, the first release under Dunford's name explained "My First Bicycle Ride" backed with a description of "The Savingest Man on Earth." The label listed no composer for either title, but Stoneman may have written them because a copy of the latter text has been found among his papers. On the second release, Dunford told about "Sleeping Late" on one side of the disc while describing a social event, "The Taffy Pulling Party," on the other. Both titles carry Dunford's name as author on the record label. It seems probable that the two also discussed with Peer the likelihood of recording more rural dramas in the fashion of the "Old Time Corn

Shuckin' Party" during the Atlanta visit because at the next session they would do more material of this type that would feature an extended cast of characters.

It is also possible that they discussed another situation during the Atlanta trip. In 1964, Ernest Stoneman told record collector Eugene Earle that he had been "gettin' on Vernon Dalhart's road." By this he meant that rather than make records for one company exclusively, as some artists did—including Peer's new "star," Jimmie Rodgers—he had more or less "free-lanced" for several different firms. We do not know exactly what Peer thought about this situation of working for competing companies. Certainly he did not object in the beginning, when he himself had switched employers in 1926 by moving from OKeh to Victor and virtually taking Stoneman with him. In the spring of 1927, Peer and his secretary-wife had even helped arrange for Stoneman to make some masters for the Plaza and Cameo-Pathé concerns, albeit the songs had already been done for other companies; in fact, with the exception of "The Old Hickory Cane," they were titles he would never cut for Victor. It seems likely that by the end of 1927 Peer began taking a dimmer view of such action. He and Stoneman agreed that henceforth he would use his own name only for material recorded for Victor and Edison. Since Edison Blue Amberol Cylinders and Diamond Discs could be played only on Edison phonographs, this company did not really compete in the same market with Victor. On the other hand, Columbia, OKeh, Gennett, Plaza, Pathé, and Brunswick comprised Victor's main competitors. Since Stoneman had already broken with OKeh—not long after Peer's departure—the restriction seemed to be directed at Gennett. Although this firm actually controlled only a small portion of the market, it would seem probable that Peer's real purpose may have been to take Stoneman's name out of the Sears, Roebuck catalogs. Most Gennett masters that reached consumers did so through their extensive sale in these catalogs. Although many of the recordings were already marketed on the Sears labels of Silvertone, Supertone, Challenge, and Conqueror under a baffling assortment of pseudonyms, these would provide Peer and Victor some degree of protection from this brand of competition. Relatively few discs bearing the Gennett label actually sold—existing royalty sheets show few Gennett sales reaching four digit numerals—but the mail-order market may have offered Victor stiff competition. From then on, material by Ernest Stoneman on Gennett bore the name Justin Winfield, while that marketed in the catalogs carried such credits as Uncle Ben Hawkins, Uncle Jim Seaney, and the Virginia Mountain Boomers.[52]

From modest beginnings in 1924, Ernest Stoneman had seen his recording career increase regularly each year. In 1925 and 1926, the number of masters cut and sides released had grown to nineteen and fifty-one, respectively. His output in 1927 would be sufficient, to use modern terminology, to fill the equivalent of five long-play albums. Although 1928 would be a slightly slower year, it would still be a quite successful one.

The activities began in late February with another trip to Atlanta. As Kahle Brewer did not make this trip, Uncle Eck Dunford handled the fiddling chores and George Stoneman took the banjo position formerly occupied by Bolen Frost. Irma Frost remained and a local country schoolteacher named Sam Patton came along to play a teacher part in one of the two skits. The first rural drama, entitled "Possum Trot School Exhibition," effectively re-created the atmosphere and much of the style of a special day at a southwest Virginia mountain school with its spelling bee, special readings, and string musical entertainment (perhaps not unlike that which Emmet Lundy had described in the 1880s). The voice characterizations of Dunford and Frost constitute the most outstanding quality on both that skit and the second one, "Serenade in the Mountains," which re-creates another nearly vanished social institution called the "belling," or "shivaree." In these events, a group of neighbors surround the house of a newlywed couple at a late hour of the evening and create sufficient noise that the young lovers must come out and treat the crowd.

In addition to the skits, the Blue Ridge Cornshuckers—this name had now pretty much replaced Dixie Mountaineers on the Victor releases—recorded nine more selections. A surprisingly large proportion of this material remains unreleased, which seems unusual considering the high quality of that which Victor did release. The only two straight string-band numbers came out as opposite sides of the same disc. They paired a British ballad (Child 289) that Stoneman had learned from Eck Dunford, "The Raging Sea, How It Roars" (previously recorded as "The Sailor's

Song" in 1925) with the Victorian sentimental classic "Two Little Orphans." These sides rank as one of the really great string-band recordings of the decade, with the music of Dunford and the two Stonemans in a nearly flawless execution and the vocals rendered in clear, crisp fashion. The other released side, "Sweet Summer Has Gone Away," featured mostly the singing of Dunford. The unreleased cuts raise a number of unanswerable musical and lyric questions. "Tell Me Where My Eva's Gone" was another vocal primarily featuring Dunford. Uncle Eck received prime credit on two likely monologues, "Uncle Joe" and "Old Uncle Jessie." Two cuts featured Ernest and Irma, "Once I Had a Fortune" (released as an instrumental for Edison) and "Claude Allen." The latter ballad dealt with the most violent incident in Carroll County history. In 1912, four people died in a shooting spree that accompanied the conclusion of a controversial trial in the Hillsville courthouse. Claude Allen and his father, Floyd, subsequently received the death penalty for their part in the affair, and Sidney Allen, an uncle of Claude, served a long prison sentence. Ernest, a youth of nineteen at the time, later told his children about seeing a posse search for the Allens while he hid in a tree. Although separate ballads about both Claude and Sidney have entered tradition, the song recorded by Ernest is believed to be a different one. Stoneman once possessed either a typed or a handwritten text, but apparently it has been lost. The final tune of the session, "Stonewall Jackson," featured a lead guitar instrumental by George Stoneman. In later years, several recordings of his banjo work made it onto records, but George's guitar talents have been lost to modern listeners unless this master surfaces someday.[53]

Two months after the Victor sojourn in Atlanta, Stoneman went to New York for another Edison session. Although some uncertainty exists, it is believed that Kahle Brewer, George Stoneman, and perhaps Eck Dunford made up the Dixie Mountaineers for this trip. The band recorded twelve songs in two days, and it proved to be Brewer's final session. With his wife expecting a baby, Kahle took regular employment with the Virginia highway department and made no more distant trips to urban recording studios. He managed to get some good fiddle breaks on the entire session, especially "Sally Goodwin" and "Careless Love," which had some short vocal refrains but tended to be largely fiddle tunes. The Dixie Mountaineers recorded four songs they had recorded earlier, but eight, including the two previously mentioned, had not been released before (although four had been done at the "rejected" session of September 1927). The new material included three Victorian sentimental pieces: "There'll Come a Time" (1895) by Charles K. Harris, "The East Bound Train" (1896) by James Thornton and Clara Hauenschild, and "We Parted by the Riverside" (1866) by Will S. Hays. The first two of these would appear to have been covers of the songs that Charlie Poole and Dock Walsh, respectively, had done earlier for Columbia. Ernest also rendered fine vocal versions of the traditional ballad "Down on the Banks of the Ohio" and the comedy favorite "The Old Maid and the Burglar." They had opened the session with a recut of a fine hymn "He Was Nailed to the Cross for Me," which had been rejected the previous fall.[54]

Following the departure of Brewer, Stoneman began to search for other musicians to accompany him to recording sessions. He soon met two youths in their late teens at a fiddling contest in Elizabethton, Tennessee, who filled the bill quite nicely. Herbert and Earl Sweet, who lived near Damascus, Virginia, played fiddle and guitar and had some different songs in their repertoire. Ernest arranged a trip to Richmond, Indiana, the central headquarters of Gennett. Since Ernest now traveled to most of his sessions by automobile, this allowed him and the other musicians to see a little of the Midwest. In addition to the Sweet Brothers, Ernest also took George Stoneman to play banjo, as well as George's twenty-year-old son by his first wife, Emma Bruner. Young Willie Stoneman contributed two vocals to the group efforts.[55]

The recordings began pleasantly enough, with seven numbers being cut on July 5, 1928. Ernest confined his role to that of leader and backup musician, and primary label credit went to either Willie Stoneman or the Sweet boys, who faced no contract restrictions. The string-band sides, some of which included prominent vocals by Ernest, used the innocuous name Virginia Mountain Boomers. After Willie Stoneman had recorded "Wake Up in the Morning" (a variant of the better-known "Midnight Special")[56] on the morning of July 6, the recording machine broke down and the group had to wait until the ninth before they could resume their work. During their two-and-one-half-day wait, the Virginia

Mountain Boomers spent their time in a variety of useful activities. They toured the Starr Piano Company's facilities in Richmond and saw not only how phonograph records were manufactured but also how pianos and vacuum brakes were made. Ernest recalled that the engineers in the brake division took him for a ride in their Ford car, demonstrating the effectiveness of the brakes, and offered to put a set on his auto, but he feared they might be dangerous—because they stopped so quickly—for driving in the Virginia mountains. While they were practicing their songs at the rooming house where they stayed, the son of the owner, a chiropractor named Wilcoxen, heard them. The Wilcoxens had never before heard that type of music, and the doctor asked them to play that Sunday in his church and later that afternoon for a big picnic. Ernest remembered that both musicians and listeners enjoyed themselves a great deal and that it gave them extra opportunities to practice their material.[57]

On Monday morning the group returned to the studio and during the next two days recorded ten additional songs. None of the material had been done previously by Stoneman except a new recording of "John Hardy," which Gennett released under a pseudonym, Justin Winfield. The numbers included fine versions of "New River Train," "Say, Darling Say," and "Rambling Reckless Hobo" and unusual instrumentals like "East Tennessee Polka." The Sweet Brothers contributed another one of their tunes, and the entire group did a fine string-band adaptation of an old Green Leonard fiddle tune, "I'm Gonna Marry That Pretty Little Girl." After their session the Boomers returned to Virginia; except for Ernest and George Stoneman, none of them ever recorded again.

In late October, Ernest returned to Bristol to perform on what would be (although he could hardly have known at the time) his last Victor recordings. By this time, Jimmie Rodgers had become Victor's star performer in the old-time-tune field, and discs by a Scott County–based vocal trio, the Carter Family, had begun to outsell Stoneman's. Nonetheless, Ernest still commanded some prestige with Peer and cut some sixteen masters, although six would go unreleased. In addition to Ernest, the personnel consisted of Hattie, Eck Dunford, and Bolen Frost. With the exception of two sides that reverted to the older name, Dixie Mountaineers, the releases now carried the name Stoneman Family on the labels, which may have been Victor's response to the growing popularity of the Carters. Actually, the group was no more and no less a family act than it had been since 1926. Eck Dunford sang a solo vocal on one master about an oldster courting a young girl; it was reminiscent of "The Mountaineer's Courtship" and was called "Old Shoes and Leggins." He also fiddled and sang "Angeline the Baker" (related to Stephen Foster's "Angelina Baker") for the reverse side. "Down to Jordan and Be Saved" featured Eck's solo voice on verses, with choral backing and Ernest's harmonica. Dunford apparently composed this sacred offering while Ernest wrote the reverse hymn, "There's a Light Lit Up in Galilee," which had a somewhat similar vocal arrangement. Ernest reverted to his familiar role of major vocalist on a new recording of "We Parted by the Riverside" and "The Broken Hearted Lover," a song that would later become more well known in a Carter Family variant as "I'm Thinking Tonight of My Blue Eyes." The group performed their last rural drama skit with a smaller cast made up only of Uncle Eck and Ernest. In "Going Up the Mountain After Liquor," the droll Dunford described an encounter with a bear, while Stoneman asked an occasional question, played banjo, and chuckled at Uncle Eck's account of his misadventures. The sides that became the final Stoneman Victor release (40206) featured Ernest and Hattie. One side bore the title "Too Late," while the other and more interesting, "The Spanish Merchant's Daughter," consisted of a dialogue between a young man and his reluctant lady friend, whose father had always instructed her to reply "No, Sir" to all inquiries for her hand. The Stonemans learned this number from Dunford, and in a sense it represented something of an opposite version of "The Mountaineer's Courtship."

The unreleased titles included a pair of gospel numbers, "Beautiful Isle o'er the Sea" and "Twilight Is Stealing over the Sea." Two other numbers of likely lyric love, "Willie, We Have Missed You" and "I Should Like to Marry," may well have been intended for another release. The title "Minnie Brown" remains an unknown item, while a text of the tragic event song "The Fate of Shelly and Smith" survives in the Stoneman Papers. This ballad told of the tragic death of two laborers in a rock slide.[58]

Some three weeks after his final Victor visit, Stoneman also made his last trip to the Edison studios in New York City. Although Edison records had more durability and at least as good a sound quality as those of rival concerns, the pioneering firm in the phonograph industry had steadily lost ground to other companies throughout the 1920s. The main reason for this was consumers' inability to play the thick 80-RPM Edison discs on any other brand of machine. Purchasers of phonographs and records had increasingly been attracted to phonographs and 78-RPM discs that could be played on any other type of machine. In 1928, Edison belatedly introduced a thin disc that could be used on other machines. However, by this time it had little impact and came too late to rescue the recording division from its increasingly minuscule share of the market. Nonetheless, Edison apparently had reason to be satisfied with Stoneman's work and had continued to record him. If we assume that it continued its standard fee of seventy-five dollars per side, he must have been equally happy with the company. In a sense, neither Stoneman nor the Edison management could avoid the firm's decline. Although the Edison recordings by the Dixie Mountaineers were never sold widely and became increasingly scarce as the company's recording division approached extinction, the quality of their music remained as high as ever.

As a band for the Edison sessions, Ernest took Eck Dunford and George Stoneman to New York with him. At least three of the songs had been numbers he had probably learned from the Sweet Brothers, since they had done the vocal work on them at Richmond, Indiana, in July. "Fallen by the Wayside" (1892) was a Charles K. Harris ballad about a "fallen woman" that Charlie Poole had cut earlier. "The Prisoner's Lament," a temperance ballad, seems to have been an original Herbert Sweet composition, while "My Mother and My Sweetheart," which Edison never released, was another piece of Victorian sentimentality. The description of a youth having to leave home, "Goodbye Dear Old Stepstone," could also be considered in the same category and has been traced back to the 1880s. Ernest also redid the Macon cover, "All I've Got's Gone," that he waxed for OKeh in 1925 and cut a master of "Midnight on the Stormy Deep" that Edison apparently released only on cylinder. He recorded a full-string-band rendition of "Remember the Poor Tramp Has to Live" and the archaic Anglo-American ballad "The Pretty Mohea" (usually known as "The Little Mohee"), which he apparently learned from John Cox's *Folk-Songs of the South*. Neither of these two was released, although Edison did release his two final offerings on both Diamond Discs and the new series of thin lateral-cut discs. Both were R. E. Winsett sacred compositions, "I Remember Calvary" and "He Is Coming After Me."

In all, 1928 had been another good year for Ernest Stoneman. The number of masters he had cut came down from his 1927 high, but only from seventy-one to sixty-nine. However, the number of those released would be only fifty, as opposed to fifty-eight in his peak year. Although Victor would never again call him for a session, it did continue to release his material into the early part of 1930, and he no doubt expected to be contacted again sometime during 1929. The Edison firm would cease phonograph-record production a few months after his November 1928 visit. The only company with which he still maintained a good relationship, Gennett, could not use his name on its record labels and his income from that company depended directly on record sales. Through the advantage of hindsight, we can now see that Ernest Stoneman and his growing family stood in a situation that could best be described as poised for disaster. Even if one dismisses foreknowledge of a coming depression, we can see that his situation had become mighty shaky, to say the least.

At the beginning of 1929, Ernest and Hattie Stoneman did not have this advantage. They could, of course, see that they owned clear title to more than two acres of land (and had access to more from the adjacent Frost holdings). They had a comfortable home with more modern conveniences than those of their neighbors. The musical group had numerous records on the market and could presumably expect that regular releases and more sessions would follow. By January 1929, they counted six children—Eddie, Grace, John, Pattie, William, and Nita—and Hattie expected the seventh come summer. Besides, Ernest was gaining a minor degree of regional and perhaps even nationwide fame as a singer of old-time tunes. The preceding five years had been good times for him, since that fateful day when he heard the voice of Henry Whitter and accepted the personal challenge of improving upon his fellow mountaineer's singing style. Who could foretell what prosperity the next five years might bring to the Stonemans?

A group of Galax musicians—and largely Stoneman kin—photographed by Eck Dunford about 1910. Standing (left to right): Burton Stoneman, J. William Frost; seated (left to right): Sophinnia Leonard, Myrtle Stoneman Hawks, Betty Leonard. In the mid-1950s, Mike Seeger borrowed this picture from Hattie Stoneman and used it as the cover for *The New Lost City Ramblers Song Book.* This and all photographs not otherwise credited are from the Patsy Stoneman Murphy collection.

Uncle Eck Dunford and his wife, Callie Frost, photographed sometime before her death in 1921.

Ernest and Hattie Stoneman on their wedding day at the Galax Methodist Episcopal Church, November 10, 1918. Virginia Patton is on the left.

Kahle Brewer about 1924. This photograph was made about the time Stoneman and Brewer met and first began to play music together. Courtesy of Kahle and Edna Brewer.

Ernest Stoneman and the Dixie Mountaineers, 1926. Left to right: Bolen Frost, banjo; Hattie Stoneman, fiddle; Ernest Stoneman, guitar; Irma Frost, mandolin; Walter Mooney, hymnbook. Mooney (1876–1965) later led a family gospel-singing group that sang in many churches throughout the Galax area.

Ernest Stoneman and the Blue Ridge Corn Shuckers, 1928. Standing (left to right): Iver Edwards, Eck Dunford, Hattie Stoneman; seated (left to right): George Stoneman, Ernest Stoneman, Bolen Frost. Courtesy of Ivan M. Tribe.

The Pilot Mountaineers about 1930. Left to right: Frank Jenkins, Oscar Jenkins, Ernest Stoneman. Courtesy of David Freeman.

Guide sheet for a Stoneman radio show from 1936. Although mired in poverty at the time, Ernest and Hattie managed to remain active in music, if only in a small way.

```
                    The Dixie Mountaineers.

        Program For  WMAL. Jan  12  36.  8.15.PM.

      Theme
        Chicken Reel.

        Well Howdy folks this is the origonal Dixie Mountaineers
      from The Mountains of Va.& Nc. and we have just lots
      of songs and music right from the hills.
        and we also claim that we are the only hillbilly
      string band that has a homemade bass banjo.

      and remember folks we never took any music lessons
      so you can know just about what to expect.

      our first song is .    The Log cabin in the lane.

      now that song is very old but here is one that is not
      near so old    we call it    The Old black dog.
        And now if the ladie  that plays the fiddle will just
      change places and get here  close to the mike we will
      play    The Old Black dog.

      And while the ladie fiddler is here we will play

        The Girl i left in sunny Tenn..

      Now we are goin to ask the fiddlers to change places
      again  so we can give the man fiddler a chance to be
      heard too  we will play an other very old one .

      now if you are ready we will play. Old sally goodin.

      And this one will be just an old dance  peice
      we call it Rag time Annie.  Go ahead Bill and strick er up
      after this we will say good by tillthe same time next week

          Theme   song
                    Chicken reel
```

The only known photograph of all the Stonemans, taken at the Washington train station about 1942 or 1943. Back row (left to right): Billy, Eddie, Grace, John, Patsy; middle row (left to right): Hattie, Jack, Gene, Dean, Scott; front row (left to right): Veronica, Jimmy, Donna; far right: Ernest holding Van.

Patsy and Pop in costume to perform their old favorite "The Mountaineer's Courtship." The picture probably dates from about 1944–45 when they entertained servicemen in the Washington area.

Pop Stoneman with his Autoharp about 1951.

After the Stonemans won the contest at Constitution Hall in 1947, Pop had this publicity still made. It contained all family members except Patsy, who had gone to California. Billy had just returned from the navy. Top (left to right); Roni, Van; standing (left to right): Scott, Hattie, Ernest, Grace, Dean, Gene, Eddie; seated (left to right): John, Billy, Donna, Jimmy, Jack.

Pop Stoneman with the Stoneman brothers, early 1950s. Left to right: Scott, Pop, Eddie, Billy, Jimmy.

Scott Stoneman, champion fiddler, about 1955.

The Blue Grass Champs about 1958 on WTTG-TV, Washington. Left to right: Donna Stoneman, Lew "Childre" Houston, Jimmy Stoneman, Van Stoneman, Scott Stoneman.

The Blue Grass Champs about 1955. Left to right: Jimmy Case, Scott Stoneman, Jimmy Stoneman, Donna Stoneman Bean. With the addition of Porter Church on banjo, this group emerged as winners on an Arthur Godfrey show, starting the second upward climb of the Stonemans in music.

4

Depression and Disaster

1929–41

Although 1929 has become memorable as the year of the great Wall Street crash that ushered in the Great Depression, the fact is that prosperity and optimism prevailed through most of the year. Record companies released more hillbilly discs, some eight hundred different ones, than in any previous year of the business and conducted many sessions at various sites throughout the nation. One of the more significant recording artists, however, namely Ernest Stoneman, experienced considerably less than a good season, even before the crash and its negative impact.

In March 1929, Ernest went to Richmond, Indiana, for another recording venture. Eck Dunford accompanied him as fiddler, along with two Grayson County youths. Fields and Sampson Ward had grown up under the musical tutelage of their fiddling father, Davy Crockett Ward, and banjo-picking uncle, Wade Ward. In 1927 their group, generally styled the Buck Mountain Band, had gone to Winston-Salem and participated in a session for OKeh Records. The boys apparently aspired to record again and struck up a relationship with the more experienced Stoneman. Fields, eighteen, played guitar and sang, while Sampson frailed the banjo. The foursome recorded fourteen numbers under the band name of Grayson County Railsplitters. Gennett ledgers show the names Ward and Winfield as prefacing the name of the band on some cuts while that of Ward alone appears on some of the others. Fields remembered more about the trip to Indiana than about the session, recalling that Ernest ran the car off the road and into the ditch more than once on the long trek. Ward insisted that he was the leader and may well have been, as he later came into possession of the surviving test pressings. After the session, some type of disagreement developed with the company and Gennett never released any of the material. In 1964, Stoneman told Eugene Earle that the dispute involved Gennett and "the Ward boys" and that he had no part in it. Doubtless, a more detailed explanation could have been given. Eventually, in 1967, eleven of the numbers appeared on the album *Fields Ward and the Buck Mountain Band* (Historical LP 8001) along with some cuts from the July 1928 session featuring Ernest and the Sweet Brothers. At the time, however, the most that can be said for the experience would be that it got the year off to a bad start.[1]

Meanwhile, Ernest apparently began to search for additional musicians with whom to record. Unfortunately, his contract with Peer prevented his name from being used on any Gennett sessions. However, he soon found a pair of highly skilled talents in a father and son from Dobson, North Carolina, one of whom had already made a recording trip to Richmond and the Gennett studios. Frank Jenkins had been about forty-seven when he went with fiddler Ben Jarrell, banjo picker–promoter DaCosta Woltz, and a twelve-year-old harmonica wizard named Price Goodson to cut several tunes under the name DaCosta Woltz's Southern Broadcasters. Jenkins had also played banjo on these recordings, which would be considered by many experts to be among the best-ever pieces documenting the early sounds of Galax–Mount Airy musicians. By 1929, this middle-aged tobacco farmer had come to favor the fiddle considerably more, while his nineteen-year-old son Oscar had become quite adept on banjo. In the last year of life, Ernest met Oscar again and recalled how he had helped Oscar and his dad put up three barns of tobacco so they could go to Richmond. "We cured them out in three days," he explained to a *Winston-Salem Journal* reporter, and then "we'd practice between chunking the fires."[2]

Actually the musicians went to Chicago first, where they made two sides for the Paramount label owned by the New York Recording Laboratories, a division of the Wisconsin Chair Company of Port Washington, Wisconsin. Although this firm had considerable success in marketing its 12,000 series of race records, its hillbilly series never quite made it commercially. This was unfortunate because the musical quality of Paramount's 3,000 series of old-time tunes compares favorably with those of its competitors. The technical quality of Paramount seems to have been a major problem with consumers, for as one critic put it, Paramount discs sounded like sandpaper even when new. Through its subsidiary Broadway label, Paramount also marketed its product by way of Montgomery Ward catalogs, but one could hardly expect to do as well with Paramount as with Victor or Columbia. Nonetheless, using the name Oscar Jenkins' Mountaineers, the three musicians waxed two sides for the firm in its Chicago studios. The first song, entitled "The Railway Flagman's Sweetheart," could be considered another recomposition of "The Broken Hearted Lover." The second number, "The Burial of Wild Bill," had a more interesting history. Captain Jack Crawford, who styled himself "the poet scout," wrote it as a poem shortly after the funeral of Wild Bill Hickok, who was killed during an 1876 poker game in Deadwood, Dakota Territory. Ernest, unaware of all this, had simply taken a reprint from the pages of the *New York Clipper* and set a tune to it. While in Chicago, the Mountaineers played for a week at radio station WLS, already recognized for its wide audience and broadcasting of down-home-style musical programs.[3]

Arriving in Richmond, Indiana, the Mountaineers recorded nine songs under the name Frank Jenkins' Pilot Mountaineers. Four of them, like the two Paramount sides, consisted of strong Stoneman songs backed by the able string band of the Jenkins fiddle and banjo, together with his own rhythm guitar. Two, in fact, were the same songs, while the other two included a second version of "When the Snowflakes Fall Again" and the hitherto unrecorded "A Message from Home Sweet Home," which Ernest had learned from an untraced phonograph disc. Two of the tunes, "Sunny Home in Dixie" and "Old Dad," showcase the fiddling expertise of Frank Jenkins in a manner that equals and perhaps surpasses the earlier work of Kahle Brewer and Herbert Sweet as Stoneman-associated fiddlers. The four vocal numbers were released only on the Sears-owned Conqueror label under the pseudonym of Alex Gordon, while the fiddle tunes were released on Gennett in Jenkins's name and on Supertone as Riley's

Mountaineers. Three numbers, the topical "The Murder of Nellie Brown," Thomas B. Ransom's sentimental favorite "I'll Be All Smiles Tonight" (1869), and the old minstrel piece by Henry Clay Work, "In the Year of Jubilo," all remained unreleased.[4]

Following the September 12, 1929, recordings in Indiana, Ernest, Frank, and Oscar returned to their mountain homes. At the time, they probably never realized that they would never record together again. In fact, more than four years would pass before Ernest would have another session, and it would be forty years before Oscar Jenkins had another opportunity to enter a studio. The three friends would do some radio work together in the next three or four years, but phonograph-studio work would henceforth be exceedingly scarce.[5]

Back in Galax, the Stoneman family continued to grow. On May 10, 1929, Hattie had given birth to Jack Monroe Stoneman, her seventh child. Within a very few months she would become pregnant again. By that time, the young couple would gain an increasing awareness that things had not been going well. Edison went out of business as a recording company, and at Victor, Ralph Peer must have noted that Stoneman record sales lagged far behind those of some of his other artists, especially Jimmie Rodgers. In fact, the last four Stoneman Family releases on Victor and the only ones for which complete figures exist document an alarming decline. "We Parted by the Riverside"/ "The Broken Hearted Lover" (Victor 40030), released in March, sold only a little above the average number of copies, 8,114 (6,000 to 8,000 considered average), while the next one (40078) did not even make it to average with 4,958. "Going Up the Mountain After Liquor" (40116), released on September 20, managed to sell some 4,534 copies, but by the time "The Spanish Merchant's Daughter"/ "Too Late" (40206) hit the store shelves in late February 1930, the economy had begun to register the effects of the Great Crash and only 2,700 buyers could be found. As the nation sank ever deeper in depression, record sales plummeted even lower. Ralph Peer continued to schedule sessions for the Carter Family and Jimmie Rodgers, and by 1932–33 their Victor releases sold even fewer copies than Victor 40206. The enormously influential Carter rendition of "The Wabash Cannonball" sold but 1,700 copies after its release in November 1933, and those by Rodgers did no better. Largely dependent on working-class consumers for sales, hillbilly recording ventures became increasingly curtailed. Income from all record sales in 1933 constituted only 7 percent of what it had been in 1929. By 1933, phonograph records that sold well in 1925–28 at seventy-five cents each sold poorly at thirty-five cents each on budget labels. For Ernest Stoneman, 1929 had been a slow year, but those that followed would become disastrous.[6]

The recollections of the Stoneman children lack such quantification data. Nonetheless, their perceptions convey some awareness of a differing condition. Patsy recalls:

> I started noticing things were changing. Although I'm sure I heard the word "Depression," it didn't mean anything to me, not then anyway. But I soon learned. The first changes . . . was that the hired girls were not there anymore. I sure did miss all the attention they had been giving me. . . . It was during this time that our sister Nita got very sick. She was a pretty thing and had hair that looked like gold silk. . . . She stayed sick for a long time and at times she would sit on the couch and look out and watch the rest of us kids play.[7]

Worsening financial conditions did not, however, impede the course of nature. On June 12, 1930, Hattie gave birth to twin boys named Dean Clark and Gene Austin Stoneman. The latter suggests that Ernest and Hattie possessed considerable admiration for major figures in the world of mainstream popular music. Born somewhat premature, the fact that they even survived seems testimony to the hardiness of the entire clan. Patsy continues: "Things were getting worse for us, and the [last] woman who had helped keep house left. Her name was Martha Weatherman, and I heard later that she had gone to the 'Poor House' over in Abbington [*sic*]. . . . There wasn't many people around our house and laughing anymore. Daddy would be gone most of the time, and when he would come home, there wasn't the big crowd to follow him in, just worried looks."[8]

Apparently, during much of this time, Ernest had been searching for work, either as a carpenter or as a musician, and having scant success. It was about this time that one of Hattie's distant kin, Galax City Attorney H. A. Melton, wrote a "To Whom It May Concern" reference letter vouching for Stoneman's good character and abilities as both carpenter and musician. Such a letter may have served to help him find employment and to identify him as an honorable individual in a time when police in many communities in the rural and small-town South were only too willing to jail or run out of town strangers who might appear threatening to already hard-pressed local budgets. In March 1968, Ernest recalled some radio work at WSJS in Winston-Salem. He told a reporter about the local textile-mill tycoon: "One time, Mr. P. H. Hanes sent his chauffeur to pick us up, and we went over to his house and played for him for about two hours." "Us" likely referred to Frank and Oscar Jenkins, who apparently stuck with Ernest musically during at least part of the Depression.[9]

Community fiddler's conventions provided a small source of income to cash-poor musicians. Walter Couch, a young fiddler from Elkin who later recorded for Bluebird, recalled playing at these events in 1930–32 with Frank and Oscar Jenkins and Ernest Stoneman. The latter would come down from Galax and more or less make his headquarters at the Jenkins farm near Dobson and, Couch thought, perhaps stay for as long as a month at a time. Different towns staged their contests on successive weekends, and many of the contestants went from one convention to another. Enthusiastic crowds attended the affairs, with cash prizes of five dollars being the maximum amount awarded.[10]

Such opportunities to play music for pay, however, tended to be increasingly few and far between. In the meantime, a small army of creditors began to gather. Beginning in Carroll County on March 8, 1930, and extending until July 2, 1931, and in Grayson County between November 10, 1930, and July 22, 1931, a series of "vendor's lien" litigations against Ernest and Hattie Stoneman deprived them of their properties. Remembering what he had been told, Gene Stoneman said, "Anyhow, daddy had a grocery bill, it came to little over $500.00 and back then that was a lot of money, so he lost his house over that much money." In addition to the grocery bills, there also existed a note for $250.00 at the Bank of Galax and another for $165.76 at the First Bank of Fries. After July, three properties passed into the hands of S. Floyd Landreth, court-appointed trustee, who was also a local lawyer, banker, and politician. The Stonemans continued, however, to occupy these lands until they had been resold, for by all accounts they lived in the home Ernest had built until the summer of 1932. During this time, Ernest worked fervently to rebuild the career that had been so good to him through 1926–28, and he probably retained some shred of hope that he could hit upon something that would either enable him to recover his losses or at least to maintain his family in minimum comfort.[11]

The children possessed only a vague awareness of the happenings outside their home, but they do remember something of the internal developments. Youngest daughter Nita remained in poor health. She seemingly got a little better in the summer of 1931, but then her condition worsened again. To quote Patsy once more: "Sometime about then, Nita told Mommy that she was going to die, and she wanted her bangs cut so she could be pretty when she died, and that she wanted Daddy to come home before she died. Mommie just cried all the time, and she didn't want to cut Nita's bangs. I guess she felt that if she did, that what Nita said would come true. But Nita kept asking her, until finally she cut her bangs and tried to get in touch with Daddy."[12]

The winter of 1931–32 took a rough toll in the Virginia mountains for those who had little source of heat. According to Patsy: "It seems to me that . . . was the winter we almost froze to death because there was no coal to heat our house. Grandpa and Granny were doing all they could to keep us alive, and I remember Grandpa coming from his grannery with baskets of corn. He would put them in our stove to try to keep us warm. You could hear the corn popping and see the tears dropping off of Grandpa's face, but somehow we did survive that winter."[13]

The return of warmer weather did not bring about any improvements in Nita's condition, and Hattie found herself "in the family way" once again. Patsy tells the story in her own words best:

Nita was in bad shape, and Mommie got hold of Daddy somewhere, I think he was in New York [actually Washington], and told him to come home because Nita wanted to see him before she died. I think that Nita died in the morning, and that Daddy got there just a little while after she died. I remember that when Daddy come in I was screaming so bad that they couldn't stop me, and I was leaning on a table that use to hold Daddy's Autoharp. He picked me up and carried me [to] a bedroom and told me that Nita had gone to Heaven and that she was an Angel now and wouldn't want to see me crying. After she was buried, whenever I would go out to play, I would always pretend that I was at a funeral, and sing about whatever I had buried. The side of the hill was covered with little graves that I had dug by the time we had to leave Galax.[14]

As Patsy recalls, "the only thing we had left was the house, and some furniture, and a car." Of course, she didn't realize that the house was really gone too, and that the somewhat benevolent Landreth merely allowed them to continue living in it temporarily. On August 4, 1932, Hattie gave birth to her tenth child, a son named Calvin Scott Stoneman. Patsy remembered "there was a window I could peek in . . . and I watched him being born. I don't remember that it frightened me, but I do remember that someone put him in my arms right after he was born." The birth of Scotty provided hardly a pause in the decline of the Stoneman fortunes. Patsy continues: "While Mommie was still in bed after having Scott some men came and took our furniture away. She was laying on a small bed with Scott, and that was the only piece of furniture that was left. When our couch was being carried out, the cushions fell off, and some of the things that Nita had played with fell out, and Mommie screamed."[15]

During these months, Ernest finally landed a job of sorts in radio. In Winston-Salem he had met a man named Bill Dougan, whom Patsy believes may have served Ernest as "a manager." At any rate, the two conceived a rural drama for radio that bore some resemblance to the skits that had been on records earlier, such as the Skillet Lickers' famous "A Corn Likker Still in Georgia" discs or Ernest's own "Possum Trot School Exhibition." The radio dramas were extended versions of these skits, which interspersed exaggerated Appalachian dialogue and musical interludes. Such shows did indeed have considerable promise. The program "Lum and Abner," which lasted more than a quarter of a century, originated about this time in Cleveland, Ohio, with a setting in the Ozark community of Pine Ridge, Arkansas. Stoneman and Dougan seem to have been more influenced by a radio series based somewhere on the East Coast called "Moonshine and Honeysuckle" that enjoyed a less enduring run. They titled their original creation "Irma and Izary" (a corruption of Ezra) and constructed a minimum of thirty-two quarter-hour episodes. The series would initially be aired on a Washington suburban station, WJSV, in Mount Vernon Hills, Virginia. Ernest played the character "Raief Crutchfield," while Irma Frost would play the female lead as "Irma Adkins." Frank Jenkins was a fiddler named "Highpockets," and Oscar also had a part. Other characters bore such names as "Izary Stillin" and "Zeb Adkins," the father of "Irma." The four also performed the musical interludes. The series began its run in late February 1932, and Stoneman and Dougan hoped they could sell it to one of the networks.[16] The *Grayson-Carroll Gazette* carried a brief announcement of the beginning of the program: "Ernest Stoneman, who with several others has been broadcasting old time music from several northern radio stations will be 'on the air' at 9:15 each evening this week over station WJSV, Mt. Vernon Hills, Va., in a sketch called 'Isary and Irmia.' "[17]

The "lye-soap opera or mountain family saga" had hardly begun when there occurred an incident that captured national attention. On March 1, 1932, the infant son of America's most admired young couple, Charles and Anne Morrow Lindbergh, vanished, with his abductors leaving only a ransom note. Hoping that the Lindbergh misfortune would provide his sagging career with a much needed shot in the arm, Ernest penned a topical ballad entitled "The Little Lost Eagle" in the days immediately following the tragedy. The musicians performed the song on their program, and Ernest invested a few of his increasingly scarce and precious dollars in having some sheet-music copies printed. Although a fine example of the event-song genre, it did not become a "Wreck of the Old 97," "Death of Floyd Collins," or "The Titanic." Failure to get the song on disc probably guaranteed it a limited audience. The sheet-music cover bore a confident slogan: "A Voice from the Heart of the Nation" with "Words and Music by IRMA and IZARY As Sung in Their Story of Mountain Life Over Station WJSV." However, the inside revealed only a printing of a handwritten musical score, and the cover photo of Stoneman, Frost, and the Jenkins boys looked more like the four malnourished musicians they actually were. It presents a sad contrast to the studio photos taken at Galax in 1927 and 1928. "The Little Lost Eagle" captured the tension and tragedy associated with the plight of the distraught Lindberghs quite well and deserved a better fate than its subsequent consignment to the scrap heap of hillbilly culture:

THE LITTLE LOST EAGLE

The Little Lone Eagle was stolen today,
Kidnaped by a villain who took him away;
By a three-section ladder he entered the room;
He turned all life's sunshine to darkness and gloom.

The Little Lone Eagle was tucked in his nest,
Lindy and Anne both thought him at rest,
Little did they dream their skies had turned to grey,
That bad bold kidnapers had stolen him away.

Big Eagle, his father, found deep in his bed
A note from the child thief, and here's what it said:
"We're holding your baby for money, for gold,
Don't call in the law or your boy'll be found cold."

"I'll pay any ransom," Big Eagle did say,
"Just bring back our baby to us right away."
To hear his soft cooing for Daddy again
Is worth more than money, it's greater than fame.

Sad days have now passed, still the baby's away,
From the home of his parents where once he did play,
The heart of the Nation is sorrowful, sad,
It beats on in pity for the boy's famous dad.

From Maine to our West Coast each Mother today,
For the dear Eaglet's parents hourly does pray,
And we of the mountains reflect how they feel,
"Oh God, restore Lindy," is our prayer of appeal.[18]

Unfortunately, "Irma and Izary" didn't do much better. As Ernest later explained, it "didn't click" because his contact with the networks, one John Engels, asked for "too much." One network, NBC, wanted the program but only wished to pay $150 (per week, one would assume). The Jenkins boys then became discouraged and returned to Dobson, leaving Ernest to play all the dramatic voices. In between broadcasts, he survived by whatever labor or musical work he could find, which apparently was not very much.[19]

Meanwhile back in Galax, chances that Ernest might be able to repurchase his property evaporated quickly. Not only did he lose the acre Hattie had obtained from her parents in 1929 and the 2.21 acres he had purchased from F. B. and Vergie Leonard in 1927, but Elisha, who had co-signed Ernest's bank loans, lost his 51 acres near Iron Ridge. Luckily, the eighty-three-year-old found refuge with his second son, Ingram, in the coal camp of Elbert, West Virginia. The Frosts also seem to have lost their little farm as well, but were allowed to remain as tenants. However, no such refuges could be found for a couple with nine children and an attractive homesite. John Leonard, a neighbor and steadily employed foreman at a Galax furniture factory, purchased the property for his oldest son about the time of Scott's birth. Patsy recalled an encounter with one of the Leonard children:

> I had been sitting on the fence steps that divided our land from the Leonard's place playing with Beulah Leonard, and she had laughed and told me that her daddy was going to take our house. I called her a liar and got as big a rock as I could pick up and chased her with it. When I caught her I hit her smack dab in the middle of her back and just about killed her. There sure was a big stink raised about it, because I hurt her pretty bad. But I just couldn't believe that it was true. But it was true, because right after they took our furniture, the Leonards took our house. So now all we had left in the world was a car.[20]

Hattie and the nine surviving children now had no place to go, but the Frosts' little three-room home. Grace recalls that conditions eased when "Gene, Jack and myself went to stay at Aunt Phinney's," referring to Martha Frost's sister, Sophinnia Norman (1873–1935). Grace had unpleasant memories of this situation:

> That was the worst time of my life. . . . Aunt Phinnia was real good to Gene, as he was real small, but she sure mistreated Jack and myself. . . . Thinking back on it now, I know she must have been mentally ill, but not bad enough to be put away. . . . I don't know how long Jack, Gene and I stayed at her home, but it sure seemed long to me. Aunt Jack [the children's term for Irma Frost] finally told Mommie that she should go get us and bring us to Granny's, that if we were going to starve, we would do it together. I wasn't at Granny's long before we got a letter from Dad saying he had a place for us and telling us to have Aunt Jack's boy friend, Emmit Moore, drive us to Alexandria, Virginia. Well, we didn't get far, only to Roanoke . . . before 3

or 4 of the children broke out with measels, and the old car was shimming, so we had to turn back to Granny's.[21]

By the next day, all the children, and Hattie as well, had measles except Grace, and within two or three days, she too came down with the ailment—a more severe case than the others. Grace remembered when the illness really hit her:

I got up and went outside on the back porch in freezing weather and broke the ice on the water bucket and drank all the ice water I could hold. Anyway the measels went in on me and I don't remember anything [for] three days. I came too when I heard Dad's voice and Mommie was telling him I was too sick to make the trip to Alexandria. Dad had come up after us himself. Anyway, I got up in bed and said I could make the trip. So everyone started packing and getting ready. Dad had a one seated Whippet with a rumble seat which he had put a canvas top over to keep out the wind.[22]

In retrospect, the Stoneman exit from Galax could probably best be described as an escape. Ernest told Hattie and the children he had to be in a rush, as he needed to get back to work. The reason for his hurried attitude soon became apparent when the county sheriff appeared on the scene. Patsy described what happened next:

He told Daddy that he had papers to take the car. Oh God, the look on Mommie and Daddy's face, and Mommie's tears. It was just awful. The Sheriff said that he hated to have to do it, but it was his job. Daddy said "I'll tell you what; we will have to be going through Galax anyway, so why don't you get in the car with us and we will go over to Galax and get this straightened out and we can just go on." The Sheriff said that would be alright, and he pushed in with Daddy and Mommie and whatever kids she had in the front with her, and we started across the flat to the gap near Granny's garden. When we got to the gap, Daddy told the Sheriff that he would have to get out and open the gate and the Sheriff got out, opened the gate, and Daddy pulled through. When the Sheriff closed the gate and come back to the car, Daddy said "When you crossed that fence line, you are in a different county. So unless you have a warrant for this county too, you can't take the car." We left the Sheriff standing there and headed for Alexandria. Daddy said, "I hated to do that, but I don't have any other choice." . . . Well, we were heading for Alexandria, to what I'm sure all of us hoped would be better. Little did we know that some of the worst was yet to come and that the Depression would last for us a mighty long time.[23]

The circumstances surrounding the Stoneman departure from Galax left Ernest with much bitterness toward his home community and those of its residents he considered "fair-weather friends." To quote Patsy again: "I guess Daddy had already learned that the ones who use to be his so called friends were the first to turn on him. Not long before Daddy died, he said that he did not want to be buried in Galax because of the way he had been treated by so many of them there."[24]

After a three-hundred-mile ride in an overcrowded car, the exhausted and impoverished Stonemans arrived in Alexandria. The new home Ernest had found for them at 1205 King Street "was a big old house that must have been abandoned for some time." Patsy recalled that "lots of the windows were out and it looked like the place was about to fall down." Ernest had gathered up some old furniture, most of which Patsy thought "must have been thrown away by some one else." The family patriarch spent most of his time "trying to find . . . work." He seemingly picked up a day or two of labor or carpenter jobs here and there, but generally he had only limited success. His most dependable but only occasional work made him a "non-certified" substitute railway postal clerk. One of these assignments came in December 1932 when he received notice to report to Train 95-5 on the run between Washington and Hamlet, North Carolina. One could hardly expect even to subsist with a wife and nine hungry children on such sporadic work, but somehow the Stonemans managed to stay alive, although one is tempted to believe that it could best be described as "just barely."[25]

Patsy's recollections of this time concern her own experiences in urban poverty more than those of her father. An atypical instance took place

one freezing night, Grace and I were asleep, and during the night I woke up needing to go to the outhouse. When I tried to move my feet I found out that I could hardly do it. After twisting around for a few minutes I finally got raised up and looked to see what was wrong. When I saw a man laying across our feet that I didn't know I started screaming and wetting all over him. Poor old man, it was an old colored man that had no place to sleep, and he kept telling Mommie and Daddy that he didn't mean no harm but that he was freezing and had no place. He had found the only place that was room for him to lay down.[26]

Ernest still tried to supplement his meager income through music, but that, too, provided insufficient—although helpful— amounts. Eddie Stoneman, who had left school and picked whatever he could find, recalled: "My father worked as a carpenter whenever he could find a job which were not easy to come by in the early thirties. He and I played music wherever we could find a place to play for a dollar or two each performance to help out the meager salary he got. We played for supermarket openings, automobile show room openings and any other place we could find."[27]

Finally, after nearly four and one-half years since his last record session, Ernest managed to arrange for another trip to the studio. Certainly he must have had hopes that this would relaunch his career in records. The American Record Corporation had been organized in 1929 and during the next few years acquired the rights to such labels as Banner, Brunswick, and Vocalion. In January 1934, American brought Ernest to New York and he took not-quite-fourteen Eddie along to assist. The latter has clear recollections of the incident: "I was still playing the banjo. . . . my trip to New York was . . . very frightening. . . . We could only afford a hotel room in 'Hell's Kitchen' which is frightening to a native New Yorker. . . . I was afraid to walk on the street except to go to and from the studio to record. But I never forgot that experience in my young life."[28] A Mr. Connor directed the recordings, which the father and son made over a three-day period. Ernest thought he would drop by the Victor offices to see whether any of his old friends were around. Connor found out and became incensed, believing Ernest may have gone to Victor to do a session when American was paying his expenses. He told Ernest that if Ernest worked for Victor, he would guarantee that Ernest would never work again for the American Record Corporation. However, Ernest managed to restore calm. He and Eddie cut nineteen sides, but only six were ever released. Sales must have been exceedingly low because these discs are at least as scarce as those of Stone-man's final Edison offerings.

He had recorded many of the songs earlier, although several of those that remained in the vaults he had never done before. They included such numbers as "After the Roses Have Faded Away" (that he would later preserve on television in the mid-sixties), "Meet Me by the Seaside," and the hymn "I'll Live On." The only released number totally new to Ernest was "Nine Pound Ham-mer," a work song that his friends the Hill Billies had done a few years before. More memorable cuts included a pair of numbers he had helped the Sweet Brothers do in 1928 and some from the ill-fated session with Fields Ward the following year. The first, a comedy song about courtship, was titled "There's Somebody Waiting for Me," while the second, a sentimental piece from the turn of the century by Harry Von Tilzer and Andrew Sterling, first bore the title "My Only Sweetheart." He used these titles again in 1934, but since both titles use the line "Somebody's waiting for me" in the chorus, the names of the songs became confused. Stoneman continued to sing the Sterling–Von Tilzer composition for the rest of his life under the latter title, and the children have recorded it twice since his death, all using the name "Somebody's Waiting for Me." Oddly enough, the tune survived in the reper-toire of Fields Ward, who recorded it again in 1971 under the title "In a Concert Garden."

Somewhat ironically, the last cut recorded from the 1934 ses-sion to be released was another waxing of "All I Got's Gone," which by now had become a true song for the hapless singers. The six sides released from the session, all on the Vocalion label, did poorly. It would be Ernest Stoneman's last appearance before a recording microphone for twenty-three years.[29]

Whatever fee Ernest and Eddie received from their trip to New York came in quite handy because another baby arrived within a month. On February 7, 1934, Hattie bore a daughter, Donna La-Verne. She became the first child of the household to be born in a hospital, and Hattie named her after one of the nurses who had helped her: Donna LaVerne McLaughlin. Mother and child came home from the hospital to inhospitable conditions. Patsy remem-bered: "It was awful cold in our house . . . and Mommie took the mumps, and they settled in her brests . . . and I was the only one to take care of them [Grace also being ill]. We put two beds in by the old wood stove and I['d] sit up at night to be sure that them and Donna stayed warm. One night I was sitting there with Donna wrapped up in my lap, and I fell asleep. I woke up and looked over at Mommie and there was a big rat trying to eat one of her eyebrows off! Poor Mommie, she was so sick."[30]

Although hard times prevailed in the Stoneman household during that period, happy moments were not entirely lacking. Patsy remembered that "when spring came, things didn't seem so bad." Not only was there an old airfield nearby that provided them with ample play space, but a family living across the field, named Favil, gave the Stoneman children additional playmates. Unfortunately, the Stoneman kids "got our first case of itch from" the Favils and "it looked like we would never get rid of it." Ernest went to a doctor and got some medicine, which apparently didn't work, and finally "one of the colored people told Daddy to use sulfur and lard." You applied this folk remedy in a mixture which you were supposed to leave on for nine days and then burn all the bedclothes. Patsy said it "sure smelled awful, especially after nine days, but we kept it on us." Even humor could emerge from the worst situation: a traveling salesman showed up at the door "while we were all covered with all that yellow greasy stuff." Hattie retreated, but the kids invited him in and he sat in a chair: "My brother Jack kept walking around him and scratching, finally Jack leaned on the man's arm and said, 'We got the itch but we ain't supposed to tell you.' The salesman got out of there as fast as he could, and we never saw him again."[31]

The children eventually recovered from the itch, but there seemed no cure for the economic doldrums. Patsy recalled that Ernest found several days of steady labor for a Dr. Jacobs doing "painting and carpenter work." The doctor worked in some kind of food-testing lab and got them a goodly supply of macaroni and spaghetti, which they ate raw, dry, and hard for three or four days before someone told them you were supposed to boil it in water first. But in the final analysis, "no matter how he tried there was never enough to feed us all. There were times that I seen the tears in his eyes, and Mommie and him started fussing an awful lot. Nothing seem[ed] to ever go right, and it must have been harder on them than it was on us kids. Lord knows that was hard enough. I have never been able to understand how they survived. Even though they would fuss and fight a whole lot, I'm sure they loved each other very much and that there must have been some tender times for them."[32]

Ernest, and sometimes Eddie and Hattie as well, continued also to pick up a music job now and then, "mostly for groceries or for a dollar or so." They sometimes played at WJSV radio, and Hattie even sold a few patterns for the bonnets she wore on radio and at their shows. Al Hopkins had been killed in a car wreck on October 21, 1932, and the Hill Billies did not survive him as an act, but his brother Joe stayed around Washington, and he still played now and then with Ernest. Another band member, Tony Alderman, also settled in the area and kept in touch. So, too, did Frank and Oscar Jenkins, who periodically came back to the city. Patsy believes that not only did the music help a little with putting food on the table, it also kept Ernest's spirits buoyed because "he still thought that maybe he could make a living that way again."[33]

Sometime in 1934, probably in the summer, Ernest lost his part-time job at the Railway Mail Service, and, in Grace's words, "things continued to be bad in Alexandria so after two years or so we went back to Galax." Actually, Ernest and Eddie seem to have remained in Washington, picking up whatever labor jobs they could, while Hattie and the nine younger kids returned to the mountains for the remainder of 1934 and at least the first three months of 1935. They lived in what had been an abandoned log cabin, near Aunt Phinnia's place, that Hattie's grandfather had lived in years before. Aunt Phinnia and Hattie were both very superstitious. "Both said they were born with a veil over their face," which Grace said they claimed gave them the power that "they could see things before they happened." At any rate, they both got extremely alarmed one day, contending that "they saw a gray casket coming over the hill." Grace looked, too, but "saw nothing." Not long after that, on February 23, 1935, Aunt Phinnia's only son, Dowe Leonard, met his death in a shooting affair, which gave the women reason to insist that they had a premonition of his death and the casket being "carried over the hill." Grace remained skeptical.[34]

Although conditions were about as bad in the cabin as they had been in Alexandria, a plentiful food supply existed, thanks to their garden and the Frost farm. Meanwhile Ernest had located another place for them to live—at 4768 Reservoir Road in the District of Columbia. Hattie and Grandma Frost had canned a lot of wild greens and other garden vegetables to help get them through the winter. Ernest came to get them with a small trailer hooked to the back of his old car. They packed auto and trailer with the jars of canned goods, flowers that Hattie took back to plant in the new yard, and especially children. Periodically the radiator would boil over on the mountain roads and they would have to stop to add more water. At a gas station, they refilled the fuel tank and the kids all went to the rest room. Thinking everyone was back inside and ready to go, Ernest took off down the road. Within a few minutes the children began screaming and hollering, and a car behind kept blowing the horn frantically. Ernest kept grumbling and said "Dad blame it, you've got room to pass" and waved his arm to signal the driver. Patsy says:

> Finally the car started past us, and we looked over at it and there was our brother Gene, just crying his heart out and hanging out the window. Daddy pulled over . . . and Gene got out of the car and come running as fast as he could. . . . When we had left the gas station, Gene was in the toilet, and when he heard us leaving he tried to catch us with his pants still down around his knees. The man at the station had put him in his car and tried to catch us. . . . When we got Gene back in the car . . . Mommie turned to Daddy and said, "Ernest Stoneman, you are trying to get rid of my younguns, and at this rate I won't have one left when we get to Washington."[35]

Contrary to Hattie's fears, the overextended nuclear family did make it to their new home intact. Like their Alexandria residence, "it was another old house," but it did have twelve rooms and running water. The owner told Ernest that they "could live there until it was sold." Patsy remarked that "we lived there a good while because nobody could afford to buy anything." Grace remembered the "home for unwed mothers . . . right across the street" and an ice-cream store nearby. Patsy's best memories concerned the adjacent fire station and the friendships made by the children, contending, "Those firemen were to be a blessing to us for the next couple of years." When their basement filled with water because of leaky pipes, the boys from "#29 Engine Co." came over and pumped it out for them. Later they provided thrills for the children by showing—and even letting them play with—the fire engines and other equipment. Most significantly, when "Daddy did everything he could to feed us, but we were hungry most of the time until the firemen discovered what shape we were in. Bless their hearts, there was Capt. Anderson, Lt. McGee . . . , one we called 'Bunny,' Carl Davis and several more that was real good to us. They gathered as much food . . . as they could, and when Christmas came we just couldn't believe it! They would gather toys and cloths and repair everything for our Christmas. [Later] the fireman's wives started making us things."[36]

Until they moved to Reservoir Road, school authorities had never quite caught up with the Stonemans; even then it took them until February 1936. Eddie, Grace, and John attended Pine Ridge Elementary School near Galax before poverty began overwhelming the family, and Patsy had gone there a little, but in Alexandria they had managed to avoid school altogether.[37] Grace had unpleasant memories of her school experiences: "Fourteen in fourth grade, I was the most uncomfortable, self concious person in school. I did not have suitable clothes, was made fun of, called 'hillbilly,' told to get the hayseed out of my hair, and of course, so much taller than the other children that I think that hurt me worse than being hungry. It was hard being so old in the school."[38]

Patsy had similar experiences, especially by being "so much bigger than the rest of the kids that were in the first grade." However, encouragement from the firemen brightened her attitude. One got her some better clothing, while another provided learning incentive by giving her a nickel for each letter of the alphabet she mastered and others promised her a dollar for each A she earned on her report card. She came in with eight A's on the first card, "and believe me I collected!" This must have temporarily provided her with the status of being the richest Stoneman. Patsy's first teacher, Mrs. Adams, also proved helpful and "was always good to me." She eventually not only helped Patsy quite a bit but even arranged for her to skip a couple of grades. Sadly, she had considerably less success with young Jack, who began in the same class with Patsy. The mischievous boy constantly either created problems for the hapless teacher or sneaked out of the room and went home. Once he stretched chewing gum across the aisle between two seats and ruined her dress. Before the "school year was out," Patsy said, "Jack had been sent home and told not to come back that year."[39]

In addition to laboring, Ernest, sometimes with Eddie and sometimes with Hattie, continued to pick and sing at WJSV and whenever an opportunity arose to make a dollar or two; sometimes they even played at private parties for food and whatever leftovers they could carry home. On one occasion, Ernest had a neighbor who could make a noise like a train whistle and was going to take him to do the radio program. Patsy said the man put on a suit for the event and left "just beaming." However, when Stoneman "started playing Old 97, he stepped up to the mike, and just froze." Patsy remarked, "It made Daddy so mad that he wouldn't give him another chance."[40]

In the summer of 1936, several of the children went back to the Frost farm near Galax. Eating out of the garden and canning food for the winter helped to ease the ever steady pressures on the limited food budget. Patsy's favorite memory of that summer concerned a day when a neighbor named Roy Leonard, who had a "Club House" where he and some friends could gather "to drink and play cards," along with a radio, allowed them to come up "one night and listen to Daddy on the radio. I was sure proud, I guess I always felt that Daddy was pretty great!"[41]

Unfortunately, being great was not enough to guarantee one a minimal living standard. A weekly radio program paid little or nothing, but it did keep Ernest Stoneman in show business a little bit and may have helped him find a show date now and then. Meanwhile, he continued to subsist mostly by sporadic labor and carpenter work, augmented by such musical jobs as he could obtain. The home on Reservoir Road would prove the most desirable of the several bad places in which circumstances forced the Stonemans to live, but by the fall of 1936 they had to relocate again. Their new home consisted of "another dilapidated house" at 1816 Wisconsin Avenue NW. The school was quite near, but Patsy's main memory of it consisted of an unpleasant girl there "named Sylvia that" acted "real snooty to me, and that Dean fell off of the fence . . . and knocked his head real bad." She adds that "as usual, we stayed hungry, and there was another school . . . a good ways from our house that would give you something to eat at lunch time, but it was hard to walk that far and get back to [our] school in time. . . . All they ever had was [barley] soup . . . and some crackers. . . . But it did help."[42]

Patsy also remembered stealing ten cents from a pile of newspapers in front of a drugstore. Hattie found out about it and the next morning marched her down to the pharmacy and made her return the money. After her confession, the man at the counter let her keep the ten cents. Patsy remarked, "I sure was surprised, because Mommie had told me that I would be put in jail." She concluded that the experience "scared me so bad, and shamed me so, that I never in my life again took anything that didn't belong to me."[43]

On March 8, 1937, Hattie again became the mother of twins, a boy and a girl named Oscar James and Rita Vivian. The names apparently came from Oscar James Anderson, the friendly fire captain, and a relative of Irma Frost's husband. Irma had come to Washington a couple of years earlier, worked in a laundry, helped in the Stoneman household, and in 1936 married a man named Hilary Smith, who became generally referred to as Smitty. Rita's middle name came from Captain Anderson's wife, who helped by gathering up some baby clothes, two cribs, and whatever else the folks from Engine Company 29 could locate. Rita remained with the Stoneman household only a short time. Early on the morning of June 12, Hattie arose and gave the sick child her bottle; two hours later, she checked on Rita again and found the infant dead. Patsy remembered that "Mommie was screaming real bad and everybody was crying." Hattie opened the front door and noticed "a green scarf tied around the door knob," which she interpreted as a symbol of death and henceforth forbade the children to "wear anything green." The police came and took the corpse for an autopsy, which revealed that the child had died of a broken vein in her head as the result of having whooping cough. Ernest found that the burial insurance he had "was no good," but "he managed to get Rita a little coffin." Destitute as usual, most of the Stonemans piled into their rattletrap car and "started for Galax to bury her."[44]

The journey back to the Stonemans' Blue Ridge homeland seems to have been an especially pathetic one. Along the road, they had a flat tire and Ernest had to leave on foot to get it fixed while Hattie and the children had to wait beside the jacked-up auto for his return. As usual, fatigue, hunger, and thirst took their toll on already dismal spirits. A couple watched from a distant farmhouse and the man finally walked over to take a closer observation: "He looked at us a few minutes and at the little coffin. Then he told us to come up to his house and get some water and a little bit to eat. So we went and they gave us a drink of water, and I think they gave the smallest ones some milk, and we all had some corn bread. We set under a shade tree in their yard until Daddy finally came back and put the tire on, and we were able to leave."[45]

Finally they arrived at the Frost farm and placed Rita's coffin "in the back room on a table in front of the fire place." A little later they "buried her next to . . . Nita at the grave yard on the side of the mountain toward Galax." The children remained at the farm for the summer. Grace had not accompanied the family on this mission of woe, as she had "got a job housekeeping for $2.00 a week plus room and board." She recalled, "I did cleaning, dishes, ironing etc. and lived there with them" while the rest of the family went to Galax. Ernest, and perhaps Eddie, spent the summer "working around D.C. and sent all the money he could home."[46]

By fall, when the family returned from the mountains, Ernest had found another residence at 203 Anacostia Road NE. Patsy thought the "neighborhood there was even worse than the others." In retrospect, she believed it provided "an education for some of us," as "sex and stuff like that had not been mentioned around us at all." They soon found out plenty because the community contained "several women and girls" that folks called "supporting themselves outside of work." Patsy described one neighbor girl as somewhere near her in age "but she sure had been around. Two men had already been put in jail for living with her, both at the same time. . . . It got to where she would come down to our house and hang around . . . Eddie and John. She smoked cigareets and . . . later on . . . I learned that she had died with all kinds of deseases while living with a couple [of] men. I was told that she even had bite marks all over her lower body, and that they were even infected."[47]

Coping with the struggle for daily existence probably occupied more of the Stonemans' time than learning about the seamier side of slum life. Grace helped ease the pressure a little by "working out," but "as far as us having enough to eat, it just seemed like we never would have." Patsy related that "the kid's bellys would stay swelled looking most of the time, and their knees looked about three or four times as big as their little legs." On one memorable instance, she recalled that "a bum came to our house and asked for some food. Mommie told him that we didn't have any-thing. . . . He left . . . but near evening he came back with a cou-ple loaves of bread and a can of Pet Milk for us. When people saw him doing that, they said that it was a miracle because he had never been known to do any kind of work before. He had gone to some store and worked to get bread and milk for us."[48]

Heat competed with food as a serious need during the winter, and on one occasion Patsy and Billy became desperate enough to attempt stealing again. They went down to the railroad yard, where stationary coal trains could be found. However, at the mo-ment Patsy prepared to throw a big lump down to Billy, a railroad policeman flashed a light in her eyes and asked her what she was doing. Quite honestly, Patsy replied, "I'm stealing coal." The stern cop started to take them home, but when he saw "the shape all of us was in," he told the near adolescents to be down by the coal cars about ten that night. When they got there, he already had two full sacks waiting for them and repeated this process sev-eral more times in the future. Eviction constituted another serious problem for the hapless family, and representatives of the land-lord carried their belongings out more than once.[49]

In March 1938 a *Washington Times* reporter learned of the Stone-mans' desperation and wrote a lengthy piece about the family's plight. Since it makes up the fullest contemporary description of the Stonemans during the Depression, it will be quoted verbatim:

> Threatened with eviction from their dilapidated home at 203 Anacostia Rd. N. E., Mr. and Mrs. Ernest Stoneman and their 11 children looked out on a cheerless world today.
>
> They need $15 to make up the balance of the $25 rent for March and they need food—especially milk and eggs for the children. Meanwhile, Stoneman, a carpenter, can't find work either in his line or any anything else.
>
> Mrs. Stoneman, an attractive blonde of 36, who is soon ex-pecting another child, was putting the finishing touches to an

already clean house. Neat bundles of the family's meager belongings [illegible] the Stonemans have no money to pay for shelter elsewhere.

Billy, 10, a pale lad made listless through infected tonsils, was holding the baby whose legs are too thin for a youngster a year old. The children are beautiful with blue eyes and pale golden hair and white skin. Though clean sweet, and well behaved they are obviously undernourished. Little Donna, aged four, had dark circles around her violet eyes. Scott, a mischevious imp of five with ash blond curls, dimples and an infectious smile piped, "I'se dot bad tonsils, too!"

While Patsy, a bright little girl of 12 with dark curls hugged Dean, 7, on her lap, she had fainted one day at the Bennings School, her mother said. Patsy added, "Now when I'm hungry I just say so." Jack, 9, and Gene, twin of Dean piped, "And so do we!"

They have, Patsy said, become experts on packing. Since they first occupied the house at 203, the Stonemans have been nearly evicted three times. Each time fate stepped in and saved them. Once the attorney for the property, himself the father of three children, gave Mr. Stoneman enough work to pay the rent for two months. "So," says Patsy, with a wave of her hand, "we just unpack again and hope for the best!" The Stonemans are a jolly family, despite their troubles. They had a time recollecting names and ages "because there's so many of us."

After the reporter had written them down they counted again just to be sure while the littlest ones squaled with glee. Even Mrs. Stoneman looked a bit non-plussed when asked to tabulate her brood. Here they are: Eddie, 17; Grace, 16; John, 14; Patsy, 12; Billy, 10; Jack, 9; Dean and Gene, 7; Scott, 5; Donna, 4; Oscar, 1 year.[50]

The citywide publicity calling attention to the Stonemans' plight brought about no massive aid efforts, but it did result in a few short range benefits. The firemen "from #29 Engine Co. . . . sent some things for us," a few mothers from the school gave the children some clothing, and "some people brought us some food and cloths [sic]." Negative aspects often accompanied minor improvements and good intentions, for Patsy explained how a dress that she then wore had previously belonged to a girl at school, and she would tell everybody that it was her dress, and we were poor dumb "hillbillies." . . . I took that for a good while, until one day a girl told her . . . the dress looked better on me than it ever had on her. Needless to say I became friends with [that] girl. In fact she would let me use her comb. That was sweet of her except that I caught lice from it. So head lice spread through our family like wild fire. I tried to get rid of them. I even put coal oil and clorox on my head. I don't remember that it killed the lice but it almost killed me.[51]

Whether from eviction or from opportunity, the Stonemans soon left Anacostia Street for another run-down home by Capital Airport toward Bladensburg, Maryland. They lived there only a few weeks, but during that time Hattie gave birth to her youngest daughter, Veronica Loretta Stoneman, on May 5, 1938. She received these names from two sisters of Hiliary Smith. Patsy recalls that afterward "Mommie . . . stayed in the hospital a good while," remaining there until at least Ernest's birthday on the twenty-fifth. Patsy baked him a birthday cake, which "looked awful . . . but I knew it pleased him." A friendly family named Talbert lived nearby and the Stonemans seemed to have enjoyed their brief residence.[52]

After Hattie came home from Gallenger Hospital, the Stonemans moved back to a Washington house on Higdon Road NE near a reform school. Patsy recalled that "our neighbors there seemed to be nicer than the ones in Bennings, and the house wasn't as bad as most we had lived in since leaving Galax." One of the first major events in the family after the move occurred after June 15, 1938, when the not-quite-seventeen Grace came in and announced that she and her boyfriend, William H. "Jack" Jewell, had run away and got married. Grace had started going with Jack when they lived in the Bennings area, and neither Ernest, Hattie, nor Aunt Jack liked him in the least. Said Patsy: "Aunt Jack almost had a fit, and Mommie and Daddy sure hollered about it." Grace knew her husband had a few flaws but said he "really impressed me with his looks, his muscles and all the attention he gave me." Somewhat naïvely, she "really believed that love would conquer all and in time he would change." In the final analysis, the deed had been done and Ernest concluded, "You have made your bed, now you will just have to lay in it."[53]

Some problems that never seemed to leave the Stonemans, underemployment and underfeeding, remained with them throughout the decade. Ernest seldom had regular work for more than a day at a time, and the little jobs Eddie had never brought in much cash. Their musical jobs did not pay much, either. In 1979, Eddie reminisced to a *Washington Star* staff writer: "Dad and I played for Arthur Godfrey [on radio] back in 1935 or 1936, and he got us a couple more jobs. We went down once and played in a contest at the Gayety Theater, where first prize was a basket of food and $10. In 1937, we played as Ernie and Eddie on radio station WJSB [probably WJSV], singing mostly old-time religious songs, but we got so much fan mail that they got jealous and they let us go."[54]

The children never seemed to be fed sufficiently. "Hunger," Patsy recalled, was "still with us," while "Mommie's health began to get bad. . . . She always said she had headaches, and would take whatever kind of pills she could find to ease it." A little later, Eddie, upset at not finding any work, wandered into a police station and "told them that if he didn't get some help for his brothers and sisters, that he was going to rob some place." He further "told them that he could not go back to the house and look at all us hungry kids." This caused sufficient alarm that "police brought him home, and looked at us all standing there hungry, and scaired of them." Whether Eddie put on an act to get police attention or had really reached that state of desperation cannot be determined, but his action did have positive effects:

> Any way, they went to the reform school and got some of the boys from there to carry us stuff out of the big garden that they had. The news paper people came again. They put our pictures in the paper, and asked people to help us. Some people who run shoe stores said that they would each give us a pair of shoes and the police would come in the patrol car and carry one or two of us to a shoe store. . . . People would send us some cloths and boxes of food. But the boys from the reform school came a good many times to bring stuff from their garden.

Unfortunately, this form of philanthropy ended when one of the boys from the school dropped by and came in "just like he belonged to us," as had been the case when he brought food. Soon, however, "the police came after him" and "after that the reform school boys couldn't bring stuff to us any more."[55]

During this Higdon Road residence, Patsy said, she grew "up some [and] started having my monthly period." Also, Hiliary Smith took Eddie somewhere, likely a YMCA, and came back announcing that he would "be in the Golden Gloves, and fight as a featherweight." Eddie's career ended when he broke his hand, but he told a reporter in 1979 that he "had 63 fights, [and] didn't lose but one" until his accident.[56]

In the summer of 1939, Patsy and the younger children went back to Galax with Hattie. By fall the family found themselves in a little house on a section of Minnesota Avenue called Cracker Box Row, from the similarity of the houses. They weren't there very long before Ernest found another "old house . . . on a farm owned by a man named Kitson" near Franconia, Virginia. Three or four memorable incidents took place during the several months the Stonemans lived there. Most significantly, young Oscar James, commonly called Jimmy, "fell off a bed and went into convulsions." Said Patsy: "After that we learned that he had Epilepsy." Second, Patsy went to school for the last time that year (1939–40). She still had to face the humiliation of being "called dumb hill billie and other things." A boy who aggravated her a great deal referred to her as "turkey legs" one day when they were near the top of a staircase and Patsy "hit him so hard that he landed at the bottom and was hurt pretty bad." The principal summoned her "into his office and really read the riot act." Nonetheless, she had less trouble with name calling from that point on, and the one she had knocked downstairs "seemed to be afraid of me." Patsy met a boy named Sam Hopkins, who befriended her and of whom she says, "I thought I was really in love with him and I thought so for a long time." She and Sam remained friendly even after the Stonemans moved back into the city. Patsy also remembered the farm owner's brutish son, George. One evening while she was carrying a sack of groceries toward home, George "grabbed me . . . and tried to drag me into [an] old shed." She managed to escape and somewhat later "his house caught fire and burned down." She remarked, "Everybody thought I had done it, but I hadn't. I was just glad that it happened." Not long afterward, the Stonemans moved to Minnesota Avenue SE.[57]

While the family still lived in Franconia, however, Ernest had begun to pick up more musical jobs. Patsy often joined him and Eddie and helped by playing guitar or banjo or doing whatever she could to help out. One time when Uncle Ingram and his family came to visit them, Patsy asked him if she could take one of his daughters along and showed considerable surprise when Ingram, who had been drinking quite a bit, yelled that "no daughter of his was ever going into a bar room and that Daddy was no good to let his children do it." After that, Patsy remembered, "we didn't see Uncle Ingram for a long time." Another minor but memorable argument between Ernest and Hattie took place on Sunday afternoon and culminated when "Daddy said he was leaving. He drove away and some of the children began crying but Hattie said he would be back" because "he left his guitar." Patsy said he came home by suppertime.[58]

Back in the District of Columbia, there were more changes in the Stoneman household. While Eddie and Patsy had been playing music at a "Pythian Temple," the former met a girl from North Carolina named Katherine Copeland. Too bashful to ask her for a date, he got Patsy to ask for him, and a serious romance soon developed. They planned marriage, but as Eddie had no money, he recalled that "I pawned my fiddle to get the four dollars for the marriage liscense . . . and pay the preacher." Sam Hopkins took them to Marlboro to get their papers, and the ceremony took place next day, November 24, 1940, "at Grace Baptist Church." In spite of their limited income, the young couple managed. Wrote Eddie: "I was working as a carpenter's helper at the time, but unfortunately that job did not last, and I went to work at a meat packing plant making hot dogs for a salary of $12.00 a week. We paid seven dollars a week for our apartment and that left five dollars for food, but I played music for two dollars a night whenever a musical job was available. But we managed to eat three meals a day and have clothes to wear."[59]

Patsy credited much of Eddie's success in marriage to Katherine's skill at budget management. With Eddie's low salary, it certainly came in handy for the next several years. With Hattie expecting another child and her health none too good, Patsy "hadn't bothered to go to school since . . . Mommie needed me at home, so I hadn't even registered." On December 31, 1940, Hattie gave birth to Van Haden Stoneman, who would be the youngest of the children to survive (according to family tradition, Hattie carried a total of twenty-three children, including four and perhaps five sets of twins, so she likely had at least one and perhaps two or three miscarriages during the war years).[60]

Hattie remained in the hospital for several days after Van's birth, and Patsy, left at home to take care of the other children, faced two crises, one of them major. The first took place when "the truant officer" came and inquired about "Patsy." She reacted thus: "I looked him right in the face and said that she was in Galax with our Grandmother. I'm Pattie Inez," she told the school official, who told her that when Patsy returned, she should register. In retrospect, Patsy said, "I've always felt that he knew . . . but saw how bad I was needed at home."[61] The second crisis involved considerably more danger and adrenalin:

> Jimmy and Roni set the upstairs bedroom on fire. I don't know how they got the matches but . . . the first thing I knew there was smoke boiling down the stairs. I hollered to all the kids . . . but I couldn't find Jimmy and Roni, . . . so . . . I tried to get into the bedroom. . . . I had to break in. . . . They fought me like crazy and . . . I had to drag them out. I run back . . . and don't remember how many buckets I carried before . . . the firemen arrived and . . . I was passed out at the top of the stairs. One . . . carried me out and . . . I didn't mind that nearly as bad as I minded seeing one of the firemen throwing the old pee-pot out of the window, and it was full, with "things" floating on top. . . . The firemen said that I was a hero for saving the kids, but I didn't feel like one, I was just ashamed.[62]

Some months later, when school had ended for the season, "Mom and the rest of the kids went back to Galax to see Granny," but Patsy remained "to keep house for Daddy." Ernest finally found his onetime benefactor, Dr. Jacobs, who had some work at a house he owned "down at the Island." Patsy evidently didn't realize that Daddy would be gone for several days, and he in turn "must have forgot" that she remained "at the house." Within a few days, Patsy realized she would have to do something on her own. She decided to stay with some neighbors until Ernest returned:

I couldn't go to Grace because she was having such a bad time. Jack Jewell was about the worst thing that could ever [have] happened to Grace. He would be beating on her a whole lot, and she was having a hard time having a place to live and some food for herself and her baby. Jack seemed to think that his drinks were more important than taking care of them. Eddie and Katherine was just sharing a place with her uncle . . . so I went to a drive-in and got a job as a curb girl. I was way too young to be working there because they served beer, but I lied to get the job.[63]

A couple of days later Eddie dropped by, found out where Patsy worked, and really "pitched a fit." He not only threatened to call the police, get her employer's license revoked, and have Patsy sent to reform school, he also planned to give her a severe whipping himself. Patsy decided that at sixteen she would no longer take orders from an older brother, so she ran "into one of the neighbor's house, and straight out the back door." She then called Sam Hopkins, and with what little money they both had, she purchased a train ticket to Galax, Virginia. By that time, the government had initiated the pre–World War II defense buildup, and the train had "a lot of soldiers on it." She enjoyed the ride to Radford, Virginia, a great deal because one of the soldiers "had a guitar, and all of us on the train sang and played . . . most of the way and the soldiers got me something to eat." Once she arrived at the Frost farmstead, Patsy learned that she had traded the discipline of an over zealous and protective big brother for that of an overly suspicious, guilt-ridden mother.[64]

Sixteen-year-old Patsy found Galax and being back at her grandparents' farm as enjoyable as ever and perhaps even more than before, partly because she had matured to the point of attracting "a lot of so-called boy friends." Hattie manifested feelings considerably less than positive, however, partly because of the mess Grace found herself in as the result of an early marriage and partly because Eddie had written her and suggested that Patsy had been involved in near-delinquent behavior. Because of crowded conditions, Hattie began insisting that Patsy spend some time up at Ginny Patton's, four miles away. Virginia Patton was Grandma Frost's half-sister and lived up at the Green Leonard cabin, where the late Aunt Phinnie formerly dwelled. The latter's widowed husband, Emmitt Norman, a heavy drinker and laborer at the furniture factory, also lived at the remote cabin. Norman, who many years earlier had fathered Ginny's woods colt, posed more of a threat to Patsy's honor than any of the adolescent boys that hung around the Frost farm, but Hattie seemed unaware. However, the drunken old man attacked her one night, and Ginny slugged him with "what looked like a rocker from the rocking chair" and screamed, "So you are trying to do to her what you did to me." Nonetheless, "Mommie didn't believe what he had tried" but continued her objections to relatively harmless hand holding that accompanied visits to church services at Hickory Flats or going to the movie theater in Galax.

Oddly enough, the boy most attracted to Patsy, Thurman Leonard, was the son of John and Mary Leonard, who had taken over the former Stoneman home in 1932. At any rate, after Patsy brought her younger siblings home from the movies in Galax one night later than expected, Hattie literally flew into her with a razor strop, administering a very severe and humiliating beating. In a fit of anger, Patsy drank a bottle of Grandma Frost's heart medicine and got pretty sick as result. In retrospect, Patsy believes that much of her mother's anger stemmed from her anxiousness to get back to Washington and that as a result she had "become real upset" and a "nervous wreck" who took her "frustrations out on us kids." At that point, Patsy wrote fire Captain O. J. Anderson and "Daddy," obtaining bus fare to go back to Washington. Thurman Leonard rode the bus back to the District with her, returning to Galax the same way. However, from the summer of 1941 on, mother-daughter relations continued to deteriorate.[65]

Back in Washington, Patsy found conditions much more pleasant than before. Ernest had been working pretty steadily, and "Eddie didn't act so mean to me." The fairly steady work probably was the reason Ernest had not found time to get back to Galax and bring Hattie and the others back home. Besides, she reminisced, "Daddy and I had always been able to talk about things" and "I stayed with him until he started the house in Carmody Hills."[66]

By late summer 1941, the defense expenditures of the most recent federal budget began to catch up with the impoverished Stonemans. Eight years of the New Deal had left them virtually untouched. Although hundreds of thousands of unemployed and underemployed Americans had found temporary federal help since the founding of the Reconstruction Finance Corporation in late 1932, neither it nor any other program, including the WPA seems to have helped the Stonemans. In fact, the only public assistance they received during this entire period apparently came from the few free meals they got at school and the food supplies provided by the boys at the reform school. Private charity—initiated through efforts of journalists, municipal police and firemen—helped them through some of their direst difficulties. Patsy thinks she and Billy visited a welfare office one time and obtained something. Whether Ernest followed this route by his own choice or whether the Stonemans represented a portion of some underclass that New Deal programs bypassed or overlooked must remain unanswered at this time.[67]

The Stoneman situation in the fall of 1941 can best be explained in Patsy's words:

> Daddy started getting work enough to go out to the edge of Maryland and put the down payment on a couple [of] lots, and started trying to build a place to keep us. It wasn't much of a place, but at least it would belong to us. The place was called Carmody Hills, and it would be our home until all the rest of the kids grew up. Daddy had a job with the government doing carpenter work, and was able to gather some of the wood and stuff that was used or discarded. The war was a horrible thing, but I guess that's why Daddy was able to get some steady work. It's a good thing that Daddy was able to move out to Carmody Hills because it had got to the place where nobody would let us live in any rented house, we just had too many kids. I was glad not to have to live in some of the places that we had been. . . . And bed bugs seemed to be in every one of them. Carmody Hills was almost a pleasure after that. I'll admit that [it] must have been full of people that had been run out of someplace else . . . but would you believe that most everyone there had an outhouse. We didn't even have water in the house, but Daddy dug a well.[68]

The house Ernest built could hardly be considered imposing by any means. It consisted of one large square room, roughly twenty-eight by twenty-eight feet square, with a half-basement underneath. He located it in the only place he could afford land: a suburban slum area three miles outside the District of Columbia in Prince George's County, Maryland. He ran out of money before it could be properly roofed, and cold weather arrived before he could get it finished. He got a big canvas that would suffice for a roof until he got enough money to purchase tar-paper roofing. With Patsy's help, he gathered some old furniture and finally went to Galax to get Hattie and the children. It snowed before he returned from the Blue Ridge, and one corner of the big tarp came loose and the snow blew in on Patsy as she slept. When Ernest finally made it back with Hattie and the others, "she didn't seem to think it was so bad, and there was plenty of room for her to plant flowers . . . and none of the kids thought the house was bad either."[69]

During that winter of 1941–42, Ernest and Hattie Stoneman and their eleven children still remaining at home settled into their new home at 307 Seventy-fourth Place NE. Their struggle with poverty, though hardly over, had passed through its direst phase. Ernest could expect to have steady work for a least the duration of the war. Furthermore, the increasing concentration of military personnel in the Washington area would provide a broadening audience for whatever musical talents he could offer. By now, not only did Ernest and Hattie have entertainment potential, but Eddie, Patsy, and even some of the younger children manifested interests in the cultural heritage that had first bloomed in the rugged hills of the Blue Ridge. While George Stoneman, Eck Dunford, the Wards, the Lundys, and others would continue to make music in the mountains, the Stonemans of Carmody Hills would not only maintain the heritage of the past, they would expand upon it, infusing newer sounds into the traditional music of their forebears as past generations had done before them.

5

The Road to Recovery

1941–55

World War II had a considerable impact on the Stonemans and
thousands of other families in the American underclass, Appalachian and otherwise, as the struggle for daily existence became
transformed into a struggle for national survival. Although they
remained poor, the threat of starvation no longer hovered around
their heads. Like most mountain people, the Stonemans manifested a deep-seated patriotism and shared in the desire for the
defeat of the Axis. Patsy recalls that when the Japanese "bombed
Pearl Harbor, Daddy had tried to join the Army, but they just
laughed and said that he should go back home." Being age forty-
eight did not exactly make Ernest prime military material, and besides, the recruiter argued, "it would break the army to feed all
his kids."[1]

Although two of Ernest and Hattie's children, John and Billy,
would eventually enter military service, the immediate short-run
effect of the war on the Stonemans was an improvement in their
monetary and musical situations. The national defense buildup
not only created conditions whereby Ernest Stoneman found
steady work at the carpenter's trade, but it provided an audience
for his music as well. Patsy remembers that they began to play at
a lot of army barracks: "We would get on the bus with . . . other
entertainers and go to the army camps and sometimes we would
eat with them. I use[d] to think that all the other people on the
bus was big stars, and it was a thrill for me to be with them. All

of them would sing and play on the way to the Army camps, I did enjoy them. Daddy always tried to play for the service men."[2]

Despite the easing of their economic situation, the legacy of a decade of poverty continued to dog the personal lives of the older Stoneman children. Eddie and Katherine fared somewhat better than the others through a combination of Eddie's hard work and Katherine's tight budgeting. About a year after his marriage, Eddie bought a lot in Carmody Hills adjacent to his dad's holdings and began constructing a small house on it. During this time he and Katherine moved back with Ernest and Hattie so that what had been rent money could go for building materials. He recalled carrying pieces of lumber home on the streetcar and working weekends and evenings until they moved into the kerosene-lighted two-room cottage on May 14, 1942, nearly three months before the birth of daughter Barbara, and that spring Eddie began adding a room to his little home. Rejected for military service, the young family man worked throughout the war, switching jobs. He worked at a service station as a twelve-hour-a-day "gas jockey," and by the last year of the war, his earnings had increased to thirty-five dollars weekly plus whatever else he could pick up from music jobs.[3]

In contrast to Eddie and Katherine's modest attainments, Grace suffered through a series of disasters. Her choice of a spouse, coupled with the position of women in society, accounted for much of her difficulty. She had given birth to her first child, William E. Jewell, on May 23, 1939, and on March 10, 1942, Grace and Jack became parents a second time with the birth of Steven. All this time, Grace's husband continued his heavy drinking and became increasingly violent, while never holding a job for very long. The couple also lived in Carmody Hills, a few blocks from Ernest and Hattie's home. On December 26, 1943, Grace gave birth to her third child, Frederick. However, on the last day of the following February, tragedy struck the Jewell household:

At 5:00 AM my oldest son woke up screaming and when I got there he . . . continued to scream "Get Boss [nickname for Steve] before something gets him." . . . When I leaned over the crib my baby was stiff. He was dead. I couldn't believe it. I picked him up and shook him and screamed. When I finally realized he was dead something came over me. I got real quiet and lay him down and covered him. I . . . had to find a phone. I stopped at my mother's house down the hill and knowing [she] could be a hysterical woman, I told her, "Now look Mom, I don't want no screamin' hysterical and on goin' on, but little Freddie's dead." Mommy just said, "Oh no, Grace." From there I went to my mother-in-laws to use the phone and make arrangements.[4]

Shortly afterward, Jack Jewell received his draft notice and entered the navy.

Military discipline did not bring any improvements in his behavior. Grace wrote that "he went AWOL, came home and beat me, choking me unconscious twice. They had to put seven stitches in my mouth. He broke my jaw bone, and left me in the hospital for a week. While I was in the hospital, they had to take shovels to scrape blood off the floor and wash it off the windows. He said he didn't remember doing it, he was in [such] a drunken stupor."[5]

Grace's physical recovery did not end her problems. A few weeks later, the bank repossessed their modest home and "set the furniture out" on the curb. Still, Grace tried to make her marriage work, recalling that "I went through a lot more with that man." Jack's drinking seemed beyond control and there were problems "with all his other women," too. The military bureaucracy also had difficulty with Jewell, since "in the four years that Jack was in the service, 3½ of those years, he spent in the brig or naval penitentiary, so the government had as much trouble dealing with him" as Grace did.[6]

Finally, Grace, having been reared in a family in which divorces had been almost unknown, "knew the situation wasn't going to get any better." She also concluded that she must "bring my children up in a different environment." She consulted a congressman and found that she could collect her back allotment checks. By early 1948 she had managed to receive this past-due assistance and recalled that "when I finally received my back checks, it enabled me to pay for the divorce." In the meantime, she passed a civil-service test and went to work for the federal government.[7]

John Stoneman, something of a loner and bashful by nature, began courting a girl from Jonesville, Virginia, named Bonnie Deeta Yeary. Their courtship lasted about a year, and finally Patsy volunteered to act as an intermediary. Deeta, also quite bashful, told Patsy that she would accept John's proposal if made. Soon afterward, on September 12, 1942, the couple married and moved into a tiny shack that Ernest helped John fashion from "a big wooden shipping crate." Later the couple purchased a lot "up on the next street" and John and Deeta started a house, constructing and living in the basement first. Patsy recalled that "Deeta was never afraid to tackle anything in the line of work, so she and John built the house, and both of them worked day jobs so they built most of it on weekends." Their first child, John Stoneman, Jr., was born on February 11, 1944. A few weeks later, John received his draft notice and immediately enlisted in the marines. Patsy recalled that he weighed a little less than the minimum requirement, but someone told him that eating bananas would increase his poundage. The banana diet evidently worked, and in May, John went to Parris Island, South Carolina, for basic training. Less interested in music than the others, John played some guitar and Autoharp and had a high tenor voice. Although he performed with the rest of the family on rare occasions, he generally contented himself with his job at the Thomason Dairy and went his own way.[8]

The war years brought new problems for Patsy. When Hattie returned to Carmody Hills just before Christmas 1941, she and Patsy continued to have emotional clashes. One night when Patsy returned home from a date, Hattie began to administer a severe beating with a razor strop. Patsy yelled for Ernest, who nailed the leather to the wall. Later that night, Patsy decided to leave home as soon as possible. Obtaining a waitress job at Jerry's Drive-In on Bladensburg Road, she arranged to share a room with two other girls. After another altercation, Patsy did as she had planned and never again lived at the Carmody Hills home, although she made brief visits.[9]

Being on her own brought about change in Patsy's life, but not necessarily for the better. Although she did satisfactorily in her job at Jerry's, she soon met a man and married him one week later. Her choice of a husband did not prove a satisfactory one, and as she reflected some forty years later, "it seemed that I was so lonely that I wasn't very particular." On May 4, 1942, Pattie Inez Stoneman became Mrs. Charles Streeks. Commenting on her husband's background, she said "he was the only son of a fairly middle class family, and the apple of his mother's eye." The latter condition proved a trying one because "she thought he had married beneath him and never let [anyone] forget it." A week after the wedding, Patsy recalled, her mother-in-law "asked just how many children that my mother had, and I told her. She said 'All I can say is that any woman that has that many children is not much better than a dog.' It just so happened that I had a frying pan in my hand at the time, and when she said that, I hit her across the face with it and she landed in the dining room. . . . That is not the way to start off a marriage."[10]

Patsy continued to work as a waitress for the next five years, but Charles "did not work but 6 months the whole time . . . the rest of the time I supported him by working." A year or two after the wedding, Patsy "became pregnant" and carried the fetus for seven months. One morning about 3:00 A.M. she awoke with labor pains and sent her husband to summon a physician: "The pain was unbelievable, and I was frightened so bad. Here I was all alone, waiting for a doctor to get there. With the baby half in and half out I fell into the living room floor and remained there for an hour or so. Finally I managed to get myself up on the couch where my baby girl was born, and where she died."[11] About 8:00 A.M. Patsy's mother-in-law entered. Rather than seeking a doctor, later events showed that Patsy's husband had sat outside the house on the curb until daylight and then went to his mother's house. Mrs. Streeks told Patsy she wasn't fit to have her son's child anyway. Finally she did summon a physician, who provided some help for Patsy and took the dead child away; Mrs. Streeks subsequently ordered it cremated.

These incidents taught Patsy much about how to hate, but she managed to try making her marriage work for a couple more years. At times, Charles began drinking heavily and beating his young wife. After a particularly rough night, Patsy decided that if they didn't split, she would probably kill him. Instead, she went to a lawyer, who suggested that she "pack his clothes and set them on the floor" and keep doing this until he left. After a couple of times, the errant husband got the message, took his belongings, and departed.[12]

Shortly afterward, Grace separated from Jack, moved in with Patsy, and they shared the apartment. Charles Streeks came around now and then "trying to bum money." One day his mother called Patsy and begged her to take him back. Patsy found out that he had beat her up, too, and told his mother "that she had him now and as far as I was concerned she could keep him." That, for all purposes but the formalities, ended the marriage. Meanwhile, Patsy continued to work as a waitress and play musical instruments with her father as circumstances permitted.[13]

Billy Stoneman became the first in the family to enter the military service. At age sixteen, with six years of elementary school completed, he went to work for the Pennsylvania Railroad in Baltimore as an electric lineman. However, he wanted to join the navy, and Ernest signed for him as soon as he turned seventeen. He enlisted exactly six days after his birthday and went to the naval training station at Sampson, New York; he was home from boot camp at the time Grace's infant died. Then the young sailor received his assignment on the USS *DeHaven*. During 1944 and 1945, the ship engaged in heavy action in the Pacific Theater and took part in the liberation of the Philippines. Billy served as third machinist's mate on the *DeHaven*, continuing his four-year enlistment after the cessation of hostilities. He was discharged at San Francisco in the fall of 1947, listing his job preference as musician in the Washington, D.C., area.[14]

The remaining Stoneman children, too young for military service, remained at home. Some went to school for a time, participated in the family's musical activities, enjoyed some benefits from less-crowded quarters, and got acquainted within the Carmody Hills community. Carmody Hills could be described best as a low-class suburb. Patsy pictured the community as she first knew it:

> To begin with, I guess that Carmody Hills wasn't too bad when we first moved there. There wasn't all that many families that lived there then, and most all the neighbor kids were kind'a young so they still hadn't got into full steam. But you can just imagine what it was like with my nine brothers, all different ages, roaming around the neighborhood meeting all the rest of the kids. Most of the fathers were real hard drinkers, and

my brothers thought that was something new, and would hang around them to watch the things they did when they were drunk.[15]

By and large, the populace of Carmody Hills did not immediately take to the Stonemans, with their sizable number of children, some of them already becoming unruly. According to Donna, some of the residents opposed allowing this large family of Appalachians into their community and circulated petitions to "kick them out" of the neighborhood. At the same time, she describes many of the residents as alcoholics, wife beaters, and child abusers who ranged from being little better to considerably worse in character than the Stonemans. Furthermore, there must have been other Appalachian and Southern families within the community whose past experiences could not have been very different.[16]

Popular or not, the Stonemans remained in Carmody Hills for more than twenty years. With the passing of time, the family achieved some degree of community acceptance. As time went by, Ernest managed to replace the tarp with roofing shingles, and electric lights replaced the kerosene lamps. Some neighbors came to appreciate the Stonemans' music, and a few even commented that their practice sessions on the porch constituted some of the best they ever heard. Ernest increasingly came to be called "Pop" during this period as more children began to join in with their dad and mother in musical activities.[17]

In addition to playing service clubs and wherever else they could pick up a few dollars (or even free food), the Stonemans began to make regular appearances at a place called Armstrong's Restaurant and Tavern on Central Avenue about five miles east of the district line. At various times over a period of three or four years, the family played there, usually on Sunday afternoons and evenings and sometimes on Friday and Saturday nights as well. Pop built a stage with a rail around it to prevent the drunks from falling onto it. Mr. Armstrong paid them but little, and most of their income was derived from passing the hat. Jimmy, possibly as young as five when their work started, received the responsibility of taking up the collection, but his persistent attitude alienated some customers and Mr. Armstrong and Ernest finally decided that less-offensive but equally appealing little Donna would do the hat passing. Jimmy and Donna comprised the younger children in the family at that time, while Scott, Dean, Gene, and Patsy also worked in the group. One night Hattie became jealous of some woman who socialized a bit with Ernest and decided that she would no longer fiddle while he flirted. After that, he began grooming Scott as a fiddler, and within a few months Scott turned into a top-notch bow wielder and won his first national championship in the contest at Warrenton, Virginia, while still in his teens.[18]

By 1947, Eddie, who had become proficient on the electric lead guitar, and some of the older boys had pretty much gone on their own musically, playing in a style more akin to the contemporary honky-tonk sounds of Eddy Arnold and Ernest Tubb. Pop and the aforementioned younger children favored the songs and music Ernest had performed since his youth. During that year, Connie B. Gay, a youthful promoter affiliated with new (November 1946) radio station WARL, initiated a talent contest in Constitution Hall "to pick the winners from that for his show" he planned to start. Says Patsy:

> My older brothers thought that Daddy and the rest were "Old Hillbillies," so they decided they would have a better chance if they played by themselves. I didn't go but Mommie and Daddy took all the youngest kids and went. Eddie and the other boys went on before Daddy and Mommie, and was standing beside the stage when they went on. To say the least, they just tore the crowd up! And when Eddie saw what was happening, they all walked out on the stage. . . . Somebody was running up and down the [aisle] hollering "Tear'em up Mom." So I guess you could say that the family were setting off on another life.[19]

Winning the contest initiated the beginning of a climb back up the commercial-music ladder for the Stonemans. Winning the contest got them twenty-six weeks of appearances on Connie B. Gay's local country-music television program "Gay Time." However, the return to more than local prominence would be a very slow one for the Stonemans; another decade would pass before they would achieve any more than local prominence in the Washington area. The TV program did make the Stonemans' children celebrities of a sort, yet, it placed them in the somewhat awkward position of having been on television before they had even seen one. Classmates who had once made fun of them as "dumb hill-billies" now sought their autographs.[20]

Patsy, tired of bill collectors trying to make her pay debts accumulated by her estranged husband, enamored of a young sailor from Mississippi who was being transferred to the West Coast, and having a disagreement with Connie B. Gay, decided to go west for a while. After one particularly rough Saturday, she made up her mind to leave. She says that "after the show, I went up to Daddy, told him bye, and kissed him, then, I left, heading for California."[21]

A few weeks later, Billy returned from the navy and rejoined the family. Ernest had a professional photograph of the group made, showing all the family members except Patsy. They were clustered in front of the old Chevrolet "covered wagon" that Ernest used to transport the family; it bore a sign reading "Stoneman Family, songs, music, dancing will be at _____ ," with a space to be filled in showing their current venue. Underneath was a caption: "Now Playing Gay Time Constitution Hall." For Ernest, this accomplishment represented the beginning of a comeback, so he renewed his correspondence with Ralph Peer. Through much of 1948, the American Federation of Musicians imposed a ban on recording, and since Ernest had joined the union, he apparently waited until the ban was lifted before he contacted the publishing executive. His letter reflects both his current situation and his optimistic spirit:

> I know you will [be] surprised to hear from me. Well I have 15 [in] my family and 10 of them play and sing as you can see inclosed photo and we are now playing a show [in] Wash. D.C. called (Gay Time). Played 27 weeks in Constitution Hall. Was on station WNBW television NBC chain from Boston to Richmond, Va. We have a big following here. I lived in Wash. D.C. 15 years and I have the largest family of hillbillys on radio, television, and stage in the country. We are billed as the sensational Stoneman Family and I would like to have a list of songs that I can play and sing on NBC television programs that is under your control. Also I have songs I have written and like to get published. And also I am planning to do some recording soon as we belong to the union now and the recording ban has been lifted.

And also I am looking for a booking agent to take charge of our bookings as we are going to do lots of work in the Intertainment field. If you are interested in some of my songs or any phase of my work, please write me by return mail.

Inclosed is a photo of my family and also one of some of the small children playing at a club here near Wash. D.C. [Armstrong's] We was at this club one year. Went from there to (Gay Time) Constitution Hall.

Your old friend,

Ernest V. Stoneman

P.S.
Would like some bookings in N.Y. if you can give me some advise on any of my ideas or I could come to your office in the near future and talk things over, please let me know and I would arrange same.[22]

At the bottom of this letter, a notation initialed by Roy Horton indicates that a return mailing took place a week later. Beyond that result, it seems that relatively little came of the Constitution Hall–"Gay Time"–television exposure the Stonemans received in 1947–48. After their run at Armstrong's, the Stonemans moved to the Club Hillbilly and worked there more or less regularly for a year or two. Connie B. Gay either owned an interest in this place or had considerable influence in its management. A 1950 copy of Ernest's Maryland income-tax return suggests that only $263.40, or 6 percent, of his income for that year came from music. He derived the remaining $4,293.01 from his regular carpenter's jobs at the Wertherman Corporation of Seat Pleasant, Maryland; Ray S. Eccleston of Laconia Park; and the more-or-less regular job he had held since the war at the U.S. Naval Gun Factory (according to Pasty, he worked for the former two employers while he was laid off at the gun factory).[23]

Connie B. Gay also contacted the editors of *Life* magazine and encouraged them to do a feature on the transplanted hillbilly musicians. Photographers and writers came out and gathered material for several days. However, a polio epidemic in the Carolinas and the Berlin Blockade in Occupied Germany suddenly took precedence over their human-interest story and the editors omitted the article at the last minute. The Stonemans were left with copies of a few photographs rubber-stamped on the reverse side with "LIFE Magazine Cop[y]right Time Inc. Reproduction Not Permitted" for souvenirs of the incident.[24]

Although their brief encounter with regional fame brought the Stonemans only minimal financial rewards, it did help with their sustenance and, more significantly, boosted the spirit of optimism that continued to fuel Ernest's hopes and plans. Donna remembered that Daddy often found the coins and encouraged them to see motion pictures of Roy Acuff, the Grand Old Opry star, who had replaced Jimmie Rodgers as a symbolic figure in the image of hillbilly musical success.[25]

Meanwhile, the individual Stonemans continued their daily lives, which tended to be filled with the problems and minor success of normal existence. Generally, the difficulties encountered by people of limited economic means who are adjusting to a changing urban environment and have a limited education restricted their opportunities. Only their involvement with music as a family and as individuals made their experiences atypical.

Eddie Stoneman and Katherine continued to live in Carmody Hills until 1965. On September 22, 1948, Katherine gave birth to their third child, a boy named Wayne. Eddie continued at the service station for several more years, eventually working his way up to a mechanic's weekly salary of eighty-five dollars. During most of this time he supplemented his income with work as a musician, favoring the electric lead guitar. Generally he worked as part of the Stoneman Brothers, which usually included his brothers Bill, Jack, and sometimes Dean and Gene. A pair of nonfamily members, a fiddler named Slim Tanner and a steel guitarist known only as "Shotwell" often worked with them, too. As he became older, Eddie played music somewhat less frequently, rested more, and spent more time at home. He became a maintenance employee of the federal government in 1960 and left Carmody Hills in 1965.[26]

After her divorce from Jack Jewell, Grace Stoneman remarried on December 4, 1948. Her second husband, George Jewell, a cousin of Jack, could best be described as a hard-working, serious, sober individual. Still, he could be emotionally difficult, and Grace's life could not really be called a happy one. On February 6,

1950, Grace gave birth to the couple's only child, a daughter christened Donna Kay. Grace continued in her job at the Government Printing Office until 1955, after which time she remained home as a housewife. Although her musical participation as a Stoneman Family member remained minimal, her interest in their activity tended to be high and she maintained a close relationship with all of her brothers and sisters.[27]

John Stoneman received his discharge from the marines in 1946 and returned to Carmody Hills. On April 3, 1947, he and Deeta had a second son named Stanley. John continued working for Thomason Dairy for several years until it went out of business, after which time he worked for Prince George's County. He sometimes played a little music with the rest of the family, but not often. Although a heavy drinker at times, he never missed work, and in rare instances, Grace says, he could dress and look the part of a "Philadelphia Lawyer."[28]

Patsy Stoneman's personal life continued to be plagued with hardship and difficulties. In the later summer of 1947, she left the D.C. area for California in the company of a Mississippi sailor named R. H. Cain. Although separated from her first husband, she had not obtained a divorce. She was in California in September 1947 when Billy Stoneman received his naval discharge and returned briefly with her brother to Washington. Soon afterward, Patsy returned to California and married Cain the following spring. She later heard—erroneously, as later events would show—that Charles Streeks had been killed in an automobile accident. This eased somewhat the tension related to legal and moral implications in her marriage to Cain.[29]

After R. H. Cain's discharge from the navy, he and Patsy returned to Mississippi, where they farmed for several years. Their relationship deteriorated with the passing of time. Cain's harsh attitude toward women, Patsy's inability to have a child (she suffered a series of miscarriages), and the tension caused by her questionable marital status contributed to the situation. Loneliness and the backbreaking labor of the farm, of which Patsy performed a disproportionately large share, coupled with the failure of most of the provincial local populace to accept her as anything other than "that girl from the North," further complicated the circumstances. Adoption of three young girls brought Patsy a measure of temporary satisfaction. Then health problems and other difficulties intervened and conditions deteriorated again.[30]

Patsy had minimal direct contact with her family. She made two or three visits in a ten-year period, and they made but two or three visits to Mississippi. Through all of her experiences, however, she gained a toughness of constitution that would earn her much respect as a survivor. She became an individual who could cope with adverse conditions. In later years, Patsy would assume a matriarchal position and become the family member to whom the others would look for leadership in times of difficulty and duress.

After his return to Carmody Hills, Billy Stoneman married Barbara Brooks, a fifteen-year-old friend and classmate of Donna. The couple had four children, Gary, Michael, Jody, and Ricky. Billy played music with his brothers and other family members, being a skilled banjo picker, and had what most folks described as the best singing voice in the family. He also worked at a variety of jobs in the Washington area. As time went by, the emotional stresses related to his naval combat experiences took an increasingly heavy toll on his mental stability. Unfortunately, he did not take the time to receive a thorough physical examination at the time of his navy discharge, with the result that he received little help from the Veterans Administration.[31]

A onetime relative and longtime friend of the Stoneman family described Jack Stoneman as having the most intelligence of any of Ernest and Hattie's children. Somewhat sadly, he added, "almost nothing ever worked out right for Jack." Patsy wrote that the environment of Carmody Hills had negative effects on her brothers. With the exception of Jimmy, she said, "as the boys got bigger, [neither] Mommie nor Daddy just couldn't seem to handle them. They were learning to drink pretty much, and was always into something." Jack, and later Scott, developed serious alcohol problems. Although he became a skilled bass player from his late teens onward, Jack's drinking had a considerable negative effect on his musical career and personal life. Family members recall Daddy's firing Jack during their Constitution Hall appearances. Jack played off and on with the family group and with various others for years, but his problems increased. He joined the navy but went AWOL and had a series of behavioral difficulties. Following his discharge he met a young widow named Anna Jean Todd James, who had two young daughters. After a stint in the merchant marines that took Jack to Ireland and Sweden, he married Anna Jean and settled down for a time, driving a bus and playing music part time. In 1957 he got into difficulties with the law that involved the theft of some scrap iron in a railroad yard. The judge put him on probation for a year. A family letter at the time suggests he had become something of a nuisance; "Jack is on a year probation. I guess they got tired picking him up all the time. They said they are sick and tired of looking at him." Jack, making himself more of an innocent victim, believes that a man named Buck Gott set him up in the situation so that he could steal Jack's wife. With the help of Anna Jean's brother-in-law, they then got him sent away to the Jessup's Cut workhouse for a year.[32]

Gene and Dean Stoneman managed to lead more sedate lives. Gene played guitar off and on with the Stoneman Brothers and other part-time bands for several years. In 1952 he married a Carmody Hills girl name Peggy Edelen. Shortly afterward, Gene received his draft notice and spent much of his army career in West Germany. His musical abilities helped him get into Special Services, and he helped entertain. After his discharge he and Peggy had a daughter, Robin, born on August 17, 1957. They purchased an old house in Edgewater, Maryland, and Gene's carpentry talent came in handy in remodeling it. Over the years, Gene's musical horizons broadened and he developed an interest in jazz music as well as country. Eventually he found regular employment in the federal bureaucracy as a jack-of-all trades. As he puts it, "I do lock work one day then dig a ditch the next."[33]

His twin brother, Dean, who always remained much smaller in stature, survived an accident-prone childhood. Among other things, he hit a cartridge with a sledgehammer, in essence shooting himself in the eye. Years later he lightheartedly described the situation: "It felt like a bee or hornet had stung me. . . . Well, I started bleeding like a stuck hog, so to the hospital I went. Of course they operated on me and of course I lost the sight of that eye, and from that day on it had bothered me to a[n] extent."

In spite of his injury, Dean managed to get into the military service and later got to "drinking right heavy, quite a bit, intirely too much."[34]

Fortunately, Dean "managed to pull out of that before I completely ruined my life." He married a girl named Faye Casper on August 31, 1957, and they had five children: Teresa, Darrell, Debbie, Laurel, and Julia. Like several of the others, Dean played music on a part-time basis for several years, a bluegrass mandolin. Much of his singing and playing favored a style not unlike that associated with Bill Monroe, and "Mule Skinner Blues" became one of his trademark numbers. Dean worked several years for Trailways as a bus mechanic and later worked as a truck mechanic for the city of Bladensburg. Finally, to use his own language, he reached the age where "he don't want to go out and get his teeth kicked in, or his ear busted or whatever."[35]

Unlike the older children (except Patsy in later years), who generally made music a part-time occupation, the younger Stonemans made show business their prime career occupation. Therefore, somewhat greater attention will be focused on their lives and musical activities. Scott, the eldest among this number, merits more space in this narrative, but his briefer life span makes less detailed information available than one would like.

As a youngster, Scott Stoneman manifested a larger degree of musical talent than the other children. He also possessed an impish nature that could be not only amusing, but at times quite repugnant. Scott became proficient on all string instruments. In fact, he helped teach others to play the instruments of their choice. As a child, he worked to emulate such things as trains and chickens with the fiddle. The photograph taken at Armstrong's does not show Scott with a fiddle, but he has one in the picture taken at the time of the Constitution Hall concerts. Although Eddie and Billy fiddled from time to time, Pop decided that only Scott possessed a "fiddle wrist." He won fiddling contests often from the age of sixteen, defeating such competitors as Curly Fox, although the oft-mentioned championships at Warrenton, Virginia, seem not to have carried the adjective "national" before 1951. At any rate, his creative prowess with the bow won him wide respect among musicians. The arrival of well-known professional fiddler Chubby Wise in the Washington area to work on the

"Gay Time" programs provided Scott with both an expert instructor and a challenging competitor. In later years, Chubby told how he and Scott used to trade licks and technique information and tell the other one that he was "the best in the world."[36]

More than any other Stoneman, Scott also interacted a great deal with other musicians in the Washington area. He made friends with Jack Clement while Clement was stationed there during military service and also with the young Louisiana mandolin picker Buzz Busby, who came to the District as a young FBI worker in 1951. Later, after Clement left the service, he, Scott, and Busby went to Boston, where they worked for Aubrey Mayhew on the Hayloft Jamboree at radio station WCOP. He also toured as a sideman with respected bluegrass vocalist Mac Wiseman. Scott did record sessions with Busby, country singer Pete Pike, and young bluegrass singer Bill Harrell. With Clement and Busby, he made a recording on the Sheraton label during their stint in New England and made friends with the Lilly Brothers during their long stay at Hillbilly Ranch. He also worked with Benny and Vallie Cain's group.[37]

In his personal life, Scott exhibited less regularity but some creativity. He drank some from his mid-teens but tended more in the direction of such activities as upsetting outhouses or tying two cats together by the tail and throwing them over a clothes line. In one notable instance, he defecated in the neighbor's piano. He hated pianos and horn music, sister Roni says. In March 1954, Scott married a Maryland girl name Cecile Phipps and they had a daughter named Sandra on December 2, 1956, but the marriage endured for only eight years. Donna believes that he became a serious drinker only after he began traveling extensively with other musicians. Something in Scott's nature seemed to make him try the impossible just to see if he could do it. This characteristic could sometimes make him a creative genius, but it also carried the potential for personal disaster.[38]

When first Grace and then Patsy left home, this made eight-year-old Donna the youngest girl remaining at home. In Ernest and Hattie Stoneman's world, girls, above all else, existed for the purpose of helping their mothers in the home, especially with housework and the younger children. If educational authorities and Pop found it difficult to make the boys attend school, Hattie often preferred that Donna remain out of school. As a result, she acquired only a seventh-grade education and says she was a poor student. She remembered some of her teachers as being helpful and concerned, while others tended toward indifference, if not outright hostility.[39]

Earlier, Donna had been a somewhat undernourished and often ignored little waif. Hattie's cousin Mary Helen Melton and her husband, Troy Leonard, offered to adopt her but Hattie decided against it. So Donna spent about eight years as a household servant while her mother tended her flower garden and looked after the yard. Grace said that at first she thought Donna seemed to be meek but later concluded that she was afraid. After an exasperated Hattie complained that Grace and Patsy had run away and married, Donna recalled giving her mother a big hug and crying, "I'll never leave you Mommy." This, coupled with Donna's interest in music, won her a degree of acceptance. A pair of dancing feet distinguished her stage presence from her first work with the family about 1941 or 1942. Since she was so tiny anyway, the mandolin seemed like the only instrument she could handle and still dance on stage. Scotty taught the basics of the instrument, and she worked wherever Pop and the other kids did until the summer of 1950.[40]

In 1949, while the Stonemans worked in a club called the Wagon Wheel, they became acquainted with a couple of regular patrons, Crockett and Gertie Bean, both of whom had younger brothers. Donna preferred the former's brother Bob because he had a clean-cut appearance and drank ice water. Donna said that because there were so many foul-mouthed, tobacco-smoking, alcohol-consuming roughnecks around Carmody Hills, she would settle for no less than a boyfriend or husband with neat, clean habits. Bobby fit the bill, and compared to Jack Jewell or Charles Streeks, he certainly looked like a prize indeed. Only a year older than Donna, he had a tenth-grade education and worked with Crockett on the county road crew. Because of his smooth manners, many people thought he had been to college. The couple dated for a time, split up briefly, and then resumed dating. Pop liked Bob, and Donna recalled that at mealtime he would say, "Have a tater, Bean."[41]

During the summer of 1950, Patsy invited Donna to come down and spend the harvest season on the farm in Mississippi. Bobby went, too, and they traveled by bus to Attala County. While there, the couple decided to marry. Patsy signed approval for both of the underaged couple, explaining to the marriage-license clerk that Bobby was an orphan boy who worked on the farm. Donna recalled that the justice who married them that September 30 "was drunk. . . . He looked down . . . and said 'this ain't no marriage license, it's a hunting license' . . . but he married us." Back in Maryland, the young couple moved in with Bob's mother and went on with their lives. Donna played music with Pop and the others as before; Bob got her a nice instrument and bought her records by Bill Monroe and other musicians that featured lead-mandolin work. Donna soon learned to become a real virtuoso, but no one ever quite put her in a category with Scott as an instrumentalist. Reflecting on her marriage to Bob a decade after its termination, Donna said, "We both were too young." At the time, however, it appeared that she had fared much better in matrimony than either Grace or Patsy in their initial efforts.[42]

Since Jimmy Stoneman had been diagnosed as an epileptic in early childhood, he received something of a protected status within the family circle and by the family when on a musical engagement. Ernest always took Jimmy with him wherever he played. Like Donna, Jimmy became a lifelong teetotaler and avoided the pitfalls of barroom musical work. As a child he suffered some disadvantages from having poor eyesight and being placed in the rear of the classroom without anyone realizing that he needed visual correction. His most vivid childhood memory stems from the time when younger sister Roni fell into the outhouse. Jimmy finally got Hattie's attention, and the mother rescued the helpless child. Jimmy recalled that "you could hear the suction when she yanked her out."[43]

As a musician Jimmy learned to play several instruments, including guitar and fiddle. However, his talents on the "whumper" gained the most attention in the early years. Pop made this from an old bass drum, but it looked like a huge banjo and served the function of a bass fiddle. Connie B. Gay allegedly so named it from the sound it made. Jack played the whumper in the beginning, but as he became less reliable, he often would send Jimmy, whom he had taught to play in his place. As time went by and a regular bass replaced the whumper, Jimmy became the full-time bass player, too.[44] Although he became known around the District for his whumper and bass playing, he did his first record session as a fiddler. The manner in which this came about is complex, but also significant. For the first time, it involved the Stonemans with a character known as Billy Barton.

In the spring of 1953, Bob Bean received his draft notice and entered the army, going to Fort Knox, Kentucky, for his basic training. After returning from the initial army experience, he went back to Fort Knox, taking Donna with him. When this phase ended, Bob received an assignment at Fort Lewis, Washington. When Bob and Donna arrived in Washington, they turned on their radio and heard a hillbilly music program hosted by Billy Barton. The latter, a Kentuckian whose real name was Johnny Grimes, had gained some renown as primary composer of "A Dear John Letter," a song that went No. 1 and remained in the Top Ten for twenty-three weeks in the last half of 1953. Barton's own recording career had not had much success, but he did have a contract with the King label.[45]

Donna went up to the radio station to meet Barton and soon was a member of his band. She found him to be a likable but fickle type of country promoter that some folks might call a con artist who had an eternally optimistic nature and lots of big ideas. She said Billy usually talked with a cigarette dangling out of his mouth. He had a female vocalist–wife name Wanda Wayne, who also recorded for King. Billy referred to Donna as "little Donna Dean, the mandolin queen," and she also did occasional duets with him, such as Tommy Collins's hit "You Better Not Do That." Donna thinks Wanda exhibited jealously from time to time, but neither ever had any romantic inclinations toward the other. Billy did need a fiddler, however, and Donna convinced him that her younger brother Jimmy could handle the fiddle as well as anyone. So seventeen-year-old Jimmy made the cross-country trip by bus from one Washington to the other. Billy opened a night club in Olympia for a time, and Donna and Bobby lived in an upstairs apartment over the place. Things went well for several weeks, and then Billy shot and wounded a soldier during a scuffle and the Military Police forced the club to close. After that, they relocated in Boise, Idaho.

Billy then scheduled a recording session in Cincinnati. Bobby's army career was scheduled to end in a couple of months, so they agreed that Billy, Wanda, Donna, and Jimmy would travel by auto to Cincinnati and also play some show dates with Billy in the vicinity of his family home in London, Kentucky. The trip to Cincinnati proved to be a tragicomedy of errors. Billy traveled in an old rattletrap stretch-bus car and showed himself as something less than a careful driver. During a snowstorm in Montana, they crashed into a tractor-trailer. Donna, who had just eaten a bologna sandwich, remembered sitting beside the highway with a cut on her head, wondering whether she would vomit. Billy and Wanda had an argument, and so, too, did Wanda and Jimmy. A little later they were picked up by a couple whose car Billy had nearly run off the road when he passed them several minutes before he crashed. The couple had a retarded child who kept pointing at Billy and screaming, "That's a crazy man, Mommy!" In the midst of all this confusion, Jimmy had an epileptic seizure, Wanda continued arguing, and Donna thinks she threw up her sandwich. At the hospital, a doctor put seven stitches in her head.

The crash ruined their vehicle beyond repair, and none of the four had any more cash than a little pocket change. Billy had a few possessions, which he sold and agreed to buy gasoline for some folks traveling east in exchange for the ride. The rest of the journey proved just as difficult, for the old car in which they now traveled had no heater and cardboard in one window, and the six passengers nearly froze. Finally they reached Cincinnati, where they met with Syd Nathan in the King studio.

The session, held on January 14, 1955, did not go well, either, from Donna's viewpoint.[46] Syd threw a near fit, opposed the use of a mandolin on Billy's recording, and virtually ejected her from the studio. In contrast, even though Jerry Rivers was available, Nathan loved Jimmy's fiddle work and gave him the introductory break on "Pardon Me Old Buddy," a comic novelty love song that everyone hoped would be the hit of the session. The number, in the vein of some recent Tommy Collins hits, deserved a better fate than it received. They recorded additional masters and then went to Billy's home in Kentucky. They played in a couple of Holiness churches. Billy felt insulted in the first one because the audience did not applaud, and in the second the preacher denounced them as sinners playing worldly music.

The group did not make any money, and Billy's father got drunk and chased them away with a shotgun. They moved in with Billy's cousin. Donna decided that they had no future in Kentucky and that when Bob sent her his service check they would get bus tickets and she and Jimmy would return to Carmody Hills. About this time they got a telegram signed by Ernest V. Stoneman saying he needed them for some dates around Washington. A day or two later, Donna received the ninety-one dollar check from Bob and she and Jimmy took off for home. They returned to Carmody Hills, relieved to be back. Soon afterward, Bob returned from the service, and then Scott began organizing the band known as the Blue Grass Champs, of which Donna and Jimmy would become members.

The two younger children made minimal contributions to music at this time, but events from their childhood nonetheless helped to shape their careers. Like Dean, Roni seemed to be especially accident prone. That both survived seems nearly miraculous in retrospect, but for Roni—in a somewhat embellished form—their accounts became the source of some of her later comedy routines. The most noted of her flirtations with danger occurred about 1946:

> We had an out house that was the king of all out houses because the hole was DEEP: When you have that many children using that dude, the hole has to be deep! Now, we didn't have a two-seater we had a two-by-four. Either you leaned over it or you climbed up on it like a chicken. One day, when I was about eight years old, I had to go to the out house. I passed Jimmy, playing in the yard, I told him not to come near the out house because sometimes, my brothers would get sticks and beat on the outside while I was inside. He yelled at me and said he wouldn't. I went inside and there, in the corner, was a mud-dawber's nest, well . . . I climbed up on that two-by-four like an old chicken and that old mud-dawber started BUZZIN' around and every time he'd make a dive at me I'd go "Wh-o-o-o-p!" and I'd lean

backwards. About the third dive he made at me, I went backward, head over heels and fell into the "Pits of Hell" (what else could I call it?) but I did land feet first. I sunk up to my chin and needless to say, I was hollering—"HELP! HELP!" Poor little Jimmy came into the out house (he finally got the door open) and looked down into the hole (thank God I saw his face!) Just my luck to see something else comin' at me and no place to run. The first words he said were, "What's the matter Roni?" . . . so slow, (he always talked slow). What the Hell did he think was the matter? Here I was down there in the out house hole, with just my chin stickin' up, fighting for my life, (maybe that's why I got a long neck to this day!) It'll sure grow in a hurry when you're in that kind of shape. He went up to the house to get Mother. She was washing dandelion greens (they're pretty good if they're fixed right). Jimmy said, "Maw . . . Maw!" And she replied, "Honey, what is it?" Jimmy answered, "Roni fell in the outhouse, Maw." Mama replied, "Lord, God!" (which was her favorite phrase). She came running down to the out house and looked down to see me, still hanging in there; and she started prayin'. And she prayed, and she prayed, and she prayed. I thought—'S-H-I-T!' If she didn't finish prayin' and get me out of here, I was gonna die! I knew better than to tell her to quit prayin' and get me out because she would have taken a stick and pushed me under (it would have been easier to have another one, than clean me up!) She finally pulled me out by the hair of my head and all the neighbors came and formed a bucket brigade. . . . Was it cold! I was naked too! Mama had to take all my clothes off me and all the neighbors saw me naked with shit all over me. . . . They laughed and laughed at me. Mama got the trusty ole soap that Grandma made and washed me down with it—"Oo-o-o-o-ee!" That stuff stinks, (for those of you who don't know.) We were sleeping seven in a straw-tick bed. The straw-tick bed for the bed-wetters. The ones who were more mature slept in Grandma's feather-ticking she sent us. There is nothing worse than pissified feathers. Even though Mom and Katherine, (Eddie's wife) washed me up real good with that lye soap, I still had an ungodly smell on me. I started to get into bed that night and six feet kicked the shit out of me and they yelled, "Mama, the out house kid ain't sleepin' with us!" Mama made me a pallet out of straw on the floor and there I slept for the next three months.[47]

A less dangerous but nevertheless painful example of Roni's accident prone childhood took place when "Scott tied a wagon to an old bicycle and set me in it and I wanted to please him so I sat there. He went very fast and the wagon turned over. I took a dive onto the pavement, skinning my whole chest. One huge scab— it hurt!"[48]

With such incidents almost a daily event in the Stoneman household and occurring to Roni almost on a weekly basis, one defense mechanism she learned early in life resulted from her discovery that she could make people happy, usually without even trying. As she says, "I had something going for me, you know, like being able to make people laugh even if it were laughing at me not with me." She could always see humor in her own appearance, such as describing the first time she got a factory-made garment: "Most of the girls that wore" tight skirts "had pretty figures to put in them," but Roni's figure was "like a fence post stuck in the ground, [and] I thought I looked good anyway."[49]

Sometimes her humor came across as being in less than good taste. One of her planned efforts at humor caused her to be disciplined severely. For a time in the 1940s the Stonemans had a Sunday morning radio program on a little station in Morning Side, Maryland, where the children would sing gospel songs. Roni planned her attempt at satire well, but her timing was not right:

> Came my turn I looked around, knowing, if I was to get a whippin', I was gonna make it worth my while. I cocked my eye over at daddy, keeping on him while he moved the orange crate over for me to stand up on. With all the gusto I had in me, I announced, "I am going to sing a song for all the shut-ins, called, 'The Little Rosewood Casket' " and knew every word and sang it as hard and loud as I could, all the time staring at my father while he squirmed in the chair with his mouth drawn up into a bow. After I finished singing, telephones started ringing and daddy reached for me. He didn't even wait until we got home. The ground was wet with tears and plowed up with the dust of my hurt. He liked to kill me! Over the air you could hear, "Oh, I won't do it no more daddy, oh God, don't kill me!" Mama gave it to me when I got home, (oh boy! What a warped sense of humor they had!!—Kill joys!) I had. . . . It truly was worth it. . . . Singing that song wasn't the nicest thing to do, but, Damn! it was fun![50]

Despite her sense of humor, Roni could and did reveal a serious side, such as her recollection of her first formal date:

I met a young man on the telephone and we made a date. He knew my girlfriend Mary and she had been talking to him on the phone. I came in and she told me to say "Hello" to Bobby Fink. She had met him in Hyattsvlle, Maryland, where she had gone to an Easter Egg Roll. Well, I talked to him, he liked me pretty good I guess; he came to see me the next day. Then he asked me to go on the Wilson Line with him. This was a pleasure boat that cruised from Washington to Virginia and back again. I didn't know what that meant, but I really wanted to go because it had a trio on board, to entertain called the "Crew Cuts." They were my heroes. Mama said I could go, if I did the housework for a whole week and I did. He came to pick me up in front of our house which was a real 'shacky' place, but Mama had a pretty yard. Daddy was sitting in the yard and I had to finish the dishes before I could even get in the car with him. He got out and came to the door and I was still washing dishes at the table, we didn't have running water. I was embarrassed that he caught me doing dishes so I asked him to stay in the yard and talk to daddy while I finished my work. Friends in the car would tease him about the junky old place I lived in. (I was ashamed for him, but he didn't say anything.) I put on that old coat (Mama made me wear a coat) it was patched all the way around the hem, (it was awful looking . . . the dress wasn't much better!) When I got into the car, the young man and lady were in the front seat and they said "Hello" to me. She was so pretty, a senior in high school in Washington . . . oh, she was pretty. Now, don't get me wrong . . . girls ain't my bag, but you can imagine how I felt, I was ashamed again for my date. We got to the boat and it started getting dark and the band came on. Bobby took me down to see the band, bought me a Coke and I was so excited! I'd never seen horn music in person. I felt like I was in another world. Then he took me to the upper deck and said the moon was pretty and he kissed me, my second kiss in my life. I liked it! . . . He was good at it, and he kept kissing me and he kissed me some more in the car, and I liked it . . . I'd have been a damn fool if I hadn't of. He never tried to take advantage of me, he probably knew I was green as grass . . . boys can tell things like that. Well, we got to my house, and were met by three brothers on the front porch and they were drinking. Bobby walked me to the door and said goodnight to my mother.

My brothers started calling him, "Yankee Boy," first they tried to borrow money from him, (that humiliated me), the icing on the cake was when they siked the dogs on him. (They could be assholes, when they wanted too). Bobby barely made it to the car, jumped in and drove off. Of course, I was not talking "tacky" mouth then. I was very innocent and sweet; Bobby knew that. The next day, he called me on the phone at Mary's house. She came and got me and he asked me to marry him. I was very young then and afraid, and besides, I didn't know him, even though he was very nice to me. If I had married him it would have saved me a lot of heartaches, sorrow, pain, and grief.[51]

Roni had two or three teenage romances, including one with a neighbor boy named Chuck Davis. She cared a great deal for him, but she had serious reservations because of his drinking habits. Like Donna, Roni has witnessed enough of the negative side of alcohol consumption in Carmody Hills to be exceedingly cautious about drinking. At the age of sixteen, Roni—already an accomplished banjo picker in the style of Earl Scruggs—met Eugene Cox. Nearly a decade older and a man of moderate habits and temperament, Gene

was very quiet and played a little bit on the banjo and he had a new Gibson Mastertone, (I'd only heard of them in books, I never imagined I'd see one in person) because they cost quite a bit of money, five or six hundred dollars back then. I'd get to play on it when he came calling on me. I taught Gene how to play, "Foggy Mountain Breakdown." I also taught him the three-finger roll on the banjo. He was very nice to me and didn't try to take advantage of me. He liked my parents very much, respected them. Nine months later [on April 27, 1956] I married Gene Cox. He was out of the Navy, and I thought he was a "real man"; someone to be the father of my children. I wanted a family of 15 and I wanted to live on a farm. I wanted to buy pretty shoes and dresses for my children to go to school in. I often day-dreamed about this when I was a little girl. I was married three months and became pregnant. I was very happy when I first married Gene. I had my first bedroom to myself, even my first dresser drawer and we lived in a little apartment with running water. I was in paradise![52]

She did not remain in paradise long. Gene's lack of ambition made their marriage a difficult one. However, in one respect, their union did result in a partial fulfillment of her ambitions: the couple had four children by the time she reached age twenty-four.

Being the youngest child in the huge family placed Van Haden Stoneman in a somewhat unusual position. By the accounts of most of the other children, Hattie had her favorites, and Van held this position from the time of his birth. They point out that he got more food, received fewer household responsibilities, and played the all-around role of the "spoiled brat." Although laconic by nature, Van conceded this to a degree, calling himself "actually the baby of the family and also being the 'baby' of the family."[53] Nonetheless, Van developed into a versatile and talented musician. He became adept on bass fiddle, Dobro, rhythm guitar, and both clawhammer and Scruggs-style banjo. In later years he would carry the major share of lead vocals, and his voice also blended well with the others. He became the band's front man.

As the older children worked increasingly on their own, some even went away for a time, as Donna and Jimmy did. Pop, still employed at the Naval Gun Factory and less enthusiastic about working weeknights, organized a band built around himself and young folks in their midteens. He called the aggregation Pop Stoneman and his Little Pebbles. Roni and Van came from his own household, together with Peter "Zeke" Dawson and Larry King. The former, a boy about Roni's age, became a protégé of Scott and developed into a pretty good fiddler. Zeke later recalled that he would spend many hours and evenings in the Stoneman household, learning and practicing music. Some weeknights he would start the five-mile trek to his parents' home on foot, only to have Pop pick him up within a few minutes and drive him the distance, even though he would have to rise at 5:00 A.M. to go to work. Zeke doesn't think he ever knew a more admirable man than Pop Stoneman. King played bass fiddle, and a boy named Bill Brazeale, an epileptic who owed his life to Scott, sometimes worked with the Little Pebbles picking the Dobro. This group worked more often in Maryland because child-labor laws tended to be less restrictive there. Zeke recalls that they worked at Armstrong's and also at the Charles Hotel in Hughsville, while

Van remembers the USO shows. Both remember the time Van purchased a brand-new Martin D-28 guitar and leaned it up against the trunk of Pop's car. Since Pop and Van both thought the other had put the guitar away, the Little Pebbles backed out of their driveway on their way to a show date. The occupants of the car heard a loud crunching sound. Realizing what had happened, Pop called Van a "dad blamed idiot" as they jumped out to find both the guitar and its hard-shell case a total wreck. Zeke says Pop just shook his head and sent Van to get another guitar. Van remembered that he couldn't even play the show and subsequently cried all night long.[54]

In retrospect, if the war years and the decade that followed had not been good times for the Stonemans, they were a considerable improvement over the years of depression that preceded them. As the older children grew to adulthood and some moved away, it eased the financial burdens somewhat. However, several of the children continued to have problems that could be costly at times, even though Ernest had steady employment.

Musically speaking, the family's accomplishments had also been modest, but nonetheless encouraging. The appearances in Constitution Hall, on local television and radio, and club work had given them something of a name in the Washington area. Scott's fiddle championships and work as a professional sideman made him a respected name among fiddlers. Donna and Jimmy had gained some professional experience outside the family circle, and all the Stonemans had worked enough together that they had become seasoned veterans within their field. One hopeful sign could be detected in 1953, when Ernest's income from music reached $522.50, almost double what it had been in 1950.[55] On the negative side, Ernest had also reached the age of sixty. His chances of reaching the top again diminished in proportion to his age. But his spirits remained high, and he continued to personify his own motto: "Don't Quit."

6

Struggling Upward

1956–63

Shortly after Donna and Jimmy returned home from their experience in the Pacific Northwest and in the Ohio Valley with Billy Barton, Scott Stoneman formed a new band. Sanford "Sam" Bomstein owned a club at the corner of New York Avenue and Twelfth Street called The Famous. Located adjacent to the Trailways bus depot, the place attracted a large crowd of transients, especially servicemen, many of them hillbilly-music fans. Although some Stoneman musical aggregations had played there earlier, the club had really become a true country-music center when Roy Clark and band worked a lengthy engagement there. Bomstein needed a dynamic group to follow that of Clark and selected Scott to assemble one. The young fiddle champion got a young guitar picker named Jimmy Case and filled out the band with sister Donna, whose quality mandolin and wholesome attractiveness would be appealing, and brother Jimmy, whose bass fiddle provided a solid rhythm. Bomstein also wanted the group to have a new name and selected Blue Grass Champs, since they did a lot of Bill Monroe-style numbers. In Donna's view, either Bomstein the businessman or brother Scotty the innovative musician could be considered the founder of the Blue Grass Champs.[1]

Although the term "bluegrass music" had not yet come into general use, the band quickly became such with the addition of Porter Church. Described by Sam Bomstein as a "Tennessee banjo player," Church had been born on the Tennessee side of Bristol in

1934 but grew up on a tobacco farm north of town on the Virginia side. He had worked at WCYB radio with various bluegrass music veterans, including Ralph Mayo, and had kinship ties with the Stonemans (his older brother Jim married Ingram Stoneman's daughter Erma). Coming to Washington, Porter sat in one night with the Champs. At that time, Bomstein paid each band member $12.50 a night and they collected additional tips from a bucket, placed at the foot of the stage, that was called the "pitch pot." Donna recalls a sign beside the bucket: "If you don't pitch in the pot tonight, tomorrow you might not have a pot to pitch in." Either some local union rule or a Bomstein regulation limited the number of salaried band members to four, so Church gained provisional membership by playing for the tips in the pitch pot. To the best of his recollection, he nearly always made more money than the regular band members.[2]

The Blue Grass Champs played six nights a week at The Famous and quickly became one of the most dynamic and popular musical combinations in the Washington area. When they won the band contest at the Warrenton, Virginia, national championships, they really lived up to their nickname. Donna recalls that many national figures in country music caught their show when passing through Washington and gained a highly favorable impression of the Champs.[3]

Meanwhile, Pop Stoneman continued working at the Naval Gun Factory and played weekend dates with his Little Pebbles. He had a radio program at WPGC and did an occasional guest spot with the Champs. Soon, however, a rather atypical development would briefly place him in the national spotlight.

Televised quiz shows became one of the more popular fads of the mid-1950s. Such programs had been popular on both radio and television for several years, but substantially larger cash prizes, prime-time positions, and the fact that the people in charge of the program sought out colorful personalities as contestants all helped to increase their appeal. "The $64,000 Question" on CBS started the trend, but other networks soon emulated it with similar programs. Folks like Gloria Lockerman, a winsome black teenage spelling champion, or Dr. Joyce Brothers, an attractive young psychologist and boxing expert, became instant celebrities.[4] As the quiz show's popularity soared, Ernest Stoneman began to see such programs as a possible vehicle for self-advancement.

Sometime in the winter of 1955–56, Ernest wrote to CBS about the possibility of being a guest on "The $64,000 Question." Grace remembers her father confidently telling her that he would soon be on the program. Grace reassured him and kissed his bald head, saying "Sure, Daddy," but she considered it an idle dream. He said the producers had been seeking interesting people and he really knew of no one whose background exceeded his own when it came to interesting experiences. Since "The $64,000 Question" had an excess of applicants, especially elderly ones, Ernest's application went into a pool being considered for NBC's new large-cash-prize rival show titled "The Big Surprise."[5] Program officials accepted him and on March 3, 1956, he went before the cameras on what would be the last night Jack Barry emceed the show before giving way to Mike Wallace. As with some of the other contestants, much of the public could identify with the aging carpenter. Television viewers in southwestern Virginia in particular took notice of one of their own. The editor of the *Galax Gazette* wrote with some degree of pride:

> Many long-time Galax citizens remember the day when the name Ernest Stoneman was synonymous with the best of the old time music in this section and when many of his recordings were on sale at all record shops in Galax and over the country. . . . As if to prove to any doubters in Galax and area that he was the true Ernest Stoneman who used to be hereabouts, he proceeded with permission of the quizmaster, to play on the autoharp, and sing, in true old mountain fashion "That Good Old Mountain Dew."
>
> Hundreds of TV viewers in Galax and Grayson and Carroll counties will be waiting eagerly for "The Big Surprise" program next Saturday night, March 10, at 7:30, when Mr. Stoneman will be back to try to go on toward the big money on WSLS-TV Roanoke.[6]

Although extremely limited in formal education, Ernest Stoneman nurtured a lifelong curiosity about the world and amassed a large storehouse of geographical facts within his keen mind.

While his own travel experiences had largely been confined to trips to recording studios or searches for work during the dark days of the Great Depression, he continued his thirst for geographic information. Loose pages from almanacs delineating data about bridge lengths, mountain altitudes, and lake sizes later found among his personal effects indicate that he treasured such material almost as much as his carefully typed or written song-lyric sheets. Accordingly, he chose travel as a category for questioning on "The Big Surprise." By the time Pop's winnings reached five thousand dollars when he correctly named the eight states that bordered Tennessee, the metropolitan dailies began taking notice. A feature titled "No Frills for Pop" revealed that "so far he's made no changes in his way of life which includes having no phone at his modest home."[7]

Stoneman doubled his winnings the following week but stumbled at twenty thousand dollars in a slip of the tongue, answering "Austin, Texas," instead of "Santa Fe, New Mexico," in response to a question about capitals in the Spanish Southwest. Rules of the game provided for rescue by a viewer, and a Percy Lintz in Detroit saved him by properly answering a current-events question. Pop then correctly responded to another twenty thousand dollar four-part interrogatory "dealing with National Parks." By that time, fellow Marylanders had become sufficiently supportive that Senator John Marshall Butler, a Maryland Republican, had Mike Wallace read a message when Ernest came before the cameras "telling Pop the state was behind him." That proved to be his last success because on his try for fifty thousand dollars, his luck ran out and game-show fans found new heroes.[8]

Even before Ernest Stoneman's five-week string of appearances on "The Big Surprise" had run their course, he began to capitalize on his new fame. Sam Bomstein announced that "that amazing hillbilly Ernest Pop Stoneman will be our guest at 'The Famous' tonight, March 28," with the Blue Grass Champs. Later on, in August, he took his Little Pebbles to Galax, where they won first place in the band contest at the Old Fiddler's Convention, which also celebrated the town's fiftieth anniversary. Their rendition of "Bile Them Cabbage Down" took the prize. Van Stoneman recalls that he, along with Roni and Zeke Dawson, assisted Pop that weekend. The Pebbles apparently played several numbers outside the competition. The *Galax Gazette* noted that Pop apparently en-joyed himself and visited with kinfolk and old acquaintances, no doubt his cousins George, Bertha, and Myrtle being chief among them. Roni recalls playing a bluegrass tune on George's banjo when they visited at his house. She said the aging clawhammer master told her then that he wanted her to have the instrument after his death, but she never pressed the matter. Zeke remem-bered how the folks around Galax seemed to look up to Pop and thought his prestige helped them win the contest more than their talent. Winning ten thousand dollars made him a hero again to the hometowners, and they forgot the besieged debtor who had left town hurriedly in the fall of 1932. Ernest likely forgave, but could never forget.[9]

One might wonder what Ernest Stoneman did with his cash windfall. Patsy says much of it went to pay his debts, help the children, and perhaps make a few modest home improvements. Zeke Dawson recalls that Pop bought decent-quality instruments for those of his children who lacked them, one being the Martin D-28 that Van accidentally left in the driveway.[10]

At about the same time that Pop Stoneman began aspiring to success via the quiz-show route, the Blue Grass Champs aspired to spread their fame beyond the doors of The Famous. Their ini-tial effort resulted only in another bad experience. Billy Barton, recovering from his failures in Kentucky, relocated in Grand Junc-tion, Colorado. He urged the Stonemans to join forces again. Scott and Cecile, Donna and Bob Bean, together with a guy named Chris Christesen and Jimmy, made the long trek to Colorado by car, but things fell apart there soon after their arrival. The ever optimistic Bill, accompanied by a guitar picker called "Lonesome Luke," decided they would move south and the musical entou-rage shifted to Albuquerque, New Mexico. They did find some club work there but hardly made enough to cover expenses. Billy hoped to impress a man he believed had lots of cash and the ca-pability to promote them. Donna says they spent most of their re-maining funds to buy groceries so she could cook a pork-chop dinner with all the trimmings for the man, but he wound up try-ing to borrow money from them. Billy then concocted a scheme to get Bob to help secure a long-term club engagement by conning the owner into thinking they were about to accept a lucrative offer in Las Vegas. This ended when Donna threatened to leave Bob if he participated in such chicanery. Donna recalled that in her first twenty years of marriage, that was the only time she ever considered a separation. She then adds that at that moment she couldn't have bought a bus ticket out of New Mexico, let alone back to Washington. The experience of a few weeks in the Southwest with Billy Barton convinced the Stonemans that they would be better off back at The Famous. Finally they managed to scrape enough pennies together to get gas money for returning to the District, where local club patrons would keep them working steadily.[11]

Not long after Ernest Stoneman's modest success on NBC television, the Blue Grass Champs scored a triumph of their own on the CBS network. Sam Bomstein, in his efforts to promote them, encouraged them to try out for "Arthur Godfrey's Talent Scouts," a popular program in which relatively unknown aspiring professionals could gain national exposure and perhaps, with a little luck, launch a more substantial career in show business. Donna recalls that they auditioned three times before program officials accepted them—on condition that the girl would sing. Scott, Jimmy, and Jimmy Case all sang more than Donna, but the band accommodated. They worked up an arrangement of "Salty Dog Blues" that featured Scott doing his solo vocals on the verses, with Donna coming in to sing harmony on the chorus. Scott, Donna, and Porter Church all took instrumental breaks. Their appearance marked one of the first times that a full bluegrass band appeared on a prime-time network program. Godfrey liked them and so did the audience. Their competition came from a California pop vocalist named Ann Leonardo and a classical violinist named Gino Sambucco. The Champs thought Ann Leonardo would win, but the applause meter showed the Blue Grass Champs as the clear favorite. Porter Church recalls that each member made $680 for that one song and still considers it the most financially lucrative half-hour of his life.[12]

A victory on the Godfrey program meant a week of guest spots on his daily TV variety show. Arthur took an obvious liking to Donna and suggested to her that he might hold the Champs over for a second week and also that they get to know each other better. Donna, who took her marriage vows most seriously, replied with a paraphrase in verse to a popular country song of recent vintage:

"I'll bring my father, my mother, / my sister and my brother / Oh you'll never get Donna alone." Godfrey chuckled and said that he would have them back for an extra week anyway. Almost simultaneously with this event, Scott Stoneman engaged in some personnel manipulations that may have influenced the decision of Godfrey show officials to retain the band for the extra time.[13]

As the Blue Grass Champs' popularity increased, numerous local musicians hoped to become members of the group. Among these was a girl Dobro and steel guitarist named Peggy Brain, who had dated Jimmy Stoneman. As Jimmy recalls, he had proposed to Peggy and she had refused. Scott suggested to Peggy that she could get into the band only by marrying Jimmy. As Peggy's opinion toward matrimony shifted, Scott convinced the show directors that he could get a girl singer who could duet with Donna. Scott then fired Porter Church to make room for Peggy, and she appeared with them on the second week of the daytime Godfrey show. In Scott's defense, Donna recalls that Porter created a problem at one point on the show when he "froze" on the "take-off" of "Dear Old Dixie," which caused problems with the program directors. Jimmy thinks Peggy and Donna did only one song together the whole week, but hardly anyone noticed (except, perhaps, the unfortunate Porter Church).[14]

On July 4, 1956, Oscar James Stoneman and Peggy Brain became Mr. and Mrs. Perhaps, because musical expediency rather than love had been its basis, the union did not turn out to be a happy one. Peggy remained with the Champs long enough to play Dobro on their initial recording session the following winter. Band members recall her association with the band as a stormy one in which she quit several times. Some animosity developed between Donna and Peggy that could be blamed more on spectators than either girl. Jimmy said that after Peggy would finish a vocal, "the public being cruel like they sometimes are, would yell 'let the little one sing' meaning my sister, Donna, who did not sing solo at the time." Peggy came to resent this unfortunate circumstance, and it created dissension. In late November 1957, both Jimmy and Peggy quit the band, he for six weeks and she permanently. On December 2, 1958, Peggy gave birth to a daughter, Jeanette Joyce Stoneman, whom Jimmy called the "one good thing that came out of this marriage." The pair struggled on for a time, but, as Jimmy says, laconically, "after five years the marriage ended." Patsy adds that Jimmy subsequently allowed Peggy and her second husband to adopt the child but adamantly refused to sign a statement saying he had abandoned Jeanette, which in fact he had not.[15]

Despite personnel changes, the Blue Grass Champs continued to play and prospered to a degree. Donna says they increased their standard fee to three hundred dollars for an appearance at a firemen's carnival or country-music park, such as New River Ranch or Sunset Park. Bob Bean came into the picture more as a part-time manager, and Arthur Godfrey even had the family back on his other network television show, "Arthur Godfrey and His Friends," in the spring of 1957. Donna remembers that they did the popular bluegrass standard "Roll in My Sweet Baby's Arms" on the program. Back in the dressing room, she overheard the McGuire Sisters asking one another how anyone could have the nerve to sing a song with such vulgar lyrics over the air. Known for their high moral standards and as the products of a strict upbringing by a minister mother, the McGuires had made a point. Donna, something of a moral Puritan herself, like most country folks who sang and heard the words, had never really given much thought to the meaning of "lay around the shack . . . and roll in my sweet baby's arms."[16]

Back in Washington, Scott increasingly drank to excess, which produced difficulties. Donna says Sam Bomstein fired Scott from The Famous more than once, and Jimmy remembers a vicious argument in which his brother called Bomstein "a baldheaded Jew" on stage. The latter tolerated Scott's drinking to a point, said Jimmy, but the last insult went too far. After Bob Bean became manager, tensions between him and Scott increased still more. As a result, Scott came and went as a band member several times. Patsy wondered—in retrospect—how one could be fired from his own group, but it did indeed happen, and more times than one.[17]

With Scott in the band, the Blue Grass Champs were a superior group; however, even without him they were a pretty good one. He dropped in and out several times over the next decade. Pop Stoneman also appeared frequently as a guest vocalist, and Porter Church came back two or three times. Billy Stoneman filled in on banjo or guitar on several occasions. For a brief period, three musicians who would form the nucleus of the Country Gentlemen—Charlie Waller, John Duffy, and Bill Emerson—even had temporary fusion with the Champs. For quite a while however, the leading non-Stoneman in the band would be a fellow known as "Cousin Lew Childre."[18]

Donna believes that Childre's real name was Lew Houston and that he came from Alabama, which seemed about the only thing he had in common with the real Lew Childre (a country musician whose career went back almost as far as that of Ernest Stoneman). Zeke Dawson says he claimed to be a nephew of the original Lew and that he came close to fitting the stereotyped image of the "slick" talking and acting hillbilly musician. He played a decent Dobro with an electric pickup (something the entire band had used since the mid-fifties, responding to a need for more volume in the noisy clubs) and contributed a nice song on occasion, but otherwise the Stonemans seem to know little about him. On one of their television shows in 1959, he gave his age as twenty-three and said he and his wife had a little girl. Don Owens joked that when Lew first came to Washington, he worked on a garbage truck for a weekly salary of forty dollars and all he could eat. According to Bob Bean, Lew later came to Nashville and worked as a sideman with Conway Twitty. The Stonemans think he eventually was killed in an auto crash.[19]

The Blue Grass Champs continued to work at The Famous but also branched out to work in other clubs as well. Sam Bomstein bought another club called the Ozarks and they worked there part of the time. Doug Adkins, a serviceman from Oak Hill, Ohio, became a regular weekly visitor to this club while he was stationed in the Washington area and recalled the Champs as an excellent and exciting band, with Donna being a real crowd pleaser. Another favorite spot was the Hotel Charles in Hughsville, Maryland, and a place called Dairy Land. They worked still other clubs, whose names they have forgotten, sometimes on a more or less regular basis. Some places they seem to have worked only once or twice. The February 1957 issue of *Cowboy Songs* carried a short feature on them as an up-and-coming group: their first coverage in a national country-music magazine. Unfortunately, the article contained a serious mistake: it referred to them as the "Stoveman Family." Sometime during this period they got an offer to join "Ozark Jubilee" in Springfield, Missouri, on ABC-TV but rejected it because some of the band members wanted to stay in Washington.[20]

The Stonemans, regular figures on local television, got a program on WTTG-TV Channel 5 in Washington, D.C. Using the 1954 Bill Monroe number "I'm on My Way Back to the Old Home" as a theme song, the Blue Grass Champs presented a weekly half-hour of spirited bluegrass and country music. By this time young Van Stoneman had become lead vocalist and guitar player in the band, a position he would occupy from that time onward. Van recalls Pop complaining to Scott, "Doggone, you are going to hire all my pickers out from under me." But Van realistically adds, "Of course that was why he was teaching us anyhow . . . so we could join Scott later, when we got good enough. That's the way I felt about it anyhow."[21]

Following the Blue Grass Champs on WTTG-TV came another country-music program called "The Don Owens T.V. Jamboree." Owens, a popular country disc jockey on WARL, did much to popularize bluegrass in the D.C. area, sometimes sang himself, but primarily assembled a variety of country and bluegrass musicians to carry most of the load. Eventually the two shows merged, with the Stonemans remaining as the principal performers, and remained on the air through 1960. Pop, Van, Donna, and Jimmy appear to have been on most of these telecasts, along with Lew Childre and Porter Church. Scott was there sometimes and a non-Champ, such as Luke Gordon or Jimmy Haynie, appeared on many programs. Owens, in the role of a congenial host, hurled good-natured insults at Lew and sometimes Pop, Porter, and Van (mostly about Van's size).

The Stoneman repertoire at the time largely reflected the better-known country and bluegrass favorites of the middle and late fifties. Van sang such numbers as Marty Robbins's "Story of My Life," Johnny Cash's "Home of the Blues," and "There You Go." Jimmy, who had a fine country voice reminiscent of Jim Reeves, soloed on such songs as Webb Pierce's "Crying over You" and Porter Wagoner's "I Thought I Heard You Calling My Name." Donna sang less than the others but specialized in Bill Monroe's "I'm Breaking In a Brand New Pair of Shoes" and could also do "Sitting on Top of the World." On rare occasions she sang the Davis Sisters' "Rock-a-bye Boogie" and Sue Thompson's "Mama Don't Cry at My Wedding." Scott, in addition to his fantastic fiddling, vocalized on such pieces as the Louvin Brothers' "I Don't Believe You Met My Baby" and Marty Robbins's "Running Gun." In addition to his Dobro instrumental, Lew "Childre" Houston contributed an occasional vocal, such as Warner Mack's "Is It Wrong?" or "That's What It's Like to Be Lonesome," which both Bill Anderson and Ray Price popularized on the national charts. As music scholar Richard K. Spottswood reflected, the crowds who flocked to The Famous, the Ozarks, and the Hotel Charles expected to hear the current hillbilly hits of the day, and the Blue Grass Champs provided it at live shows and on television.[22]

Unlike his children, Pop Stoneman remained much closer to his traditional roots. By now, he had returned more to playing Autoharp than guitar, and his songs more often than not tended to be those old ballads such as "The Titanic" and even the hymns like "The Great Reaping Day" that he had recorded back in the twenties. He also did songs from that era that he had not put on wax such as Vernon Dalhart's "Prisoner's Song" and the Carter Family's "Wildwood Flower." Donna says that he did quite a few songs of the forties including "Detour," "Remember Me," "I'll Be True While You're Gone," and Bill Monroe's "Will You Be Loving Another Man" (by which he demonstrated how well he could adapt a bluegrass song to his old-time style). The newest song Zeke Dawson can remember Pop singing was "Before I Met You," a Lester Flatt–Earl Scruggs favorite from 1955 that made the Top Ten country charts for Carl Smith in late 1956. Donna recalls an instance at a dance about that same time when someone asked Pop to play the then current Elvis Presley hit "Hound Dog" and Pop complied, but with much less than satisfactory results.[23]

The Blue Grass Champs did do some recording in this period, but on a limited basis. Early in 1957 they waxed two sides released on a label called Bakersfield. Both numbers were Scott Stoneman originals. Scott sang a country-type number that looked at life somewhat pessimistically, "Heartaches Keep On Coming," on one side, while an instrumental, "Haunted House," graced the other. The latter featured as much of Peggy Brain's Dobro, Jimmy's bass, and Donna's mandolin as it did of Scott's fiddling, which might be why it received relatively little more than local attention. A couple of years later the Champs did two more sides, this time for the Blue Ridge label, which Don Owens then owned. One side featured Pop singing "Hand Me Down My Walking Cane," with his Autoharp being the most prominent instrumentation. Except for the others helping out on the chorus, and no harmonica, it sounded remarkably similar to the version he waxed for Edison in 1927. "Jubilee March" highlighted Lew Childre's Dobro with a nice acoustical guitar break by Perry Westland, an extra musician Don Owens hired for the session. Like the Bakersfield effort, the Blue Ridge release primarily reached the regional audience.

The group also recorded some material for a Washington record distributor named Ben Adleman. These sessions did nothing for their career, since only five sides were released and those came out several years later as the B side of a Jimmy Dean album on a budget label. They are historically significant because they contain the only numbers that feature solo vocals by Billy Stoneman ("Wine Bottom Blues" and "Daddy Stay Home"), whom most of the children considered the best singer in the family other than Pop. They also contain Roni's first recorded singing: a rendition of the popular 1902 number "Bill Bailey, Won't You Please Come Home." The Stonemans also backed an area-based country artist named Luke Gordon on some recordings, but again they had no more than a local impact. Compared to Ernest Stoneman's efforts in the 1920s, these trips to the studio, although they were musically satisfying, had little influence on the development of the Blue Grass Champs' careers in country music.[24]

The thrusting of Ernest Stoneman and the Blue Grass Champs into prominence via network television in 1956 made the urban folk-music audience aware of the Stonemans and vice versa. Folk-music scholars in the 1950s slowly began to realize that there was a close relationship between the traditional noncommercial songs and tunes they studied and the music found on pre–World War II commercial hillbilly and blues records. In 1952, Folkways Records released an anthology containing eighty-four selections of such music by both black and white musicians. The editor included two numbers by Ernest and Hattie Stoneman, namely "The Mountaineer's Courtship" and "The Spanish Merchant's Daughter," in the collection. Another song, "Old Shoes and Leggins," featured Eck Dunford's fiddle and vocal with accompaniment by the Stoneman band. Whether Harry Smith, who edited the set, realized that Ernest and Hattie Stoneman lived in suburban Washington cannot be determined from his notes, which stated only that "these artists (Stonemans, Brewer, Mooney, Dunford) . . . are probably from the vicinity of Galax, Virginia."[25]

The rediscovery of Ernest and Hattie Stoneman via network television soon led to their appearance on Folkways Records. Mike Seeger, a young folk scholar and musician, taped the session at the Stoneman home at Carmody Hills. The album *Old Time Tunes of the South*, featuring the Stoneman Family, came out in 1957. Although side B of the record contained songs by other traditional Appalachian musicians, the A side had ten songs and tunes spotlighting Ernest and Hattie Stoneman as folk musicians. Pop sang, played guitar, Autoharp, harmonica, and clawhammer banjo in various combinations on nine cuts; Hattie provided fiddle backup on two numbers, banjo on one. In addition, she performed a fine solo clawhammer-banjo rendition of "Cumberland Gap." A couple of the songs had Van Stoneman playing bass fiddle. Folkways technicians recorded one song, "Wreck of the Old 97," at a Saturday night "Paul Jones" dance in which Ernest, Hattie, and Van were augmented by Gene Stoneman on rhythm guitar and Gene Cox on a bluegrass-style banjo. After twenty-three years, the Stoneman name was finally on a record label again. While the record never reached a large number of people, it did introduce the Stoneman name to the urban folk-music audience, some of whom knew of him through the *Anthology of American Folk Music* set.[26]

At almost the same time, Folkways released a single-volume anthology entitled *American Banjo Scruggs Style*. This album contained thirty-one cuts of various bluegrass banjo pickers, ranging from such veterans of the art as Snuffy Jenkins and Earl Scruggs's brother Junie to seventeen-year-old Rick Rittler. The victor and runner-up in the banjo contest at the 1956 Gambrills, Maryland, music festival had been Eugene and Veronica Stoneman Cox, respectively, and each did a banjo tune for the album as the other seconded on rhythm guitar. Gene picked out "Wildwood Flower," a tune normally favored by guitarists while Roni performed

"Lonesome Road Blues" (this was said to be the first time a female had played bluegrass banjo on disc).[27]

By the time the Folkways Recordings became available to the public, the band known as the Little Pebbles had pretty much disbanded. Pop increasingly appeared as a featured vocalist with the Blue Grass Champs, and Van joined as their regular guitar player. Roni became an expectant mother and then, after March 20, 1957, had little Eugene to keep her occupied. Larry King took his white bass fiddle and dropped out of the music. Zeke Dawson worked with other local musicians, most notably Johnny Hopkins. He then served in the army and after his discharge went to Nashville, where he has enjoyed a long career as a sideman for such notables as Ray Price, George Jones, and especially Loretta Lynn. Since 1984, Dawson has worked as fiddler in a band more akin to his Appalachian roots, Wilma Lee Cooper's Clinch Mountain Clan.[28]

Meanwhile, Veronica Stoneman Cox increasingly found her life as a young housewife and mother a difficult one. Gene Cox, described by both Roni and Zeke Dawson as "mild-mannered" and "easy-going," had a similar approach to his role as a family breadwinner. According to Roni, "Gene had a good job" because "he was foreman over all the women at the plant and they liked him." However, after only a few months of their marriage, "he stopped showing up for work." People from the coil factory "came to see why he stopped" coming to work and "told him he had a future with the company." Continuing her story, Roni related that

> not long after this visit, he completely quit working here I was pregnant; begging him to go back to work. Not long after that, I was thrown out of my apartment, I couldn't pay my rent, so I had to put my three rooms of furniture in storage before the landlord took it from me. I couldn't pay for storage either and my furniture was put up on the auction block, but I didn't know that then. (I couldn't do anything about it anyway) . . . by this time I was living at my mother-in-laws. Her husband, (they found out) had TB and I was afraid to keep the baby at their house. I couldn't go home because mama and dad didn't have anything; they had no room for me and I knew it. I found out I was pregnant again . . . these rough periods in my life, I would many times be evicted by landlords. I found out, the law is that the landlord can keep all your possessions except the baby crib

and baby clothes. I can't tell you how many times I carried that baby crib around from place to place with the baby clothes piled in it and underneath it all I hid my electric fan. I'm ashamed now, looking back over my life, that I put up with the torments I did. My young life was not a pleasant one.[29]

With virtually no place to go, Roni scraped together sufficient funds to purchase a bus ticket to Mississippi and paid an extended visit to Patsy. The latter had become increasingly disenchanted with Deep South farm life, but a visitor from home, even a destitute one, could provide some comfort and cheer. Finally, Gene Cox's father went to a TB sanatorium and Gene's brother Aubrey gave Gene some money to bring Roni home from Mississippi to live with him and his mother. The health climate in the Cox home may have improved, but finances remained as precarious as before, Roni says:

During this whole term of my pregnancy, my husband, wouldn't even try to get a job. I was desperate. I prayed a lot and cried a lot. I begged him to try and get work. Just before the baby was born (about a month I'd say) he went fishing with his brother instead of job hunting. While he was gone, his mother told me to get out . . . that my family had more than hers and she could only take care of Gene and not me. I found a carriage in the trash and after cleaning it throughly with Lysol (I loved my babies and didn't want them getting sick) moved my few worldly goods and my baby out from that place. Not having a carriage mattress, I used my son's (Eugene, Jr.) clothes spreading them over the bottom of the carriage and covering them with a blanket to provide a comfortable place on which to lay my child. I walked the three miles to my mother's house barefooted. I traveled over an asphalt road and the hot tar bubbles covered every inch of the surface and my feet were blistered by the time I got to mom's house. I did not own a pair of shoes. Mama said I could stay as long as I needed to, but I felt so bad about it. I so wanted a better life for my children than I had experienced, but it all seemed to be in vain. I prayed some more. Three weeks before the baby was born, I found a little place (basement apartment) up the road from mama. I rented it by the week. Gene wanted to move back with me too. I was glad; mama didn't have room for us. All the time I stayed at mama's Gene had stayed at his mama's. He still wouldn't find work. We

moved into this little place anyway, and borrowed money from
his brother. . . . I had a good doctor with Eugene, but with
Becky, she was born at Prince George Hospital [on April 15,
1958]. I'd gone to the clinic a few times and the interns there,
delivered Becky. She only weighed six pounds so it was a fairly
easy delivery. I hadn't gone through the agony I'd experienced
with Eugene. This is something I hate to say, but I feel I must.
The Welfare Department paid for her delivery, but *I WAS
NEVER ON WELFARE.*[30]

After Rebecca's birth, Roni returned to her tiny basement apartment, where she immediately faced a new crisis:

Becky was three days old when I had to leave our place and go
back to mama's. It had rained an awful lot (right after my baby's
birth) and the water level became knee-deep where we lived. I
had to pile one chair on another and make Junior sit on it and he
was only 13 months old. I had to place Becky on top of two other
chairs, just to keep my darlings from getting wet. I got the old
mop and started soaking up the water. I'd wring the mop out
into a pail and dump the heavy bucket out in a sink that was
located way in the back of a small hallway, under some steps.
This area belonged to the woman upstairs, but she allowed me
to use it to dump excess water. The woman upstairs had a baby
two months old; she was still resting and being taken care of.
Here I was, sopping up a flood, with a baby three days old. Two
days later it started raining again, so I went to stay with mama.
The people upstairs wouldn't fix the hole in the wall to stop the
leak. I finally had to move out of there; but she did give me
some baby clothes for my little girl and they lasted me a long
time for Becky. I was so *pleased* with those baby clothes.[31]

Roni's life continued to be a difficult one, but through her musical abilities she found a means to survive. She relates that

even though times got harder, my heart would break, because I
knew, deep down, I was getting closer to raising my children in
the manner I always hated, I didn't go for aid. I knew as long as
I had my health and the knowledge of prayer, I felt God would
give me strength to better myself and carry me through. I
started playing bass fiddle in the clubs around Washington,
D.C. and three months after Becky's birth, I found myself pregnant again. At four months I miscarried. The hours were long
and hard, the bass was rough to play. I did six shows a night, six

nights a week and played for tips. My husband still suffered from his "do nothing, no-job" disease. God provided for me a way. During my visit to my mother's one evening, a Baptist preacher came in and started discussing the future of my soul and told me if I didn't stop working clubs, I was going to Hell! I told him I believed it was wrong, however, I had to have a way to make a living. He told me God would provide. I *hated* playing those clubs, but they fed my babies. There was nothing else I could do. The *nerve* of that Baptist preacher passing judgement on me! I had a better Christian attitude than he did. The Good Lord knew I was helping to feed my babies the only way I could. If I was going to hell for feeding my babies, then I was going to get there by not passing GO and not collecting $200.00 [a reference to the popular game Monopoly]!!³²

Roni lost her job playing bass but soon found another one playing banjo for Benny and Vallie Cain and then in a band led by Johnny Hopkins. The latter had an able country group that worked clubs in the Washington area, including The Famous when the Blue Grass Champs played elsewhere. Zeke Dawson had worked a stint with them earlier when Pop Stoneman's Little Pebbles dissolved following Roni's initial pregnancy and Van's joining the Blue Grass Champs. Roni played banjo in the Hopkins band. By this time, numerous "ladies of the night" frequented the place. Roni, while no stranger to poverty, remained relatively naïve regarding much of the darker side of life. Regarding the prostitutes who hung out at The Famous, she remembered: "They took care of me, protecting me from whatever was out there in that old world. I did not know they were in a questionable profession at that time. I just thought they were pretty ladies and they were *wonderful* to me."³³

Working six hours a night for six days a week with Johnny Hopkins did not pay more than a few dollars per day, but it enabled Roni and her little family to subsist. By the fall of 1959 she found herself pregnant again. With no maternity clothing, Roni "cut holes in the waistline of the skirts and slipped shoestrings through so" she "could expand the skirts" as her midriff increased in size. At this time Roni had virtually no possessions other than a few items of clothing and her banjo. "I didn't even own a pair of stockings or lipstick," she said. "Every penny I made went for my babies." As she entered the final months of her pregnancy, the hookers who loitered around The Famous, together with the employees, planned a surprise. One night at closing time, someone in the crowd called to her:

"Come in here Roni, (kitchen area) we have something for you." I walked in, not knowing what was going on. They had held a baby shower for me at their house; since they didn't think I'd go there, they brought the shower to me. They fashioned little gowns, sweaters, booties, diapers, and everything one would need for a baby. My sister Grace, had given me a baby shower with my first one, but those items were worn out and long gone. That shower was the sweetest gesture; those "ladies" had shown me more Christianity than that Baptist preacher.[34]

A few weeks later when the moment arrived for her "blessed event," in early May of 1960, Roni experienced her most difficult childbirth:

I had to wait until it was time to deliver before checking in at the hospital. My time came, I went to the clinic and was met by a young, rude, crude doctor. He took me back into an examining room (a nurse also present). He made a nasty remark to me and gave me some pills to hold off the labor and sent me home. I found out later that the baby's buttocks was already out. I had carried the baby 10 months and was *very much* overdue. I got home somehow and managed to look out the window toward the street. The street was moving up and down; from the pills I'd been given. I was in real pain and had to go back to the clinic. . . . I started hemorraging. Interns there, took me to another examining room and they kept examining me, not knowing what they were looking for. I was in *agony!* They kept discussing my problems and finally decided to call a specialist. He had each one feel the "protrusion" and make the diagnosis. One intern suggested that it was my bladder. At this, the specialist became angry and stated, "*Hell* no, *you* knot head, it's the baby's buttocks!" He looked into my eyes and told me he was going to help me, I reached for his hand and said, "Thank you, thank you doctor." He numbed me and then started to turn the baby with his hands and Barbara was born, feet first. I forgot all of the pain I had just been through upon seeing that beautiful baby. She weighed eight pounds, ten ounces.[35]

At three, Barbara began to have seizures, and two years later, Roni learned that the child had suffered brain damage. Over the years, Roni has taken considerable interest in the needs of special children, especially their schooling. Reflecting on the experience, she said, "It has been a long, hard climb for [Barbara] and God allowed my legs to be strong to make the climb with her."[36]

Barbara's delivery hardly ended Roni's difficulties. In the spring of 1961 she had her second miscarriage at a time when the other children "were ill with the measles and mumps." Exhausted, Roni lay down on her bed. Gene "came in from visiting his mother" and inquired as to what "was running out from under the bed." Upon closer examination, he exclaimed "Hell! It's blood!" With three children already sick and no cash to pay a physician, Roni had little choice but to suffer in silence.[37]

By this time, Roni had become the regular banjo picker for the Blue Grass Champs. While carrying Barbara, she had an opportunity to fill in for Porter Church. She recalls the pride she felt when the others complimented her on how much her picking had improved. Not long after that, Church quit for the second time. Jimmy Stoneman recalls that Porter had an off-stage argument with Peggy, broke his banjo in disgust, and departed. Roni then became the banjoist. With three (and then four) small children and a husband to support, the increased income hardly took her away from poverty's door. Looking back in 1982, she bitterly recalled:

> It was getting more *impossible* for me to work, feed and clothe the children and keep an apartment, all by myself. The nightmare was only beginning. After each night's work I'd get in around three or four in the morning, (not playing around, just working). I'd get up at six to feed the babies. I took in washing during the day and did it all by hand. I had no luxuries, just a scrub board. . . . My hands were very strong from wringing out those clothes. I got a dollar a basket. Doesn't it seem ironic, that years later, I would get a part on a wonderful successful TV show called, "Hee Haw" as Ida-Lee, the lady at the ironing board. I guess God prepared me well. People say I do the part so naturally . . . they can't believe after they see me, that it's really me. They say I'm wonderful doing the part. . . . If only

they knew. Fifteen years with this kind of life, sometimes sleeping in cars with my babies because there was no place else to go . . . it was extremely harsh.[38]

As the younger Stonemans married and moved out of the household, the "baby," Van Stoneman, eventually found himself the only child remaining at home. Since many continued to live nearby and economic or domestic difficulties often forced them to return to 307 Seventy-fourth Place, this hardly meant Van had great freedom of space, especially with increasing numbers of grandchildren in the extended family. Like several of the others, Van found romance at a fairly early age. He met a southern Maryland tobacco farmer's daughter named Helen Alvey. They married on September 18, 1958, a few months before Van's eighteenth birthday. Their first child, Van, Jr., was born in 1960 and their second, Randy, in 1966 just after the Stonemans relocated in Nashville. In his musical training with the Little Pebbles and later the Blue Grass Champs, Van had less opportunity than either Scott or Jimmy to serve musical apprenticeships outside the family. He filled in on bass fiddle for the older group during Jimmy's absence and also learned the rudiments of emcee work from Scott, who had alternated with Jimmy Case as the band's original front man. Of Scott's emcee work, Van remarked that the man really had "charisma" and "could make those people set there and laugh their heads off" and then "turn around and make them just about cry." Through such an apprenticeship, Van learned to front a show pretty well—a skill that became increasingly handy as Scott's drinking and resulting absences made an alternate emcee a near necessity.[39]

Van got a little experience now and then filling in with other local or visiting bands. He recalled one such instance when Ralph and Carter, the Stanley Brothers, came to town with virtually no band. They had used a lead guitar heavily in record sessions at this time (either Bill Napier or George Shuffler), but circumstances forced them to use Van on Dobro instead—an instrument virtually foreign to the generally distinct Stanley sound. Van helped them play out their few show dates in the Washington area, with Carter finding the Dobro rather appealing, but the musically conservative Ralph was reluctant and uneasy.[40]

As the Stonemans moved into the sixties, Scott, Donna, Jimmy, Roni, and Van had become more or less full-time musicians. The others, while still playing music on the side, subordinated their artistic talents to the necessity of working day jobs in order to support their families. Two of them, Jack, having serious bouts with alcoholism, and Billy, increasingly afflicted with the aftereffects of his war experience, encountered special problems. Bob Bean, with some degree of business sense and steadier personal habits than Scott, took on more managerial responsibilities. Pop reached retirement age and, nearly seventy, now had more time to devote to music, but simultaneously he realized that his active years as a professional were numbered. Years of hard labor had taken their toll on his physical frame, but his voice, musical ability, and sense of determination remained as strong as ever. Hattie could still fiddle pretty well, but years of poverty and attempting to cope with a large household of unruly boys strained her physical and mental health. Zeke Dawson remembers that many people simply considered her less than sane as she walked around the household muttering to herself, dipping snuff, sweeping the porch, tending her flower beds, and hollering, "Lord God, Ernest!" when something went amiss (which happened often). Yet, he says gently, he came to realize that a real, genuine, and tender human being lived within her tired body.[41]

The Stonemans who followed music professionally believed that if they expected to hit the big time, their big break would have to come soon. During the winter of 1961–62, they received a call which raised their hopes and also created some anxiety. Billy Barton, erstwhile singer-songwriter turned promoter, telephoned them at The Famous. Donna recalls that he urged them to come to Nashville. He could get them on the Grand Ole Opry and he also had a couple of record labels. "You're great, You're sensational" he told them. Although prior experiences with Barton had proved financially elusive, even disastrous, the family decided to take another chance. After all, Barton had never been based in Nashville before and the hope of a place on the Grand Ole Opry, long had had a nearly magic allure for them. As a child, Donna told her teachers, "We don't need education, we'll be musicians and play on the Grand Ole Opry." Now, through the help of Billy Barton, it seemed that the Stoneman childhood dream might become reality.[42]

Whether a "flim-flam man" or not, Van gives Billy Barton credit. "He did get us a guest shot on the Opry," Van recalled, and "we tore the house down."[43] Barton recalls that it took nearly all his persuasive talents to get the Stonemans on the show. Finally he promised to pay the Opry manager five hundred dollars if they did not go over well. It worked, and Billy says he didn't even consider it a risk. Showmanship, featuring Scotty's fancy fiddle work complete with his acrobatic tricks, took the audience by storm in his exciting arrangement of "Orange Blossom Special." Donna did some fancy mandolin picking, and Roni's driving bluegrass banjo also impressed the audience. For their second number, the Stonemans performed another spectator favorite, "White Lightning No. 2." Their arrangement of this George Jones hit of 1957 utilized impersonations. Roni emulated Kitty Wells, while Jimmy sang with voice inflections like Ernest Tubb. Finally, Pop came in with a chorus borrowed from "Good Old Mountain Dew." Opry fans demanded, and received, an encore. Backstage, the veterans of the country-music world muttered less praiseworthy remarks about these young upstarts from Washington. Particularly angered stood one of the more respected and influential Opry veterans, Hank Snow, disgusted that the wild applause and encore had severely reduced his own air time. While scoring a home run with the fans out front, the "good ole fashioned hoedown" that Scott had orchestrated produced a strikeout among significant elements within the ranks of the Nashville establishment.

Billy Barton also got the Stoneman Family, the name he preferred to Blue Grass Champs, into the recording studios. The group waxed a single containing "White Lightning No. 2" backed with "Sadness," a song that featured Jimmy vocalizing in a manner that emphasized the Jim Reeves quality in his voice. On a second single, Opry announcer Grant Turner did a recitation while the Stonemans provided instrumental and choral support.[44] Barton released both discs on his Gulf Reef label, but they had a negligible effect on the country-music industry and market.

Billy had another label on which he recorded material intended for album release. Donna says he had a great slogan for this enterprise. "If it's hot, you know it's on Fire," he said of Fire Records. Scott recorded an album of fiddle tunes and the group

cut material for a second effort. Unfortunately, an inferno destroyed the Fire studio soon afterward and the master tapes for
the Stoneman Family's initial LP went up in flames and smoke.[45]
Barton said he would build another one and start over, but his
efforts came to nothing and rumors of self-initiated arson made
the rounds in Music City U.S.A.

Meanwhile, the family had been living in four little apartments,
all of them in a house owned by Billy's wife. Bookings were almost nonexistent, and the Stonemans' meager resources vanished
rapidly. Donna earned a few extra dollars by picking mandolin on
a Capitol Records session for Rose Maddox, and Ken Nelson produced an album of bluegrass material for the powerful vocalist.
Don Reno and Red Smiley played banjo and guitar for the session,
augmenting the sound with the fiddle of Mack Magaha and bassist John Palmer. Bill Monroe did the mandolin picking at the first
day's session on March 19 but had to leave town. Knowing that
Donna was available, Reno and Smiley manager Carlton Haney
suggested that she be hired to complete the album. Haney, familiar with Donna's skill through her few appearances on the New
Dominion Barn Dance and sharing show dates with the Tennessee Cutups, knew she could handle the job. Although virtually
unknown to Nashville session sidemen, diminutive Donna came
through in fine style on March 20, playing on seven of the album's
twelve cuts.[46] Exhaustion of their funds and no lucrative bookings
soon drove the hapless musicians back to Washington, in Donna's
words "with our tails between our legs."[47]

In their old haunts, the Stoneman Family worked in much the
same manner as they had before. They probably had made more
of an impression than they realized. Don Pierce of Starday
Records took an interest in the aging musical patriarch and his
bluegrass-picking offspring. Once dubbed the smallest of the
major record labels, the almost wholly country-oriented Starday
firm specialized in signing formerly bigger stars whose careers
had sagged, up-and-coming youngsters, and those who performed the more traditional styles. As a result, Starday's roster included such acts as Red Sovine, George Jones (whose early efforts
the company kept repackaging in new covers), Johnny Bond,
Hylo Brown, Carl Story, Stringbean, and the Lonesome Pine Fiddlers. Now and then a Starday song did quite well on the charts

and a modest market existed for the albums of country figures who had appeal, albeit somewhat less than those who recorded for Columbia, Decca, Capitol, or RCA Victor. Furthermore, some Washington-area bluegrass musicians had recorded earlier for the company, including the Country Gentlemen, Buzz Busby, and Bill Harrell. The Stoneman Family appealed to Don Pierce for two reasons. First, Ernest Stoneman was clearly a man with a past, although somewhat farther back in time than the artists Pierce normally pushed. Second, Pierce wanted to market bluegrass and the whole band assembled fell pretty close to that category. Bob Bean thinks the Starday executive contracted with Ernest Stoneman not long after the family returned to Carmody Hills from Nashville to do an album for Starday.[48]

Deciding they needed a bus, Scott and Bob Bean obtained a 1949 Flxible with the help of one Don Dixon. Bob says they threw a few pieces of furniture into the vehicle and headed for Nashville to do their first successful long-play album session. This event took place in mid to late July 1962.[49]

The recordings at Starday Sound Studio resulted in sixteen numbers, many being of excellent quality. Pierce put fourteen of the songs in the album and placed two additional instrumentals in the various-artist bluegrass albums that often appeared in the Starday catalog. Although several family members demonstrated their abilities, Pop clearly emerged as the featured performer, singing lead on six songs, three of which he had not previously recorded. It must have given him some satisfaction finally to put his World War II tribute to generals MacArthur and Wainwright, "The Heroes of Bataan," on disc after holding it for twenty years. Donna did her first original mandolin speciality, "The Girl from Galax" (in reference to her mother), and Scott performed his arrangement of the old Grayson and Whitter classic "Lee Highway Blues," which he retitled "Talking Fiddle Blues." Roni sang "Nobody's Darling But Mine," with Donna joining in on the chorus. Scott sang lead on "That Pal of Mine" and "Going Home," and recited a temperance tract called "Guilty," which seems ironic in view of his own bouts with demon rum. Van sang lead on a number called "Out of School," a teenage romance. "White Lightning No. 2," a number that had appeared on disc earlier that year on the Gulf Reef single and apparently had impressed Pierce, received a new treatment for Starday. Released in late fall 1962, *Er-*

nest V. Stoneman and the Stoneman Family: Bluegrass Champs (SLP200) was a musical success, although hardly a best seller. Public reception of the album encouraged Pierce to invite the Stonemans back to Nashville for another one. Scott did not return to Maryland immediately, having agreed to play fiddle with Jimmy Martin and the Sunny Mountain Boys.[50]

Returning to their old haunts by the end of the month, the Stonemans and their kin appeared to make a near sweep at the Warrenton Jaycees' National Country Music Contests held on August 5. The Associated Press reported that "Scotty Stoneman of Galax [sic] won his eighth consecutive fiddle championship" at Lake Whippoorwill Park. Furthermore, Gene Cox took the top prize in banjo competition, while "Van Stoneman and the Stoneman Brothers of Washington took first place in the band category." Pop took second in "miscellaneous," being nosed out for the lead by C. G. Mathers, Jr., of Radford. Roni probably sat out the competition that year, since she gave birth to her fourth child, son Robert, a week after the contest on August 12, 1962.[51]

By early 1963 the name Stoneman began to attract attention in more distant locales, such as Texas. On February 21 the family headlined a Beaumont City Auditorium concert called the National Folk Festival of 1963. Sigma Nu fraternity at Lamar Tech (now Lamar University) sponsored the show, and the advertising suggests that it aimed more for the collegiate folk audience than the country-music fan. Along with "The Sensational Stoneman Family (direct from Washington D.C.)," the concert featured RCA Victor recording artist Walter Forbes, a young Georgian whose musical styles showed a blend of old-time country, bluegrass, and urban folk influences; Allen Reynolds, a folksinger of some renown; and Jack Clement, Scott's old pal. Clement had since gone on to work for Sam Philips at Sun Records, perform rockabilly material himself, and compose several hit songs, chiefly for Johnny Cash. According to one story, he told Scotty that in his Cash hit "Ballad of a Teenage Queen" he had used Donna as a model for the girl in the song, although Clement modestly says he has told several girls that they were the teenage queen in the lyrics. According to Bob Bean, Clement, who had maintained occasional contacts with Scott and other Stonemans, hoped he could put together a package tour similar to the one that played in Beaumont.[52]

Although no "National Folk Festival Tour" followed the Texas concert, the Stonemans did break into the college folk scene. On December 29, 1962, folklorist Archie Green, aided by Dick Spottswood and Doyle Moore, conducted an extensive interview with Pop Stoneman in Carmody Hills. Green combined academic interest in folksongs and labor history and became one of the first academically trained individuals to appreciate fully the cultural value of old-time hillbilly music. While seeking out and interviewing older musicians for research information relative to his publications, Green also helped—in some instances—to reactivate their performance careers. After his visit with Ernest Stoneman, he arranged for the family to appear in concert at the University of Illinois under the auspices of the Campus Folksong Club on the night of May 18, 1963. F. K. Flous, a student reporter seemingly more impressed by Scott, Roni, and Donna than Pop, wrote a highly favorable review of their program:

The concert of Appalachian folk music presented by the Stoneman Family Saturday night was distinct from all previous such efforts for two reasons.

It had more action than any group that the Campus Folksong Club yet presented; the performers not only played and sang, but danced, jumped and crawled around the stage as well. And, more important, it has a certain quality not usually attributed to folk music concerts—sex.

You see, it's like this folks: the Stoneman Family consists of Pop Stoneman, who plays the guitar, his son Van, who also plays the guitar, Scott who plays the fiddle, and Jim, on the bass.

Then come the two daughters Donna, who plays the mandolin, and Ronnie, who picks a mean banjo. Not to get ecstatic or anything, but man, it's enough to wring your withers. Ronnie sails onto the stage like a new Chris-Craft; Donna moves like a PT boat maneuvering for the kill. Both are dressed in tight skirts that seem barely capable of confining their obvious charms.

Your reviewer ordinarily tends to be a connoisseur of fiddling, but he could not keep his eye on the fiddler Saturday night. Every time a good bit of rhythm came along Donna started doing a little dance and Ronnie began jumping into the air, picking the daylights out of her banjo at the same time. To sum it up, the concert was as much visual as it was aural.

The high point of the action was no doubt the performance of the fiddler, Scott, who spent the first part of the evening playing the part of the village idiot, skulking about the stage, dispensing corn-fed humor and generally trying to make a shambles of his kinfolks' efforts.

He really stole the stage however, when he gave a classic exhibition of trick fiddling—holding the bow between his knees and moving the fiddle over it, lying on the floor and arching his back while he played the fiddle under his "bridge," playing the instrument while holding it behind his back.

The whole performance was not only wildly entertaining but significant. The Stonemans, making only their second appearance before a college audience, had made no effort to remodel their efforts into "folk music." They simply presented the same act with which they entertain audiences in their native Appalachians. The result was straight country music, with the real brand of wild country humor and liberal use of sex.[53]

The $500 fee the Stonemans received for this engagement seemingly exceeded their normal charge for an appearance, but not when one considers the distance they traveled. On May 5 they appeared at Sunset Park in West Grove, Pennsylvania, for $350 and on July 25 at the Westminster, Maryland, fireman's carnival for $225.[54]

By mid-1963, Patsy Stoneman, after a fifteen-year absence from the scene, reemerged as an active musician. Life in Mississippi had become nearly unbearable for the independent-minded woman. The years of hard labor, frequent miscarriages, and rough treatment combined to make her much embittered toward her situation, although her hopes brightened in the late fifties when she and R. H. Cain managed to adopt three young girls named Diane, Brenda, and Linda. Then came an illness, which doctors diagnosed as breast cancer, that would necessitate an operation. R. H. began complaining that he couldn't keep anyone around who couldn't pull their own weight in terms of the workload. Patsy went to Memphis for her surgery and planned to convalesce at her parents' home in Carmody Hills. While there she planned to obtain a legal divorce from Charles Streeks, who still lived and had not died in an auto crash as she once believed. In the meantime, Cain sought and received a divorce in Mississippi on the ethically shaky grounds that Patsy abandoned him. The court granted him custody of their adopted children. Physically unable to play a guitar when she first returned, Patsy went to work as a waitress for Sam Bomstein at The Famous as soon as her health permitted. The wages and tip money she received enabled her not only to sustain herself, but also to pay the legal fees for her divorce.[55]

Freed from two bad marriages but upset over the loss of her beloved adopted daughters, Patsy began to put her life back together. She organized a band that could at times be classified as either bluegrass or country, depending on membership. Red Allen, Buzz Busby, Porter Church, Bill Emerson, Ed Ferris, Roy Self, Scott Stoneman, and the Yates Brothers (Bill and Wayne) all served in the group during the five years Patsy kept it together. In 1963 they worked a lot at such clubs as the Oakcrest and Schola's, with Patsy and each band member earning ten dollars nightly plus an average of about three more in tips.[56]

Patsy was married again, to Don Dixon, on May 4, 1963. Dixon had become acquainted with the family a year or two earlier when he made a bus available for their use. Later he helped them buy the 1949 Flxible. The marriage proved a happy but short-lived one. The couple bought a home in suburban Elkridge, but Don died as the result of a May 3, 1964, automobile accident—living just long enough for them to have been married a year. The widowed Patsy kept working, primarily with her own band but doing occasional dates with the Stoneman Family.[57]

In the fall of 1963, Don Pierce arranged for the Stoneman Family to record a second album at Starday Sound Studio in Nashville. About this same time, Mac Wiseman needed a bluegrass band to back him for a three-week engagement at a Las Vegas club called The Mint. Roni got Dean and Faye to look after her children during what would be a month's absence, while Bob Bean remained in Maryland at his first job. Accompanying Scott on the trip was a woman named Gloria, who the rest of the family say made a valiant effort to keep the brilliant but erratic fiddler straight.[58]

The session produced fourteen new masters. Eight of them featured Pop, whose work from the first album seemingly impressed Pierce. Scott fiddled "Orange Blossom Breakdown," a rendition of

Ervin Rouse's classic train-fiddle tune that many experts consider the ultimate version. Scott also sang solo on "Turn Me Loose," a recomposition of an old Galax song titled "Let Me Fall," which included heavy Dobro by Van and mandolin by Donna. Van sang lead on an original entitled "Family Life," a lyric he based on his brother Jack's experiences. "Little Suzie" was a clever song, written and performed by Scott, about a mischievous girl. Patsy says that in his childhood Scott himself did most of the tricks he attributed to the fictional tomboy. Pierce chose not to release the final two numbers cut at the session. "Poor Ellen Smith" featured Jimmy Stoneman in what Van considered a unique arrangement of a traditional murder ballad that originated in the Mount Airy region in 1893. Van sang lead on another of his own compositions called "Out Running Around." The album released the following summer bore the title *The Great Old Timer at the Capitol*. The cover photo showed the Stonemans in the middle of Pennsylvania Avenue with the U.S. Capitol in the background. The picture first appeared on the cover of the *Washington Post Magazine* on November 3, 1963.[59]

With their second album "in the can," the Stonemans piled into their vehicle for the long trip to Las Vegas. Mac Wiseman led the way in his car, the Stonemans following him in their bus. An inexperienced Van did much of the driving and at one point nearly crashed into Mac, who hesitated in the lane when he missed a left turn. On another occasion, with Scott at the wheel, the bus nearly collided with a semitrailer truck on a long, narrow bridge, with rubber from both vehicles touching each other. In retrospect, Van believes "it was only [through] God's will that we made it across alive."[60]

Once they arrived in the Nevada entertainment center, the Stonemans settled in for their stay at The Mint, where they performed four one-hour shows nightly. The family would do their set and then Mac would take center stage as they became his band. Pop, who contributed only extra rhythm, could have retired from the scene while Mac sang, but chose instead to remain "in his chair on stage." The elderly musician probably wanted to demonstrate his stamina, but he also may have found it easier to remain in the chair because "he was crippled in one hip with arthritis." Although he had "pretty much been the star of the show anyhow," Pop stayed at his post, often falling asleep while continuing ever more slowly to pick his guitar. If someone awakened him, Pop suddenly began picking more rapidly.[61]

While in Las Vegas, Ernest met a man named John Kelly, who was quite impressed with the Stoneman stage show. Kelly had connections with booking agents throughout Nevada and the Far West and urged the Stonemans to return to Washington, get their business settled, and move to the West. When the family got back to Washington in the last half of November, they began preparing to depart. Bob Bean quit his job to become a full-time manager. Gene Cox would go to Las Vegas, where he had a job picking banjo for Judy Lynn. Hattie would remain in Carmody Hills until the family became more or less settled. Meanwhile, Kelly began having delays in his lucrative booking arrangements, but Jack Clement in Beaumont, Texas, thought for sure he could find sufficient work in that region to keep the Stonemans occupied until the arrangements in the Far West could be finalized.[62]

At the age of seventy, Ernest Stoneman, now accompanied by his five youngest children, set out once again to make his mark in the world of commercial music. Nearly four decades had elapsed since he went to New York by train and sang "The Titanic" for Ralph Peer. In those days only a few others—John Carson, Henry Whitter, Dave Macon, and Riley Puckett among them—had preceded him along that path. Now only he remained alive and picking. His determination to succeed remained as high in 1964 as in early days and the odds were more challenging. Still, he continued to exemplify his own oft-repeated motto: "Don't Quit."

A brochure advertising the Stoneman appearance at the Golden Bear, Huntington Beach, California, July 1964. Standing (left to right): Van, Roni, Scott, Donna, Jimmy; kneeling: Pop.

Patsy Stoneman when she headed her own band, about 1966.

The Stonemans just after they won the CMA Award, 1967. Standing (left to right): Van, Roni, Jerry Monday, Donna; center: Pop; seated in front: Jimmy.

The Stonemans as they appeared from mid-1968 to early 1971. Standing (left to right): Patsy, Van, Jimmy, Donna; seated: Roni.

The Stonemans, 1971 (without Roni). Left to right: Van, Patsy, Jimmy, Donna, Jerry Monday.

The Stoneman lineup, spring 1973. Top row (left to right): David Dougherty, banjo; Buck White, mandolin; center, Patsy; bottom (left to right): Van, Jimmy.

The Stonemans were guests on "Hee Haw" in October 1981. Left to right: Chuck Holcomb, Roni, Patsy, Van, Donna, John Bellar, Jimmy. Other "Hee Haw" cast members are seated at the picnic tables to the lower right.

The Stonemans, 1989. Top (left to right): Van, Jimmy; bottom (left to right): Patsy, Donna.

Roni Stoneman as Ida Lee Nagger on the "Hee Haw" set about 1988. Courtesy of Roni Stoneman.

Donna Stoneman, 1990. Photo taken for use either as an evangelist or solo gospel singer. Courtesy of Donna Stoneman.

7

The Golden Years—Again

1964–69

The route taken by the Stonemans on their journey for success led from Washington, D.C., to Texas and thence to California. Nashville, however, was their ultimate destination. Jack Clement, who had acquired considerable business acumen, reasoned that if they attracted sufficient notice on the West Coast, the record producers, television financiers, and booking agencies in Music City U.S.A. would be much more receptive to them than before. Clement's deductions proved correct, although they reaped much more in the way of publicity during their two years in Texas and California than they did in terms of financial rewards. New Year's Day 1964 found the six musical Stonemans making preparations for their move to Beaumont, Texas. Before that happened, however, Jimmy Stoneman needed to get some things taken care of in his personal life. In 1962, a year after his divorce from Peggy, he met a secretary named Mary Grubb Urich. Some years older than Jimmy, she had four sons by a previous marriage: Tom, George, Bobby, and Jimmy, ages fifteen through eight. Under a new Maryland law, county-court clerks could perform marriage ceremonies, so, on January 2, Jim and Mary became the second couple married at the courthouse in Upper Marlboro, Maryland, under the new legislation.[1]

Ten days later the Stonemans and some of their families took off for Beaumont. Jack Clement secured some work for them at the Tap Room, a club owned by two friends named Bob Webster and

Russ Bennett. Clement, who had come to Beaumont in 1961 and opened a recording studio in the East Texas city, recalled of the Stonemans that "they sounded real good." The patrons at the Tap Room "loved it," and the Stonemans began getting other gigs as well. For instance, in mid-March they played four days at a club near La Porte, The Colonel's Quarters, and Roni remembers working in the roof garden of a classy hotel in Houston.[2]

Jack Clement also rushed out a new single for the regional market and endeavored to restructure their image. The disc, the first of many Stoneman efforts produced by Clement, featured a stomping bluegrass rendition of the traditional song "Big Ball in Town," retitled "Big Ball in Houston" and backed with "Little Maggie." The group performed the latter in a style seemingly influenced less by Grayson and Whitter or the Stanley Brothers than by the folk-music hootenanny fad and the Kingston Trio. Clement consciously strived to sell the Stonemans as a folk-music band and to tone down the hillbilly connotations formerly associated with them. Avoiding the rhinestone-cowboy stereotype of modern country and western, he went more in the direction of a collegiate folk act. The main change occurred when he dressed Pop and the boys in little "beanie or umpire caps," stylish narrow ties, and cardigan sweaters. Clement conceded that the caps looked silly but they apparently worked to the Stonemans' advantage, especially when they began auditioning for network television specials.[3]

After nearly three months in Texas, the Stonemans traveled on to California, where they appeared at the UCLA Folk Festival in late March. D. K. Wilgus, a professor of folklore, and Eugene Earle, a serious collector of vintage country records, had been instrumental, together with Archie Green, in organizing the John Edwards Memorial Foundation, an archive dedicated to the preservation and serious study of early country music. Earle conducted an interview with Pop Stoneman on March 27. The Stonemans also formalized their management contract with Clement, giving Jack control of their career for a seven-year period.[4]

Following the UCLA performance, the Stonemans appeared at the Monterey Folk Festival in Northern California, where they made an immediate hit. Joan Baez and Judy Collins also played there that year, and Donna saw them for the first time. In April the Stonemans recorded a new album for World-Pacific, *Big Ball in Monterey*. The cover carried the tag "Live!" but it actually was done at the studios of World-Pacific Records in Hollywood. Clement produced the recording and purposely aimed it at the urban folk and general-music audience. Donna considers the California album as the "first of the better sounds."

Whereas the Starday efforts had been built largely around Pop, the World-Pacific disc emphasized Scott's talents and attempted, partly through use of canned applause, to capture the group as the dynamic stage act they had become. Much of the material came from country tradition, both old and new. Scott fiddled and sang his way through "Fire on the Mountain" and vocalized on the 1909 sentimental ballad "I Wonder How the Old Folks Are at Home," which he picked up from Mac Wiseman. From fairly recent bluegrass tradition he took "Lost Ball in the High Weeds," which Jimmy Martin waxed in 1956 as "You'll Be a Lost Ball." Scott sang solo lead on a new Jack Clement–Allen Reynolds composition called "Take Me Home." Van did likewise with Harlan Howard's "Busted," which had done well for both Johnny Cash and Ray Charles. Jimmy Stoneman made his initial vocal-solo release by doing the Merle Travis song of life in the coal mines, "Dark as a Dungeon," a hillbilly hit of the forties that won acceptance in the folk idiom. Scott played banjo while Van picked Dobro on an instrumental version of "Dominique," an international pop hit by Soeur Sourire, the Singing Nun from Belgium. "Darlin' Corey," "Ground Hog," "Little Maggie," and "Big Ball in Monterey" all had true folk origins but had won acceptance by the urban crowd, too. Clement recut new versions of the last two songs for World-Pacific, making "Big Ball" a California song. Finally, Pop sang the sentimental favorite of 1899, "The Girl in Sunny Tennessee," with Autoharp accompaniment instead of the guitar and fiddle he used in 1926. The album was released in midsummer and *Billboard* reviewed it with favor: "Instrumentally or vocally the Stoneman Family make great country and bluegrass music. Banjos, Fiddles, bass, and autoharp are handled with such grace and verve that it is almost impossible for one not to be in rapport with the group or the music they play. The selections are diversified enough to appeal to almost anyone's taste. Topnotch package."[5]

Here and there one did take exception to this positive view. Professor D. K. Wilgus of UCLA, who liked the Stonemans' Starday material, lamented that the Stoneman Family "is now becoming a casualty of the urban revival," with its new album "a succession of pop-folk arrangements." To the folklorist, their stylings had become too slick and commercial for the true folk taste. The Stonemans, as nearly always, concerned themselves more with the basics of daily sustenance and survival than whether the purity of their musical virtue had been compromised.[6]

The Stonemans appeared on two network television programs that spring. On May 7, 1964, they were guests on "The Steve Allen Show." As Donna recalled, Allen disliked country and hillbilly music, but with the boys wearing the umpire caps and sweaters, he loved them as "an authentic folk group from Maryland." Allen introduced them as the "Stone Man Family," and they performed "Darlin' Corey" and Pop sang "The Girl in Sunny Tennessee." As a finale, Scotty fiddled "Orange Blossom Special." A month later they did a CBS network special, "Texaco Star Parade Starring Meredith Willson." Then they added "He's My Friend" from Willson's Broadway hit *The Unsinkable Molly Brown* to their repertoire.[7]

As always, personal appearances were the major Stoneman activity in California. Donna believes the first and most frequent of their club shows tended to be at the Hollywood Troubadour, although the exact dates seem forgotten. The Stonemans did work two days at the Golden Bear in Huntington Beach in late April and came back for two weeks in July. At the end of April they worked at the Ash Grove in Los Angeles and did another two weeks there, which ended August 2. During that period the Ash Grove showcased quite a few traditional country and bluegrass acts, including Maybelle Carter, Lester Flatt and Earl Scruggs, the New Lost City Ramblers, Hylo Brown, Doc Watson, and the Kentucky Colonels.[8]

In May the group worked two weekends at the Mecca in Buena Park, and in June they appeared several times at Disneyland. Although all of their festival, television, and club appearances in California succeeded in bringing them considerable attention, they hardly reaped major financial rewards for the struggling musicians. According to fragmentary information from surviving contracts, their most lucrative pay in California came from their work at Disneyland, where they received two hundred dollars per day twice and three hundred dollars per day four times. The Mecca paid the best among their club engagements, for which they grossed one thousand dollars for six nights' work. Their pay at the Golden Bear was considerably less. The Stonemans earned no more in California than the Blue Grass Champs did in Washington, D.C. Living expenses on the West Coast undoubtedly exceeded those in Carmody Hills, but hope for a better future in music continued to sustain the six musicians and their families. They literally lived the life in the song "Better Times a' Comin'."

> Pick away on the old banjo,
> Keep that guitar strummin',
> Put more water in the soup,
> There's better times a' comin'.

Sometime during their California experience the Stonemans returned to Texas and worked a stage show with Johnny Cash. It occurred during one of the darker periods in Cash's life. At that time he was doing an adaptation of the old traditional ballad "The Legend of John Henry's Hammer" in his stage show. In the course of the song he would hit a steel bar with a Coca-Cola bottle to create the sound of a hammer. For some reason he could not get the sound he wanted and angrily gave the bottle a fling to the side of the stage, where it struck a waiting-in-the-wings Roni on the shinbone. Roni yelled in agony and Johnny became quite alarmed and tried to comfort her and ease the pain. In the long run, the incident came to be simply one of those memorable events that take place on the road.[9]

Returning East in mid-August, the Stoneman Family played a two-week engagement at a Virginia Beach club called The Shadows. They received one thousand-eight hundred dollars for the job, which suggests that their California experiences may have increased their earning capacity back East. Donna recalls that Scotty began teaching her a few tricks on the fiddle during their stint at The Shadows, and had they stuck with it, their stage presence likely would have increased even more. The group also played some of their old Washington haunts again. In early

October they spent a week at a Kent, Ohio, club, the Blind Owl, which, like many of the California locales, catered to a college audience.[10]

In mid-October the Stonemans went to New York, where they appeared as guests on "The Jimmy Dean Show." An hour-long musical variety show on ABC, Dean's program was the major network fare for country-music fans in the years between the demise of "Ozark Jubilee" and the start of "The Johnny Cash Show." Although he was a native of Texas, Dean, like the Stonemans and Roy Clark, first gained prominence in the Washington area. Beginning with "Big Bad John" in 1961, a string of hits made him a national star, and television viewers found his Texas drawl and easygoing manner appealing.

Poverty continued to dog the musical family during the Dean experience. Donna says she and Bob used their last dime to go to a rehearsal on the subway. The petite Donna managed to squeeze through the turnstiles with her husband and thus economize. At the rehearsals the hungry Stonemans twice cleared the refreshment table, prompting Dean to make inquiries as to where the food had gone. A $500.00 advance alleviated their dire needs slightly and later each Stoneman received another $171.75.[11]

A few more club dates, including a trip to Boston, occupied the band for the remainder of 1964. In late December the Equitable Trust Company of Baltimore repossessed their bus because of their "failure to meet the installment terms." With their contract "in arrears to the amount of $1,509.36," there was no practical alternative to giving up their vehicle. Patsy went with Donna and Bob to Bob Simon's Mobile Home Sales in Aberdeen to retrieve the stage clothes and other personal items that had been stored on the bus.[12]

With the other Stonemans in California, Patsy and her band had moved into some of the night spots formerly occupied by the Blue Grass Champs. The leader and each band member received twenty-seven dollars at the Hotel Charles and twenty-five dollars at The Famous for the one night each week that the Patsy Stoneman Show appeared there. This suggested that the Stonemans may have prospered just as much by remaining in Washington, albeit without the national TV exposure and extensive travel.[13]

Despite this modest success, Patsy jumped at the opportunity to play some shows with the family group. Scott found himself fired again after another drinking binge. This time Bob and the others decided they would try to get along without him for more than the customary few days. Donna says the Stonemans without Scott would be like the Lewis Family without Little Roy, but life had to go on as best it could. Bob Bean told Patsy that some of the West Coast contracts required six Stonemans on stage and they needed "a warm body" Stoneman to fulfill that obligation, so Patsy took temporary absence from her own band, leaving it in charge of Red Allen.[14]

Without their own bus, the Stonemans traveled in automobiles, leaving on January 16, 1965, for Denver. They opened there on the twentieth at The Exodus. Patsy recalls the weather as being snowy and dangerous most of the trip. The group rolled into Denver on the evening of Tuesday the nineteenth; while the others slept on Wednesday morning, Pop decided the stage needed enlarging. Accordingly he went to work with his carpenter tools and by that night had a bandstand that would accommodate six pickers and a mandolinist who danced around more than the average musician. "For my gang it takes a big stage," the elderly Autoharpist told Pat Hanna of the *Rocky Mountain News*, who took an obvious liking to the old-timer.[15]

Following their Denver experience the Stonemans drove on to California, where they began a three-week return engagement at the Hollywood Troubadour at eight hundred and fifty dollars per week in early February. Their earlier visits to the Ash Grove and the Troubadour had made them enough of a drawing card that they could now earn a living wage on such club work, provided they kept working steadily. When periods of slack employment occurred, however, their cash reserves drained rapidly. To tide them over through such times, the Stonemans attempted to set up a system whereby they would each draw a weekly salary of sixty-five dollars, which would maintain them on a modest but regular wage.[16]

During their Troubadour stint the Stonemans began to enjoy some of the advantages of having a little more money. In Denver their cash reserves had been so low that they stayed in a run-down hotel called the Bellview, which Patsy described as "about the worst I have ever seen." In Los Angeles, their motel belonged to Sandy Koufax, the Dodger pitcher, and Hollywood stars took in their show. Kathryn Grayson came to see them and became sufficiently acquainted for a young friend to get a few banjo lessons from Roni. Mitzi Gaynor nearly went wild with enthusiasm over Donna's dance steps. She had the whole band come down to her practice studio while Donna taught her some footwork techniques. The heroine of *South Pacific* discussed the possibility of using Stonemans in some of her own routines, but things never went beyond the talking stage.[17]

Before the Troubadour stint ended, the Stonemans began rehearsals for another network special, "The Danny Thomas Show." Other guests on the program had much bigger entertainment-business reputations, including Mary Tyler Moore, then best known as Laura Petrie on "The Dick Van Dyke Show," and Andy Griffith, known for a number of Hollywood films as well as his own situation comedy. The folksy Griffith hailed from Mount Airy, North Carolina, which was only a few miles across the state line from the Stonemans' hometown of Galax. Griffith also had a country-music background, having started with Roy Hall and the Blue Ridge Entertainers at WDBJ in Roanoke during World War II. The fictional setting of his own series, "Mayberry," resembled an idealized Mount Airy, and members of such bluegrass bands as the Dillards and the Kentucky Colonels had appeared on it. Griffith seemed like an ideal figure to do a number with the Stonemans.[18]

Before the special aired on April 23, the Stonemans went to Calgary, Alberta, where they taped a "Let's Sing Out" program for Canadian television. The relatively well-known Oscar Brand and the less-renowned Logan English worked the show with them. Patsy did not go on this trek, but she had worked in the Thomas special. She believed she needed medical attention and returned to Washington. During her weeks in California she began receiving flowers from a fellow back in Maryland named Murph, who had paid some attention to her earlier. Now she began to take the man seriously.[19]

Resuming her career as a musician and country band leader, Patsy's group "found several more places to play and wasn't hurting too bad for money, not that I was rich, but I could hold my own." After a lifetime of material deprivation, she began to "dress fairly nice for the first time in my life" and feel somewhat "secure." Of her social life, Patsy says: "Murph took me to the nicest restaurants . . . and showed me there was something to eat besides pinto beans and purple hull peas." When she went back West in May to play two weeks with the family at the Silver Nugget, "Murph flew out to see me[,] carrying an armload of roses." That romantic gesture proved "the clincher," Patsy said. "I knew then that I wasn't going to let him get away from me."[20]

Medical conditions necessitated another surgical experience for Patsy before she and John J. Murphy, Jr., became man and wife on August 25, 1965. Her new husband worked as a legislative representative for the Bricklayers, Masons, and Plasterers Union, of which his father was president. After the nuptials the newlyweds went to the home of noted bluegrass picker Smiley Hobbs, where they spent most of the evening looking at his collection of model trains. Patsy realized that she had a few years of seniority on Murph, but she found the number larger—fourteen—than she had thought. Nonetheless, the couple bought a home near Lanham, Maryland, and lived there until Nashville beckoned. In regard to her domestic life, Patsy says Murph was "the best thing that has ever happened to me."[21]

Although Scott Stoneman's antics led to another musical and personal break with his family and he did not go West with them in January 1965, he soon reappeared in California. By March he joined forces with the Kentucky Colonels, which worked many of the same Pacific Coast clubs the Stonemans had worked in 1964. A solid band, the Colonels included Roger Bush on bass, Billy Ray Latham on banjo, and Roland White on mandolin. The latter's brother Clarence, an unusually gifted rhythm and lead-guitar picker, was the band's hitherto most distinguished member. The addition of Scott on fiddle gave the group a second and equally innovative instrumentalist. Scott stayed with the Colonels about six months, working largely in clubs like the Ash Grove and the Cobblestone. Although the Colonels made no studio recordings, several cuts from their live shows have appeared in albums, particularly after they attained near-legendary status. Scott and Roland White assisted Lester Flatt, Earl Scruggs, and the cast of

"The Beverly Hillbillies" at a Columbia session in June 1965, playing fiddle and mandolin, respectively.[22]

Personal problems continued to dog Scott. He went through two marriages, both short, to women named Ann and Paula. The latter composed a novelty song that Scott eventually recorded, "The Martian Band." Donna, who had been so close to Scott and his first wife, Cecile, worried a lot about Scott's erratic behavior and spent more than one sleepless night because of concern for her wayward brother. She recalled that at some of the California clubs Scott's fans would shout requests for "Orange Blossom Special," so she finally adapted it to the mandolin to satisfy their demands. In 1966 he rejoined the family after what they politely called "a year long leave of absence," but it proved temporary. He joined forces with Patsy for a time but did not begin to give any indications of stabilizing until 1972.[23]

In the meantime the remainder of the Stoneman Family continued to work on the nightclub circuit in the Far West. Hattie came out and joined Ernest sometime that summer, and the Stonemans had their main public-relations photo retouched, removing Scott from the picture. Gene Cox continued as a banjo picker with Judy Lynn's eight piece band. Although she worked most often in Las Vegas, Judy also played show dates on the western rodeo circuit. By this time, Gene and Roni lived in a situation somewhere between still being married and being separated. For a time, Gene says, the two kept an apartment in Las Vegas and Roni stayed there between Stoneman engagements. In September the family worked several days at the Commercial Hotel in Elko, Nevada, and Van took sick. Gene had some free time and left Las Vegas long enough to fill in on guitar for a couple of days. Cox had occasionally substituted as a Stoneman sideman ever since his marriage to Roni, although this would be one of his last efforts with the band.[24]

In February 1965, Jack Clement moved to Nashville and began producing records for major artists and labels. Having produced the Stoneman Family's World-Pacific album, he sought an opportunity for them in Music City, for he considered them a country act despite his efforts to help promote them as a folk group in California. In early November, it seemed that their time had come. He saw an opportunity to take them into a nightclub in Printer's

Alley, the Black Poodle. If they proved successful there, doors would open elsewhere.[25]

The Black Poodle stint indeed seemed to provide the ideal place for the Stonemans to showcase their talent and stage presence. As Clement recalled, people in Nashville who had never come to a country nightclub act before or since flocked to the Poodle. Music-industry folks, doctors, lawyers, merchants, and established musicians all turned out to see what quickly came to be known as "those singin', swingin', stompin', sensational Stonemans." They signed a contract with M-G-M Records and began cutting sessions for a new album. Rehearsing and session work in the daytime, coupled with the club work at night, made for a tiring grind, but with real commercial success near, the Stonemans endured the fatigue. If Pop, seventy-two and crippled with arthritis, could hold up, the children told themselves, they, too, could bear the long hours and the pressure.[26]

Finally, with material for an album in the can, the family took several days off from the Black Poodle. From New Year's they would be scheduled to return on a more or less permanent basis, or so they thought at the time. In the meantime, Van decided to drive Hattie, who had been on the road with the family for four or five months, back to Maryland with his wife, Helen, who would be spending the Christmas holidays with her family in Mechanicsville.

Van made the trip in a nearly worn-out 1952 Mercury he bought in California from Kentucky Colonels mandolin picker Roland White for thirty-five dollars. The car "had the valves all stuck up on it, it wouldn't run over 35 miles an hour without backfiring and spitting, and everything. Anyhow, I drove it on in. Pop said we would move to Nashville in that . . . until finally the valves broke and it ran perfect all the way to Gallup, New Mexico where the clutch linkage broke. I couldn't get it fixed, so I drove it all the way to Nashville without pushing the clutch."[27]

After taking Helen to her parents' home, Van went to visit his older brother John and "see my nephew Johnny." They went out to buy some cigarettes and on the way back to Carmody Hills, the exhausted musician fell asleep at the wheel and had a nearly fatal crash: "The police said we had to have been doing about 85 mi[les] an hour; we hit a tree, broke my leg, burnt my legs, turned ligaments loose in my legs. I was in very bad shape and my nephew was there with me in the hospital in Washington D.C."[28]

Van was very depressed about the whole event, particularly when "Pop and them came over and said that the show has got to go on, and they left without me."[29] When the Stonemans returned to Nashville to begin a renewed and extended tenure at the Black Poodle after New Year's Day 1966, Van's absence forced them to hire their first nonfamily band member since the days of Lew Houston and Porter Church. They found one in the personable and talented Jerry Monday. The Iowa native had come to Nashville seeking some kind of work in country music. When the Stonemans first saw the young man, he seemed nearly destitute. Like Jimmy Stoneman, Jerry suffered from epilepsy, and Donna says Pop took him under his wing, bought him some prescription medicine, and Jerry and Jimmy quickly became close friends. As Patsy observes, their common health problem created something of a bond between them, and they looked out for each other. When Van returned, Pop had taken such a liking to Jerry that he decided to keep him, primarily as a Dobro player but sometimes on harmonica or drums, depending on the arrangement. Van seemed somewhat resentful, and he and Jerry never got along very well. However, Pop liked Jerry and felt protective toward him, while the others appreciated his kindness toward Jim.

Musically, Monday fit into the Stonemans' act quite well, worked with them regularly for two years, and later filled in for others at various times. They referred to him as "Jerry Monday, the Stonemans' Man Friday." He did occasional solo vocals on their programs, such as "I Guess I'd Better Hang My Britches Up," and played at their record sessions through April 1968. For a short time he even had kinship connections, being briefly married to Eddie Stoneman's daughter Barbara. Donna says Jerry liked to pick and jam with other musicians a good bit, and she thinks her niece got tired of constantly waiting for him.[30]

Meanwhile, the Stonemans' appearances at the Black Poodle made them the talk of Nashville's music circles. A business that had been about to close only a few weeks earlier and turned to country entertainment as a virtual last resort suddenly became the "in place" for Music City U.S.A. Iowa fan Harry Beardsley heard them at the Poodle and wrote, "They are a great group and it is because of them that my enthusiasm for country music is at an all time high." *Record World* commented that the club's talent booker, Dottie O'Brien, and co-owners, Bob Carney and Cadillac Wilson, "flipped over the freshness and vitality of this family act," adding that "the sound of the Stonemans is a unique blending of contrast modern harmony and traditional bluegrass instrumental licks; the quiet stability of Family Bible and the rollicking mobility of Ground Hog; the reserved Van, Jerry, and Jim and the exuberance of Ronnie and Donna."[31] Reflecting on events of the past four months, *Music City News* said: "Nothing has ever had the effect at 'the Poodle' that the Stonemans had. They literally captivated the audience and, as the word spread, even die-hard Pop fans and local founding fathers came to see what the ruckus was all about. Presently, even Monday, Tuesday, and Wednesday nights have SRO crowds."[32]

After years of struggle and near starvation at times, Jack Clement's efforts began to produce results. For the first time since 1927, the Stoneman name had again become a hot property. In cooperation with a Chattanooga businessman, Gene Goforth, vice-president of a company known as Jet Star Productions, together with Clement, started a syndicated television series. Initially sponsored by Gingham Girl Flour, the half-hour program debuted on ten stations on April 30, 1966. First filmed in black and white at WSIX-TV in Nashville, the shows soon went to a color format. Original carriers of the show included a new UHF station in Chicago, WFLD, and nine VHF channels in the South, ranging from WLTV in Bowling Green, Kentucky, to WRBL in Columbus, Georgia. Some of the stations, such as WCYB Bristol, WBT Charlotte, and WIS Columbia, had long-established traditions of radio and television programming in country music. In May, stations in Florence (South Carolina), Louisville, Savannah, Knoxville, and home station WSIX in Nashville added the program, and by the end of June the number increased to eighteen and included such major midwestern outlets as Cincinnati, Fort Wayne, and Indianapolis.[33]

Unlike some of the other popular syndicated 1960s television shows, "The Stonemans" initially had neither guest stars nor regular comedians. The producers decided that sufficient versatility within the group precluded a need for guests and that Roni did enough comedy to provide plenty of laughs. Bob Jennings, a dee-jay at WLAC radio, was announcer and shared emcee chores with Van, and sometimes the others introduced songs. A typical early program featured the entire group doing a rousing bluegrass version of "Roll in My Sweet Baby's Arms" before a short rendition of their theme song, "Cripple Creek." Van, still subdued because of his accident and standing rather stationary, led the singing on "Mama Don't Allow No Music Playin' Round Here," which allowed each member of the group to do a solo break on his or her instrument. "Foggy Mountain Breakdown" featured Roni's banjo talents on an Earl Scruggs tune that had not yet received the attention it would get from its use as a movie theme the following year. Roni then sang solo verses on "My Dirty Lowdown, Rotten, Cotton-Pickin' Little Darlin'," while Donna's mandolin and harmony vocal on the chorus offered strong support on this Jack Clement song from their new album. The group then sang the Meredith Willson song "He's My Friend," which also appeared in their new album. Pop and Roni did the longtime Stoneman favorite "The Mountaineer's Courtship" with the latter in costume. Jennings talked a bit with Pop, who told one of the family's favorite anecdotes about the time back in Lexington, Virginia, when Pop left Gene in the outhouse. He also displayed some of his knowledge about historic bridges, and a few bars from their theme ended the program. Donna displayed her dancing skills on most numbers, and Roni also pranced around a bit.[34]

By March, Van had recovered sufficiently for the Stonemans to hit the road. They played in Iowa, making a guest appearance on fifty thousand-watt WHO in Des Moines, swung up into Minnesota, and then went to Chicago, where they spent two weeks at Sammy C's Rivoli Club and also guested on the locally popular WJJD "American Swing Around" program hosted by Chris Lane. Back in Nashville by early April, they returned to the Black Poodle, where such established figures as the Glaser Brothers and Billy Grammer had filled in during their absence. In the meantime, their first M-G-M single, "Tupelo County Jail," hit the country radio stations, accompanied by a full-page ad in *Music City News*. Jack Clement, with some timely help from Jet Star Productions, Bob Bean, the management at the Black Poodle, and, of course, the Stonemans' own talent, had finally set the stage for the long-struggling family to go places commercially.[35]

Shortly after release of "Tupelo County Jail," the Stonemans' initial M-G-M album, *Those Singin', Swingin', Stompin', Sensational Stonemans*, appeared on record shelves. In addition to the aforementioned songs, the album contained two old-time numbers featuring Pop, "A Message from Home" and "Blue Ridge Mountain Blues." Two Bob Dylan compositions, "Girl from the North Country" and "It Ain't Me Babe," maintained their links with urban folk music. Bluegrass versions of "Mule Skinner Blues," "Ashes of Love," and their theme, "Cripple Creek," illustrated their debts to the stylings of Bill Monroe and his followers. Critics generally saw the album as a strong beginning. Writing in the *Chattanooga News–Free Press*, Bill Hagan said, "Family acts are nothing new in show business, but few families can boast the flair and enjoyment in what they're doing as the Stonemans."[36]

By late summer the Stonemans began receiving media attention labeling them one of the hottest new acts in Nashville. The *Chicago Tribune Sunday Magazine* ran a lengthy article titled "The Big New Sound of Country Music" by associate editor Clarence Peterson. A Ron Bailey color photo called "Country and Culture" showed the family standing in the foreground with Nashville's Parthenon as a backdrop. Peterson characterized the Stonemans as "successful" and excessively busy, "rarely finding time to rest." The journalist obviously admired Pop for having so much determination that despite his crippled condition he could still walk with "just plain old fashioned grit." Shortly afterward, *Music City News* featured pieces on the Stonemans and Jack Clement. The Bill Brittain–bylined article on the family did little more than recap their recent successes, but the account of Clement's efforts as a "musical maverick" with creative ideas as an independent producer said more. In analyzing Jack's role in his management of the Stonemans, the anonymous reporter characterized the family band thus: "Here is a traditional group with a modern sound—not folk in the hootenanny sense and not exactly country in the bluegrass sense, despite their brilliant use of banjo and mandolin. The Stonemans are truly a blend of many things with their own exceptional talent and their tremendous success initiating Nashville's Black Poodle to an All-Country format is proof that the sky is the limit to the appeal of well-managed Country Music."[37]

While the media increasingly used such words as "success" to describe the Stonemans, this did not mean an immediate and steady cash flow into their individual coffers. Donna recalls that each member enjoyed a relatively steady income of about two hundred dollars a week from their work at the Poodle, but their expenses also increased. For Van, who did not really begin work until March, dire poverty continued longer because of his accident and the expenses that accumulated therefrom. He, Helen (soon to have another child), and Van, Jr., remained in Carmody Hills for a few weeks with Hattie at the home place. Finally they came by bus to Nashville, where Jack Clement and Bob Bean met them. Their only possessions were a few clothes and a television set that the pregnant Helen carried since Van remained on crutches. With no money in hand, they had to stay in a rundown Sixteenth Avenue house that Jack Clement owned. Besides the TV, an old couch and a mattress for sleeping were the only furniture, but as Van laconically puts it, "we got by." Finally he went back to work, sitting on a stool or standing in a stationary position as he did in the early television programs.[38]

Although success for Van had been delayed because of his accident, confidence in their future rose for some of the other Stonemans. Pop bought a home in the Hermitage Hills suburb "not too far from the Andrew Jackson Mansion," reported Bill Brittain in his "Dateline . . . Music City" column. Hattie joined him there after twenty-five years in the shack in Carmody Hills. Jack remained at the old home briefly, selling, trading, and trashing those items not taken to Nashville. Unfortunately, Patsy thinks, he junked many papers and other items that should have been kept. Jack later joined his parents in Nashville. Roni, Gene, and their four children moved into a home in Donelson. Bob and Donna moved into a fine split-level brick house on Sailboat Drive at the corner of Edge-O-Lake several blocks from the busy intersection of Bell and Murfreesboro roads.[39]

The activity in Nashville lured Scotty back into the family fold, although only temporarily. He rejoined the group on May 16 after what the press called a "year leave of absence." The family's initial M-G-M album was a modest success, received fine reviews, and "Tupelo County Jail" hit the charts for three weeks in June, making it to No. 40. Since fiddles were not really "in" at the time, Jack Clement persuaded Scott to experiment with a bowed banjo, which he did on the song "Five Little Johnson

Girls," another of the Memphis songwriter's novelty compositions. Released in August, the number did not begin to attract attention until fall. It appeared on the *Billboard* charts on October 8 and remained there for the rest of the year, reaching No. 21, although in some areas it did much better. While neither a major hit nor one that attracted covers, it would stand as the Stonemans' most popular single release.[40]

Meanwhile, the family continued to be received well by audiences. They went to New Orleans for a two week engagement at Al Hirt's nightclub, beginning June 27, where they played to "sell-out crowds" nightly. They also played a return engagement at the Rivoli Club in Chicago and in September spent two weeks at the Flame Room in Minneapolis, where old-time record collector Willard Johnson conducted the first of three interviews with Ernest Stoneman. Johnson gave special attention to discussing the sources of songs in the Stoneman recorded repertoire.[41]

During the increasing absences from their base at the Black Poodle, other musicians appeared at the now all-country club. Although established Nashville acts worked there with enthusiasm, outside performers played, too. Among them was Patsy Stoneman, who appeared there the week of September 4 and did a return engagement the week of October 23. By this time Scotty had joined forces with his older sister, having fallen out with the group again. Some months later the pair and some other musicians, including Jack Stoneman on bass, did a Cedarwood Music session from which a single was released. One side, "Big Wheel in Nashville," had been written largely by Scott's wife, Paula, and was intended to be Scott's tribute to his one-time musical sidekick Jack Clement, who indeed had become just that.[42]

If 1966 proved a good year for the Stoneman Family, 1967 would become the pinnacle of their rejuvenated career. With an increasingly popular syndicated television program, now considered "the new status symbol for country artists"; a second album release from M-G-M plus a third in the works; and their third chart-making single, "Back to Nashville, Tennessee," remaining in the *Billboard* listings for twelve weeks, things indeed seemed to be going their way. That summer they were finalists for the Country Music Association's Vocal Group of the Year.

There was a new experience for the Stonemans that year: motion pictures. To be sure, neither of the two films ranked as major Hollywood productions, but were movies just the same. Typically, such fare consisted of light and weak plots, with a little humor and plenty of opportunity for about a dozen musicians or groups to showcase their talent on the screen. The first film, *The Road to Nashville*, featured Doodles Weaver in the principal dramatic role as a somewhat inept agent recruiting talent in Music City; musicians Connie Smith and Marty Robbins have key speaking parts. In an early scene the Stonemans rehearse Donna's mandolin tune "Donna Mite," after which she inquires, "How did you like that, Daddy?" Ernest tells her, "Well, I'll tell ya, that's good! One more rehearsal and I'll think it'll be fine," to which Donna moans, "Oh-h-h!" For the brief exchange, Donna recalls that she and Pop had to join AFTRA. Later the group, including Jerry, performs "Tupelo County Jail" and "Cripple Creek" while Pop rocks away in his familiar rocker.[43]

In the second film, *Hell on Wheels*, which premiered in Nashville on June 16, 1967, Robbins, Smith, and the Stonemans appeared again. Like the earlier effort, it originated with Robert Patrick Productions, but this time top acting honors went to John Ashley, already a veteran of several beach and race-car flicks, and Gigi Perreau, a former child star then in her mid-twenties. Robbins, almost as well known for his love of the speedway as for his music, drove cars and sang. The Stonemans performed "Five Little Johnson Girls" and "Doin' My Time" (which the producer deleted from the film because Acuff-Rose wanted too much money).[44]

M-G-M Records released *Stoneman's Country* in the spring of 1967; it was the family's most successful commercial release. Three tracks had been cut the previous summer, including the charted singles "Five Little Johnson Girls" and "Back to Nashville, Tennessee." Several weeks later the Stonemans returned and did two additional masters, "Bottle of Wine," a Tom Paxton song that became the B side of "Back to Nashville," and a still unreleased Jack Clement lyric titled "Queen Bee." In February at two sessions, they recorded eleven more songs, of which seven filled out the album. As on the first M-G-M album, the numbers reflected the diversification Jack Clement had been constructing in his image of the Stonemans. "Shady Grove" and Pop's rendition of his old favorite "Remember the Poor Tramp Has to Live" reflected their traditional roots. "Winchester Cathedral," a recent hit of English origin, was another foray into pop music. Their covers of current hits like Jack Greene's "There Goes My Everything" and Lynn Anderson's "Ride Ride Ride" constituted current Nashville influence. So, too, did the Jack Clement song "Got Leavin' on Her Mind" and the Jerry Monday original "Colorado Bound." Following its release, *Stoneman's Country* spent several weeks in the *Billboard* album listings and was doing relatively better than any of their singles.[45]

In the second season of syndicated television programs, some changes were made. By now the filmings took place at WSM-TV and all were in color. From time to time, guests appeared on the program. At first they tended to come from the extended family— Hattie, Scott, Jack, and especially Patsy—but later there were other guests. Donna believes they worked gratis in return for the media exposure as the number of stations carrying "The Stonemans" increased to thirty-seven. The guests included traditionalists like Stringbean (Dave Akeman) and Grandpa Jones, mainstays of the country scene like Little Jimmy Dickens and Bobby Lord, current favorites such as Bobby Bare, and aspiring newcomers as typified by Tammy Wynette. Ventriloquist Alex Huston and his dummy Elmer were one of more unusual acts. Pop generally did a solo number on each show, after which the family would gather round a mailbox. Bob Jennings would randomly select one or two fan letters with questions that various family members would answer while Roni supplied humorous commentary. The latter feature added to the program's wholesome down-home quality, creating an idyllic scene of an elderly father and his grown children clustered around a mailbox beside the front porch, enjoying themselves with their music. In the United States of 1967, where social unrest was rising and traditional values seemed increasingly threatened, thousands of working-class and rural Americans found comfort in the Stoneman Family, their blending of old fashioned virtue and modern exuberance, and all that it represented.

Complete data on Stoneman personal appearances in 1967 are lacking, but that which exists suggests that their earnings had improved a great deal since the California days. In May 1964 they had received $1,000 for six nights at the Mecca, but in January 1967 they worked six nights at the Pla-Room in Atlanta for $2,000. Whereas a day at Disneyland in 1964 had yielded $250, appearances could now result in fees of $1,000 on February 11 at the Milwaukee Auditorium and $1,200 the next night at Freedom Hall in Louisville. At times the Stonemans might work for less, such as when they worked at Municipal Auditorium in Chattanooga on March 10 and in Birmingham on March 12 for $900 each time. However, such places were not all that far from Nashville and besides, a very active promoter like Carlton Haney could furnish them with abundant work. Their willingness to work cheaper for Haney may have been rooted in their common experience at the New Dominion Barn Dance in Richmond a decade earlier and may have influenced the situation. The Stoneman Family also began to play as an opening act for country superstar Eddy Arnold, usually at $1,000 per concert, working with the Tennessee Plowboy at Salisbury, Maryland, on April 8; at Anderson, South Carolina, on April 21; and at Sioux City, Iowa, on May 13. Overall in 1967, the Stonemans played at such geographically diverse sites as Fort Worth, Texas; Rochester, Minnesota; Toronto, Ontario; and Cleveland, Georgia.[46]

A concert that must have produced bittersweet feelings for Ernest was staged on May 6 at the VFW Hall in Hillsville, Virginia, only a few miles from Galax. A Stoneman kinsman named Clyde Lineberry booked the event and it must have represented something of a homecoming for the elderly musician, although it may not have been advertised as such. No one recorded his thoughts that day, but he must have felt good about coming back to Carroll County yet saddened that he was becoming, if not the last leaf on the tree, one of the few still remaining. His cousin George had died in March 1966, having accumulated many prizes at the Galax contests, and Burton had passed away a decade earlier.[47] Uncle Eck Dunford had been dead since 1953, and Willie Stoneman and Bolen Frost had died recently. Edna and Kahle Brewer still lived near Galax, although Ernest had long ago lost contact with them and did not realize that his premier fiddler was still alive. He seems to have known only of Herbert Sweet and Oscar Jenkins, both teenagers at the time of their recordings, as living reminders of his early career as a country musician.

Grace and Patsy drove down from Maryland for the Hillsville concert because they saw it as a memorable event. The two sisters arrived before the family—late because of an appearance on the Mike Douglas TV show in Philadelphia the previous day—got there. Bob drove up to the Corner Restaurant at the intersection of Routes 52 and 221 in Hillsville in the limousine in which the family then traveled. Pop looked out the window, grinned, and said, "Well, look at all the Stonemans." Patsy says he was really in high spirits that night and there were still folks around who at least knew him from earlier days. She couldn't remember Bertha or Myrtle Hawks as being there but recalled the presence of Bolen's widow. "Daddy," she thought, "viewed the incident as something of a triumphant homecoming." Some months later he and Hattie drove up to Galax and had markers placed at the graves of her parents and also where Juanita and Rita had been buried under such humble circumstances in the dark days of the Great Depression. That, Patsy believes, was Ernest's way of saying farewell to the Virginia of an earlier day.[48]

At times the hectic schedule the family maintained proved difficult for them. Sometimes they resorted to air travel to make their show dates. Donna recalls one such instance in which she, Jimmy, and Roni missed a plane to Atlanta and hired a man with a small four-seater to transport them. Jimmy sat in front and the two girls crowded into the rear. Once in the air, the pilot explained that he had just obtained his license and this was his initial trip by himself. Jimmy began having seizures and Roni went into a series of hysterical screams, but somehow they made it to their destination. At the time Donna thought such close calls seemed worth it when the family could attract a crowd of ten thousand in Nashville's Centennial Park and police escorts seemed necessary to protect them from enthusiastic fans.[49]

By the time *Stoneman's Country* came out, the family had returned to the studio to produce another single for the hit market. The results, while far from a disaster, failed to equal their earlier efforts. The song "West Canterbury Subdivision Blues," another Jack Clement offering, had a relevant theme concerning a rising middle-class husband who lost his lady by giving her too many material things and too little of himself. However, both the title and the allegorical style were too complex for country audiences, who preferred the simple direct messages in the songs Jack gave them earlier in such lyrics as "Ballad of a Teenage Queen." The flip side, "The Three Cent Opera," was a clever piece that featured some nice mandolin work by Donna, but it was hardly geared for hit status. Released in July, the Clement number hit the *Billboard* charts on August 5 and remained there through most of September but rose no higher than forty-ninth. This did not necessarily constitute a serious problem, but perhaps it did cause some concern.[50]

On October 20, 1967, the Country Music Association held its first annual awards night. The association had been formed to give more dignity and prestige to the industry and enjoyed considerable success in achieving its goal. Nominees for Vocal Group of the Year included the longtime studio-support Anita Kerr Singers, the Browns, June Carter and Johnny Cash, the Statler Brothers, the Stoneman Family, and a new duo, Tammy Wynette and David Houston. At the time, only Wynette had less experience in Nashville, but "My Elusive Dreams" had hit the top recently, and except for the Kerr group all the other nominees had had bigger hits within the preceding twelve months. However, the Stonemans, with their dynamic showmanship, managed to attract enough votes to win the coveted award. Pop had not felt well that day and decided to go only at the last minute. Arriving late, he encountered Doug Kershaw in the lobby and generously gave his ticket to the Louisiana Man, thinking he could obtain another. Finally gaining admission, the patriarch came through the door and down the aisle just in time to see Donna and Roni on stage accepting the prize from Ernest Tubb on behalf of the entire family. " 'Tweren't nothin' . . . but talent," snapped a brash Roni, while tears filled the eyes of the more humble Donna as they graciously took the trophy in hand. For Pop, he had almost missed the recognition he had sought so long. For the Stonemans, it appeared that Nashville had finally accepted them, but they had little opportunity to rest on their laurels because next morning they departed for an October 23 opening at the Horseshoe Tavern in Toronto.[51]

Back in the recording studios, the Stonemans did four more numbers which, together with previously unreleased material, provided sufficient tracks for their third album, *All in the Family.* The old pop standard "The World Is Waiting for the Sunrise" received the Stoneman treatment, as did Doug Kershaw's "Rita Put Your Black Shoes On," Jack Clement's "Tell It to My Heart Sometime," and an otherwise unknown piece by one Johnny Fitzmorris titled "It's a New World Everyday." Leftover songs from previous sessions included a rousing bluegrass rendition of "Old Slew Foot," Pop's oldie "Katie Klein," Roni's version of "Dirty Old Egg Suckin' Dog," Jimmie's "In the Early Morning Rain" and the western favorite from the forties, "Cimarron." The last, along with "Tell It to My Heart Sometime," became the next M-G-M single release, but it failed to score on the charts. According to Patsy, "Tell It to My Heart" allegedly became No. 1 in Czechoslovakia, but it had little effect on the Stonemans' career in America.

The Stonemans' second full year in Nashville had been a success in that their popularity had soared. They had been recognized as the top vocal group in their business and had been in demand for club appearances, package shows, fairs, and parks. Their syndicated television show ranked second only to that of Porter Wagoner among such programs coming out of Nashville, and fans found their M-G-M albums quite appealing. True, they had not enjoyed a giant hit that fans would identify with them for generations, such as Ernest Tubb's "Walking the Floor over You" or Roy Acuff's "Great Speckled Bird," but "The Five Little Johnson Girls" had done quite well and a couple of others had attracted considerable attention. After all, it had taken longer in Music City for many artists to hit it really big.

Pop had begun to receive recognition as a living symbol of the early days of country recordings. In Donna's home on December 29, 1967, Bob Jennings conducted a lengthy interview for the archives at the Country Music Hall of Fame. Two months later, Bill Littleton of *Billboard* interviewed both him and Maybelle Carter concerning the Bristol Victor sessions in which both had participated during the summer of 1927. Mrs. Carter, already somewhat steeped in the Carter-Rodgers legend, seemed hardly aware that many acts participated in the recordings Ralph Peer made that week or that Stoneman helped arrange them and cut twice as many masters as herself, Sara, and A. P. during the Bristol proceedings. Of course, neither seemed to realize that out in the hinterlands, folks like Tweedy Brothers, Eck Robertson, and Doc Roberts, whose recording careers predated even that of Pop

Stoneman, still lived, but then they had never counted for much in Nashville. By 1968 only the experiences in Music City, and perhaps California, seemed relevant. It had taken a long time, but Pop had finally made a dent in both places to complement all those early accomplishments that excited history and folklore buffs but few others.[52]

The negative side to all this was that the man advertised as America's oldest recording artist, whose career extended from cylinder to stereo, had begun to feel the burdens of age. Rightly or wrongly, Pop believed that the others wanted to drop him from the group, so about Christmastime he asked Patsy whether, if he were dismissed by the others, he could work with her band. Donna recalls that "Daddy" showed increasing physical strain on the road, had difficulty keeping food—even the buttermilk and corn bread that became his ever-present staple—in his stomach, and found it necessary to make even more frequent rest-room stops. Still, the determination, willpower, and "just plain grit" that had carried him so far would carry him just a bit farther.[53]

The year 1968 started with a light schedule in January, and then the pace quickened. The Stonemans worked some one-nighters in Iowa and Texas and followed it with a week-long tour in the Carolinas promoted by Roy Martin, which began on February 3 and paid three thousand dollars (one of their most lucrative weeks thus far). After a week in Indianapolis at the Crazy Horse Saloon beginning on February 19, they came back to Nashville for a week at the familiar Black Poodle. The Stonemans then commenced another week-long engagement at the Pla Room in Atlanta that ended March 9. After that, they did a series of one- and two-night stands in North Carolina, Virginia, Texas, Alabama, and Kentucky. In Winston-Salem, Pop had a reunion with his onetime musical associate Oscar Jenkins. They recalled their work on radio there during the Depression and how Pop helped Frank and Oscar with their tobacco crop before the 1929 recording ventures.[54]

In between these personal-appearance dates, the Stonemans continued taping television shows and working on their fourth album for M-G-M Records. Their first trip to the studio yielded a pair of songs. "You're Gonna Be Sorry" was a cover for one of Dolly Parton's initial RCA Victor efforts, while Van authored "The Love I Left Behind." Some days later, they returned to recording, where they mastered four additional numbers. "Wrinkled, Crinkled, Wadded Dollar Bill" and "Christopher Robin" came from the pen of a new Nashville songwriter, with the latter becoming the plug side of a new M-G-M single. The author, Vince Matthews, has been described as a Jack Clement protégé who had a minor hit in 1967 with "Bob" as recorded by the Willis Brothers. The whole group turned in a superb bluegrass rendition of the not-yet-overworked standard "Roll in My Sweet Baby's Arms" along with a Bill Monroe–composed instrumental called "Bluegrass Ramble."

After five days in early April at the Stage House in Minneapolis, the Stonemans returned to Nashville to put the remaining five tracks on the album at Bradley's Barn outside town on April 12. The first three songs were "Baby Is Gone" by Jack Clement, "Don't Think Twice" by Bob Dylan, and "Hello, Dolly!" from the recent Broadway hit musical of the same name. The group then took a one-hour break before finishing. While Pop tuned his Autoharp, the others conversed in the cool night air, during which time Donna allegedly said, among other things, that "Daddy's gonna die before we can get an album by him released." Returning to the studio, Roni and Donna dueted on an old favorite, "The Baby O," while Pop twanged away on the Jew's harp, getting blood on his lips in the process. Pop then performed another of his old favorites, "The Nine Pound Hammer." With their album now complete, the Stonemans prepared for an early-morning flight to Amarillo, Texas.[55]

The family spent Friday taping television commercials. For Saturday they scheduled four brief shows in the Texas Panhandle towns of Amarillo, Borger, Dumas, and Pampa. The appearance in Amarillo gave Pop a special thrill because a police escort whisked them downtown. The family had come a long way since he gave the slip to the Grayson County sheriff on the county line near Galax back in the fall of 1932 when he and his pack of hungry kids left the Blue Ridge for Washington, D.C. Even when he had returned from his successful trips to recording studios in the twenties, he had generally attracted little notice. Now people called the Stoneman Family stars. In spite of the mental satisfaction Pop got, his physical situation was quite another thing. According to Thurston Moore, "Pop was feeling pretty bad; in fact he wasn't sure he could make it through all four shows. But he said he was "a goin' to try." He made it through the first three with the aid of quarts of milk and plenty of Stoneman determination, but after the third show he asked to be taken back to Amarillo." The family returned to Nashville early enough for church on Easter, and Donna decided to go. Pop expressed pride in her decision, but he certainly didn't possess the stamina to do much of anything. On Monday he went to Vanderbilt Hospital.[56]

Tests at the hospital indicated that the elderly musician needed surgical attention, so on April 22 doctors performed a five-hour operation. They removed 65 percent of his stomach along with his gall bladder, which contained eighteen stones, and repaired "some hernial damage that he had suffered during an accident several years ago." On the positive side, Pop held up pretty well otherwise for "he lost no blood pressure and his heart remained strong." Recovery, however, was quite another challenge. Ernest never regained the ability to take food by mouth and had further problems with fever, infection, and pneumonia. After two weeks, X-rays revealed a blood clot and he began to hemorrhage. As soon as the pneumonia had been relieved, physicians operated again on May 16, primarily to make intestinal repairs. Resurgence of the pneumonia and Pop's inability to consume and digest food hampered his recovery. Patsy and Grace came down from their homes to help in his convalescence. During one of their conversations at the hospital, Pop asked Patsy to take his place in the band should he fail to recover.[57]

Meanwhile, life had to go on for the remaining Stonemans. This meant fulfilling all show dates and keeping busy because they needed money to pay those medical expenses Pop incurred which were not covered by Medicare. The day after their dad entered the hospital, they worked in Athens, Georgia, and spent the next two weekends in Milwaukee; Detroit; Kitchener, Ontario; and Chicago. They went South again in early May and after working a high-school auditorium in East Peoria, Illinois, went to New York City to open the week of May 14–18 at the Nashville Club in the Taft Hotel. They received three thousand dollars for the Taft gig, one of their most lucrative nightclub engagements.[58]

Music critic Leslie Rubenstein interviewed the Stonemans during their week in New York and found their "free-wheeling combination of bluegrass, folk, 'pure' country, contemporary country, and pop" much to his liking. Furthermore, he concluded, in whatever category one might put the Stonemans and their music, "it was great." He also noticed that "Daddy" somehow slipped into every other sentence. Offstage, Donna, Van, and especially Roni filled Rubenstein's ears with stories from their past and the central role Ernest had played in leading them through the hard times. Rubenstein went back another night and learned more of their fascinating story. Jim joined in the conversation this time, since the critic seemed especially interested in his well-worn bass fiddle. "Daddy," however, continued dominating the conversation. Van concluded by saying, "I'm just doin' it for my Dad; I love my Dad." With Pop Stoneman missing from the stage and perhaps near death, the younger generation finally began to realize that Pop was the cement that glued them together. Sometimes they might have regarded him as a quaint remnant from the past, but now they seemed to sense that he was much more.[59]

By the end of May, Pop felt well enough to receive visitors. Along with Jack Clement and the family, some of the elder statesmen of the Nashville establishment came down and posed for pictures with his physician, Dr. Bernard, and the family patriarch. These included Roy Acuff, Grandpa Jones, and Minnie Pearl. This helped Pop's morale quite a bit and contributed to his feeling of belonging. As soon as he was able, they would take him to the recording studio and let him record as much material of his own choosing as he wanted.[60]

The first week of June brought some improvement in Pop's condition, although problems remained. Patsy went back to Maryland for a few days, then returned. Conventional medical wisdom suggested that he needed to get up and move about, but he resisted the idea as much as possible, preferring "complete rest." Perhaps careful observers could have noted that the grit and determination which had carried him so far had started to wear thin. Yet Paul Soelberg, who wrote publicity releases for the Stonemans, could write privately on June 7, with some optimism, that "apparently he's doing much better, because the doctors are talking about turning him loose in a day or so, probably to send him to the Medicenter." He added: "It is probable that some of the nursing care can be stopped."[61]

With this cautious optimism, the family left Nashville for nine days of work, beginning at the fairgrounds in Murray, Kentucky, on June 8. On Sunday they worked Steve Lake's Chautauqua Park in Franklin, Ohio, in the afternoon and headed for Toronto, Ontario, where they would open on Monday night at one of their favorite haunts, the Horseshoe Tavern. They would end their six-day stint on Saturday night, then stop Sunday afternoon for another show at Ponderosa Park in Salem, Ohio.

Patsy and Grace returned to Nashville on Monday. Any optimism they might have possessed on their arrival quickly vanished when Pop went back to the operating room on Tuesday for another ordeal under the knife and his condition gradually worsened. In Toronto, Donna remembers praying that if "Daddy would not be able to recover, then she hoped that God would take him with a minimal amount of suffering." In retrospect, she believes that God responded to her prayers. The Stonemans terminated their Toronto trip when called back to Nashville: "Daddy" was dying! Just before noon on June 14, 1968, the man whose career as a recording artist spanned forty-four years passed away.[62]

The family arranged for removal of Pop's remains to Roesch-Patton Funeral Service at 1715 Broadway. Meanwhile, letters and telegrams of condolence began to arrive from folklore scholars, such as Alice Gerrard, Ralph Rinzler, and Mike Seeger, and ordinary fans like the Al Brown Family of Chattanooga, who wrote, "Our whole family of seven extend our sympathy to the Stoneman Family. We loved Pop Stoneman and will miss him very much." Sixty-eight individuals and organizations sent flowers, with Sam Bomstein of The Famous back in Washington being the first. People who booked the Stonemans on the road, such as Steve Lake at Chautauqua Park and Jack Starr at the Horseshoe in Toronto, did their part, as did such Nashville institutions as Moeller Talent, the Grand Ole Opry, the Black Poodle, Acuff-Rose, the Nashville local of the American Federation of Musicians, and Tootsie's Orchid Lounge. Fellow Nashville musicians who sent flowers included Roy Acuff, Skeeter Davis, George Hamilton IV, Carl Tipton, Buck Trent, Billy Grammer, Pat McKenney, and the Wilburn Brothers. Business associates included Jack Clement, Bob Jennings, Jim Vienneau of M-G-M, and Raymond

Patterson of Jet Star. At the funeral home, former in-laws Cecile Howard, R. H. Cain, and others paid their respects. Pop Stoneman had been much appreciated, and his friends let the family know it.[63]

The funeral was held on Monday. The Reverend Richard Bruehl conducted the services, and Paul Soelberg delivered the eulogy. The nine living sons served as pallbearers, with various representatives of the Nashville music industry serving in an honorary capacity. They laid him to rest in Mount Olivet Cemetery. Patsy recalls that Dr. Stanley Bernard, the chief physician attending Pop at Vanderbilt Hospital, shed tears throughout the service. Never before, he told her, had he ever become so emotionally involved with a patient.[64]

For the other Stonemans, life and work continued. Not only did Pop want them to go on with their careers, but financial necessity required it. Five days after the funeral, the family played a show in West Jefferson, North Carolina. Patsy did not consider her debut as a regular member of the group a particularly happy one and had a difficult time getting through the Autoharp numbers. Although it was emotionally challenging, she had always been a survivor and was the one who would carry the main share of the load.[65]

Fortunately, the months immediately following Ernest's death ranked among the busier and more lucrative in the Stoneman experience. In addition to several one-nighters in July, the family journeyed to California for an appearance at Disneyland on the twenty-first, followed by four days of rehearsal and taping for "The Smothers Brothers Comedy Hour." Although they received only $1,000 for the latter, a guest slot on a prime-time ABC variety show paid much more in terms of publicity. In August they worked several state and county fairs, mostly in the Midwest, and three parks, including a return to Chautauqua in Franklin, Ohio. They grossed a minimum of $11,550 for eleven days of work that month.[66]

That summer the latest Stoneman single record, "Christopher Robin," entered the *Billboard* country charts and remained there for eight weeks, but it rose only to No. 41. The M-G-M public-relations people gave the number something of a buildup with ads in *Billboard* and similar trade papers, asking, "Where Is

Christopher Robin?" and "What's the Story on Christopher
Robin?" So although "Christopher Robin" may not have matched
expectations, it proved to be the last hit record the Stonemans
would have.[67]

Still, their albums continued to get a favorable reception. *Record
World* commented of *The Great Stonemans*, "These folks—all happy
and sassy—make some sweet and fun loving music here," while
Billboard's reviewer wrote: "Here is another winner by this great
act." One song, "Wrinkled, Crinkled, Wadded Dollar Bill," attracted so much airplay that M-G-M officials considered releasing
a single of it and probably wished they had chosen it instead of
"Christopher Robin" as the pick hit of the album. Moreover, the
firm began recording a Stoneman Family Christmas album in August for late-fall release and initiated plans for a Pop Stoneman
memorial effort, supplementing material from earlier albums with
songs from television-show sound tracks.[68]

September proved more financially rewarding than August. After a Labor Day weekend trip to work the Ohio State Fair on August 31, they stopped over at Bill Monroe's Brown County
Jamboree in Bean Blossom, Indiana, on Sunday, September 1.
They contracted the show for only $750, but Donna recalls that
"the father of bluegrass" was so pleased that he gave them an extra $100. Back in Nashville after Labor Day, they completed their
Christmas album and then played five more consecutive days on
the road at fairs in Huntsville, Alabama, and Cleveland, Tennessee, plus two days in Knoxville, with an excursion to Lake Norman Music Hall in North Carolina sandwiched between the two
fair shows. On the thirteenth they began an extended package
tour that began in Rochester, New York, and closed in Akron,
Ohio, on the twenty-ninth, with only three days of nonplaying,
mostly consumed by travel. During the trek they worked four
days in New York, three in Canada, three in Ohio, two in Pennsylvania, and one each in Connecticut and Rhode Island. Although such months could be physically exhausting, they did
bring in cash—some $16,100—which was probably the second-
best single gross for a month in the group's history. Since 1967,
the individual Stonemans had been drawing a weekly salary of
$250. Had they worked as much in every month, they could have
given themselves a substantial raise.[69]

As the coming of fall curtailed outdoor appearances, the tour schedule eased somewhat and the family filmed more television shows and concentrated on new songs. For a new single, they waxed in November another song co-written by Vince Matthews and an as yet unknown Brooklynite named Eddie Rabbitt, "God Is Alive and Well," backed with a number by Donna, "Travelin' Man."

In the meantime, *A Stoneman Christmas* made a positive impression on the critics. *Billboard* called it "a bright-sounding album," adding that "the noted Stonemans are right on target for the holiday season with this package" containing "standards such as 'Blue Christmas,' plus specially written material such as 'A Stoneman Christmas' and 'Santa Played the Autoharp.' " Al Freeders called it "a sparkling package of Christmas songs beautifully conceived by the Stoneman Family. This is their first offering of yuletide greetings and the blending of voices makes this a must for your Christmas list. The production by Jack Clement adds that something special—like a red bow on a gift package. 'A Stoneman Christmas,' 'Blue Christmas' and 'Let's Put Christ Back in Christmas' are the Stonemans' way of extending a happy holiday wish."[70]

In retrospect, *A Stoneman Christmas* tended to be the album effort that virtually all family members would praise most in later years. Some preferred the more traditional material that featured lots of Pop's singing, Scott's fiddle, and bluegrass-oriented instrumentation. Others liked the material that emphasized the Nashville sound. A few may even have preferred their later trends toward folk-rock or efforts to identify with music of the counterculture. But whatever differences may have developed in viewpoint, all loved and felt tremendous pride in their Christmas recordings and the image that the album cover projected—that of middle-class family contentedness. It must also have been what Pop had wanted for the family. Back in the days of Washington and Carmody Hills, Christmas had been a holiday for other folks; now it became a time of celebration for Stonemans, too. Their fans must have felt the same way because 5,760 of them bought the album during the brief time it was on the market that season.[71]

Looking back at 1968, it had certainly been a memorable year for the Stonemans. They had experienced the joys of success and the sorrow of Pop's death. Again they were nominated for Vocal Group of the Year and for instrumentalists as well. Although they didn't win—and only winners were announced—strong rumor placed them a close second in both categories. If the Stonemans looked to the future, that appeared bright, too. With Jerry Monday's departure just before the Christmas-album sessions, the Stonemans were now a total brother-sister act. Although Pop was no longer there, his influence and some of his music (largely at Patsy's insistence) remained. The Stonemans' audience seemed as big as ever, and their potential apparently had not been reached. However, in earlier times when the road looked smooth and clear, it had proved rough and dark upon closer examination.

8

Living without Daddy
1969–85

As the tumultuous decade of the sixties drew to an end, the Stoneman Family stood at a musical crossroads. Like the rest of the
American public of which they were a part, they saw the fabric of
society appear to be unraveling in widely differing directions.
During his own lifetime, Ernest V. Stoneman had symbolized tradition, in both culture and values, with unwavering steadfastness.
In the twenties he shared in the material comforts of the times,
and in the thirties he suffered through tougher years than most
because of the Depression. Over the next quarter of a century, his
fortunes improved somewhat, but he maintained the frugal lifestyle to which he had grown accustomed by necessity. Musically,
he sat in his rocker and sang the tried and true songs of his heritage while his children kept one foot nestled in the roots of traditional country and bluegrass and moved the other around
somewhat. With Pop gone, their fingers continued to pick as
surely and steadily as ever, but, they seemed considerably less
certain about where to put their feet and which direction to take.

Some of their dilemma began to show even while Pop was
alive. In his December 1967 interview for the CMF Archives, Bob
Jennings asked Pop what he thought about all the things happening with young people. Pop admitted having problems understanding them and remarked that many reminded him of an
early-day comic-strip character named Bathless Groggins. Although Pop did not share their rejection of the traditional forms of

patriotism and religion, he also realized that some of them found his music quite appealing. Pop appreciated anyone who liked his music. By the same token, the younger Stonemans could appreciate people who liked their renditions of Bob Dylan compositions. Within the band, Roni and Donna tended toward the forces of modernism, identifying first with the Nashville sound and then finding themselves drawn toward the "underground" and music of the counterculture. Patsy recalls Roni's running around saying things like "That's where it's at, man" and "That's what happening" in reference to industry trends. Clothing-wise, their offstage dress increasingly showed such influence, too, particularly in the case of Roni, but Donna even went so far as to iron her hair, which Patsy disgustingly says "ruined it." To the older fans whose Stoneman image had been fixed by the two initial seasons of syndicated television, such scenes may have been something of a shock. Patsy represented a more traditional approach in musical tastes but was broad minded enough to incorporate the Nashville sound into her old-time and bluegrass heritage. Van and Jim, less strong in their personal convictions, became objects of contention whom the others sought to influence.[1]

For the Stonemans not involved in the musical group, their lives tended to stabilize during the sixties. Eddie, John, Gene, and Dean Stoneman all lived in the Greater Washington area, regularly employed and rearing their children. Eddie and Gene entered General Services of the Federal Government as mechanic and laborer, respectively. Dean went to work as a mechanic for the city of Bladensburg and retired on disability in 1985. John stayed at the Thomason Dairy until it closed and then worked for the state of Maryland. John, who had never been very interested in music, excluded himself from it completely as he grew older. The other three played now and then. Eddie favored electric guitar and did some work in the clubs, but as he grew older preferred to spend more time at home. Gene and Dean played more for their own amusement than anything else, with the latter taking a more active interest. Dean favored the mandolin and displayed more Bill Monroe influence than any other Stoneman. As he grew older, it could be safely said that if the family had a bluegrass purist in the ranks, it was Dean. Gene played guitar, manifested an interest in jazz, and could sing a decent vocal on a country song.[2]

Billy Stoneman continued to be plagued by mental problems that were aggravated by his war experiences. Although he had occasionally worked with the Blue Grass Champs and even recorded a couple of items as a member, his behavior became increasingly more erratic. Life for Billy and Barbara indeed proved difficult, but she endured, working in low-status jobs, rearing the children, and taking care of her sick husband as well as circumstances permitted. The other Stonemans have much admiration for her courage. Grace, in her understanding manner, describes Billy's situation best: "So many times he hasn't known who or where he was. He's disappeared for weeks at a time. I have the saddest looking picture of him I cut out of the newspaper that read 'Where is Billy Stoneman?' ??? . . . Whenever he does get better, even partially well enough to come home, he takes up his interest in his guitar and his banjo, singin' and writing songs as usual. Of course none of his songs have been published because his mental condition and circumstances prevent him from doing anything with them. All of his songs are sad . . . depressing songs."[3]

Jack Stoneman also continued to have problems. After the house in Carmody Hills had been sold, he came to Nashville and lived with his parents, but difficulties with alcoholism still plagued him. He had a job in music for some time as bass player with Carl Tipton and the Mid-State Bluegrass Boys, which had an early-morning television show on WTVF, Channel 5, in Nashville. Patsy says his work with Tipton ended when he made a remark about the leader's toupee in retaliation for a Tipton comment about Jack's showing off his new false teeth to the TV audience. Jack played bass on one of Tipton's albums and also on the singles that Scott and Patsy did on the JED label. In the early seventies he went back to Maryland for a while and played bass for Buzz Busby and Leon Morris, then returned to Nashville.[4]

Back in Music City, Jack described himself as "living in one hotel after another and . . . drinking away to much [*sic*]." He voluntarily checked into a rehabilitation center, Samaritan House, for three months. There he met a woman of similar background named Nola Story, and they subsequently had what he describes as "a whirl wind courtship." They married in 1978, and for about eight months their lives stabilized. Jack played bass for various musicians on the road and in clubs, while Nola did home nursing work. Then one night Nola "came in with two other nurses drunk and that's when everything started going down hill." Within a few months, both had deteriorated as their old habits returned. Jack finally left and three months later met Nola on the street. They decided to try to make it again, and Jack took her to a hotel room. A few hours later, the manager awakened him. Nola had set the bed on fire and skipped with every dollar Jack owned ($280 in traveler's checks). He got a divorce, went back to rehabilitation, and even obtained a GED and high-school diploma from Glencliff High School, making him the most educated Stoneman of his generation. Still, things did not go well, and none of his attempts at reform endured for long. As his niece's former husband says, Jack was probably the most intelligent member of the family, but almost nothing ever worked out for him.[5]

Scott Stoneman's restlessness continued, too. He worked off and on with Patsy's group from the fall of 1966 to the spring of 1968. In between he cut a fiddle album, with backing provided by Bill Emerson and some other Washington musicians, which came off musically successful despite the rumor that most of the players had been drunk at the session. Released on the Design budget label under the title *Mr. Country Fiddler,* it reportedly sold ten to fifteen thousand copies. Scott also worked some in East Tennessee—his second wife, Paula Brogan, came from Jimmy Martin's hometown of Sneedville—where he fiddled for Cas Walker on Knoxville television. He stopped playing in Patsy's band about the time his marriage to Paula collapsed. By early 1968, he had remarried after meeting a girl from La Follette, Tennessee, named Mary Madison. Although he never completely left music, he went to work in a factory that made fiberglass boats. Scott and Mary parented two children, Ernest Scott and Kerin. By the fall of 1972 he had gone approximately a year without drinking and started attending church on a regular basis.[6]

Grace and George Jewell lived in Riverdale, Maryland, until 1974. Bill and Steve, her children by her first husband, grew to adulthood and gave Grace ample reason to be proud of them. She and George's daughter, Donna Kay, whom Grace describes as excessively spoiled by George, had an unsuccessful first marriage to a man named Bill Bassin, who became a close and lasting friend to the Stonemans. Bassin came to consider Grace his second mother, and in his later career as an academic he dedicated a textbook to her. Donna Kay's second marriage lasted longer, produced three children, and eventually ended in disaster. By this time George and Grace had left the D.C. area for the serenity of Rhodesville, Virginia, about an hour's drive from the metropolitan area.[7]

The Jewells continued as they had before, with Grace as a dutiful and diligent housewife and George as the steady, dependable (if not particularly understanding or affectionate) provider. About 1978, George began suggesting a separation and said perhaps Grace should go to Nashville to be closer to her family. Soon he insisted, promising to send her support money. Grace learned that after thirty years of marriage, George had fallen for a younger woman with experience as a home wrecker. The Jewells divorced and divided their property. George came out of his second romance a few months later sadder but wiser. After he retired, George Jewell also moved to Nashville, and Grace eventually came to regard her former husband as one of her best friends.[8]

The formal members of the Stonemans as a musical group might appear on the surface to be at the zenith of their professional careers after years of struggle to achieve what had happened to them since 1966, yet most of them also faced difficult circumstances and personal crises from time to time. Patsy needed to gain confidence as a group member and in her early months found it necessary to commute between Nashville and Lanham, Maryland, where Murph continued his job as a labor-union lobbyist. While in Nashville, Patsy stayed at Bob and Donna's house. She soon came to admire the house across the street facing Edge-O-Lake Drive and finally got the opportunity to buy it. Murph sold their home in Maryland, gave up his lucrative job in Washington, and brought their furniture to Nashville. He arrived barely in time for Patsy to say good-bye before hitting the road for a tour. Domestic life for a musician could be a real challenge.[9]

By the time Patsy made Nashville her home, Roni made hers in Winston-Salem, North Carolina. Although still married to Gene Cox when she came to Nashville, the marriage had virtually collapsed and they grew further apart. In March 1968 the Stonemans had been hired to assist in the primary-election campaign of an aspiring North Carolina congressman named James G. White. George Hemrick, a Winston-Salem school principal, served on his staff. Hemrick possessed some significant characteristics that Gene lacked, including education, culture, and connections, all of which impressed Roni. When Pop died, George sent a wreath. When the Stonemans went to California to tape the TV show with Glen Campbell and the Smothers Brothers, George flew out to visit the set. When the Stonemans prepared their Christmas album, George wrote a special narration for it entitled "Christmas without Dad," which seemed tailor made for them. June Carter, who also had been on the set at the Campbell-Smothers taping, pulled Roni aside and gave her some negative warnings about Hemrick and urged her not to marry him. Roni, however, felt swept off her feet for the first time since her midteens. On October 11, 1968, she and George married during the deejay convention in Nashville. Thereafter, Roni made her home in Winston-Salem and commuted from there for show dates and record sessions. In time, it would distance her from the rest of the family in more ways than mere miles.[10]

In the short run, however, Roni felt happy, secure, and appreciated. What's more, her sense of humor shown brighter than ever and in places where it had never been seen before. When she and George attended a Washington ball for the Democratic Club of North Carolina, George introduced her to the state's respected longtime senator Sam Ervin, telling him, "My wife is a singer." Insisting that she "must sing for us," Ervin led her to the bandstand, where orchestra leader Lester Lanin presided. The "guy had a stick and a bunch of tails and britches," she explained. Roni broke into a rousing rendition of one of her M-G-M recordings, "Dirty Old Egg Suckin' Dog." Columnist Don Rhodes reported that "when the initial shock wore off, the audience burst into laughter and loud applause."[11]

The new year of 1969 started off well for the Stonemans. They opened New Year's Day in Des Moines, Iowa, then traveled to Philadelphia, where they grossed fifteen hundred dollars. A week later they worked three dates in Nashville and after a few more days made a northern swing, working in Ohio, Michigan, and

Bridgeport and Norwalk, Connecticut, before finishing on Saturday, February 1.[12]

Back in Nashville, they all gathered at Bradley's Barn Tuesday and Wednesday, February 4 and 5, to do some light overdubbing on the seven cuts from television-show sound tracks for the *Pop Stoneman Memorial Album*. Jack Clement chose to reuse four titles from earlier releases; the new numbers included two sacred songs, "Hallelujah Side" and "Where the Soul Never Dies," and two Autoharp numbers. One, of recent composition, was arbitrarily assigned the title "No Name for It Yet"; the other had been Pop's favorite Autoharp tune: the very unwaltzlike "Stoney's Waltz," which he did twice for Folkways. "I Love Corrinna" was one of the few songs in Pop's repertoire from black tradition, and he had first recorded "The Birds Are Returning" (better known as "Sweet Fern") at the time of his ill-fated session with Fields Ward. The album closed with Pop and Roni's version of "The Mountaineer's Courtship." Rushed into print by May with a good scholarly liner by Norm Cohen of the John Edwards Memorial Foundation, the album sold 12,114 copies during the next four years before being relegated to the cutout bins. With Nashville influences kept to a minimum, it represented one of the last attempts of a major record company to market newly recorded old-time music. In all, the *Pop Stoneman Memorial Album* was a fitting tribute to a country-music pioneer whom the Nashville establishment came to appreciate too little and too late to benefit him personally.[13]

The album, along with the single "God Is Alive and Well"/ "Travelin' Man," turned out to be the Stonemans' swan song for M-G-M Records. *Billboard* saw the gospel-tinged single quite favorably, with reference to its "infectious rhythm and compelling lyrics line with a top vocal performance." The magazine further predicted that the "potent rouser" would "hit with sales impact and spill over into the pop chart as well." Reality was quite different. Although the song attracted some airplay, it failed to register on either the country or pop charts. "The deejays didn't want us to go gospel," Donna says. Some 6,077 consumers bought it, which suggests that it did have genuine appeal among individuals, since almost no jukebox distributors would have purchased the disc.[14]

For the Stonemans as a business entity, March 1969 constituted a key month in their careers. From April 1964, the principal
management decisions had originated with Jack Clement.
However, Cowboy Jack's reputation as an independent record
producer had grown by leaps and bounds since he moved to
Nashville in 1965, and 1969 found him with more work than
he could properly handle. Clement produced for Ben Colder
(Sheb Wooley), Tompall and the Glaser Brothers, and Charlie
Pride in addition to the Stonemans, and by the end of the decade
the emergence of Country Charlie as the first black superstar in
what had hitherto been the preserve of white folks dominated
Clement's work schedule. From time to time, personal problems also intruded into his business life. He had always been
known for occasionally bizarre conduct that shocked the Nashville establishment. For example, he and Big Joe Talbot once
put laundry detergent in the fountain at the Country Music
Hall of Fame, which, according to one embellished account, "created such a mountain of suds that it swept down Sixteenth
Avenue and engulfed Columbia Studios." Such activity, along
with record production and music publishing, took up much of
Clement's time, so he willingly gave up management of the
Stonemans to the newly organized corporation of Bean, Murphy,
and Soelberg.[15]

Bob Bean had by now established himself as the road manager
of a successful group and felt sufficiently competent to take charge
of booking and whatever additional details might arise. Jack Murphy, having just arrived in Nashville from Washington, would
look after "administration and accounting details." Paul Soelberg,
who had come to the Stonemans via previous work for RCA Victor on the West Coast and as a PR man for Jack Clement, "will continue to manage the public relations program and also will
assume new duties relating to marketing and market expansion."
The Moeller Talent Agency did not seem to be doing as good a job
as Soelberg thought could be done with the act, and furthermore
it did not really have experience in some areas where he thought
the group could be worked. So, while the Stonemans continued to
work the dates Moeller had booked for them, Soelberg endeavored to broaden the family's appeal. Bean, Murphy, and Soelberg
assumed managerial control on April 1, 1968. Jack Clement con-

tinued as a record producer, but otherwise his connection with the group was terminated.[16]

Some evidence suggests that Clement thought the Stoneman's progress had stopped and asked why. Soelberg penned a lengthy letter to Cowboy in mid-March, suggesting that the new corporation would be an initial step in accelerating their professional development, followed by a switch in record labels. The Californian thought a contract with RCA Victor would be a major change for the better and intimated that M-G-M was doing virtually nothing to promote the family. Clement apparently accepted this explanation and went to work persuading RCA executives to sign the Stonemans to their roster of country talent. Soelberg, having previously worked for RCA in the San Francisco area, believed the firm would engage in the type of promotion needed to propel the family to superstar status.[17]

In retrospect, Jack Murphy believes that from a business standpoint Soelberg had some decent ideas and that in terms of public relations he did all the right things, but in the most expensive manner. Certainly his expenditures exceeded the Stonemans' budget. Murphy cites as an example his desire to announce the Stoneman management switch with a full-page advertisement in *Billboard*. He and Bob considered it somewhat extravagant but relented because the arrangements had already been made. Paul then had similar ads placed in *Cashbox* and *Record World*. The new corporation, formed with a fifteen hundred dollar loan from Soelberg's mother (living in California), as well as funds supplied by Murphy and Bean, set up operations in Suite 412 in the West End Building. Murphy recalls that they did not economize on office furniture and equipment, either. *Billboard's* news article on the event unintentionally gave a negative connotation to the management change with a banner headline reading "Firm Forced [instead of formed] to Handle Stonemans After Shift From Moeller Talent." Perhaps the incident should have been taken as a bad omen.[18]

Meanwhile, the Stonemans continued to honor the bookings the Moeller agency had obtained for them. For not doing much, Moeller had found twenty days of work for them in May—eighteen as part of another package tour at $850 per night in Canada and the northeastern states, plus two additional dates in Florida at $1,000 each. Never before or again would the family enjoy so large a gross income, $17,300, in a single month.

While the Stonemans remained active on the road, Jack Clement began planning their next album. He apparently chose to record the material at Bradley's, since his own studio was still under construction, and then, as an independent producer, to market the masters to an interested firm, preferably RCA Victor. Clement enjoyed some prestige with the firm, largely on the basis of his successful development of Charlie Pride into a major figure: the Afro-American country singer had eight straight Top Ten hits in a recording career that commenced about the same time as the Stonemans. Furthermore, Clement had been an assistant to Chet Atkins between his Memphis experiences with Sun and his Beaumont operation.

The sessions began in July. As in some of the earlier M-G-M work, extra musicians and vocalists assisted. Patsy remembers Billy Grammer, among others, while studio backup vocalists like Commercial Hurshel Wigginton and Joe Babcock, who had been on their Christmas album, were also present. The first song proved a difficult hurdle. Jack Clement and Alex Zanetis wrote "Two Kids from Duluth, Minnesota," which carried a subtle anti-Vietnam war message and not only didn't fit the Stonemans' style very well but gave them trouble with the phrasing. The song required numerous takes before they had a satisfactory track, and both Clement and Zanetis imbibed a considerable quantity of liquor during the session. By the time they finished, tempers had become rather short. Fortunately, the rest of the recording was smoother, especially on older familiar tunes like "Banjo Signal," "Wildwood Flower," and perhaps the still-unreleased "We Live in Two Different Worlds." Roni did an original specialty, "All the Guys That Turn Me On Turn Me Down," and Van wrote "Weed Out My Badness." The flirtations with Broadway-oriented pop material gave way to Creedence Clearwater Revival's "Bad Moon Rising" and First Edition's "But You Know I Love You." Other rock songs included "In the Plan" and "Tecumseh Valley." They concluded with a nice cover of Kris Kristofferson's "Me and Bobby McGee," then a Roger Miller hit but, at a length of 5:50, much too long to attract much airplay. Whatever misgivings the family may have had probably vanished when RCA Victor purchased the masters, signed the Stonemans to a contract on July 28, and threw a party in their honor on August 5.[19]

On the road almost as heavily as ever, the Stonemans worked 134 dates in 1969, nearly as many as in 1968. They probably took in more revenue—a total of $115,545.79—than in any other year in the group's history. They had signed with the most prestigious record firm in the world and the one that seemed natural, since it brought "Pop" his biggest successes in the twenties. As a musical aggregation, the family apparently had survived the loss of its key member.

The Stonemans' surface prosperity obscured a number of potentially serious problems. By the last half of 1969, the number of stations carrying their television program dropped to nineteen, roughly half of what it had once been. About this time they stopped filming new shows, and by 1972 the number of carriers had fallen to three. Despite taking in a record amount of money, the Stonemans actually operated at a deficit that year. Salaries received the highest priority, and even then no one received any in the last week of November and all of December. Whereas four Stonemans had annual earnings of $11,750.00 and one of $10,450.00 (Patsy received only $200.00 a week through June), each member, after deducting expenses, generated only $7,117.00. Bean, Murphy, and Soelberg made up the shortfall through Bean's and Murphy's not collecting their $125.00 weekly wage as road manager and bus driver (after July), respectively, and leaving a large number of unpaid bills, chiefly to Moeller Talent Agency, which had booked most of their appearances that year. Had individual members of the Singing Stonemans, Incorporated, drawn weekly payments of $137.00, they would have had a solvent business. Murph also points out that maintenance of the bus they purchased in February proved a drain on their finances to the tune of $9,439.15.

Even before the release of *Dawn of the Stonemans Age* early in 1970 the group had gone back to the RCA studios to commence work on another album. From then on, the recordings contained neither additional session musicians nor vocalists, but only the five Stonemans doing all the picking and singing. At three additional short sessions in March, they completed the effort. In the meantime, the first album, characterized by liner-note writer Ed

Kahn of the John Edwards Memorial Foundation as "a new eclectic musical journey drawing from a wide variety of musical experience," hit the market. Dedicated Stoneman fans bought and appreciated the effort, but it generally seems to have missed the broad audience that its producer and Paul Soelberg had so earnestly sought. Traditionalists found too little of the tried and true, while the Now Generation apparently found it a move in their direction, but not sufficiently so to entice many to buy it. By and large, the same thing seems to have held for their next two RCA albums as well. On balance, despite Soelberg's high hopes that a switch in labels would produce a much-needed shot in the arm for the Stonemans' recording career, their M-G-M offerings had more impact. Although RCA released four singles and three albums in roughly twelve months, none of them registered on the charts.[20]

Paul Soelberg did try to introduce the Stonemans to a broader audience, particularly the West Coast youth and counterculture elements. They spent most of January 1970 in Los Angeles, Berkeley, San Francisco, and San Jose. This gained them an April booking in a place generally frequented by the hippie crowd, Fillmore West, but they encountered some unexpected problems. Donna inhaled so much marijuana smoke that she had to see a physician. On another occasion Jimmy suffered an epileptic seizure on stage, but the audience thought he was high on drugs and that it was all part of the act. While Jim suffered, people kept yelling, "Go, man go!" and "Right on, man!" In retrospect, Patsy isn't sure whether they succeeded in broadening their appeal to new fans, but she feels fairly certain that it did them no good with their traditional fans, who increasingly identified with the value system encompassed by the term "Silent Majority."[21]

On March 26, 1970, the Stonemans completed their second album with a song written especially for them, "Proud to Be Together (Happy to Be What We Are)." The principal writer, Cathy Manzer, met the group at a mid-March club date in Phoenix, New York. Impressed by her abilities, Roni invited her to accompany them back to Nashville when they ended their engagement on March 21. Donna had the idea and Cathy came up with the lyrics on the twenty-third. They cut it three days later and in early May it became the B side of their third RCA single release. *Record World* apparently much preferred it to the plug side, another adaptation of a Creedence Clearwater Revival song. In a critique aimed at Jack Clement, the reviewer wrote: " 'The Cowboy' definitely gave the plug to the wrong cut [because] 'Who'll Stop the Rain' is a monster." Because it had no extra musicians, backup singers, or musical gimmickry, the album entitled *In All Honesty* generally fared better. The cover photo, an ill-advised attempt to remake the Stonemans into what looked like a group of misplaced flower children, could more accurately be described by Donna in later years as "anything but honesty." Apparently, fans who remembered the wholesome youths in gingham dresses and sweaters only four years earlier did not become excited in an affirmative manner. Even those who saw their covers of rock songs as "competent" and liked their work on antiwar songs conceded that bluegrass instrumentals like "Colossus" and "Somebody's Waiting for Me" were "the honest-to-goodness Stonemans."[22]

By the time *In All Honesty* had been reviewed, the material for another album had been completed. It reflected something of a trend back toward the Stonemans' roots, with three numbers associated with old-time music and only two from contemporary rock. The remaining cuts all had country origins, including "Jimmy's Thing," which ranks as one of the few bluegrass instrumentals dominated by a bass-fiddle lead. One could only have wished that *California Blues* had been the title cut for their initial album and single on RCA rather than a virtual farewell.[23]

By late summer 1970, Paul Soelberg who had championed the switch from M-G-M, had grown most unhappy with RCA. Reflecting his disillusionment, he wrote: "The assistance we needed, the kind of help that could come only from a sincerely interested record company, was not forthcoming, although the record company expressed interest. In fact, it was only after considerable prodding by the Stonemans' management that any activity of any kind occurred. But the efforts were not as extensive as we felt were needed. Very little initiative was displayed, although a half-page ad in *Rolling Stone* was purchased (three months after the release of *In All Honesty* and four months after the Stonemans' Fillmore West appearance)."[24]

Such argument, needless to say, now became a justification to change record companies again. Surprisingly, the Stoneman organization lost confidence in RCA before the opposite happened.

Bob Bean and Paul Soelberg went to Jack Clement and asked him for help in obtaining a release from their contract. Although no longer engaged in active management of the group, Cowboy apparently harbored some reservations concerning the wisdom of this decision, but he accommodated it. Within the Stoneman group, there developed some feeling that Clement and the writers at Jack Music had been giving their best songs to other singers for the past couple of years. Roni contended in 1985 that individual Stonemans had no idea that the decision to leave RCA had been initiated by their own management.[25]

Meanwhile, some doubt could be raised about the quality of the Stonemans' own operation. Their work schedule for 1970 showed the number of days booked dropped from 134 to 128 and total earnings fell to $94,189.96. Patsy holds that the effort to capture "the youth and college markets" had been more than offset by a corresponding decline in their traditional audience. Their fifteen days in California in January had grossed only $1,600.00 in cash, cost $2,420.00 in motel bills, and resulted only in their Fillmore West booking. An April 10 concert at Abraham Baldwin College in Tifton, Georgia, probably had no connection with their effort to score with the underground. In fact, only an unusually busy August and a November appearance on Johnny Cash's network TV show prevented Stoneman income from declining further.[26]

The end of 1970 brought an end to the initial unity of the second generation of musical Stonemans. During the course of the year, tension had mounted within the group. Roni and Donna manifested unhappiness with Van for failing to exercise more leadership and sometimes less than responsible behavior on the road. Those within the family further argued that George Hemrick endeavored to convince Roni that she had not received her just due in either money or credit for their accomplishments. Furthermore, Roni expected another child in February and had learned earlier that George suffered from personal problems. Roni increasingly began to feel needed at home. She called on her brother Scott to finish that particular tour. Then Jerry Monday filled in for most of her dates from November 12 to the end of the year. Hattie Georgia Hemrick was born on February 9, 1971. Roni continued on leave for several months afterward but eventually decided to leave the group.[27]

The Stonemans started 1971 in a positive manner with four solid weeks of booking in Las Vegas at three thousand dollars per week, beginning January 5, and Jerry Monday continuing as Roni's replacement. Donna remembers that month particularly well for two reasons. First, she met one of Elvis Presley's body guards, who was a solid fan of the Stonemans. He offered to take her to meet Elvis, who was also working in the city. Second and more significantly, Donna learned that her twenty-year marriage had problems that she had never hitherto suspected. It wore on her and caused her much stress and tension, which at times ahead would drive her seriously to consider suicide. Still, for the next year and a half, she continued her regular work with the band. Except for a three-week period in late November and early December 1968 when she had an operation, Donna almost never missed a show.[28]

As the Stonemans continued to work show dates in Florida and the Midwest after their Las Vegas stand, Bean, Murphy, and Soelberg tried to line up another record contract. The effort bore fruit on January 16, 1971, when they signed with Capitol. This firm had a successful history of developing such major country and western figures as Tex Ritter, Tennessee Ernie Ford, the Louvin Brothers, Buck Owens, and most recently Merle Haggard. Moreover, the Kingston Trio, the original pop collegiate folk group a decade earlier, had been a Capitol contractee. The Stonemans had a session on May 4 and cut four vocal tracks, one of them titled "Who Really Cares?" The band members must have thought the question asked in the lyrics applied to them later that year when Capitol Records staged a major shake-up in its country and western division, fired the Stonemans' producer, George Richey, and eliminated the artists under his direction from the Capitol roster. A pair of checks for the sessions, totaling $894.51, turned out to be the only thing the Stonemans had to show for their contract. Bob Bean thinks the masters remained uncompleted, with some instrumental tracks still blank.[29]

Despite the Capitol debacle and Roni's absence, the Stonemans continued to fulfill their engagements and worked regularly. They guested on the Grand Ole Opry a couple of times and alternated one-day/night stands with multinight club appearances. Jerry Monday remained with them most of the year, although Cathy

Manzer filled in several dates during July and August. Gene Cox even did the Disney, Oklahoma, Bluegrass Festival with them in mid-July when a five-string banjo seemed a necessity. When the year ended, however, their total working days had declined to 117 and their gross earnings to $87,042.15.

Before year's end, the corporation of Bean, Murphy, and Soelberg had been dissolved. Paul Soelberg simply proved too expensive. As Jack Murphy reminisced, Paul's heart was in the right place but the Stonemans simply couldn't afford him, not that his salary was extravagant, just his ideas. The public-relations specialist went on to occupy a similar role with Porter Wagoner and Dolly Parton, who at the time were a pretty hot act in Nashville, and Murph reflected that he eventually proved a mite costly for their organization, too. In August, business control of Singing Stonemans, Incorporated, passed to BOJAC Management, Incorporated, comprised of Bob Bean and Jack Murphy.[30]

If most living Americans remember 1972 as the year of tension, stress, and turmoil associated with more antiwar protests, Watergate, and the Nixon-McGovern election campaign, it proved an equally difficult year for the Stonemans, although for very different reasons. Changes in personnel and the collapse of their management corporation plagued the family throughout the year. Somewhat surprisingly, through all of this turmoil the Stonemans actually worked more dates and grossed more income than in either of the two preceding years.

Since Jerry Monday quit for the final time at the end of 1971, the band found itself in need of another member. Cathy Manzer, the young lady from New York who came to Nashville with the Stonemans in March 1970, had filled in several times during the previous summer and had the advantage of availability. Logic suggested that the family needed either a banjo picker or a Dobro player. Although Cathy's instrumental talent was limited to the electric organ, the others convinced themselves, on the basis of her excellent singing voice, that she would fit into their act. Patsy would have preferred bringing Scott—equally adept at either banjo or fiddle—back into the fold. However, Bob Bean staunchly opposed his return, and so did Donna to a somewhat lesser degree. So while this move distanced the Stonemans even more from their earlier fans, some family members believed it would broaden and enhance their appeal. In retrospect, one is tempted to wonder why, with bluegrass festivals enjoying steady growth in the late sixties and early seventies, the Stonemans increasingly took steps to alienate themselves from a growing market. Other essentially bluegrass acts, such as Mac Wiseman, Jim and Jesse McReynolds, and the Osborne Brothers, sought to broaden their appeal by using mainstream country instrumentation in their record sessions, but they also kept their bluegrass contacts and fans.[31]

The Stonemans' 1972 road schedule resembled that of preceding years with two exceptions. First, they went to England for an April 1 appearance at the prestigious Wembley Festival, which attracted country fans from throughout the British Isles and points even farther away. The engagement paved the way for an extended tour of the British Isles lasting from October 19 through November 12. In July and early August the group visited twenty-one towns scattered through Kentucky under the sponsorship of the Rural Electrification Administration. Although neither tour paid much, they provided nearly all of the increase in Stoneman income. They received $500 for Wembley and $4,500 for the longer tour, but the promoters paid most of their expenses. George Hamilton IV and a British country band made up part of the entourage, and they kept busy nearly all the time. Audience reaction varied from average to excellent, but by and large, Donna recalls, "they really loved us." The Kentucky tour paid only $350 a day but took place on weekdays, leaving them free to play the more lucrative weekend dates elsewhere. Patsy says the fans who flocked to the shows were some of the most enthusiastic who ever watched them.[32]

The Stonemans increased their work load in 1972 but realized that in order to maintain an active image, they needed to have records on the market and being played on the radio. Since their 1971 liaison with Capitol bombed badly, they had not had a single or album release since late 1970. An album that appeared on the market in the spring of 1972 eventually proved to be their all-time best seller, but it provided them with little in the way of commercial publicity at the time. During a week of dates in Southern California in late August 1970, the family spent a day in the Disney studios taping a sound track for the Country Bear Jamboree, one of the forthcoming attractions at the soon-to-be opened Walt Disney World theme park in Florida. Small segments of the track featured the voices of Wanda Jackson and Tex Ritter, but the remainder consisted of the Stonemans singing shortened versions of such songs as "Old Slew Foot," "All the Guys That Turn Me On Turn Me Down," and "If You Can't Bite Don't Growl." When the new park opened in 1972, Disneyland Records released *Country Bear Jamboree*, an album which proved to be a steady seller in the children's market, with average sales of more than twenty-one thousand copies a year through 1982. Ironically, the name Stoneman appears nowhere on either the record or its jacket, and thousands of children would know them only by such names as Liver Lips McGrowl, Teddi Barra, and the Sun Bonnets (Bunny, Bubbles, and Beulah).[33]

To remedy their lack of current discs, the Stonemans—with no offers forthcoming from the major firms—signed with a new company, Million Records. Country singer-entrepreneur Autry Inman represented the firm, the name of which seemed indicative of the corporation's aspirations in the music world. The contract, penned on June 30, 1972, provided for the standard royalty and a minimum of six sides per year. The results turned out to be something less.[34]

Preceding the recording sessions for Million, the Stonemans suffered another personal, business, and personnel crisis in August. As had been the case in 1969, the Singing Stonemans, Incorporated, and their management firm continued to lag behind in payment of debts. Moeller Talent Agency topped the list of creditors, but there were others as well. As Murph recalls, he kept at the typewriter until it and the rest of the office furniture were repossessed. BOJAC Management, Incorporated, collapsed. The financial ledger contains the notation "Murphy quit." The fiscal crunch constituted only half the reason for Murphy's departure, the other being that Patsy, increasingly unhappy about the musical directions the family was taking and locked in a personality clash with Cathy Manzer, quit the band on August 13, 1972, after a concert at Bruceton Mills, West Virginia. On top of all these developments, Donna, having undergone considerable stress since January 1971, decided to separate from Bob Bean and moved into an apartment with Cathy Manzer.[35]

Miraculously, the Stonemans as a musical entity did not disintegrate. Bob continued management alone and the group fulfilled its show dates, including Donna, who says the situation with her estranged husband was somewhat awkward. Beginning on September 9, they acquired a banjo player in the person of David Dougherty, an Acworth, Georgia, native and veteran of James Monroe's Midnight Ramblers. This constituted a step back in the direction of their musical roots, although the results would hardly be detected in their session for Million later than month. Dougherty's banjo can be heard on "Blue Ridge Mountains," while Donna's mandolin is scarcely audible on either it or the plug side, "The Touch of the Master's Hand." They cut two other numbers for Million that remained unreleased. In spite of Autry Inman's intentions and hopes, his company never got very far in the music business. When their contract expired, the Stonemans chose not to renew it.[36]

In England, the Stonemans planned to release a live album partly based on their April experience at Wembley and completed on their fall tour. The tracks from the latter shows display a remarkable verve and spark when one considers the stress under which the band worked at the time. Donna and Dave Dougherty render a spirited instrumental arrangement of the recent bluegrass-tinged Buck Owens hit "Heartbreak Mountain," and Van delivers a fine vocal on the ghostly "Bringing Mary Home." Such efforts also suggest that the Stonemans' flirtations with country rock may have about run their course and that they were about to return to their roots. Offstage, however, Dougherty remembers that Donna had a very difficult time emotionally. Several times he remembered seeing her throwing up because her nerves were so upset.[37]

When the family returned from England on November 12, there were more personnel changes. Cathy Manzer received word that her mother was dying and quit. Donna gave notice that she intended to drop out at the end of November and did so after two dates in Pennsylvania and Virginia on the eighteenth and nineteenth. Patsy played these shows at Bob's request as a fill-in and subsequently remained with the group. Despite her recent discomfort, Patsy felt equally uneasy outside the group, as it seemed inconsistent with the promise she had made to "Daddy" back in the spring of 1968. As a result she returned on a permanent basis. Meanwhile, after months of emotional agony, Donna also made some decisions. She concluded that she could no longer stay married to Bob and that she could no longer be a member of the Stonemans as a musical group. Believing that the others needed Bob's management and direction more than they needed her as a musician, she urged them to retain him. Donna and Patsy had become estranged because Donna resented her older sister's efforts to reconcile her and Bob; by the same token, Donna's defense of Cathy aroused Patsy's anger. Donna felt that she must get away from Bob and her family and leave music. In a temperamental fit of anger, she hurled her mandolin across the room.[38]

On another front, Donna struggled with what to do with her life. Seriously undereducated like the other Stonemans, she doubted her ability to earn a living outside music. Always attractive to men, the petite beauty had caught the eye of many rich and famous ones from the time the Blue Grass Champs first appeared on CBS television. Some had openly proposed marriage to her, while other merely suggested that the two of them could "make beautiful music together." A decision to "go with the flow" and the "way of the world" seemed tempting, yet it conflicted strongly with what Hattie taught her as a child. Donna had considered herself a proper Christian lady, but one lacking commitment. In spite of that, she says, "still I was a sinner bound for hell . . . being vain and having a bad temper." Finally, she says, "I chose the right way," made her decision to live her life for Christ, and "to follow His lead" wherever it might take her.[39]

With a Stoneman Family band that faced a near state of being reduced to only two Stonemans, the others faced some difficult decisions. Not only did Patsy return, but Scott was brought back into the circle. Although no one doubted that Jim, Patsy, and Van all exhibited sufficient musical competence, Scott, Pop, Roni, and Donna had the stage charisma that made crowds go wild. With Pop dead and increasingly forgotten by folks with short memories and Roni and Donna gone their own way, Scott now seemed the person most likely to restore the Stonemans to bluegrass and country preeminence. Fortunately, Scott's personal life had stabilized for the first time since the early years of his marriage to Cecile. He rejoined in time for a pair of show dates in Louisiana on December 2 and 3 and five more later that month, including one in extremely cold Grand Forks, North Dakota. Dave Dougherty recalls that Scott manifested congeniality and made the long ride to North Dakota and Missouri a pleasant experience. He also points out that they had a good, solid, predominantly bluegrass sound that actually seemed more pleasing to the musical ear than it did when he first joined them. Scott fell off the wagon briefly around Christmastime, but that seemed like a minor problem. A more depressing situation developed because of several booking cancellations that resulted from the departure of "little dancing Donna" and other dates that failed to materialize for the same reason. Still others came through, and the *Bluegrass Summer '73* edition of *Muleskinner News* went to press that winter with several festival ads proclaiming the future presence of "The Stonemans with Scott Stoneman."[40]

Unfortunately, Scott's reunion with his family ended almost before it started. The band played only three or four dates in January and February. It guested once on the Opry, with Scott singing and fiddling "When They Ring Those Golden Bells" as a finale. In the meantime, Roni, who had played a few dates in Winston-Salem in 1971 with Scott and a picker named Bill Stanley as Stonemans II, came to Nashville and was trying to make it as a single. She had recorded a couple of singles for Dot and had asked Patsy, the family seamstress, to make her some stage clothes. On Sunday, March 4, Patsy spent much of the day at the sewing machine. She noticed a van and some musicians over at Bob Bean's house and knew that Scott was there. Fearful that such a situation could be very tempting for a person who needed to keep far from the bottle, she went over to investigate. Horrified, she found the others gone and Scott, who had consumed considerable alcohol, gasping his last breaths. They rushed him to the hospital, but to no avail. Although there had been some early speculation that death had been self-induced, one Dr. Clark Gregg told the *Tennessean* "he did not consider the death a suicide because records indicate the musician had consumed shaving lotion on other occasions." Bob Bean further explained, "A person drinks a lot and then lies down and strangles with fluid caught in the lungs." Patsy later reflected that watching Scott's birth when she was seven and then being

forced to see him die was particularly painful. Once again, tragedy had struck the Stonemans a powerful blow.[41]

With Pop's motto, "Don't Quit," pushing them forward against
the odds, the family pressed on. Bob Bean sent a letter to promoters reminding them that "THE STONEMANS ARE HERE TO STAY."
Minimizing Donna's departure, he wrote:

> Granted there have been various personnel changes over the
> past few years, one of these being the recent death of their
> brother Scotty, national champion fiddler. When buying the
> Stonemans, though, you are not buying individuals, but in-
> stead you are buying a group with over 40 years of musical her-
> itage. The Stonemans are now recording for MILLION RECORDS.
> Their second release is expected within a few weeks. They are
> booked by TOP BILLING INC. They will be returning to England
> for another extended tour in the Fall. They are looking forward
> to bigger and better things this year and in the future. They are
> happy you will be part of these projections.[42]

Dave Dougherty does not recall that the letter brought much of a
positive response. No matter how good they might sound, the
Stonemans did not seem the same to the fans and promoters without their dynamic drawing cards.

Continued quality remained in their act, however, as they re-
cruited mandolinist Buck White for the band. A native of Texas,
White came to Nashville with his family in 1971 by way of Arkansas. The Whites had a capable family bluegrass band composed of
Buck, his wife, Pat, and their teenage daughters, Sharon and
Cheryl. Getting established in Music City proved as trying for
them in 1972 as it had for the Stonemans a decade earlier, and
Buck accepted extra jobs when he could find them. It is probably
fair to say that White never considered his job with the Stonemans
as any more than a temporary one, and *Bluegrass Unlimited* reported that "when the Downhome folks are booked with the
Stonemans, Buck will play with both groups."[43] In late spring and
early summer, Sharon and Cheryl also played some dates with the
Stonemans. By midsummer, when work perked up for Buck and
his Down Home Folks, the Whites went their own way. By the
early eighties, they finally began to receive some of the acclaim
they had deserved and sought so long.

White's departure paved the way for the addition of an international flavor to the Stoneman band in the personage of Noboru Morishige, a young Japanese fiddler. "Shige," as he became known, had been an English student at Kyoto University who also studied violin and joined a band called the Lost City Cats. He especially idolized Scotty's version of "Orange Blossom Special," calling it "just fantastic, just amazing." In April 1973 the band came to the United States to observe and play bluegrass in the raw. After July 1 the other Lost City Cats found it necessary to return home, but Shige decided to remain for a time. He met Paul Soelberg, who induced him to enter the fiddler's contest at Renfro Valley, Kentucky, and also introduced him to his own former employers, the Stonemans. His admiration for Scotty's style drew the family to him and Bob Bean soon reported that he was "overwhelming the American and Canadian audiences wherever we go." Patsy recalls that Shige could present problems on occasion when he decided unexpectedly to innovate in the middle of an instrumental by tossing in a few bars of some different tune like "Sweet Georgia Brown" without warning, but she had great respect for his fiddling ability. Shige remained with the Stonemans until 1974.[44]

From 1973 on, the Stonemans entered what might be called the postpeak period of their career. Dave Dougherty, who remained with them through October 1976, recalls that while they often sounded quite good and received numerous encores at many stage shows, they simply did not get as many bookings as they had in 1966–72. More often than not, they worked most weekends and sometimes did longer stints in clubs, some of which retained a spot in Dougherty's memory because of their rowdy atmosphere. One beer garden in Peterboro, Ontario, he said was wilder than anything in the States. Ely, Nevada, had a club with pretty rough characters who gave Patsy some real challenges. The young Georgian learned that not all of the dangerous bars on the North American continent were in cities frequented by Appalachian migrants. Economically, the Stonemans survived those years, but one could hardly say they thrived. Dougherty recalls that they always treated him as equal and became like a second family to him. He still regards them quite highly. Their attitude helped sustain him during times when work opportunities and show dates were scarce. Between engagements, he took gigs in Nashville clubs and worked part time for Tut Taylor as an instrument craftsman.[45]

While Patsy, Jim, and Van struggled to keep the Stoneman Family group together, life also went on for the two expatriate Stoneman sisters. Roni, who came to Nashville when Georgia was about a year old, did not prosper initially as a single act because she tried to score as a serious singer rather than exploit her natural flair for comedy. By this time, her marriage to George Hemrick had become rather shaky, but he found a position as director of the Adult Continuing Education center for the state of Tennessee. Eventually, their union dissolved and he returned to North Carolina.

In 1973, Roni's career took a turn for the better when she joined the cast of "Hee Haw," the most successful syndicated program and country music show in the history of television. From the very beginning Roni's comedy work was a strong feature on the program. She picked banjo and sang from time to time, but one phase of the show in particular gave her an identity which made her readily recognizable to millions of television viewers: that of Ida Lee Nagger, the bedraggled housewife at the ironing board locked in almost perpetual argument with her shiftless husband, LaVerne. The program also gave Roni a steadier income than any other Stoneman active in the music profession. She told Augusta, Georgia, journalist Don Rhodes, "Thank God and Greyhound, I got the part of being a regular on the show. I was desperate for 'Hee Haw.' " Patsy says that at first Roni expressed private disgust with her Ida Lee role and hoped she had been selected to be on the show for the same reason Barbi Benton, Dianna Goodman, Misty Rowe, and Gunilla Hutton were chosen—to look good. However, nothing succeeds like success, and by 1976 she could tell Rhodes: "I wasn't hired on that show to be attractive. . . . I like to look bad when it looks funny. That's why I like to play in 'the Nagger's' segment of the show. . . . I told him [George Hemrick] if I learned to speak like him, I wouldn't make any bread."[46]

While "Hee Haw" hardly brought wealth, it allowed Roni to live in comfort as long as she remained part of the cast. It also allowed her to remain in the public eye without benefit of hit records—she has had two single releases, participated in three Stoneman Family recording sessions, and recorded two albums— after joining the program. This has enabled her to get bookings somewhat easier than the others, whose syndicated series ran its course in 1969 (although a few stations still carried it as late as 1972–73).

About the same time Roni began her affiliation with "Hee Haw," her sister Donna emerged from several months of relative seclusion as a full-time servant of the Lord. *Bluegrass Unlimited* reported in June 1973 that "Donna Stoneman is now working as a single singing gospel songs and painting. She had her own art show in Murfreesboro, Tennessee in May." Actually, more often than not, Donna worked with Cathy Manzer, who had a conversion experience about the same time, and the art exhibit was in the game room of the apartment building on Murfreesboro Road in suburban Nashville where they shared dwelling space. Donna recalls that TV coverage from WSM news brought buyers, including fellow musicians Skeeter Davis, Dolly Parton, Jeannie C. Riley, and Connie Smith. The last-named in particular proved to be a comforting friend in Donna's postmarital adjustment. The money she earned from the sale of paintings, plus a thousand dollars, the sum total of her savings, together with her faith, enabled Donna to subsist during her first year outside the musical group.[47]

Donna let Bob keep their home on Sailboat Drive; she kept some of the furnishings. She and Cathy went to churches, gave testimony, sang, and played. Initially she hesitated to accept remuneration, but her pastor, Brother Billy R. Moore of the Lord's Chapel, a large independent congregation with a set of beliefs somewhat akin to the Assembly of God, finally convinced her of the propriety of receiving "love offerings." Rather than being commercial gospel singers in the same sense as the Blackwood Brothers or the Rambos, Donna and Cathy engaged in a much more modest form of what one might call a "ministry of music." Economically, they managed to subsist, but not much more than that. Donna says, however, that God always provided for her needs, citing as an example the time she and Cathy drove to Maryland in a car with "bald headed tires." After the church service, a man came up and told them "the Lord spoke to his heart" and told him to buy Donna some tires. Although financial returns tended to be meager, the spiritual rewards proved highly satisfying.[48]

In 1976, Donna and Cathy made their only recordings, an album entitled *I'll Fly Away* that was released on the Skylite subsidiary label Temple. Cathy did most of the singing, while Donna picked mandolin, augmented by musicians from Jeannie C. Riley's Red River Symphony band, including banjo picker Ray Edwards and fiddler Mike Hartgrove. Donna did three instrumentals, including one called "Sanctified Orange Blossom Special"; rendered a recitation in one of Cathy's songs; and sang lead on "Oh! That Joy," an autobiographical lyric of her conversion experience. Jeannie C. Riley, another Nashville born-again Christian, wrote an inspirational jacket liner.[49]

The Stoneman Family made no recordings from the time of their ill-fated session for Million in September 1972 until 1976, when they waxed a pair of albums. They did one in Nashville for an aspiring songwriter from West Virginia named Dallas Corey, who penned every song and financed the album. By the time they cut the masters, the band had been stable for two years, Johnny Bellar, a young Dobro player from Ashland City, Tennessee, having joined the three family members and Dougherty in 1974. Not all of the songs could be classed as excellent, but several were quite good and the Stonemans did some of the best pure bluegrass they had done since their Starday days. Highlights included the title cut, "Country Hospitality"; a Roy Acuff tribute song that used the tune for "Wabash Cannonball," titled "Music City Yo Yo"; a lighthearted nonsense ditty, "Iney-Iney-It-Zi-Iney"; and a pair of gospel numbers. Dougherty alternated three-finger and clawhammer banjo styles and introduced some of the songs in the manner of Uncle Dave Macon; the entire group obviously enjoyed making the album, which had a light, relaxed feel coupled with zip and verve. George B. McCeney, reviewing it somewhat belatedly in *Bluegrass Unlimited* and realizing that the Stonemans had trouble capturing their essence on disc, took note of their "wonderfully executed arrangements . . . and exceptionally good lead singing." He further wrote that "their level of performance here ranks with the best bluegrass bands that have ever come down the pike." Unfortunately, the quality of distribution has made *Country Hospitality* a relatively scarce album. Only those fortunate enough to have purchased a copy at one of their live shows in the late seventies are likely to possess it.[50]

The two other Stoneman albums from the later seventies had the advantage of better distribution but the disadvantage of an inferior product. In 1975, C. Martin Haerle, a German American who had earlier been associated with Don Pierce and Starday, inaugurated the CMH record label. For the most part, Haerle built his label around name bluegrass and traditional country performers, including Mac Wiseman, the Osborne Brothers, Don Reno, Lester Flatt, Grandpa Jones, Merle Travis, Joe Maphis, the Willis Brothers, and Carl Story. He also contracted some new acts, most notably the Bluegrass Cardinals. The Stonemans did two albums for CMH in the later seventies, the first, *Cuttin' the Grass*, at Arthur Smith's studio in Charlotte and the second, *On the Road*, at John Wagner's studio in Albuquerque in late March 1977. Both albums consisted of a mixture of older and newer material, with the second containing a little more of the traditional fare. Jim Griffith, a folklorist by training and occupation, explained the traditionalist position on the Stonemans as the "children continued the family band in the directions which it already taken—away from the older material and sounds and towards a style and repertoire designed to attract a wide country and pop audience. This is the sort of material and approach found on this record—acoustic instruments, some old and a good deal of modern material, and little hard edge to music. If this combination is for you, then you'll like the record. Like all CMH productions, it is smoothly performed. Also like a good deal of the CMH products it is a bit bland."[51]

As work was begun on *Country Hospitality*, Hattie Stoneman faced her final illness. Since her husband's death she had given up maintaining a home and lived with her various children, usually Grace or Van. At times she appeared onstage with the family, usually fiddling on a number like "May I Sleep in Your Barn Tonight Mister." She did this for the final time in Virginia in the summer of 1974. The following winter, she suffered a series of heart attacks and momentarily stopped breathing. Donna recalls praying and breathing into her mouth. Hattie opened her eyes and told them she had been in a beautiful green valley and had spoken with Ernest. In the summer of 1976, she suffered more heart attacks. Says Donna: "This time, we knew it was her time to go." Death came on July 22, 1976.[52]

Like that of her husband eight years earlier, Hattie's passing attracted the attention of the Nashville establishment. By now, however, the Stonemans no longer ranked as the reigning vocal group on Music Row but had become just another country-bluegrass band. Still, numerous fans and friends paid their respects. Vic Willis, Jimmie Riddle, and Lorene Mann visited the funeral home, while Roy Acuff, Skeeter Davis, Connie Smith, and Jeannie C. Riley sent flowers. Former Stoneman associates Paul Soelberg, Cathy Manzer, and Jerry Monday were among the mourners. The Reverend Billy Moore of the Lord's Chapel conducted the service and Grandpa Jones sang "I Will Meet You in the Morning," with Carol Lee Cooper serving as organist. The staff of the Hibbett and Hailey Funeral Home then placed Hattie Frost Stoneman beside her husband in Mount Olivet Cemetery.[53]

Not long after Mom Stoneman's death, Dave Dougherty left the band (October 1976), to be replaced by Eddie Mueller. The latter, a sixteen-year-old, spent somewhat more than four years with the group—like his predecessor—and proved to be a banjo picker of quality. Himself the product of a family bluegrass band, the youngster had won a banjo contest at Sunset Park when he was twelve. He then spent three years with his dad and uncle in an aggregation known as Eddie and the Mueller Brothers. He had been with the Stonemans about five or six months when they cut *On the Road* in Albuquerque. Eddie contributed some original tunes, such as "Tennessee Walker," and generally played a fine banjo, although he contributed less to the group vocals than Dougherty had done. At times the Stonemans carried an additional musician for brief stretches, including Mike Harris, a Canadian fiddler who lived in Nashville. The most notable short-term Stoneman sideman of the mid-1970s, Roland White, had known the family since their California days, when he and his brother Clarence led the Kentucky Colonels. After Clarence joined the rock group known as the Birds, Roland worked with Bill Monroe and Lester Flatt before settling in for a longer stint with the Country Gazette. His brief work with the Stonemans included a Canadian tour, of which the memorable club engagement at Peterboro had been a part.[54]

Until Labor Day weekend of 1977, Bob Bean continued to function as the Stonemans' manager. In the meantime, Bob married a girl named Emma Jean and they became parents of a daughter. As time went by, relations between Bob and Patsy became increasingly strained and tense. A feeling developed among the band members that they needed to know more about their finances. At the same time, Patsy became increasingly incensed about road accommodations:

> The blow-up finally came when I let it be known that I no longer would ask Murph to put our home up as collateral to keep us on the road when the family already owed him lots of money, and that I was tired of being hauled all over the country like a bunch of cattle, without any thoughts about our comfort; lots of times it had gotten to where Bob had not even made any arrangements for us to rest nor take a bath. He was getting the idea that I could stop in a truck stop and shower as well as a trucker. . . . It was at a festival in Kerrville, Texas we had been traveling about three days, the air conditioner had not worked for some time, and we had gone from one show to another without a bath. It was about 100 degrees when we arrived in Kerrville, and I said that I will take a bath before I go on or that I would not go on. Bob acted like I had asked for the moon, and we got into it. It wasn't a pretty sight, but Van, Jim and I asked a guy at a service station where we could get a bath real quick, and he told us that a new camp ground had just opened right near by, so we went to that; it was a real nice, clean place and the bath sure helped. When we returned from that lovely trip, Bob said that he was leaving because of health reasons, and he was right. . . . We were sick of each other.[55]

Although the passage of time cooled their anger, from September 9, 1977, Patsy became the unofficial manager of the Stoneman Family as a musical group. Initially, income and gross earnings increased as they worked six more dates and took in $4,266.73 more in 1978 than in 1977. The next year, however, there was a drop in both work and income, mostly because their work in Canada was cut in half. Part of the decline resulted from the passage of the Canadian Cultural Preservation Act and part was an indirect consequence of some business dealings involving Bob and a Canadian promoter. The combination of these factors, plus a slowdown in the economy, caused Stoneman appearances in Canada, once numerous, to become negligible from 1980 on.[56]

While on the surface 1978 seemed like a better year for the Stonemans, it had a negative side. Numerous unpaid bills and taxes were a serious problem. On June 5, 1978, the Third National Bank went to court to collect from both The Singing Stonemans, Incorporated, and Robert Bean. Patsy handled the matter with adroitness: "Meanwhile, I was trying to get the old bills paid when the bank informed me that they were coming out and take everything that Van and Jimmy had. I told their lawyer that I would pay $100.00 a month on the bill. He said no; then I said that if he didn't accept that amount that we would be in court next morning to declare bankruptcy. He did agree and now [1982] we almost have it paid off, as well as most everything else, including the taxes."[57]

The close of the 1970s saw the Stoneman Family in considerably less than ideal circumstances, but there was a moment of triumph. On May 20, 1979, they appeared at the Smithsonian Institution in Washington, D.C. In addition to the regular band, Donna, Roni, Gene, Dean, and Eddie appeared for the occasion. The *Washington Post* generously publicized the event, calling attention to the family's earlier activities in Washington and terming it "A Musical Circle Unbroken." Patsy later told Chattanooga writer Randall Armstrong: "Oh man! Eleven of us on stage at one time. It was great. My brother Dean got standing ovation after standing ovation for 'Muleskinner Blues.' He left the hospital to come. In fact he was operated on Tuesday and performed on Sunday. He looked like he was going to fall over when he left the stage but he was so happy!"[58]

Although 1980 proved to be the slowest year, workwise, the Stonemans had had since coming to Nashville, they did engender some excitement in high places. Randall Armstrong pointed out that the Stoneman show he witnessed at Lake Winnepausaukah Amusement Park still electrified the audience. Commenting that "in the past few years . . . the Stonemans seemed to have moved away from the spotlight and constant media exposure," he added that "the adjectives" that identified them in the late sixties still described "their act to a T." Their July appearance at a Waterford, Ontario, bluegrass festival under sponsorship of the Lions Club so impressed the organization's leaders that they wrote President Jimmy Carter a letter praising the Stonemans' spirit and musicianship. Among other things, they told the president: "Musicians from the length and breadth of North America are invited to perform, and no group of musicians exemplifies better the spirit of Blue Grass—its honesty, its earnestness, its love of a good old-fashioned time—than the splendid Stoneman Family from Nashville, Tennessee. Had you searched the corridors of Congress you could not have found finer ambassadors to send to our fair town, and we thought you might like to know that every time they come back to visit with us the members of the Stoneman Family bring a huge supply of American good-will."[59] Senator Howard Baker, Governor Lamar Alexander, and Rep. Bill Boner all expressed their appreciation to the Stonemans for the outstanding job they did in representing Tennessee and American music at the Waterford festival, with Boner inserting the entire letter in the *Congressional Record.*[60]

About this time, Patsy began to conceive the notion of a double album that would properly present the Stoneman story on disc. Their company, CMH, had produced a series of two-album sets for Don Reno, Lester Flatt, Mac Wiseman, Merle Travis, Benny Martin, and Jim and Jesse, plus four by Grandpa Jones. Why not one for the Stoneman Family? Although Pop, Mom, and Scott obviously could not participate, the more extended family members could be included, as well as some of the next generation, who had begun to come of musical age. The record company gave the green light. Patsy and Jack "Hoss" Linneman, a former session musician on Dobro for Starday, went to work as co-producers on the project and scheduled sessions at Jack's Hilltop Recording Studios in Nashville. John Stoneman, shy and never very confident about his musical abilities, chose not to participate and Billy Stoneman's health and mental condition excluded him, but ten of Pop's children appeared in some capacity, as did five of his grandchildren. At no time, however, did all of them appear in the studio at once. In fact, bad weather in Ohio prevented Roni and daughters Barbara and Georgia from making it to Hilltop Studios at all. She did her tracks in Mansfield, sending them to Hilltop for overdubbing. The regularly performing Stonemans, plus Johnny Bellar and Eddie Mueller, provided accompaniment on most of the two dozen cuts.[61]

Although somewhat less polished than the others, the semiprofessional musicians in the family provided some of the more interesting moments in the album. Gene Stoneman, showing himself to be very much a child of the fifties, resurrected one of Hank Snow's minor classics of 1953, "Honeymoon on a Rocket Ship." Dean Stoneman, the hard-core devotee of traditional bluegrass, rendered rough but rousing renditions of "Mule Skinner Blues" and "I'm Thinking Tonight of My Blue Eyes." Past critics of the family who lamented that newer Stoneman recordings lacked a "hard edge" could never had said that about Dean. Jack Stoneman sang a competent version of his favorite vocal, the 1941 Red Foley classic "Old Shep," and Eddie Stoneman, back in a studio for the first time in forty-seven years, displayed versatility by fiddling his way through "Old Joe Clark," picking out Arthur Smith's "Guitar Boogie" on his electric model, and vocalizing Carson Robison's "Left My Gal in the Mountains." Grace Jewell, ranking with John as the least-musical Stoneman, dueted with daughter Donna Kay on one of Pop's songs, "When the Snowflakes Fall Again."

As one might expect, the active Stonemans tended to be featured more than the others. Van sang lead on the songs he had done earlier, but perhaps more significantly for traditionalists, he revealed himself for the first time on disc as a capable clawhammer-banjo player in a manner that did credit to his mother Hattie and his cousin George. Jimmy soloed on Pop's standard "The Poor Tramp Has to Live," revived the Mitchell Torok hit of 1953, "Caribbean," and closed with the one new song of the entire set, "Prayers and Pinto Beans," an autobiographical Stoneman song recently composed by Patsy. Donna sang "Life's Railway to Heaven" and picked lead on two instrumentals, "Under the Double Eagle" and "Orange Blossom Special." Roni sang Merle Haggard's "I Take a Lot of Pride in What I Am" and "Lonesome Road Blues," with Barbara and Georgia joining on the chorus of the latter. Patsy played Autoharp and sang on "The Whippoor-will Song" and "Blue Ridge Mountain Blues," both songs from Pop's repertoire of the twenties.

The younger generation of Stonemans identified more with contemporary influences than their ancestral heritage. Nineteen-year-old Van, Jr., sang "Fire on the Mountain" and "Peaceful Easy Feeling," taken from the respective hits by the Marshall Tucker Band and the Eagles. Fifteen-year-old Randy vocalized on

"Amie," a 1975 Pure Prairie League song. By February 1981, the mastering complete, Linneman and Patsy sent the tapes to California. Martin Haerle enlisted Norm Cohen of the John Edwards Memorial Foundation, who, coincidentally, penned the notes for the *Pop Stoneman Memorial Album* a dozen years earlier, to write the liner.

When it was released a year later, *The First Family of Country Music* engendered more excitement than anything the Stonemans had done for a decade, including their two efforts on CMH. David Freeman, who had been critical of Stoneman Family efforts since Pop died, responded positively: "The talents of this huge, remarkable family are well presented on this 2-LP set which is considerably more successful than their earlier CMH LP's. There are several quite nice cuts here like POOR TRAMP HAS TO LIVE, sung by Jim Stoneman, and Patsy's WHIPPOORWILL SONG. Donna Stoneman returns after a long absence with her dynamic mandolin work. A pleasant variety LP."[62] Les McIntyre of *Bluegrass Unlimited* also gave favorable commentary:

> Throughout the four sides, the various Stonemans take turns at the microphone with no one individual dominating the proceedings. The result is a tremendous assortment of different types of music that still retains a characteristic that is distinctly this unique family. . . . As with any undertaking of this magnitude, there are some performances that may not be up to standards expected from a full-time bluegrass or country band. However, the purpose of this album was to showcase the musical heritage of the Stoneman family, and the love and dedication that was obviously inserted into the production far outstrips any faults that a reviewer might uncover. "The Stonemans, The First Family of Country Music" represents a stroll down memory lane for their long time fans.[63]

The most introspective review came from Professor John Morefield of East Tennessee State University, who, while letting it be known that he hadn't been all that thrilled with Donna's dancing back in the syndicated television days, revealed great respect for all the Stonemans and their music:

> One would expect competence and confidence from people who have been making music in public for most of their lives, but the Stonemans give more, a sense of involvement and intimacy.

Each sibling is featured on at least one selection and there is the impression throughout, even if the voices and fingers are not what they once were, of people who know what they are doing and know that, with the rest of the family gathered around, it is all going to turn out all right. It turns out much better than all right. There is nothing innovative here, but everyone sings on pitch and plays the right notes, something of an accomplishment for those who have not been in front of a microphone for thirty or forty years.[64]

Unfortunately, when CMH released the album, it did not put as much promotional effort into the double sets as it did when such fare as *The Mac Wiseman Story* or *The Grandpa Jones Story* were pressed. As a result, the Stoneman effort had less impact than it would have had if it had been cut five years earlier. Nonetheless, it could be called a musical success in every sense of the term and Patsy could justly take pride in her production.

Not long after completion of *The First Family of Country Music*, Donna Stoneman felt compelled to return to the musical group. After 1977 she remained friends with Cathy Manzer, but since their musical styles were not compatible, Donna generally worked as a solo gospel singer, using sound tracks for accompaniment. She wrote new gospel lyrics for bluegrass standards like "Rocky Top" and "Fox on the Run." In 1977, Tom T. Hall talked her into playing mandolin on his bluegrass-oriented *Magnificent Music Machine* album for Mercury. Receiving a call to preach, Donna began an intensive Bible study under the direction of Brother Moore at the Lord's Chapel, which led to her receiving a minister's license in October 1980.[65]

Earlier that same year, Donna spent six weeks ministering in England and Northern Ireland, having by her own account sold her bedstead and slept on the floor of her tiny apartment to save money for an airline ticket. Destitute, she recalls that she had only enough money for the flight to London. Not knowing how she would make it on to Belfast, she received a pleasant surprise when Connie Smith met her at the airport and handed her $150 in cash; tickets from London to Belfast cost $149. Once more she felt the Lord had provided. Back in the States, she preached in the Montana state prison and on Indian reservations. Along the way she appeared as a guest on inspirational telecasts, including both Pat Robertson's "700 Club" and Jim Bakker's "PTL Club." All the while, she subsisted on the bare minimum. Donna exudes confidence that God will see that her needs are supplied, but she hastens to add, "He never promised to make me wealthy."[66]

Having heard that Jimmy, Patsy, and Van had been having hard times since 1980, Donna began meditating and praying about rejoining the group. She knew her departure in late 1972 had been costly and feared they might not want her. Eddie Mueller gave his notice during the CMH double-album sessions and worked his last dates on February 5 and 6 at a pair of shows in Kansas. Patsy hired a fiddler named Mitch Fuston for several shows after that, but he didn't work out all that well. Donna asked about returning in July and went on the payroll in August. Mitch played his last show on September 5, and Patsy replaced him with a young banjo picker named Chuck Holcomb later that month. Donna did only six show dates with the Stonemans in 1981, but she had two television guest appearances, on "Nashville Live" and "Hee Haw," which reintroduced her to a wider audience. Work opportunities for the entire group tended to be meager through most of the eighties, and for about four years Donna lived in Murph and Patsy's spare bedroom. Meanwhile, Bob and Emma Jean Bean continued to occupy the home across the street until financial difficulties that resulted from a Canadian business deal forced them to sell.[67]

Roni Stoneman continued through the 1980s as a "Hee Haw" regular, where, through her Ida Lee Nagger skits, she became a familiar figure to both casual and serious country fans throughout the nation. Relatively few of them ever realized that Roni's own life in the early years of her first marriage bore more resemblance to that of Ida Lee than to the mode of living the public associated with the image of a Nashville star. In 1980 she married for the third time, to a Mansfield, Ohio, banker named Richard Adams. Of the marriage she remarked: "He married me for my body and I married him for his money and we both got cheated." Such humor, however, masks the depression that Roni feels because of her failed attempts to achieve domestic happiness and security. As in the early days of her marriage to George, Roni commuted to Nashville for her engagements. After four years she and Richard parted company and Roni returned to Tennessee, occupying a home in Smyrna.[68]

During Richard and Roni's marriage, the Stoneman Family was inducted into the Walkway of the Stars in June 1981 at the Country Music Hall of Fame. Roni's description of the event reveals much of the triumph and tragedy, along with the bittersweet character, of the Stoneman experience:

> Last year, the family's name was inducted into the "Walkway of Stars" at the Country Music Hall of Fame in Nashville, along with Boxcar Willie, (whom I love very much, he's my buddie) and the Mandrell girls. Barbara, I "hate." . . . She's so beautiful and talented, she knocked me off my queenly throne when she came to town! What a talent! She's class, what else can I say? All of the family was so pleased, dear sister Patsy had worked so hard. All my older brothers showed up from Washington and Maryland to be present at the induction. Each one had a little speech ready for the occasion. My sister Donna, who is an ordained minister and evangelist, was there in her favorite little lace dress, all prissy and pretty, (goody-two shoes!) Grace stood their [sic] so angelic and caring, and Patsy, who's proud, (ate up with it), my older brothers were there too, (unfortunately the affects of their past drinking sprees, aged them a wee bit) . . . bein' nice! . . . About a month prior to this event, my sister Grace had taken Jack, our brother, into her home. She bought him some new clothes, suits, and cut his hair. Cleaned him up real good. All the time thinking she was going to stop him from drinking (Ho, ho, ho!) it was a waste . . . she always seemed to pity Jack and would take it upon herself to save him from himself. Jack had been living at the mission and Grace, Patsy, and Donna had tried hundreds of times to help him and get his feet on the ground, away from there. He can be very talented and they do love him . . . but alas and alack, it always falls through. At this time, they decided he should be invited to the ceremony. . . . I thought then, . . . Oh Wow! Anyway, the big day arrived to take pictures with my family at the Country Music Museum. My new husband, Richard Adams, accompanied me that day. We rode over to Patsy's house to follow the family bus to the Hall of Fame. 'Fanfare' was going on that week and there were at least 25,000 fans of country music in town. I believe half of them were at the Hall of Fame as spectators for the event. All the country music newspapers were there along with *Billboard,*

Record World, Associated Press, and UPI, to record this moment in country music history. I was present with my pony tails from the show, Boxcar Willie saw me and gave me some hugs. (I hugged him back.) I said "Hey" to the family and "Hey" to the fans, signed a few autographs, and played star. I was standing there beside my darling little sister Donna, I looked over and here came Jack direct from the mission with two buddies tagging behind him. Jack had sold all his new clothes that Grace had bought him for wine. He was wearing a suit from the mission, which was two or three sizes too big for him . . . He was walking on the knees, (his feet were where his knees should have been), my husband looked at me in disbelief and said, "Oh, my God, who's that?" (He'd never met him before.) I said sweetly, "That's your new brother-in-law, darlin'," while holding back a laugh. My husband being a bankin' businessman, was quite surprised and fuddy duddy, exclaimed, "Oh, my God!" Jack pushed directly past me and moved onto Donna with his hands outstretched and in his whiskeyitis voice, spoke, "How you doin' there sis?", he wanted his buddies to know she was his sister. Donna has always told me, "Never be embarrassed of your brother, it's unchristian like." For about 15 seconds Donna lost her Christianity. She turned her head, cast her eyes to the floor and from her throat, in the key of high C gave a cat-like cry of embarrassment. All the while, Jack was pumping her arm like he was priming a well. I just stood there and grinned. Jack's face was the same color as a turkey gobbler's snout. His nose was still spread across his face from the many fights of his youth. It had been repaired several times, while he was in the pokey, by the state doctor trying to improve Jack's emotional stability. When it came time for the Stoneman's to give their speeches on how much of an honor it was to be invited into the "Walkway of Stars," we all moved up to the podium. All the country music fans kept their eyes right on us and they listened as we thanked everybody, each and every one of us. . . . Donna looked down and saw Jack as he pushed his way toward the mike and put his lips directly on the microphone and spoke in his whiskey voice, giving a 15 minute speech which nobody understood. After he finished a man from UPI asked "What did you say, sir?" If I'd been on the podium, I'd have kicked his ass up between his shoulder blades because I think he was just being downright naughty! Jack was having fun, but the family was embarrassed. . . . I think I was, at the time, too! Right after that, Jo Walker, of the Country Music Awards announced, "Ladies and gentlemen, there will be cocktails and hors d'oeuvre honoring those whose names went into the Walkway of Stars, downstairs." Jack looked at his two buddies and said, "Let's go gang!" Fortunately, I had to go back to the studio. I went back and told Grandpa Jones and Minnie Pearl and they laughed down to their bones for they knew Jack and could see the humor in it.[69]

The Smithsonian appearance, the CMH anthology and the Walkway of the Stars induction, coupled with the realization that some of Ernest Stoneman's own grandchildren lacked an understanding of the role their family had played in the development of country music, led Patsy Stoneman to take action. Always the most tradition-minded Stoneman in the bunch, she began collecting documents, doing research, and encouraging her brothers and sisters to write or orally record their life stories as they remembered them. Her short-range objective led her to put together a documentary slide presentation that not only could serve a general educational purpose but also could be a prelude to a Stoneman concert. Dr. Nat Winston, a long time family friend prominent in Tennessee medical and political circles, narrated a sound track interspersed with significant recordings, both old and new. Since the family had relatively few show dates in 1981, Patsy took some time to put it together rather accurately. Although a stickler for facts might take exception to a point or two, her history displayed more authenticity than most media presentations that came out of Nashville. She made arrangements to show the slide set at the Roy Acuff Theater at Opryland on October 31, 1981, followed by a Stoneman concert. A secondary goal of Patsy's presentation would be that it was her way of telling friends and fans that the family had endured hard times before and could hang in there "as long as there was a Stoneman left to pick." Her eventual goal would be to get the Stoneman life story into a book.[70]

Unbeknownst to Patsy at the time, the Stonemans had already made it into a book, albeit in somewhat disguised form. A *Grit* reporter and mystery writer named Marvin Kaye wrote "a novel of suspense" titled *The Grand Ole Opry Murders*. The plot centered on a family performing group of country-bluegrass musicians named Boulder that had been founded years before by their late father,

"Pappy." As the story unravels, a fictional female detective named Hiliary Quayle learns that the pretty dancing mandolin picker, Dolly Boulder, murders her two sisters, Amanda and Pearl, because they won't let her sing solo lead parts.[71]

The pattern for show dates did not change much after Donna returned to the band, except that out of mutual respect for her ministry the Stonemans ceased working in clubs. They worked several times each year, mostly during the summer, but not really enough to make a decent living from their music. Van sometimes worked at other jobs to sustain his family, and Helen also worked full time, as did Jimmy's wife, Mary. Murph, as a professional bus driver, chiefly for such country and rock stars as John Denver, Neil Young, and Huey Lewis, brought home the bacon in his household, while Patsy endeavored to promote the family by whatever means possible. Donna's ministry work sometimes brought in a little money, generally just enough to stave off financial calamity. Now and then she would receive the opportunity to preach a revival and the church would take up love offerings in her behalf. A pastor at a church in Beaver, Ohio, told how he and his wife took Donna to the post office each morning, where she would count dollar bills for money orders to catch up on car payments, liability insurance, and debts to other creditors.[72]

Now and then a better opportunity came along. In April 1984, Merwyn Conn brought them back to England, where the Wembley audience received them with as much enthusiasm as it had a dozen years earlier. Johnny Bellar and Chuck Holcomb dropped out of the band shortly afterward. Although Johnny remained with the Stonemans longer than any nonfamily member in the group's history, things had come to the point where the Stonemans simply didn't work enough to warrant carrying sidemen. Besides, Johnny wanted to do some things on his own and with his father. Later that year the Stonemans played two more memorable shows. The first, August 17 at Lincoln Center in New York City, reunited them briefly with former band member Dave Dougherty, who filled in on banjo that weekend. Some weeks later, on September 7, they performed a concert at Shenandoah College in Winchester, Virginia, where they received a Lifetime Achievement Commendation.[73]

Some hopes went awry, too. In 1978 the family inaugurated a small bluegrass festival at Section, Alabama, that might have grown into a much larger event had not vandalism at the park become such a problem that the event had to be discontinued after 1980. In 1982 and 1983, Rodger and Sally Alderman of Willis, Virginia, tried to build a festival around the Stonemans as central figures, but the results did not encourage them to try again. As one festivalgoer later remarked, the local populace in the Floyd-Willis area did not support such shows very well in spite of its relative nearness to and cultural similarity with such neighboring locales as Galax and Mount Airy.[74]

In the summer of 1985, Patsy arranged for the Stonemans to spend the better part of the tourist season at the Cherokee Entertainment Center on the Indian reservation in North Carolina. Unlike the Tennessee side of the Smokies and the Maggie Valley complex to the north, the Cherokee area had relatively little in the way of country music. Working six days a week would give them more dates than they had played in years, although for less money and an uncertain amount even then because they would be paid on a percentage basis. Still, the situation appeared to have promise; it would involve less traveling, and Roni promised to work the portion of the season that remained after the June filming of "Hee Haw." That spring, Roni married a younger man named Bill Zimmerman, and her summer commitment at Cherokee promised a reunion of the five Stonemans of 1968–70.[75]

Although the crowd sizes at Cherokee did not match expectations, the Stonemans did a little better than pay their expenses. There were some good musical moments, such as the day Everett Lilly came by, performed with the family, and reminisced about the days when Scotty worked with the Lilly Brothers at Hillbilly Ranch in Boston. The two days as guests at the Galax Old Fiddler's Convention and a festival appearance at Otto, Arkansas, on August 31 probably yielded nearly as much income as their Cherokee gig. However, Patsy expressed hope that a second season there might be stronger, even if Roni chose not to join them again.

For sixteen years the Stonemans had endured as a musical entity after the death of Ernest Stoneman, and for nearly a decade after the passing of Hattie. Emotional stress, temporary estrangement among some family members, death, and financial hardship had all been surmounted. Small differences remained, but unity was better than it had been in the late sixties. Roni still chose to go it alone most of the time but worked with the others on special shows and occasionally at other times as well. They came to regret some of their past errors, such as their management turning down Grand Ole Opry membership when they were CMA Vocal Group of the Year, not trying harder to rehabilitate and reintegrate with Scott earlier than they did, and discontinuing their syndicated television series. Of course, by the 1980s, none of these mistakes could be rectified. Life would have to go on as well as possible without these missed opportunities.

The Stonemans still faced difficult problems. As of 1985, seventeen years had elapsed since their names were attached to a recording on the *Billboard* country charts. A new type of star system had begun to evolve in which the record firms turned out bigger but fewer stars. An older artist like George Jones, who could rebound from personal and career crises time after time, was clearly exceptional in Nashville. Older established figures like Faron Young, Charlie Louvin, Jean Shepard, and Billy Walker had difficulty in getting their records produced by major labels. Even a new traditional movement focused on relative youngsters like Ricky Skaggs, Dwight Yoakum, Randy Travis, the Whites, Keith Whitley, and Kathy Mattea rather than the middle-aged stalwarts of the sixties. Other than custom labels, about the only opportunities for Stoneman recordings came from smaller specialty firms like Heritage and Old Homestead, whose owners knew and respected the contributions that various Stonemans had made to traditional music over the decades. These non-Nashville firms, valuable as they might be to collectors, stood little chance of getting their discs on the charts.

By now, Patsy Stoneman had emerged as the behind-the-scenes catalyst in keeping the family musically intact. Like Pop, she had lots of determination and "just plain grit." Also like "Daddy," Patsy was a survivor. Before joining the Stonemans as a full-time musician, she had already survived a tough childhood, two disastrous marriages, a dozen years of hard farm labor, and a sudden unexpected plunge into widowhood. Having been through these experiences, leading kid sisters and kid brothers, now in middle age, in a country band might not be too tough. It had become her turn to remind the others of what Ernest V. Stoneman had told them so many years before: "Don't Quit."

Conclusion:
An Update and a Retrospect

The Stonemans' career has not yet ended. Their engagements continue and may well extend into the next century. However, in the years since their August 1985 concerts at Galax, relatively little has changed except that the group and its members have become older.[1]

A good deal has happened to individual Stonemans in the 1980s that has affected their lives, however. Three have recently gone to their reward, reducing the number of Ernest and Hattie Stoneman's living children to nine. A brief glimpse of their recent activities will illustrate the continuing cycle of life for family members.

Eddie Stoneman retired in 1985. Shortly afterward, doctors diagnosed his wife, Katherine, as having terminal emphysema. She passed away on August 2, 1987. Her long struggle took its toll on Eddie's health and vigor, too, but he continued to fiddle, pick, and sing on special occasions, such as the Stoneman reunions held in the Blue Ridge in the summers of 1988 and 1989. His older son Doug has worked twenty-four years for Western Union; he and his wife, Dena, have three grown children. Daughter Barbara lives in Parsons, Kansas, with her husband, Marion Chenoweth, who works in printing and advertising. Younger son Wayne, a Vietnam veteran, makes his home with Eddie and services ice-cream machines for a livelihood.[2]

Grace Stoneman Jewell moved to Nashville after her separation and divorce from George. Not long afterward, in April 1978, she met a graying gentleman named Jim Dugan who fit her own and most people's description of being a near ideal man. Unfortunately, Dugan was soon found to be suffering from either Lou Gehrig's disease or some other condition quite similar to it. Grace's devotion led her to marrying him, although by the time of the ceremony Dugan could not move a muscle in his body and required round-the-clock nursing care. Grace continued to care for him lovingly until his death in March 1987, nearly thee years after their July 16, 1984, wedding. Attending physicians remarked that they had never seen a man bedfast for so long who had been cared for as well as Jim Dugan. After his death, Grace continued to live in Nashville.

Grace is also the only Stoneman to have been anything akin to a political activist. Although technically a registered Democrat for many years, she generally identified with the Republican viewpoint and conservative causes from her days in Riverdale, Maryland, when she helped elect a mayor. She exemplifies the oft-heard contention that moral and social issues frequently outweigh economic questions with many voters. In 1988 she identified initially with Pat Robertson but had no qualms in transferring her loyalty to George Bush, a man of patrician Yankee origins who has become an unabashed country-music fan.

Grace's children have been some of the highest achievers among Ernest and Hattie Stoneman's grandkids. Bill Jewell attended Kenneth Hagin Bible College in Broken Arrow, Oklahoma, but has generally worked in air conditioning and refrigeration, currently for the J and D Services Corporation. He and his wife, an employee of NASA, live in Beltsville, Maryland, and have reared three children. Steve Jewell rose through the federal civil service to the position of senior account representative at the U.S. Government Printing Office and has supervised special jobs for both the Reagan and Bush administrations. He recently took a position as head of printing at the White House. This puts him in a category with Pop Stoneman, who reportedly did the finish carpentry work in President Roosevelt's yacht during World War II. Steve and his wife have three children. After Jack Jewell's second wife died, Steve received custody of his father's two younger children and reared them to adulthood. Donna Kay Jewell mothered four children and as a divorced housewife graduated in biology from Middle Tennessee State University. She completed course work for a master's degree and then was married again to an independent trucker.[3]

John Stoneman and Deeta retired to her original hometown of Jonesville, Virginia. John, Jr., also moved to Jonesville. The other son, Stanley, a Vietnam veteran, remains in Carmody Hills, where he works as a housepainter. Billy and Barbara Stoneman lived in Carmody Hills until his death on April 10, 1990. Their four children are all grown and reside in the same neighborhood where the Stonemans began playing their hillbilly music nearly a half-century ago. A proud veteran to the end, he was buried with full military honors. Donna officiated at his funeral.

Jack Stoneman alternated between Maryland and Nashville. His efforts at rehabilitation in his battle with alcoholism continued until his death in April 1992. He preferred being in music, saying: "I am hoping somebody will need a bass man and that I get a chance at it for I won't be happy unless I am playing bass with some one."[4] But it never happened.

Gene and Dean Stoneman, both settled from their early rowdiness, lived in Edgewater and Bowie, Maryland, respectively. Gene's daughter Robin grew up and married, while Gene continued in the employ of the government, primarily as a locksmith. In 1989 he and Peggy attended the Stoneman Reunion in Hillsville, Virginia, where he and some of the family members from Nashville helped provide entertainment.

Dean Stoneman, forced to retire early because of ill health, suffered from lung cancer and emphysema in his later years, becoming frightfully thin. He and Fay attended the Stoneman Reunion in 1988 and Dean helped Patsy and Donna perform a few numbers on stage, but he declined steadily that fall and winter before expiring on February 28, 1989. Patsy authored a *Bluegrass Unlimited* tribute letter recalling how Dean, as a teenage musician, had frequently abandoned the stage when he got the opportunity to dance with a pretty girl. "Soon people were calling him 'Crazy Legs' Stoneman," she said. Gene took his twin's death particularly hard, remarking, "You know he's not just my brother, he's a part of me."[5]

Scott Stoneman's older daughter Sandra lives in suburban Maryland with her husband. Sandy takes a just pride in her dad's accomplishments with the fiddle. She has done some playing and singing locally, but in recent years she has been content to remain at home with her daughter and son, whom she proudly describes as "a little Scotty of my own." Her mother, remarried as Cecile Howard, also lives in the area. Scott's last wife, Mary, and their children, Ernest Scott and Kerin Faith, reside in Nashville.[6]

The Stonemans who remained in music fared about as well or as poorly in the latter half of the eighties as they did in the first part of the decade. In 1986 they returned to Cherokee without Roni, hiring a young banjo picker from Bryson City named Kevin Tuck. Patsy became increasingly aware that a behind-the-scenes intertribal political squabble for control of the Cherokee Entertainment Center existed and helped cause the meager attendance at their daily shows, so she terminated the contract a month early and returned to Nashville just before their employer lost his lease on the center.

The Stonemans worked very little in 1987, but did somewhat more in the next three summers. Generally speaking, they did not make an adequate living from music. Van held a variety of part-time jobs, and his wife worked regularly. Donna derived some income from preaching an occasional revival, performing weddings, or singing at a funeral. Sometimes she and Cathy Manzer would entertain at a church gathering or private party. Mostly she lived in a very frugal manner. Jimmy's wife continued to hold down a full-time job, and Murph worked to keep his and Patsy's household going. In 1986 they (Roni included) recorded several gospel tracks, which Rutabaga Records released on an album in 1988 under the title *Family Bible;* the critics generally looked upon it with favor. In *Precious Memories*, Wayne Daniel characterized it as "pleasant listening" and "straight from the heart bluegrass gospel." He particularly found the title cut and Roni's "Will the Circle Be Unbroken" appealing. Frank Childrey of *Bluegrass Unlimited* termed it "authentic country gospel . . . from true veterans," describing Van's rendition of "Sinner Man" as "spirited and creative" and labeling Roni's vocal as "soulful" in the church hymn "In the Garden."[7]

Except in those instances when Roni worked with them, the four active group members usually played show dates by themselves. Sometimes at a bluegrass festival they would temporarily add a local banjo picker, such as Tib Hart on a swing through Ohio, or an accomplished member of another band like Little Roy Lewis would become a temporary Stoneman simply for the pleasure derived from lending an assist. In addition to several festival appearances, the family played for appreciative audiences at such varied locales as Earl's Drive-In at Chafee, New York, and the Berea College Celebration of Traditional Music in Kentucky. At the latter, Van had a rare opportunity to discuss and display his clawhammer-banjo techniques.

On an individual level, the Nashville Stonemans endeavored to live their personal lives within the framework of being members of a semiactive musical group. Patsy, as she had done for more than a decade, took the lead. In 1987 she arranged an hourly radio program at station WSVT in nearby Smyrna which she called "At Home with the Stonemans." At noon on Fridays, Patsy talked about her family, with occasional commentary from Donna, Jim, Van, or whoever happened to be available, and played selections from their recordings, both old and new. Well-known guests from the country-music world, ranging from Eddy Arnold and Faron Young to Bill Monroe, came on from time to time. Even academics from the scholarly world of country music, such as Charles Wolfe of Middle Tennessee State University, made visits to the show. Anxious to get out of Nashville, she and Murph spotted a small farm near Manchester and moved there in December 1989, having finally sold their split-level brick house on Edge-O-Lake Drive. Promoting the group at every opportunity, she generally did more than such agents as Joe Taylor and Lance LeRoy to secure bookings for them.

Donna, having lived in Patsy's spare bedroom for more than three years, secured her own apartment in September 1985 on Edmondson Pike near Nollensville Road. Anxious to reassert her independence, she preferred living on her own. Jimmy and his wife, Mary, lived in the same apartment complex, as did Cathy Manzer and—until Jim's death—Jim and Grace Dugan. Donna's revival efforts have taken her to such sites as the Sand Mountain area of Alabama; Morristown, Tennessee; and southern Ohio, where she found an especially welcome reception in the town of Hamden. Maintaining her modest lifestyle, she has managed to eat, as well as pay the rent and maintain her car payments. For instance, in October 1989 she taped an instrumental with Roni on "Hee Haw" that paid $300, which came to $208 after deductions, but it was enough to cover a month's rent. In between those now-and-then play- or preach-for-pay engagements, Donna visits nursing homes and hospitals and tries to bring cheer and salvation to the infirm. A recent example in which she takes considerable satisfaction occurred when she led her former brother-in-law, Eugene Cox, "to the Lord"; Cox had been hospitalized and diagnosed as having cancer. In the spring of 1989 she met a dental technician named Ben Wilkinson and the two dated a few times. In order to have something to sell on the road, she put together a cassette tape of her gospel songs, vocalizing with sound-track accompaniment. Her fans have generally found it both spiritually comforting and aesthetically pleasing. Donna also recently played mandolin on a record session for Charlie Louvin.

Jim and Mary live nearby. Since Jim's physical condition tends toward the precarious, he hasn't sought outside employment but generally busies himself at a variety of household chores and electrical gadgetry. Mary's children have all grown to adulthood and are on their own, so when they are not playing music, he and Mary are content to live modestly and quietly. Jim does express concern for his daughter Jeannette, whom he hasn't seen for three decades, and he hopes she understands that he neither abandoned nor refused to support her.

Van lives in Smyrna. When not on the road, he worked in a cabinet shop until the fine sawdust created problems for his lungs. He then worked part time at Nissan Motors, the Japanese firm that built a large assembly plant near Smyrna. He and Helen have two grown sons and a daughter, Vickie, still at home.

Van takes considerable pride in the musical development of sons Van, Jr., and Randy, who have a band known as the Stoneman Brothers. Both boys debuted on the CMH double album. Randy subsequently filled in several times for Jimmy in 1982 and 1983, including their appearances on the PTL Club television program. The Stoneman Brothers have done a great deal of club work through central Tennessee and in Nashville. Van notes that while the boys' talents reflect the Stoneman heritage, the music is of their own generation. He describes it as being somewhat akin to that of Larry Gatlin and the Gatlin Brothers and says their harmony is particularly strong. On the personal side, Van, Jr., remains single while Randy and his wife have two children.[8]

As for Roni Stoneman, while she retains more current prominence than the other family members because of her long-running presence on "Hee Haw," she has continued her personal search for stability and happiness. Her spring 1985 marriage to Bill Zimmerman had run its course by the fall of 1986. The following September, she married a paint contractor from Bath County, Kentucky, named Larry Corya in an ostentatious ceremony. Roni worked a lot of festivals and show dates in the summer of 1989, some with her family. That Labor Day weekend, she and Larry sponsored the Scott Stoneman Memorial Fiddler's Contest near Owingsville, Kentucky, with additional entertainment by Nashville friends like Little Jimmy Dickens, Charlie McCoy, and onetime "Hee Haw" girl Dianna Goodman, as well as the Stoneman Family. They expressed hope that it would become an annual event. However, financial difficulties during the winter put the festival's future in doubt. In the recording studios in the fall of 1989, Roni cut sufficient material for both a banjo album and a country album featuring her vocal efforts, subsequently released on cassette. By spring 1991, she announced that she and Larry would terminate their marriage. That September, "Hee Haw" management announced plans for a change in format and dropped Roni and several other longtime stalwarts from the cast.[9]

When Roni's children grew to adulthood, Eugene Cox, Jr., went to work in the design department at Nissan, where his sister Rebecca already worked in personnel. Both married and had children. Bobby Cox has spent some time in what Roni calls "searching for himself." Along the way he trained to become, and briefly worked as, a card dealer in Las Vegas but has more recently been honing his skills as a "flat-pickin's" guitar player often accompanying Roni on stage. Daughter Barbara, a "special child," remains with Roni, and the younger daughter, Hattie Georgia Hemrick, recently got married.

Looking at the Stoneman Family experience in retrospect suggests that for them the myth of the rags-to-riches hillbilly has twice been close to becoming a reality. In two distinct periods, the late twenties and the late sixties, the Stonemans' musical prowess brought them a substantial income and a considerable amount of fame. As a musical dynasty, their longevity ranks somewhat ahead of their fellow Virginians the Carter Family, although in overall acclaim, influence, significance, and success their rating obviously would be somewhat less. Yet while the rags-to-riches image may be no more than a myth for the Stonemans, there can be no doubt that it has sustained them in music through what will soon be seven decades.

So while long-term financial success has eluded the Stonemans, their career accomplishments in the evolution of country music have been considerable. Many—if not in fact most—amateur, semiprofessional, and full-time hillbilly pickers and singers would like to exchange résumés with them if given the opportunity. In the twenties, only a few of the pioneer recording artists could equal or surpass Ernest Stoneman and associates in terms of the quality and quantity of things he did. Likewise, a generation later, Scott Stoneman emerged as a fiddler who combined creativeness, showmanship, and technical skill in a manner that would be virtually unchallenged. By a similar token when the Stonemans arrived on the Music City scene in 1966, the outburst of enthusiasm engendered at the time ranked them as a superb performing unit. Yet like many other show-business personalities, their tenure at the top tended to be relatively brief. While faring better than those individuals who had one hit or one starring role and were never heard from again, the Stonemans found it difficult to sustain long-term success.

Luck is a factor which is difficult to measure, and one can easily argue that in the long run the Stonemans have not been blessed with many runs of good luck. In the short run, it could sometimes work in their favor. For instance, chance undoubtedly played some part in Ernest Stoneman's effort to improve on Henry Whitter's efforts at recording, the victory of the Blue Grass Champs on the Arthur Godfrey show, Scott's fiddling championships, and the business link with Jack Clement at the moment his star began rising in the Nashville establishment. More often than not, however, the Stoneman luck tended to be bad.

Ernest V. Stoneman ranks as an authentic major country-music pioneer whose achievements have been easily documented. Yet beyond his initial use of the Autoharp—an instrument abandoned after a year or so for session work and taken up again in later years—he could hardly be called an innovator. Nonetheless, he did develop clear-set career objectives for himself. Norm Cohen writes that

> of all his recording artist contemporaries, he seemed to be the most sophisticated in managing himself—his many difficulties nothwithstanding. He took initiative in starting the recording process, and acted as an agent for Peer. He learned songs from a variety of sources, from other recordings to scholarly collections. He was, it seems, aware of the importance of what he was doing. On the other hand, as a singer he was, while not so erratic as his friend Henry Whitter, rather uninteresting to urban listeners. He sang a straight and unornamented style—good for getting a ballad across, but without the decorations and nuances of a G. B. Grayson, John Carson, Alfred Reed, Alfred Karnes, or Clarence Ashley.[10]

Once Ernest settled into his position as a self-accompanied vocalist, he reacted to changes initiated by others. When the fuller string band sound, first popularized by Charlie Poole and the North Carolina Ramblers, became fashionable, Stoneman also began working with a group. He sang with a clearer voice than Poole, whose muddled vocals listeners found difficult to comprehend. However, many Stoneman recordings tended to be covers of titles that Poole, Riley Puckett, or some other artist already had on the market. While his ability to cover material, as Charles K. Wolfe has noted, seems to have increased Stoneman's value to the firms for which he cut records, it may have unintentionally limited his capacity for musical creativeness.[11] After 1928, when musical trends began to shift away from string bands toward the blue yodel sounds of Jimmie Rodgers or the group vocals of the Carter Family, Stoneman's career began to lag and the Great Depression temporarily destroyed it. Death probably prevented Poole from suffering a similar fate, and even Rodgers experienced decline before succumbing to "that old TB." Other artists did better; the Carters continued recording, while Uncle Dave Macon and Bradley Kincaid had already become established in radio.

Patsy Stoneman deeply regrets—and justly so—that Ernest V. Stoneman has not been elevated to the Country Music Hall of Fame. Yet she can take some consolation in the fact that other worthy contemporaries, such as Poole, Puckett, Kincaid, Carson, and Mainer's Mountaineers are not there, either. Of the early pioneers, only Rodgers, Macon, the Carters, and Vernon Dalhart are enshrined. Macon's longtime association with the Grand Ole Opry undoubtedly played a key role in his selection. While Dalhart's country credentials have been questioned, one can hardly argue with the influence that his major recordings, such as "The Prisoner's Song," "Wreck of the Old Ninety-Seven," and "The Death of Floyd Collins," had on the development of country music as a cultural phenomenon and a commercial industry. Certainly anyone who has ever searched attics, outbuildings, and junk shops in search of old records can attest to the relative prevalence of his discs as compared with those of his contemporaries. At this point it seems likely that qualified old-timers will become members only when some kind of selection committee, somewhat similar to that which chooses honorees for baseball's hall of fame, made up of people who have been retired for more than twenty-five years, has a hand in the selection process.[12]

The struggle of Pop Stoneman and his family to survive the Great Depression exemplifies the grit and determination that characterized the man's entire life. Whether it typifies the strength that some observers have attributed to Appalachian people cannot be ascertained with certainty here. In his infinite mountain wisdom, Pop plainly summed it up with his simple advice: "Don't Quit."

When the upward mobility the Stonemans experienced raised them from dire to moderate poverty, the children began to emerge as musicians, too. Scott quickly attained a superior status with his fiddling skills, but beyond contest victories and employment as a band member, the fiddler who has made more than a comfortable living from such talent has been rare indeed. Roy Acuff may have attained considerable wealth, but few would link his affluence to his fiddling abilities. In fact, most noted country fiddlers have been people of modest means or even less. No less a personage than Chubby Wise, Scott's principal mentor outside the family circle, has freely admitted that if his wife had not held a regular job, too, the Wise household would have had much difficulty in making ends meet.[13] Chubby speaks of those years when he achieved the most acclaim and influence. In fairness to his employers, Chubby received pay equal to most sidemen. Rare indeed is the sideman who can virtually make a lifelong career with one employer as did Pete "Bashful Brother Oswald" Kirby with Roy Acuff. According to most people who knew and understood Scott Stoneman, his frustration in trying to make a decent living, whether within or without the family band, compounded the personal problems that eventually led to his premature death. He hardly stands as a unique musical genius whose bad habits led him to an early grave. The list runs from Stephen Foster to Hank Williams, Keith Whitley, and Elvis Presley. Some, however, most notably Presley, managed to attain considerable worldly goods. Others, like Scott, received their pay mostly in fancy adjectives and applause from their fans. Perhaps wealth would have been as harmful to Scott as it was to other tragic-hero musicians, but as things turned out, no one will never know.

As the Stonemans developed as a musical group, they also achieved a great deal. Most aspiring—and even retired—country musicians could look at their accomplishments and hope they would do as well. A brief list should suffice to make the point: appearances on a half-dozen prime-time television variety shows or network specials; three and one-half years of successful syndicated television; eight albums on major record labels (M-G-M and RCA Victor); seven more albums on near major labels (Starday, World Pacific, CMH); additional album and single releases for smaller firms; two motion pictures; one Country Music Association Award for Vocal Group of the Year, plus four additional nominations; several CMA nominations for Instrumental Group of the Year; and four trips to England, including one extensive tour.

Yet the Stonemans have not attained long-term commercial success. One is tempted to ask why, or how they could have done things differently. A really big hit record would have helped, but it never came. Between 1966 and 1968, five of their M-G-M singles were charted, but only "The Five Little Johnson Girls" reached the Top Twenty and it just barely made it. Critics in 1967 marveled that the Stonemans had achieved so much without having a major hit. Ernest Tubb had "Walking the Floor over You," Ferlin Huskey had "Gone," Faron Young had "Hello Walls," and the Browns had "The Three Bells." The Stonemans had nothing to compare with them. Pop's early success with "The Titantic" had occurred too long ago to ring mental bells for anyone other than the elderly and the scholars, and they had little influence in determining the hits.

The Stonemans themselves, in retrospect, believe—perhaps correctly—that if they had had better management and had obtained sufficient education to have exercised more control over their own financial affairs, things could be different today. Early would-be managers, such as Billy Barton, had a lot of hope but little else. Bob Bean did as well as he could, but he was not a Nashville insider. Jack Clement helped for a time, but his interests eventually became broader and somewhat overextended at a time (in the period following Pop's death) when dedicated guidance was most needed. A J. L. Frank or a Col. Tom Parker never appeared at a time when the "Children of Ernest" needed him to lead the flock to the "Music City Promised Land." One could hardly find anybody who has more grit and determination, but by the time Patsy really took hold of things, circumstances had deteriorated to the point where the most she could do was prevent further erosion. While inadequate schooling has undoubtedly contributed to their problems, the individual Stonemans have a formal education nearly equal to that of Loretta Lynn, George Jones, and Hank Williams, who managed to do pretty well in the business, although Ms. Lynn has perhaps done better at retaining her earnings. Based on her autobiographical comment on her education, she probably got more out of her training, at least in terms of steady attendance habits, than did some of the other country singers.[14]

Certainly one problem the Stonemans, and indeed all who are part of country ensembles, faced is the simple fact that a five-person group cannot charge a fee five times that of a solo act. The members have to be satisfied with less income than that of an individual star, although hopefully more than that of a sideman. In their best days, each Stoneman received a $250.00 weekly salary, which provided an adequate living in 1968, when the minimum wage reached $1.60 an hour. Average earnings for factory workers in the 1967–71 period increased from $103.00 to $146.00, which suggests that the Stonemans did better than they would have done in the labor force. By the eighties, however, conditions had changed greatly. In no year during that decade did any Stoneman—Roni excepted—earn as much in music as he or she would have made holding down a regular job at the minimum wage of $3.35 an hour. Donna, the one Stoneman who was not part of a two-income nuclear family, estimated her annual income at $5,000.00 for the decade, which included both her music and her church work. Yet in the mid-1980s she could tell someone who was so impressed with her ministry to children that she could have been an excellent elementary teacher (whose beginning salaries in the lower-paying districts were in the range of $15,000) that teaching hardly paid anything. The evidence suggests that the Stonemans have largely sustained themselves on the popular myth of the rags-to-riches country singer, or as journalist Kyle Crichton defined it in a 1938 *Collier's* article, "Thar's Gold in Them Hillbillies." The custom-styled Cadillacs and guitar-shaped swimming pools may be in someone else's garage and backyard, but the Stonemans keep trying. The music that has thus far shaped their lives continues to do thus.

The lack of an easily categorized style has not always been beneficial to the Stonemans. Sometimes they have been considered too country for the bluegrass fan, and too bluegrass for the country fan. At a crucial point in their lives, an effort to gear their appeal to the counterculture may have cost them support with both of these relatively traditional audiences. One might speculate on the question of whether, had they remained Washington based and bluegrass styled in the years when that city began to receive recognition as a bluegrass center, the Stonemans would have enjoyed a status roughly equal to that of the Country Gentlemen. In August 1988 at Massillon, Ohio, when the Stonemans and the Country Gentlemen appeared at the same festival together for the first time in several years, no fan in the audience watched the Stonemans on stage with more interest or reverence than Charlie Waller. Between shows, Waller and Bill Yates reminisced with Patsy and Donna as if they were long-lost brothers and sisters. They all came to musical maturity in the same Washington clubs, and sometimes even on the same stage together. The Country Gentlemen aren't rich, either, but they are among the most active groups on the festival circuit, while the Stonemans make visitations every now and then. Patsy likes to cite as an ideal example

Scott's onetime employer Mac Wiseman, who worked with the family at Las Vegas in 1963. Mac has perpetually straddled the fence between bluegrass and country and nearly always has stayed busy working. That is what she would like for the Stonemans to do, yet it seems an easier task for an individual than for a band.

As a longtime fan and family member outside music, Grace cites what in her opinion constitutes two serious management mistakes. The first was management's rejection of an offer to become Grand Ole Opry regulars in the late sixties. While they may have been doing well without it at the time, the Opry connection has carried many country musicians through slack periods in their careers and would have been equally beneficial to them. The second error occurred when the group did not take Scott back into the band when Roni took leave at the end of 1970. His presence not only would have kept the Stonemans an all-family group, but would have added to the art a degree of charismatic showmanship that no one else could have supplied. He might also have provided some musical stability and direction, which the band needed badly in the early seventies.

What has happened cannot be changed. The Stonemans have long since learned that they must endure the bad times as well as the good. Their Blue Ridge ancestors eked a living from the rugged physical setting where they lived and the intestinal fortitude they gave these descendants enabled them to survive the Great Depression, make the adjustment from pastoral-rural to urban-slum environment, and grapple with the continually fluctuating country-music scene. Patsy reflected on the various aspects of their musical and personal lives in her lyric "Prayers and Pinto Beans," which she composed about 1980:

> When times were gettin' hard, and things were goin' bad,
> We always called upon the ones we knew;
> Mama fed our souls with the Bible and her prayers,
> Then pinto beans and music saw us through.[15]

Along the way, they made some notable achievements but sometimes got rather battered and scarred in the process. However, nothing in the Stoneman experience ever taught them that anything in life would be easy.

Keen observers of the Stonemans have remarked that although Pop possessed a great deal of character strength, the girls exhibited most of his mettle in the succeeding generation. This certainly appears to hold true. Grace survived domestic violence that challenges the imagination, yet she emerged from these experiences with one of the kindest, gentlest dispositions—albeit blunt and outspoken—by nature that one could hope to know. Patsy would seem to be the ultimate survivor, having come through two unfortunate marriages, widowhood, arduous labor, and career reversals with a spirit and determination that would make anyone proud, even Pop Stoneman. One senses that with the Stonemans, she isn't just the mule that pulls the wagon; Patsy also loads, unloads, cleans, repairs, and also trades the old vehicle in on another one when the time comes. She may not pick or sing as well as some of her siblings, but Patsy is the indispensable Stoneman. Donna, via her unflinching faith, has lived through twenty years of life on the margin of economic disaster with a confident, cheerful countenance that should impress even the most unimaginative, unyielding atheist. She has in her possession a snapshot taken in London's Trafalgar Square where she is surrounded by a flock of birds. In her handwriting there is a semihumorous caption on the back about "preaching to pigeons." Chances are that Donna never heard of Saint Francis of Assisi, but the parallels in the picture could convince one that she is roughly a modern female, evangelical, charismatic, Protestant equivalent of that revered medieval figure who, unlike the saint, incidentally plays one heck of a good mandolin. Finally, there is Roni, who took a parody of her own early adult life and turned it into a comic figure that brings laughter to millions on a weekly basis while still searching for long-term stability in her own life.

Yes, the Stoneman women exhibit strength, yet initially some of them were drawn to men who exhibited weakness. Under normal circumstances, none would manifest a belief in divorce, yet they have accumulated ten (at this writing) and have been widowed twice for good measure. But being the kind of people they are, all have taken those ordeals in stride.

Overall, the Stoneman experience in country music in many respects mirrors in microcosm the entire history of the genre. After all, the whole evolution of the music has not been an unqualified success story. Its popularity often ebbs and flows like the tide. Styles change and individual stars come and go. Only a very few manage to stay at or near the top for more than a few years. A man like George Jones, who has had high-ranking hits in five different decades, may be exceptional, but even he has had some low periods within that same time frame. Rare, too, was a Roy Acuff, who has been virtually transformed into a living embodiment of the Grand Ole Opry, even though his major commercial successes all occurred in the forties. Among groups, both the Chuck Wagon Gang and the Sons of the Pioneers thrived for a half-century and more, surviving numerous changes in membership but maintaining a sound and style that changed little. But none has endured quite as long as the Stonemans. Before George Jones was born or Roy Acuff had graduated from high school, Ernest Stoneman made records. After the Sons of the Pioneers sang their last song in a movie, Stoneman was still cutting discs. More than twenty years after his death, his children are still making them. They are also playing shows in locales ranging (in 1989) from New York and Iowa to Florida. They've been on television screens all over the United States and Canada. For a carpenter from Galax, Virginia, who just wanted to prove to himself that he could sing better on a "gramaphone" than some fellow he knew who lived a few miles over the hills down in Fries, this indeed represents a real accomplishment. He didn't invent country music any more than Henry Ford invented the automobile, but like the Michigan mechanic, the Blue Ridge mountaineer did a lot with it. It never made him wealthy, but it gave him a great deal of satisfaction and left his children with a heritage they could carry on in their own way.

Like those of many other Appalachian people, the Stonemans' lives have been filled with problems and difficulty. Along the way they have made some wise decisions and have accomplished some noteworthy achievements. Sometimes their choices did not prove correct, but they managed to accept the negative results, pick up the pieces, and go on as well as they could. As Scott pessimistically wrote in his 1957 lyric "Heartaches Keep On Coming,"

> Once I thought when I got on top
> That all my heartaches there would stop,

But heartaches, kept on a' comin
I traveled far to dodge the strife
That comes along in this old life
But heartaches kept on a' comin'
(Chorus)

First comes the good, then the bad
First you're happy, then you're sad
Things go wrong, things go right,
That's how life goes
But one thing, I really know
It makes no difference where you go
Heartaches kept on a' comin'.

I built a castle big and tall
Filled with dreams from wall to wall
But heartaches kept on a' comin'
Then I saw my castle fall
Tumble down to earth and all
But heartaches kept on a' comin'.[16]

So even though adversity continued moving in their direction, the Stonemans, to borrow a phrase from Pop's contemporary A. P. Carter, endeavored "to keep on the sunny side." Like the children's story about the little engine that could, the Stonemans think they can, and remembering Pop's memorable advice, "Don't Quit," they continue to pick and sing. In his media narration of the Stoneman biography, Nat Winston suggested that as long as there is a Stoneman left to play, they will be there doing their part. If the current generation does not reascend the ladder of success, imagine this scenario in 2006:

The latest Music City sensation is a chubby clawhammer banjo picker named Van Stoneman (nicknamed "Little Pop"), flanked by sons Junior and Randy, and sometimes daughter Vicky and cousin Bobby. Rumor has it that the old gentleman helped pioneer something known as syndicated television.

The tendency might be to label such fantasy as ridiculous, idle results of an infertile imagination, but it is said that history repeats itself, and strange things have happened before. If you don't believe it, check out the files of *Music City News* in 1966. If you want to be really bold, read the front-page commentary in the *Bristol News-Bulletin* for July 27, 1927.

Appendix 1

Two Contrasting Five-Year Periods of Stoneman Economics

Year	Annual Income	Days Worked	Average per date
1968*	$102,167.00	141	$724.58
1969	$114,545.79	134	$862.28
1970	$ 94,189.96	128	$735.86
1971	$ 87,042.15	117	$743.95
1972	$ 98,753.00	135**	$731.50

*Data for 1968 may not be complete.
**Based on assumption that each day of the British tour was a working day.

Year	Annual Income	Days Worked	Average per date
1977	$60,277.50	90 (36)	$ 669.75
1978	$64,544.23	96 (40)	$ 672.34
1979	$52,294.66	74 (20)	$ 706.68
1980	$30,757.93	37 (3)	$ 831.30
1981	$32,230.93	22 (1)	$1401.34

Number in parentheses shows days worked in Canada and how they fell after 1978 and 1979.

Appendix 2

Stoneman Personal
Appearance Schedule, 1969

Date(s)	Place	Gross Income	Net Income*
January 1	Des Moines, Iowa	$1,000.00	$ 750.00
January 4	Philadelphia, Pennsylvania	1,500.00	1,125.00
January 13	Nashville, Tennessee	750.00	600.00
January 17	Nashville, Tennessee	500.00	375.00
January 18	Nashville, Tennessee	750.00	600.00
January 24	Elizabethtown, Ohio	1,000.00	750.00
January 26	Detroit, Michigan	1,000.00	750.00
January 31	Bridgeport, Connecticut	1,000.00	750.00
February 1	Norwalk, Connecticut	1,000.00	750.00
February 11–16	Huntsville, Alabama	2,500.00	2,000.00
February 21	Columbia, South Carolina	1,000.00	750.00
February 22	Columbus, Georgia	1,000.00	750.00
March 10–15	Mason City, Iowa	1,900.00	1,520.00
March 16	Kansas City, Kansas	1,150.00	862.50
March 21	Winston-Salem, North Carolina	1,300.00	975.00
March 23	Saint Louis, Missouri	1,000.00	750.00
March 29	Indianapolis, Indiana	1,000.00	750.00
March 30	Pekin, Illinois	1,000.00	750.00
April 4	San Diego, California	2,000.00	1,500.00
April 5	Los Angeles, California	2,000.00	1,500.00
April 12	Danville, Illinois	1,000.00	750.00
April 13	Louisville, Kentucky	900.00	720.00
April 18	Morristown, Tennessee	850.00	680.00
April 19	Abingdon, Virginia	1,000.00	750.00
April 20	Chattanooga, Tennessee	800.00	640.00
April 23	Due West, South Carolina	1,100.00	800.00
April 26	Charlotte, North Carolina	1,000.00	750.00
May 2	Montreal, Quebec, Canada	850.00	680.00
May 3	Newark, New Jersey	850.00	680.00
May 4	Akron, Ohio	850.00	680.00

Date(s)	Place	Gross Income	Net Income*
May 8	Boston, Massachusetts	850.00	680.00
May 9–10	Providence, Rhode Island	1,700.00	1,360.00
May 11	Toronto, Ontario, Canada	850.00	680.00
May 13	Kingston, Ontario, Canada	850.00	680.00
May 14	Kitchener, Ontario, Canada	850.00	680.00
May 15	Brantford, Ontario, Canada	850.00	680.00
May 16	Erie, Pennsylvania	850.00	680.00
May 17	Rochester, New York	850.00	680.00
May 18	Hartford, Connecticut	850.00	680.00
May 21	Peterboro, Ontario, Canada	850.00	680.00
May 22	Ottawa, Ontario, Canada	850.00	680.00
May 23	Syracuse, New York	850.00	680.00
May 24	Buffalo, New York	850.00	680.00
May 25	Scranton, Pennsylvania	850.00	680.00
May 30	Fort Lauderdale, Florida	1,000.00	800.00
May 31	Miami, Florida	1,000.00	800.00
June 1	Miami, Florida	1,000.00	800.00
June 7	Reinholds, Pennsylvania	1,100.00	880.00
June 8	Columbus, Ohio	1,150.00	920.00
June 14	Charleston, West Virginia	1,000.00	800.00
June 20	Clinton, New York	1,000.00	800.00
June 21	Greenwich, Connecticut	1,000.00	800.00
June 22	Cuyahoga Falls, Ohio	1,000.00	800.00
June 28	Fort Worth, Texas	1,000.00	800.00
July 4	Anderson, Indiana	700.00	560.00
July 5	Decatur, Alabama	1,000.00	800.00
July 6	Chattanooga, Tennessee	800.00	640.00
July 9	Campbellsville, Kentucky	1,150.00	920.00
July 13	West Grove, Pennsylvania	1,000.00	800.00
July 19	Lancaster, Pennsylvania	1,000.00	800.00
July 20	West Mifflin, Pennsylvania	1,000.00	800.00
July 22	Shippensburg, Pennsylvania	850.00	680.00
July 23	Lexington, Kentucky	1,000.00	800.00
July 24	Urbana, Illinois	1,000.00	800.00
July 27	Franklin, Ohio	1,000.00	800.00
July 28–31	Toronto, Ontario, Canada	1,740.00	1,479.00
August 1–2	Toronto, Ontario, Canada	870.00	739.50
August 6	Brownstown, Indiana	1,000.00	800.00
August 8	Wichita, Kansas	1,250.00	1,000.00
August 9	Freemont, Indiana	1,150.00	920.00
August 14	Springfield, Ohio (Fair & TV Tape)	1,736.08	1,418.17
August 16	Salisbury, Maryland	1,000.00	800.00
August 20	Anna, Illinois	1,150.00	920.00

Date(s)	Place	Gross Income	Net Income*
August 29	Bushnell, Illinois	1,150.00	920.00
August 30–31	Lincoln, Nebraska	2,000.00	1,600.00
September 4–5	Huntsville, Alabama	1,700.00	1,360.00
September 6	Cleveland, Tennessee	1,000.00	800.00
September 7	Beanblossom, Indiana	850.00	680.00
September 12	Concord, North Carolina	1,150.00	920.00
September 13	Philadelphia, Pennsylvania	1,000.00	800.00
September 14	West Springfield, Massachusetts	1,000.00	800.00
September 20	Lebanon, Ohio	1,125.00	900.00
September 23	Lawrenceburg, Tennessee	1,000.00	800.00
September 25	New Burgh, New York	1,000.00	800.00
September 26	Kingston, New York	1,000.00	800.00
September 27	Glen Falls, New York	1,000.00	800.00
October 4	Milwaukee, Wisconsin	1,000.00	800.00
October 5	Paris, Illinois	1,150.00	920.00
October 6–8	Birmingham, Alabama	3,000.00	2,400.00
October 11	New Albany, Indiana	1,200.00	960.00
October 16	Nashville, Tennessee	66.00	66.00
October 29	Crab Orchard, Kentucky	700.00	560.00
October 30	Greenville, Tennessee	750.00	600.00
October 31	Danville, Virginia	800.00	640.00
November 1	Lancaster, Pennsylvania	1,000.00	800.00
November 7	Jackson, Kentucky	900.00	720.00
November 8	Virgie, Kentucky	900.00	720.00
November 9	Paintsville, Kentucky	900.00	720.00
November 9	Ashland, Kentucky	85.00	68.00
November 13	Green Bay, Wisconsin	1,000.00	800.00
November 14	Madison, Wisconsin	1,000.00	800.00
November 29	Tupelo, Mississippi	280.00	280.00
November 30	Nobelsville, Indiana	1,250.00	1,000.00
December 5	Kingsport, Tennessee	1,000.00	800.00
December 6	Salisbury, Maryland	1,000.00	800.00
December 7	Uniontown, Pennsylvania	600.00	480.00
December 11–13	Atlanta, Georgia	1,500.00	1,200.00
December 15–20	Mason City, Iowa	2,200.00	1,680.00

*Net income reflects the amount remaining for the Stonemans after booking fees and other agency charges had been subtracted.

Appendix 3

Genealogical Charts

Ancestor Chart of Ernest Stoneman

James Stoneman (1735–1829)

Sarah Freeman (1751–1844)

John Hickman

Elizabeth ??

Amos Lundy, Sr. (1743–????)

Ann Collins

George Bowers (1786–1856)

m. 1809

Sarah Short (1792–182?)

Allen Porter

Margaret Porter

"Quaker" John Stoneman (1792–1874)

Elizabeth Hickman (1792–1886)

Amos Lundy, Jr.

Mary Bedsaul

William Bowers (1813–????)

m. 1833

Rebecca Porter (1818–187?)

Martin Stoneman (1812–83)

m. ca. 1840

Eliza Lundy (1820–1900)

Daniel Bowers (1845–????)

Sally ?? (1848–1923)

Elisha Stoneman (1849–1934)

m. (2) 1891

Rebecca Bowers (1868–96)

John William Frost (1866–1952)

m. (2) 1898

Martha Ann Melton (1870–1959)

Ernest V. Stoneman (1893–1968)

m. November 10, 1918

Hattie Frost (1900–1976)

The Ernest and Hattie Stoneman Family

Note: The rest of the twenty-three Stonemans were either stillborn, died in infancy, or miscarried. Abbreviations: b. = born; c. = children; d. = died; m. = married

Ernest Van Stoneman	married 11–10–1918	**Hattie Frost**
b. 5–25–1893		b. 9–28–1900
d. 6–14–1968		d. 7–22–1976

Named children

1	**2**	**3**
Eddie Lewis Stoneman	**Irma Grace Stoneman**	**John Catron Stoneman**
b. 6–30–1920	b. 8–29–1921	b. 8–20–1923
m. Katherine Copeland	m. (1) Jack Jewell	m. Bonnie Deeta Yeary
c. Douglas	c. William	c. John
Barbara	Steven	Stanley
Wayne	m. (2) George Jewell	
	c. Donna Kay	
	m. (3) James Dugan	

4	**5**	**6**
Pattie Inez Stoneman	**Joseph William Stoneman**	**Anna Juanita Stoneman**
b. 5–27–1925	b. 11–4–1926	b. 1927
m. (1) Charles Streeks	d. 4–10–1990	d. 1932
m. (2) R. Horace Cain	m. Barbara Brooks	
m. (3) Donald Dixon	c. Gary	
m. (4) John J. Murphy, Jr.	Jody	
	Michael	
	Joseph	

7	**8**	**9**
Jack Monroe Stoneman	**Gene Austin Stoneman**	**Dean Clark Stoneman**
b. 5–10–1929	b. 6–12–1930	b. 6–12–1930
d. 4–14–1992	m. Peggy Edlin	d. 2–28–1989
m. (1) Anna Todd James	c. Robin	m. Faye Casper
m. (2) Nola Story		c. Teresa
		Darrell
		Debbie
		Laurel
		Julia

10	11	12
Calvin Scott Stoneman	**Donna LaVerne Stoneman**	**Oscar James Stoneman**
b. 8–4–1932	b. 2–7–1934	b. 3–8–1937
d. 3–4–1973	m. Bob Bean	m. (1) Peggy Brain
m. (1) Cecile Phipps		c. Jeanette
c. Sandra		m. (2) Mary Grubb
m. (2) Paula Brogan		Urich
m. (3) Ann ??		
m. (4) Mary Madison		
c. Ernest Scott		
Faith Kerin		

13	14	15
Rita Vivian Stoneman	**Veronica Loretta Stoneman**	**Van Haden Stoneman**
b. 3–8–1937	b. 5–5–1938	b. 12–31–1940
d. 6–12–1937	m. (1) Eugene Cox	m. Helen Alvey
	c. Eugene, Jr.	c. Van, Jr.
	Rebecca	Randolph
	Barbara	Victoria
	Robert	
	m. (2) George Hemrick	
	c. Hattie Georgia	
	m. (3) Richard Adams	
	m. (4) William Zimmerman	
	m. (5) Larry Corya	

The Elisha and Drake Stoneman Families

Note: Only family members mentioned in the text are included on this chart.

Martin and Eliza Lundy Stoneman

Elisha Stoneman 1849–1934

m. (1) Lauretta Montgomery, July 23, 1871 (1853–88)

m. (2) Rebecca Bowers, July 16, 1891 (1868–96)

  c. Ernest Van (1893–1968)

    Ingram Boyd (1894–1973)

    Talmer (1896–1916)

m. (3) Susan Bowers Wells, May 12, 1904 (1880–19??)

Legally separated, August 20, 1913

Stephen Drake Stoneman 1861–1944

m. Lydia Bowers, May 27, 1880 (1859–19??)

  c. Emory Burton (1881–1956)

    George (1882–1966)

m. (1) Emma Bruner

  c. Willie (1907–67)

m. (2) Lillian Fortner

  c. Glenn

    Elmer

    Lawrence (1885–1900)

    Bertha (Hawks) (1886–1983)

    Myrtle (Hawks) (1894–1986)

Notes

Chapter 1: Galax, August 1985

1. All the incidents described herein were observed by Ivan and Deanna Tribe at Galax, Va., August 7 and 8, 1985.

Chapter 2: Prelude to Country Music Pioneerdom

1. John Perry Alderman, *Carroll 1765–1815: The Settlements* (Roanoke, Va.: Alderman Books, 1985), p. 222.

2. The information in the following interview and letters is garbled and inconsistent; however, the part about the kidnapped indentured servant forms a common thread, although the time, place of origin, place of destination, and even the name in question vary: Eugene Earle, taped interview with Ernest V. Stoneman, Los Angeles, Calif., March 27, 1964 (hereafter cited as Earle interview) (copy in Tribe collection); Daughters of the American Revolution, application for membership of Margaret Keller, April 12, 1923 (copy in Tribe collection); letters: Evan C. Stoneman to Ramona Aslinger, February 22, 1974; Thelma J. Bjorklund to Ramona Aslinger, July 27, 1979; Ramona Aslinger to Patsy Stoneman, September 26, 1979; Kent Stoneman to Ivan M. Tribe, February 24, 1987 (copies of all letters in Tribe collection).

3. Quoted in James Horn, "Servant Emigration to the Chesapeake in the Seventeenth Century," in Thad W. Tate and David L. Ammerman, eds., *The Chesapeake in the Seventeenth Century: Essays on Anglo-American Society* (New York: W. W. Norton & Co., 1979), pp. 56–57.

4. See David W. Galenson, *White Servitude in Colonial America: An Economic Analysis* (New York: Cambridge University Press, 1981), pp. 220–27, for data on the known destinations of indentured servants.

5. Alderman, *Carroll 1765–1815*, p. 222; Elvyn Stoneman, "James Stoneman" (one-page sheet distributed at Stoneman reunions since 1988). According to the 1790 census schedules, James Stoneman still resided in Orange County.

6. Alderman, *Carroll 1765–1815*, p. 222.

7. Ibid.; Grayson County, Virginia, *Wills*, vol. 2, pp. 4–5 (Court House, Independence, Va.).

8. Kent Stoneman to Tribe, January 26, 1987, with genealogical charts attached; B. F. Nuckolls, *Pioneer Settlers of Grayson County, Virginia* (Bristol, Tenn.: King Printing Co., 1914), p. 205.

9. Ibid.

10. Kent Stoneman to Tribe, January 26, 1987.

11. Alderman, *Carroll 1765–1815*, pp. 219–20.

12. Anecdotes related to Tribe by Grace and Patsy Stoneman, Nashville, Tenn., March 25, 1987. All interview and other orally transmitted material has been given to Ivan M. Tribe except where otherwise noted.

13. John P. Alderman, comp., *1850 Census: Annotated, Carroll County Virginia* (Hillsville, Va.: J. P. Alderman, 1979), pp. iii–iv, 66, 82–83, 102–3.

14. Ibid., pp. 1–107. Here the text compares the Stonemans to all the other households in Carroll County.

15. U.S. Census Office, *Eighth Census* (1860), "Population Schedules," Sulphur Springs Dist., Carroll Co., Va.; U.S. Census Office, *Ninth Census* (1870), "Population Schedules," Sulphur Springs Dist., Carroll Co., Va.; Kent Stoneman to Tribe, January 26, 1987.

16. For a look at delegate Hale, see Nuckolls, *Pioneer Settlers of Grayson*, pp. 119–20; for Virginia in the secession crisis, see Louis D. Rubin, *Virginia: A Bi-Centennial History* (New York: W. W. Norton & Co., 1977), p. 128. For a good perspective on the disruptions caused by the Civil War in the Appalachians, see Philip Shaw Paluden, *Victims: A True Story of the Civil War* (Knoxville: University of Tennessee Press, 1981).

17. Patsy Stoneman, interview, Cherokee, N.C., July 8, 1985; Kent Stoneman, telephone interview, Barre, Vt., January 22, 1987.

18. Kent Stoneman to Tribe, January 26, 1987; *U.S. Census* (1870), Sulphur Springs Dist., Carroll Co., Va.; Carroll Co., Va., Marriages, vol. 1, p. 27 (Court House, Hillsville, Va.).

19. Carroll Co., Marriages, vol. 1, pp. 50, 80; Alderman, *1850 Census*, p. 89.

20. Carroll Co., Births, 1891–96, pp. 56, 82 (Court House, Hillsville, Va.); Irma Grace Stoneman, autobiographical typescript, pp. 3–4 (hereafter cited as I. G. Stoneman, autobiography) (Stoneman Papers); Stella Stoneman Rutledge to Tribe, February 26, 1987.

21. Rutledge to Tribe, February 26, 1987.

22. Grayson Co., Va., Marriages, vol. 2, p. 110 (Court House, Independence, Va.); Carroll Co., Va., Deed Book, vol. 37, p. 556 (Court House, Hillsville, Va.); Veronica Stoneman, interview, Nashville, Tenn., December 13, 1985. A copy of the separation agreement is in the Stoneman Papers.

23. Bob Jennings, taped interview with Ernest V. Stoneman, Nashville, Tenn., December 29, 1967 (hereafter cited as Jennings interview) (Country Music Foundation Oral History Collection, Nashville, Tenn.)

24. Ibid.; Patsy Stoneman, interview, July 8, 1985.

25. Rosa Landreth Cox, interview, Hillsville, Va., July 22, 1988.

26. Bill C. Malone, *Country Music U.S.A.*, rev. ed. (Austin: University of Texas Press, 1985), p. 17. For a West Virginia dance description, see Ivan M. Tribe, *Mountaineer Jamboree: Country Music in West Virginia* (Lexington: University Press of Kentucky, 1984), p. 2.

27. Elizabeth Lomax, recorded interview with Emmett W. Lundy, Galax, Va., 1941 (Library of Congress, AFS Recording 4938) (All subsequent Lundy quotes are from this interview). See also Andy Cahan, "Introduction," *The Old Time Way: The Music and Times of Luther Davis, Roscoe Parish, Leone Parish* (Galax, Va.: Heritage Records, 1986), pp. 1–4.

28. Elizabeth and John Lomax, recorded interview with Emory Burton Stoneman, Galax, Va., 1941 (Library of Congress AFS Recording 4936) (all subsequent Burton Stoneman quotes are from this interview).

29. Elizabeth Lomax, recorded interview with George W. Stoneman, Galax, Va., 1941 (Library of Congress AFS Recording 4937) (all subsequent George Stoneman quotes are from this interview). For viewpoints of various rural folk on the fiddle, see Malone, *Country Music U.S.A.*, pp. 13, 17.

30. Ronald D. Eller, *Miners, Millhands, and Mountaineers: Industrialization of the Appalachian South, 1880–1930* (Knoxville: University of Tennessee Press, 1982), pp. 16–22.

31. For a description of mountain farming in an adjacent county of the Virginia Blue Ridge, see Kinney Rorrer, *Rambling Blues: The Life and Songs of Charlie Poole* (London: Old Time Music Books, 1982), pp. 25–27.

32. Eller, *Miners, Millhands, and Mountaineers*, pp. 69–75.

33. Talmer Stoneman tombstone, Iron Ridge Cemetery, Carroll County, Va.; Kent Stoneman, interview, January 22, 1987.

34. Eller, *Miners, Millhands, and Mountaineers*, pp. 124–26; Pete Daniel, *Standing at the Crossroads: Southern Life in the Twentieth Century* (New York: Oxford University Press, 1986), pp. 42–44, 103–4.

35. Ernest Stoneman said in his 1964 interview with Eugene Earle that he "worked in the cotton mill" with Henry Whitter, which I interpret to mean that this labor was done as a mill operative, in contrast to other statements about working "on a cotton mill," referring to carpentry or other construction labor.

36. For varying perspectives on the "discovery" of Appalachia, see Eller, *Miners, Millhands, and Mountaineers*; Henry David Shapiro, *Appalachia on Our Mind: The Southern Mountains and Mountaineers in the American Consciousness* (Chapel Hill: University of North Carolina Press, 1978); and David E. Whisnant, *All That Is Native and Fine: The Politics of Culture in an American Region* (Chapel Hill: University of North Carolina Press, 1983).

37. *The Galax-Carroll-Grayson Story* (Lynchburg, Va.: Progress Publishing, 1983), pp. 30–31.

38. *Roanoke Times*, November 27, 1902.

39. Patsy Stoneman, interview, July 8, 1985.

40. *Galax-Carroll-Grayson Story*, pp. 30–31.

41. Ibid., pp. 23, 27, 41.

42. For the effects of manufactured instruments on rural culture, see Malone, *Country Music U.S.A.*, pp. 24–26.

43. Jennings interview.

44. Ibid.

45. Ibid.; for perspectives on the influence of Gilded Age songwriters on early country musicians, see Malone, *Country Music U.S.A.*, pp. 15–16.

46. Jennings interview.

47. Ibid.

48. Ibid.

49. Patsy Stoneman, "Patsy Remembers" in *From Then . . . Until Now* (N.p.: n.p., 1985), p. 3.

50. Alderman, *Carroll 1765–1815*, 308–9; Alderman, *1850 Census: Carroll County*, p. 45; Grayson County, Marriages, vol. 2, p. 89.

51. Bolen, J. William, and Martha Frost, tombstones, Ballard Cemetery, Galax, Va.

52. I. G. Stoneman, autobiography, p. 2; Patsy Stoneman, autobiographical typescript, pp. 1–5 (hereafter cited as P. Stoneman, autobiography); Donna L. Stoneman, autobiographical typescript, pp. 1–3 (hereafter cited as D. L. Stoneman, autobiography); Veronica "Roni" Stoneman, autobiographical typescript, pp. 2–3 (hereafter cited as R. Stoneman, autobiography) (all autobiographies in Stoneman Papers).

53. Jennings interview; Archie Green, Doyle Moore, Richard Spottswood, interview with Ernest V. and Hattie Stoneman, Carmody Hills, Md., December 29, 1962 (hereafter cited as Green interview) (copy provided by R. Spottswood); Rutledge to Tribe, February 26, 1987.

54. Jennings interview.

55. I. G. Stoneman, autobiography, p. 1; Patsy Stoneman, interview, July 8, 1985. While Grace and Patsy are in general agreement that their father took an occasional nip from the jug prior to his marriage, both emphatically deny that an anecdotal yarn concerning his drinking which was told to me by Eddie Stoneman at Galax on August 7, 1985, ever took place.

56. I. G. Stoneman, autobiography, pp. 1, 22; Eddie Stoneman, autobiographical manuscript, p. 1 (hereafter cited as E. Stoneman, autobiography) (Stoneman Papers).

Chapter 3: The Golden Years

1. Earle interview; Jennings interview.

2. Archie Green, "Hillbilly Music: Source and Symbol," *Journal of American Folklore* 78:309 (July–September 1965), pp. 208–10; Malone, *Country Music U.S.A.*, pp. 37–39.

3. Earle Interview.

4. Ibid.

5. Ibid.

6. For detailed data on Ernest Stoneman's early recordings, see Norman Cohen, Eugene W. Earle, and Graham Wickham, *The Early Recording Career of Ernest V. "Pop" Stoneman: A Bio-Discography*, J E M F Special Series, No. 1 (Los Angeles: John Edwards Memorial Foundation,

1968), pp. 8–18. All future discographic discussions come from this source, with minor corrections. An updated discography is appended to this work.

7. Earle interview; lyrics transcribed from "The Titanic," OKeh 40288 (reissued on *The Smithsonian Collection of Classic Country Music*).

8. Earle interview; Green interview.

9. Earle interview.

10. Willard Johnson, taped interview with Ernest V. Stoneman, Minneapolis, Minn., September 22, 1966 (hereafter cited as Johnson interview) (copy in Tribe collection); Jennings interview.

11. Joseph Murrells, *Million Selling Records: From the 1900s to the 1980s* (New York: Arco Publishing, 1984), p. 20; Joel Whitburn, *Pop Memories, 1890–1954* (Memononee Falls, Wis.: Record Research, 1986), p. 415; For the best discussion concerning sales of early records, see the persuasive arguments of Norm Cohen, "Early Pioneers," in Bill C. Malone and Judith McCulloh, eds., *Stars of Country Music* (Urbana: University of Illinois Press, 1975), pp. 4–5, 21–23, and Norm Cohen, *Long Steel Rail: The Railroad in American Folksong* (Urbana: University of Illinois Press, 1981), pp. 32–34.

12. Green, "Hillbilly Music: Source and Symbol," pp. 211, 212–14.

13. Cohen, *Long Steel Rail*, pp. 321–25; Cohen et al., *The Early Recording Career of Ernest Stoneman*, pp. 4–8; Lee Kahle Brewer, interview, Galax, Va., June 12, 1985; Tony Russell, *Emmett W. Lundy: Fiddle Tunes from Grayson County, Virginia* (String LP 802, 1977), liner notes.

14. Earle interview. For Macon's comments on the song's origin, see *Songs and Stories of Uncle Dave Macon* (Nashville: WSM Radio, 1938), No. 15.

15. Herman K. Williams, *The First Forty Years of the Old Fiddler's Convention* (Galax, Va.: n.p., ca. 1978), 106.

16. For a reproduction of the Carter Family handbill, see John Cohen and Mike Seeger, eds., *The New Lost City Ramblers Song Book* (New York: Oak Publications, 1964), p. 106; the Grayson and Whitter one is in the collection of Gleaves Harmon, Woodlawn, Va., reproduced in Kip Lornell, *Virginia's Blues, Country & Gospel Records, 1902–1943: An Annotated Discography* (Lexington: University Press of Kentucky, 1989), p. 209.

17. Rorrer, *Rambling Blues*, p. 29.

18. Ibid., pp. 29–31, 73, 78.

19. Cohen, *Long Steel Rail*, pp. 275–82; Johnson interview; typed copies of both of these songs are in the Stoneman Papers.

20. Earle interview; W. T. Miller to Ernest Stoneman, May 6, 1926 (Stoneman Papers). For more on Carper, see Elbert L. Marshall, *The Bell Spur String Band* (Heritage LP 047, 1984), liner notes.

21. For reproductions of the OKeh Catalog photographs, see Cohen and Seeger, *The New Lost City Ramblers Song Book*, pp. 152, 202; I. G. Stoneman, autobiography, p. 1; Grace Stoneman, interview, Nashville, Tenn., December 14, 1985. Copies of the letterheads are in the Stoneman Papers.

22. Cohen et al., *The Early Recording Career of Ernest Stoneman*, p. 9; For lyrics to "He's Going to Have a Hot Time By and By," see OKeh 45062.

23. Earle interview.

24. Ibid.; Brewer interview, June 12, 1985.

25. Earle interview; Ernest V. Stoneman to Alfred Frankenstein, August 6, 1929 (reproduced in Cohen, *Long Steel Rail*, pp. 68–69).

26. Earle interview.

27. Cohen, *Long Steel Rail*, pp. 351–54; Starr Piano Co. to Ernest V. Stoneman, Royalty Statements, July 1, 1928, April 1, 1929 (Stoneman papers); "Sweet Bunch of Violets" (typescript in Stoneman Papers); "Kenny Wagner's Surrender" (photostat of typescript in Stoneman Papers).

28. Earle interview.

29. Green interview; Cohen and Seeger, eds., *New Lost City Ramblers Song Book*, p. 103; Pete Daniel, *Deep'n as It Come: The 1927 Mississippi River Flood* (New York: Oxford University Press, 1977), p. 6.

30. Earle interview.

31. Grace Stoneman, interview, December 14, 1985.

32. Carroll Co. Va., Marriages, vol. 1, p. 150; Callie Frost Dunford, tombstone, Old Quaker Cemetery, Galax, Va.; Oscar Hall (secretary of Galax Old Fiddler's Convention and former neighbor of Alex Dunford), Galax, Va., July 10, 1986.

33. Charles K. Wolfe, "Ralph Peer at Work: The Victor 1927 Bristol Sessions," *Old Time Music* 5 (Summer 1972), pp. 10–15; *Bristol Herald-Courier*, July 24, 1927, p. 3.

34. *Bristol Herald-Courier*, July 24, 1927, p. 3.

35. Ibid., p. 6.

36. "The Mountaineer's Courtship," transcribed from Victor 20880 (reissued on *Ernest V. Stoneman: With Family and Friends, Vol. 2*, Old Homestead OH CS 173).

37. *Bristol News-Bulletin*, July 27, 1927, p. 1.

38. Cohen et al., *The Early Recording Career of Ernest Stoneman*, p. 12; Wolfe, "Ralph Peer at Work," pp. 12–14.

39. Wolfe, "Ralph Peer at Work," pp. 13–15. In his own account of the discovery of Jimmie Rodgers—the Rodgers myth having become so persuasive by 1953—Peer did not even mention Stoneman; see Ralph Peer, "Discovery of the 1st Hillbilly Great," *Billboard* 65:20 (May 16, 1953), p. 20.

40. W. T. Miller to Ernest V. Stoneman, July 11, 1927 (Stoneman Papers).

41. Typescripts for WGBS Radio (Stoneman Papers); Jennings interview.

42. Grayson Co. Va., Deeds, vol. 58, pp. 471–72 (Court House, Independence, Va.); Earle interview; P. Stoneman, autobiography, p. 6; I. G. Stoneman, autobiography, p. 1.

43. I. G. Stoneman, autobiography, p. 1.

44. Rutledge to Tribe, February 26, 1987.

45. P. Stoneman, autobiography, p. 6. For data on worker income in Virginia, see Paul F. Brissenden, *Earnings of Factory Workers 1899 to 1927: An Analysis of Pay Roll Statistics* (Washington: Government Printing Office, 1929), p. 388. By contrast, the U.S. average was $1,280 and for West Virginia, $1,312. For Virginia in 1914, it had been $436.

46. P. Stoneman, autobiography, p. 5.

47. I. G. Stoneman, autobiography, p. 1.

48. Rutledge to Tribe, February 26, 1987.

49. Ibid.; I. G. Stoneman, autobiography, p. 1.

50. Ibid. pp. 3–4.

51. Rutledge to Tribe, February 26, 1987; Patsy Stoneman, interview, July 8, 1985.

52. Earle interview; Green interview.

53. Earle interview.

54. For background on "The East Bound Train," see Cohen, *Long Steel Rail*, pp. 316–20; for "There'll Come a Time," see Rorrer, *Rambling Blues*, p. 73.

55. Earle interview.

56. For background on "The Midnight Special," see Cohen, *Long Steel Rail*, p. 586.

57. Earle interview.

58. Ibid.; "The Fate of Shelly and Smith" (typescript in Stoneman Papers).

Chapter 4: Depression and Disaster

1. Earle interview; Fields Ward, *Fields Ward and the Buck Mountain Band* (Historical LP 8001, 1967), liner notes; see also John Coffey, "Fields Ward," *Old Time Herald* 1:4 (May–July 1988), pp. 12–16.

2. Earle interview; *Winston-Salem Journal*, March 15, 1968, p. 6. For the Jenkins experience with Woltz, see Richard Nevins, *DaCosta Woltz's Southern Broadcasters, 1927* (County LP 510, 1972), liner notes.

3. Green interview; Earle interview. For background on Crawford and his poems, see the booklet by Mildred Fielder, *Captain Jack Crawford, Poet and Military Scout* (Deadwood, S.D.: Centennial Distributors, 1983).

4. Earle interview. A test pressing of both "I'll Be All Smiles Tonight" and "In the Year of Jubilo" has recently surfaced, and the former title has been released on album. Stoneman sang it to a tune which differs from the more familiar arrangement.

5. Oscar Jenkins resurfaced in the late sixties, participating in two albums with Tommy Jarrell and Fred Cockerham, *Down to the Cider Mill* (County LP 713) and *Back to the Blue Ridge* (County LP 723). Like his father, Oscar displayed equal skills on both banjo and fiddle.

6. Jack M. Stoneman, autobiographical manuscript, p. 1 (hereafter cited as J. Stoneman, autobiography) (Stoneman Papers). Sales figures for

the Victor 40,000 series recordings in possession of Professor Charles K. Wolfe, Middle Tennessee State University, Murfreesboro, Tenn. (via David Freeman, Floyd, Va.); for data on the Carter and Rodgers sales, see Cohen, *Long Steel Rail*, pp. 33–34.

7. P. Stoneman, autobiography, p. 6.

8. Ibid., p. 7.

9. H. A. Melton to Whom It May Concern, January 27, 1930 (Stoneman Papers); *Winston-Salem Journal*, March 15, 1968, p. 6.

10. Walter Couch, interview, North Wilkesboro, N.C., July 21, 1988.

11. Gene Austin Stoneman, autobiographical typescript, p. 1 (hereafter cited as G. A. Stoneman, autobiography) (Stoneman Papers); Carroll Co. Va., Deeds, vol. 12, pp. 179, 486 (Court House, Hillsville, Va.); Grayson Co. Va, Deeds, vol. 63, p. 39 (Court House, Independence, Va.). Despite the Stonemans' property loss, they still lived in what had been their home when Nita died in May 1932 and when Scott was born on August 4 of that year.

12. P. Stoneman, autobiography, pp. 7–8.

13. Ibid., p. 8.

14. Ibid.

15. Ibid.

16. Green interview; two fragments of these radio scripts survive in the Stoneman Papers.

17. *Grayson-Carroll Gazette* (Galax, Va.), February 29, 1932, p. 1.

18. "The Little Lost Eagle," sheet music (Stoneman Papers).

19. Jennings interview; Green interview.

20. Rutledge to Tribe, February 26, 1987; P. Stoneman, autobiography, pp. 8–9. Elisha Stoneman lived with Ingram, except for a few brief months at a home for the elderly, until he died at Elbert, W. Va., on June 6, 1934. His funeral was held at the home of Bertha Hawks near Woodlawn, Va.; Ernest arrived just after the funeral. Stella Rutledge recently found a fragment of a letter in which he tried to seek admission to the Carroll County Home ("poorhouse" in vernacular English). Ironically, he was refused admission because he was considered a West Virginia resident at the time, despite having spent nearly his whole life in Carroll County.

21. I. G. Stoneman, autobiography, p. 5.

22. Ibid.

23. P. Stoneman, autobiography, p. 10.

24. Ibid., p. 11.

25. Ibid.; Railway Postal Service, Chief Clerk to Ernest V. Stoneman, December 16, 1932 (Stoneman Papers).

26. P. Stoneman, autobiography, pp. 11–12.

27. E. Stoneman, autobiography, p. 2.

28. Ibid., p. 3.

29. Earle Interview.

30. P. Stoneman, autobiography, p. 12.

31. Ibid., p. 13.

32. Ibid., pp. 12–13.

33. Ibid. p. 14; Green, "Hillbilly Music: Source and Symbol," pp. 214, 227.

34. I. G. Stoneman, autobiography, pp. 8–9.

35. P. Stoneman, autobiography, p. 15.

36. Ibid., pp. 16–17.

37. Ibid., pp. 18–19.

38. I. G. Stoneman, pp. 9–10.

39. P. Stoneman, autobiography, pp. 18–19.

40. Ibid., p. 16.

41. Ibid., p. 20.

42. Ibid., p. 21.

43. Ibid.

44. Ibid., pp. 21–23; Oscar James (Jimmy) Stoneman, autobiographical typescript, p. 1 (hereafter cited as O. J. Stoneman, autobiography) (Stoneman Papers).

45. P. Stoneman, autobiography, p. 24.

46. Ibid.; I. G. Stoneman, autobiography, p. 10.

47. P. Stoneman, autobiography, pp. 25–26.

48. Ibid., p. 26.

49. Ibid.

50. "Pair, 11 Children Face Eviction and Starvation," *Washington Times,* undated clipping, ca. March 1938 (Stoneman Papers).

51. P. Stoneman, autobiography, p. 27.

52. Ibid., pp. 28–30.

53. Ibid., pp. 30–32; I. G. Stoneman, autobiography, p. 10; Grace Stoneman, interview, December 14, 1985.

54. Quoted in Boris Weintraub, "A Musical Circle Unbroken," *Washington Star,* May 18, 1979, p. G1.

55. P. Stoneman, autobiography, p. 31.

56. Ibid., p. 32; Weintraub, "A Musical Circle Unbroken," p. G1. In his autobiography (p. 3), Eddie concedes only to have been champion in the local Golden Gloves tourney in the 112-pound class (flyweight).

57. P. Stoneman, autobiography, pp. 37–38; Patsy Stoneman, telephone interview, Nashville, Tenn., July 30, 1987. Patsy's written narrative becomes somewhat confused (pp. 33–37); the telephone interview clarified much of this.

58. P. Stoneman, autobiography, pp. 37, 40; Patsy Stoneman, telephone interview, July 30, 1987.

59. E. Stoneman, autobiography, p. 4; Stoneman, autobiography, p. 41.

60. Ibid.; Van H. Stoneman, autobiographical typescript, p. 1 (hereafter cited as V. H. Stoneman, autobiography) (Stoneman Papers).

61. P. Stoneman, autobiography, p. 43.

62. Ibid.

63. Ibid., p. 44.
64. Ibid.
65. Ibid., pp. 33–37.
66. Ibid., pp. 44, 48.
67. Patsy Stoneman, interviews, Nashville, Tenn., December 13 and 14, 1985; Patsy Stoneman, telephone interview, July 30, 1987.
68. P. Stoneman, autobiography, p. 45.
69. Ibid., p. 46.

Chapter 5: The Road to Recovery

1. P. Stoneman, autobiography, p. 44.
2. Ibid., pp. 44–45.
3. E. Stoneman, autobiography, pp. 4–6.
4. I. G. Stoneman, autobiography, p . 11; Grace Stoneman, interview, December 14, 1985.
5. I. G. Stoneman, autobiography, p. 11.
6. Ibid.
7. Ibid., pp. 11–13.
8. Patsy Stoneman, telephone interview, Nashville, Tenn., July 18, 1988 (Patsy secured this information in a phone call to Deeta Yeary Stoneman earlier that day).
9. P. Stoneman, autobiography, p. 60.
10. Ibid.
11. Ibid.
12. Ibid., p. 61.
13. Ibid., p. 62.
14. Patsy Stoneman, "Joseph William Stoneman," pp. 1–3 (typescript in Stoneman Papers); I. G. Stoneman, autobiography, pp. 20–21; Joseph William Stoneman, Military Service Discharge (copy in Stoneman Papers).
15. P. Stoneman, autobiography, p. 49.
16. Donna Stoneman, autobiographical tape (Stoneman Papers).
17. Ibid.
18. Ibid.; O. J. Stoneman, autobiography, pp. 2–3.
19. P. Stoneman, autobiography, p. 53. For accounts of the career of Connie B. Gay, see Chet Hagan, *Country Music Legends in the Hall of Fame* (Nashville: Thomas Nelson, 1982), pp. 228–34, and Joe Sasfy, "The Hick from Lizard Lick," *Journal of Country Music* 12:1 (1987), pp. 16–24, 33.
20. Donna Stoneman, autobiographical tape; O. J. Stoneman, autobiography, p. 10.
21. P. Stoneman, autobiography, p. 62.
22. Ernest V. Stoneman to Ralph Peer, November 8, 1948 (Stoneman Papers).
23. Ernest V. Stoneman, Maryland State Income Tax Return, 1950 (copy in Stoneman Papers).

24. R. Stoneman, autobiography, p. 12; reverse side of several photographs in the Stoneman Papers. The *Life* photographer is believed to have visited the Stoneman home on August 18, 1948.

25. Donna Stoneman, autobiographical tape.

26. E. Stoneman, autobiography, pp. 7–12.

27. I. G. Stoneman, autobiography, pp. 12–13.

28. Ibid., pp. 22–23; Patsy Stoneman, telephone interview, July 18, 1988.

29. P. Stoneman, autobiography, pp. 62–64, 73, 77.

30. Ibid., pp. 67–82.

31. Ibid., p. 54; Donna Stoneman, autobiographical tape.

32. Bill Bassin, interview, Nashville, Tenn., March 7, 1987; J. Stoneman, autobiography, pp. 28–30; Roni Stoneman to Patsy Stoneman, December 3, 1957 (Stoneman Papers); P. Stoneman, autobiography, p. 49.

33. G. A. Stoneman, autobiography, pp. 7–13.

34. Dean Clark Stoneman, autobiographical typescript, pp. 6–12 (hereafter cited as D. C. Stoneman, autobiography) (Stoneman Papers).

35. Ibid., pp. 6–12; Dean Stoneman, interview, Hillsville, Va., July 23, 1988.

36. Donna Stoneman, taped interview, Milton, W. Va., September 4, 1982; Robert R. "Chubby" and Rossi Wise, taped interview, Mount Vernon, Ky., July 10, 1976.

37. For an excellent account of the D.C. area in the early to mid-1950s, as it involved Scott Stoneman, Buzz Busby, and Jack Clement, see Rhonda Strickland, "Buzz Busby: A Lonesome Road," *Bluegrass Unlimited* 21:5 (November 1986), pp. 16–29. Discussions with other Stonemans, Peter "Zeke" Dawson, Eddie Stubbs, Pete Kuykendall, and Cecile Howard have also influenced this all too brief text.

38. See R. Stoneman, autobiography, p. 10, for the only written account of the incident involving Scott and the piano, but it is an oft-told verbal anecdote related by many of Scott's former associates. For Scott's marriage to Cecile, see Cecile Howard, telephone interview, Owings, Md., August 13, 1988.

39. Donna Stoneman, autobiographical tape; D. L. Stoneman, autobiography, p. 21.

40. Ibid., pp. 9–21; I. G. Stoneman, autobiography, p. 21.

41. D. L. Stoneman, autobiography, pp. 22–23.

42. Ibid., pp. 24–25.

43. O. J. Stoneman, autobiography, pp. 2–5.

44. Ibid., pp. 7–8. Dr. Nat Winston, in his narration on the Stoneman Family slide presentation, tells the story of the whumper in somewhat more detail.

45. Donna Stoneman, autobiographical tape. I have relied on Donna's extensive recollection of the entire Barton episode here, and it has been generally substantiated in conversations with Jimmy Stoneman and a March 28, 1990, telephone interview with Billy Barton, who had recently returned to Nashville. The latter is currently writing his autobiography.

46. For data on the King session, see Mike Ruppli, comp., *The King Label* (Westport, Conn.: Greenwood Press, 1985), p. 83.

47. R. Stoneman, autobiography, pp. 7–8.

48. Ibid., p. 10.

49. Ibid., p. 15.

50. Ibid., p. 16.

51. Ibid., pp. 18–19.

52. Ibid., pp. 21–22, 23–24.

53. I. G. Stoneman, autobiography, p. 24; V. H. Stoneman, autobiography, p. 1.

54. V. H. Stoneman, autobiography, pp. 2–3; Peter "Zeke" Dawson, taped interview, Nashville, Tenn., December 13, 1985.

55. Ernest V. Stoneman, Federal Income Tax Return, 1953 (copy in Stoneman Papers).

Chapter 6: Struggling Upward

1. Donna Stoneman, autobiographical tape; Oscar James Stoneman, telephone interview, Nashville, Tenn., July 26, 1988.

2. Donna Stoneman, autobiographical tape; see also Fred Geiger, "Porter Church," *Bluegrass Unlimited* 20:7 (January 1986), pp. 46–50. The quote from Bomstein comes from his introduction of the Blue Grass Champs on CBS television when the group appeared on "Arthur Godfrey's Talent Scouts" (videotape copy in Stoneman Papers).

3. Neil Rosenberg, *Bluegrass: A History* (Urbana: University of Illinois Press, 1985), pp. 112–13, 149.

4. For historical perspective on the TV quiz-show fad, see Eric Goldman, *The Crucial Decade—And After* (New York: Vintage Books, 1960), pp. 324–25, and Ronald Oakley, *God's Country: America in the Fifties* (New York: Dembmer Books, 1990), pp. 409–12.

5. I. G. Stoneman, autobiography, p. 17; P. Stoneman, autobiography, p. 96; "Pop Stoneman Strives for TV's Biggest Jackpot" (feature article in Naval Gun Factory employee newsletter, ca. March 1956, Stoneman Papers).

6. *Galax Gazette*, March 8, 1956.

7. "No Frills for Pop" (unidentified newspaper clipping in the Stoneman Papers).

8. The audio portion of Stonemans' three final visits to "The Big Surprise" were recorded by Pop's fellow old-time musician Tony Alderman and preserved in the Alderman Collection at the Smithsonian. The dialogue that preceded the questions was scripted, as a portion of them is preserved in the Stoneman Papers. The Stonemans insist that Pop's part in the quiz show was not rigged, although they do think that when the show people tired of his presence the quizmaster asked a question that they correctly felt was almost certainly beyond his capacity to answer.

9. Veronica Stoneman, interview, Hillsville, Va., July 30, 1989; Peter "Zeke" Dawson, interview, Wellston, Ohio, July 30, 1988; *Galax Gazette,* August 2, 9, 1956. A portion of the Little Pebbles group's playing at the convention has been preserved in the Alderman Collection, although not the number used in competition.

10. Patsy Stoneman, interview, Hillsville, Va., July 21, 1988; Peter "Zeke" Dawson, interview, July 30, 1988.

11. Cecile Howard, telephone interview, August 13, 1988; Robert Bean, telephone interview, Nashville, Tenn., August 10, 1988.

12. Donna Stoneman, autobiographical tape; Geiger, "Porter Church," p. 47; videotape of "Arthur Godfrey's Talent Scouts."

13. Donna Stoneman, autobiographical tape.

14. Donna Stoneman, telephone interview, Nashville, Tenn., July 26, 1988; Oscar James Stoneman, telephone interview, Nashville, Tenn., July 26, 1988.

15. O. J. Stoneman, autobiography, p. 5; Patsy Stoneman, interview, July 21, 1988.

16. Donna Stoneman, autobiographical tape.

17. Ibid.; Geiger, "Porter Church," pp. 47–49; Oscar James Stoneman, telephone interview, July 26, 1988; Patsy Stoneman, interview, July 21, 1988.

18. Donna Stoneman, autobiographical tape.

19. Ibid.; Peter "Zeke" Dawson, interview, July 30, 1988; Robert Bean, telephone interview, August 10, 1988. In addition, several tapes of the audio portion of "The Don Owens T.V. Jamboree" from WTTG-TV have been preserved in the collections of Leon Kagarise, Baltimore, Md., and Joe Bussard, Frederick, Md. The discussion of the Stoneman repertoire from this period derives from listening to these tapes.

20. Doug Adkins, taped interview, Oak Hill, Ohio, October 7, 1987; Rosenberg, *Bluegrass: A History,* pp. 112–13; Donna Stoneman, telephone interview, Nashville, Tenn., August 6, 1988.

21. V. H. Stoneman, autobiography, p. 3.

22. Richard K. Spottswood, telephone interview, August 1, 1988. For a look at Don Owens, see H. Conway Gandy, "Don Owens: The Washington D.C. Connection," *Bluegrass Unlimited* 22:5 (November 1987), pp. 68–72. According to Donna, Jimmy, and Van, Don Owens taped virtually every live show the Champs played during this period. However, Owens perished in an April 21, 1963, auto accident and the tapes seem not to have survived.

23. A demo disc of Pop's rendition of "Will You Be Loving Another Man," Peter V. Kuyendall Collection, Alexandria, Va.

24. See "Haunted House"/"Heartaches Keep On Coming," Bakersfield 45-121; "Hand Me Down My Walking Cane"/"Jubilee March," Blue Ridge 45-504; *Country Favorites with Jimmy Dean [and] The Stoneman Family* (Wyncote LP 9032, 1964).

25. See *American Music-Folk* (Folkways FP 253 No. 64, 65).

26. See *The Stoneman Family: Old Time Tunes of the South* (Folkways FA 2315).

27. See *American Banjo Scruggs Style* (Folkways FA 2314).

28. Peter "Zeke" Dawson, interview, July 30, 1988.

29. Ibid.; R. Stoneman, autobiography, p. 24.

30. Ibid., pp. 25–26.

31. Ibid., p. 25.

32. Ibid., p. 26.

33. Ibid.

34. Ibid., pp. 26–27.

35. Ibid., p. 27.

36. Ibid.

37. Ibid., p. 28.

38. Ibid.; Veronica Stoneman, telephone interview, Smyrna, Tenn., August 8, 1988.

39. V. H. Stoneman, autobiography, pp. 3, 9.

40. Van H. Stoneman, telephone interview, Smyrna, Tenn., August 1, 1988.

41. Peter "Zeke" Dawson, interview, July 30, 1988.

42. The following account of the Stonemans' initial Nashville experience relies on Donna Stoneman, autobiographical tape; Billy Barton, telephone interview, Nashville, Tenn., March 28, 1990.

43. V. H. Stoneman, autobiography, p. 6.

44. Grant Turner, interview, Nashville, Tenn., December 13, 1985.

45. A copy of the master tape for Scott's fiddle album was given to Patsy Stoneman by Billy Barton's daughter. It has been released on cassette and is scheduled for album release.

46. See the Ken Nelson files from Capitol Records (Country Music Foundation Library and Media Center, Nashville, Tenn.) and Neil V. Rosenberg, *Bill Monroe and His Blue Grass Boys: An Illustrated Discography* (Nashville, Tenn.: Country Music Foundation, 1974), p. 111.

47. Donna Stoneman, interview, September 4, 1982.

48. Donna Stoneman, autobiographical tape; V. H. Stoneman, autobiography, pp. 4–5; Van Stoneman, telephone interview, Smyrna, Tenn., August 4, 1988; Robert Bean, telephone interview, August 10, 1988. For background on Don Pierce and his company, see William Henry Koon, "Grass Roots Commercialism," *J E M F Quarterly* 7:1 (Spring 1971), pp. 5–11.

49. Robert Bean, telephone interview, August 10, 1988.

50. Starday Records, Microfilmed Ledgers (Country Music Foundation Library and Media Center, Nashville, Tenn.).

51. *Washington Star,* ca. August 1962 (undated clipping in Stoneman Papers); Pop's certificate for second place (Stoneman Papers); Veronica Stoneman, telephone interview, Smyrna, Tenn., August 9, 1988.

52. National Folk Festival (brochure in Stoneman Papers); Jack Clement, taped interview, Nashville, Tenn., December 13, 1985; Robert Bean, telephone interview, August 10, 1988.

53. *Daily Illini* (Urbana, Ill.), May 22, 1963.

54. University of Illinois, Voucher No. 5633; Work Contracts, May 5, 1963, and July 25, 1963 (all in Stoneman Papers).

55. P. Stoneman, autobiography, pp. 80–84.

56. Patsy Stoneman, Work Ledgers, 1963–64 (Stoneman Papers).

57. P. Stoneman, autobiography, pp. 84–86.

58. Van Stoneman, telephone interviews, Smyrna, Tenn., August 1 and 4, 1988.

59. Starday Ledgers; *Washington Post Magazine*, November 3, 1963, p. 1. See also *The Great Old Timer at the Capitol* (Starday LP 275, 1964).

60. V. H. Stoneman, autobiography, pp. 4–5; Van Stoneman, telephone interviews, August 1 and 4, 1988; *Las Vegas Sun*, October 23, 1963, p. 11, October 26, 1963, pp. 9–10.

61. V. H. Stoneman, autobiography, pp. 5–6.

62. Donna Stoneman, autobiographical tape; Jack Clement, interview, December 13, 1985; Eugene Cox, telephone interview, Nashville, Tenn., August 16, 1988.

Chapter 7: The Golden Years—Again

1. Jack Clement, interview, December 13, 1985; O. J. Stoneman, autobiography, p. 5.

2. Jack Clement, interview, December 13, 1985; Veronica Stoneman, interview, Nashville, Tenn., December 13, 1985; Work Contracts, March 1964 (Stoneman Papers).

3. Jack Clement, interview, December 13, 1985. See also "Big Ball in Houston"/ "Little Maggie" (Folk Festival 1140, 1964).

4. Earle interview. The contract with Clement is dated April 14, 1964 (Stoneman Papers).

5. *Billboard*, August 1, 1964, p. 60. See *The Stoneman Family: Big Ball in Monterey* (World-Pacific LP 1828, 1964).

6. D. K. Wilgus, "Current Hillbilly Recordings: A Review Article," *Journal of American Folklore* 78:309 (July–September 1965), p. 285.

7. Tape of the Stoneman portion of the Steve Allen Show (provided by Leon Kagarise); AFTRA Contract between Ernest V. Stoneman and Rinimar Corporation for "Texaco Star Parade Starring Meredith Willson," June 15, 1964 (Stoneman Papers). See also *TV Guide*, May 2–8, 1964.

8. Donna Stoneman, telephone interview, Nashville, Tenn., August 14, 1988. Show dates from this period have been compiled from surviving copies of work contracts (Stoneman Papers).

9. Veronica Stoneman, interview, December 13, 1985; Donna Stoneman, telephone interview, August 14, 1988.

10. Donna Stoneman, telephone interview, August 14, 1988.

11. Donna Stoneman, autobiographical tape; check stubs from the Dean show (Stoneman Papers); for an assessment of Dean and his network exposure, see Malone, *Country Music U.S.A.*, p. 272.

12. Equitable Bank and Trust Company to the Stoneman Family, December 28, 1964 (Stoneman Papers).

13. Patsy Stoneman, Account Book, 1964–68 (Stoneman Papers).

14. Donna Stoneman, interview, August 14, 1988; P. Stoneman, autobiography, pp. 87–88.

15. P. Stoneman, autobiography, 87–88; Patsy Stoneman, telephone interview, Nashville, Tenn., August 15, 1988; *Rocky Mountain News* (Denver), January 22, 1965, pp. 78–79.

16. Donna Stoneman, telephone interview, August 14, 1988; Compilation of Work Contracts, 1965 (Stoneman Papers).

17. Donna Stoneman, autobiographical tape; Patsy Stoneman, telephone interview, August 15, 1988.

18. Rodney Dillard, interview, Owensboro, Ky., November 14, 1991. Dillard discussed the connections between Andy Griffith and bluegrass musicians generally at this meeting.

19. P. Stoneman, autobiography, pp. 87–88.

20. Ibid., p. 90.

21. Ibid., pp. 89–91.

22. Alex Tottle, *Scotty Stoneman: Live in L.A. with the Kentucky Colonels* (Sierra Briar SBR LP 4206), back and inside liner; The Rounder Collective, *The Kentucky Colonels* (Rounder LP 0070); Neil V. Rosenberg, "The Flatt and Scruggs Discography: The Columbia Recordings, 1965–1969," *The Journal of Country Music* 13:3 (1990), p. 32.

23. Donna Stoneman, telephone interview, August 14, 1988; Patsy Stoneman, telephone interview, August 15, 1988. See also "The Martian Band"/ "May I Sleep in Your Barn Tonight, Mister," (J E D Record 10,019).

24. Eugene Cox, telephone interview, August 16, 1988.

25. Jack Clement, interview, December 13, 1985.

26. Ibid.; Veronica Stoneman, interview, December 13, 1985. The news heralding the Stonemans' forthcoming stint at the Black Poodle was in the Sunday Showcase section of the *Tennesseean* (Nashville), October 31, 1965, p. 26S.

27. V. H. Stoneman, autobiography, pp. 6–7.

28. Ibid.

29. Ibid.

30. Patsy and Donna Stoneman, interview, Berea, Ky., October 28, 1988.

31. *Music City News* (Nashville), April 1966, p. 2; *Record World*, ca. April 1966 (undated clipping in Stoneman Papers).

32. *Music City News*, May 1966, pp. 1, 3.

33. Ibid., June 1966, p. 15.

34. Reviewed from Program No. 4, "The Stonemans" (syndicated television, videocassette copy in Stoneman Papers). Patsy also has copies of some thirty-seven other programs in the series.

35. *Nashville Banner,* April 2, 1966, p. 11; *Music City News,* May 1966, p. 9.

36. *Chattanooga News–Free Press,* April 7, 1966. See also *Those Singin', Swingin', Stompin', Sensational Stonemans* (M-G-M LP 4363, 1966).

37. Clarence Peterson, "The Big New Sound of Country Music," *Chicago Tribune Sunday Magazine,* May 29, 1966, pp. 1, 20–23, 26–30; *Music City News,* June 1966, pp. 15, 23.

38. Donna Stoneman, interview, August 14, 1988; V. H. Stoneman, autobiography, p. 7.

39. Bill Brittain, "Dateline . . . Music City" (undated clipping in the Stoneman Papers); Tandy Rice, News Release, June 17, 1966 (Stoneman Papers).

40. Joel Whitburn, *Top Country Singles 1944–1988: Compiled from Billboard's Country Charts* (Menomonee Falls, Wis.: Record Research, Inc., 1989), p. 313.

41. *Minneapolis Star,* September 14, 1966, p. 8F; Johnson interviews, September 22, 1966, February 17, 1967, November 26, 1967.

42. For Patsy Stoneman's appearances at the Black Poodle, see unidentified news clippings in the Stoneman papers (probably from the entertainment section of one of the Nashville papers). See also "Big Wheel in Nashville"/ "You're Gonna Wonder about Me," (J E D Record 10,012).

43. *The Road to Nashville* (Robert Patrick Productions, 1967) (videocassette copies in Stoneman Papers and Tribe collection).

44. *Nashville Banner,* June 14, 1967, p. 16. Unlike *The Road to Nashville,* no private copy of *Hell on Wheels* has surfaced for review examination.

45. This and subsequent M-G-M recording data supplied by the Country Music Foundation Library and Media Center; all released recordings have been reviewed.

46. All personal-appearance data for 1967 and 1968 have been compiled from available copies of work contracts (Stoneman Papers).

47. Death dates for Burton and George Stoneman furnished by Kent Stoneman from genealogical charts in his possession. For George Stoneman's awards at Galax, see Williams, *First Forty Years of the Old Fiddler's Convention,* pp. 15–26, 35, 38–39, 46–53, 105.

48. Patsy Stoneman, telephone interview, Nashville, Tenn., June 28, 1989.

49. Donna Stoneman, autobiographical tape.

50. Whitburn, *Top Country Singles,* p. 313.

51. Country Music Association Awards, October 20, 1967 (program in Stoneman Papers); Donna Stoneman, autobiographical tape.

52. Jennings interview; Bill Littleton, taped interview with Maybelle Carter and Ernest V. Stoneman, Nashville, Tenn., February 1, 1968

(Country Music Foundation Library and Media Center, Nashville, Tenn.). For Littleton's comments based on this interview, see *Country*, April 1968, pp. 6–7.

53. Patsy Stoneman, telephone interview, Nashville, Tenn., July 6, 1989; Donna Stoneman, autobiographical tape.

54. *Winston-Salem Journal*, March 15, 1968, p. 6. Although Jenkins is not mentioned in the news article, there is general agreement that he and Oscar got together during this North Carolina tour. It was also during this tour that Roni met her second husband, George Hemrick, when the Stonemans furnished entertainment in the congressional campaign of James White.

55. Quoted in Thurston Moore, ed., "The End of a Career—The Beginning of Some Memories: The Story Behind the Pop Stoneman Memorial Album on M-G-M," *The Country Music Who's Who* (Denver: Heather Enterprises, Inc., 1970), pt. 7, p. 41.

56. Ibid.; Donna Stoneman, autobiographical tape; *Music City News*, May 1968, p. 18.

57. Moore, "The End of a Career," pt. 7, p. 41; P. Stoneman, autobiography, p. 92.

58. Work Contract, May 14–18, 1968 (Stoneman Papers).

59. Leslie Rubenstein, *The Great Stonemans* (M-G-M LP 4578, 1968), backliner notes.

60. Paul Soelberg to Patsy Stoneman, June 7, 1968 (Stoneman Papers).

61. Ibid.

62. Donna Stoneman, autobiographical tape. Lengthy articles on Ernest Stoneman's death appear in *Cashbox*, June 29, 1968, pp. 55, 60; *Record World*, June 29, 1968, pp. 50–51; and *Music City News*, July 1968, pp. 1, 7, as well as both the *Nashville Banner*, June 15, 1968, and the *Tennesseean*, June 15, 1968. Briefer notices appeared in such metropolitan dailies as the *Los Angeles Times*, June 16, 1968, p. G5, and the *New York Times*, June 15, 1968, p. 35.

63. Alice Gerrard to Stoneman Family, June 15, 1968; Ralph Rinzler to Stoneman Family, June 15, 1968; Mike Seeger to Stoneman Family, June 15, 1968; Al Brown Family to Stoneman Family, June 15, 1968; Memorial Funeral Book of Ernest V. Stoneman (all in Stoneman Papers).

64. Memorial Funeral Book of Ernest V. Stoneman.

65. Patsy Stoneman, autobiography, p. 92; *Record World*, July 20, 1968, p. 44.

66. For a newspaper account of the Stoneman appearance on network TV, see "Network Welcomes 'Music City West' " (undated clipping, ca. August 1968, in the Stoneman Papers).

67. Promotional Sheets for "Christopher Robin" (Stoneman Papers); Whitburn, *Top Country Singles*, p. 313.

68. *Record World*, September 14, 1968, p. 52, October 12, 1968, p. 51; *Billboard*, September 14, 1968.

69. The date of Donna's comment about Monroe's adding the extra hundred dollars is uncertain; she repeated it at my request. Donna Stoneman, telephone interview, Nashville, Tenn., November 27, 1991.

70. *Billboard*, December 7, 1968, p. 72; Al Freeders, "The Stoneman Family Captures Season's Mood," *Dayton Leisure*, December 22, 1968, p. 14.

71. M-G-M Royalty Statements (Stoneman Papers).

Chapter 8: Living Without Daddy

1. Jennings interview; Patsy Stoneman, telephone interview, Nashville, Tenn., July 12, 1989.

2. E. Stoneman, autobiography, pp. 9–12; G. A. Stoneman, autobiography, p. 13; D. C. Stoneman, autobiography, pp. 9–10; Patsy Stoneman, telephone interview, July 12, 1989.

3. I. G. Stoneman, autobiography, pp. 20–21.

4. Patsy Stoneman, telephone interview, Nashville, Tenn., July 21, 1989.

5. J. M. Stoneman, autobiography, pp. 31–35; Bill Bassin, interview, March 25, 1987.

6. Bill Bassin, "Scott Stoneman," *Bluegrass Unlimited* 4:6 (December 1969), p. 11; Patsy Stoneman, telephone interview, July 21, 1989.

7. I. G. Stoneman, autobiography, pp. 12–14; Grace Stoneman, telephone interview, July 19, 1989.

8. I. G. Stoneman, autobiography, pp. 13–15.

9. P. Stoneman, autobiography, pp. 92–93.

10. R. Stoneman, autobiography, pp. 28–29; Veronica Stoneman, telephone interview, Smyrna, Tenn., July 14, 1989; Patsy Stoneman, telephone interview, Nashville, Tenn., July 13, 1989.

11. Don Rhodes, *Down Country Roads with Ramblin' Rhodes* (Hartwell, Ga.: North American Publications, Inc., 1982), pp. 128–30; Roni also relates this story on U.S. Air Force Recruiting Service, "Country Music Time," Program No. 391 (ca. 1975).

12. For this and all subsequent data on the Stoneman work schedule and finances from 1969 through 1972, see Bean, Murphy, and Soelberg, Account Book, 1969–72 (Stoneman Papers).

13. Moore, "The End of a Career," pt. 7, p. 41; M-G-M Royalty Statements.

14. *Billboard*, December 21, 1968, p. 64; M-G-M Royalty Statements.

15. Jack Clement, taped interview, December 13, 1985. For a contemporary look at Jack Clement, see John Grissim, *Country Music: White Man's Blues* (New York: Paperback Library, 1970), pp. 194–99. Sheb Wooley (as Ben Colder) gives an embellished version of the Clement-Talbot escapade in "Country Music Hall of Fame" on *Harper Valley P.T.A.* (M-G-M LP 4614, ca. 1969).

16. *Record World*, May 17, 1969, pp. 74, 76.

17. Paul Soelberg to Jack Clement, March 14, 1969 (Stoneman Papers).

18. Ada Soelberg to Bob Bean, June 1, 1971 (Stoneman Papers); John Murphy, telephone interview, Nashville, Tenn., July 15, 1989; *Billboard*, May 17, 1969, p. 52, May 24, 1969, p. 53; *Record World*, May 17, 1969, pp. 74, 76, May 24, 1969, p. 63. The Ada Soelberg loan to Bean, Murphy, and Soelberg was dated July 28, 1969.

19. Patsy Stoneman, interview, December 12, 1985; *Record World*, August 9, 1969, p. 64; *Music City News*, September 1969, p. 12. All RCA Victor discographic data provided by Country Music Foundation Library and Media Center.

20. Ed Kahn, *Dawn of the Stonemans' Age* (RCA Victor LSP 4264, 1970), liner notes.

21. *San Francisco Examiner*, January 24, 1970, p. 12; *Billboard*, April 4, 1970, p. 20; Donna Stoneman, autobiographical tape; Patsy Stoneman, telephone interview, Nashville, Tenn., July 26, 1989.

22. *Record World*, May 9, 1970, p. 64; *Country Corner*, April 1970, p. 5; *Coast FM and the Fine Arts*, July 1970 (clipping in Stoneman Papers).

23. See *In All Honesty* (RCA Victor LSP 4343, 1970).

24. Bean, Murphy, and Soelberg, Annual Report, 1970 (Stoneman Papers).

25. Jack Clement, taped interview, December 13, 1985.

26. Patsy Stoneman, interview, Hillsville, Va., July 22, 1989.

27. Donna Stoneman, autobiographical tape; R. Stoneman, autobiography, p. 29; Holiday Inn of Mason City, Iowa, to Bob Bean, March 30, 1971 (Stoneman Papers).

28. R. Stoneman, autobiography, p. 29; Donna Stoneman, autobiographical tape; Donna Stoneman, interview, Hillsville, Va., July 22, 1989.

29. Capitol Records, Recording Contract with the Stonemans, January 16, 1971 (Stoneman Papers); Robert Bean, interview, Nashville, Tenn., December 12, 1985. See also the Bean, Murphy, and Soelberg Account Book.

30. Bean, Murphy, and Soelberg, Account Book; John Murphy, interview, Nashville, Tenn., July 15, 1989.

31. Patsy and Donna Stoneman, interviews, Hillsville, Va., July 29, 1989.

32. Donna Stoneman, telephone interview, Nashville, Tenn., August 1, 1989; Patsy Stoneman, telephone interview, Nashville, Tenn., August 2, 1989.

33. Compiled from correspondence between the Stonemans and Buena Vista Records and royalty statements from the same, 1971–82 (Stoneman Papers). See also *Country Bear Jamboree* (Disneyland LP 3994, 1972).

34. Million Records, Recording Contract with the Stonemans, June 30, 1972 (Stoneman Papers).

35. Bean, Murphy and Soelberg, Account Book; Donna Stoneman, telephone interview, August 1, 1989; Patsy Stoneman and John Murphy, telephone interview, August 2, 1989.

36. Donna Stoneman, telephone interview, August 1, 1989; David Dougherty, telephone interview, London, Ky., August 2, 1989. See also "The Touch of the Master's Hand"/"Blue Ridge Mountains" (Million 45-#32, 1972).

37. Dougherty, telephone interview, August 2, 1989. See also *Live at Wembley* (N A L LP 5005, ca. 1973).

38. Cathy Manzer, interview, Nashville, Tenn., December 12, 1985; Donna Stoneman, autobiographical tape.

39. Donna Stoneman, autobiographical tape.

40. *Bluegrass Summer '73* (Festival Edition of *Muleskinner News*), p. 88; Patsy Stoneman, telephone interview, August 2, 1989; Dougherty interview, August 2, 1989.

41. Patsy Stoneman, taped interview, Milton, W.Va., September 4, 1982; *Tennesseean*, March 5, 1973, pp. 1, 14; *Nashville Banner*, March 5, 1973, p. 7.

42. Bob Bean to "Friend," March 19, 1973 (Stoneman Papers).

43. Dougherty, interview, August 2, 1989; *Bluegrass Unlimited* 7:12 (June 1973), p. 15.

44. Bob Bean to Merwyn Conn, August 29, 1973 (Stoneman Papers); Douglas B. Green, "Noboru Morishige," *Bluegrass Unlimited* 8:12 (June 1974), pp. 26–28.

45. Dougherty, telephone interview, August 2, 1989.

46. Quoted in Don Rhodes, "Roni Stoneman," *Bluegrass Unlimited* 11:11 (May 1977), pp. 13–17.

47. *Bluegrass Unlimited*, June 1973, p. 15; Donna Stoneman, autobiographical tape.

48. Donna Stoneman, autobiographical tape; Donna Stoneman, telephone interview, August 1, 1989.

49. Ibid. See also *I'll Fly Away* (Temple LP 7706, 1976).

50. *Bluegrass Unlimited* 13:2 (August 1978), p. 34. See also *Country Hospitality* (R P A LP 1019, ca. 1977).

51. *Bluegrass Unlimited* 11:10 (April 1977), p. 23; *Bluegrass Unlimited* 12:10 (April 1978), p. 62. See also *Cuttin' the Grass* (C M H LP 6210, ca. 1976), and *On the Road* (C M H LP 6219, ca. 1977).

52. Donna Stoneman, autobiographical tape; Donna Stoneman, taped interview, September 4, 1982; *Tennesseean*, July 24, 1976, p. 1; *Nashville Banner*, July 24, 1976, p. 17; Memorial Funeral Book of Hattie F. Stoneman (Stoneman Papers).

53. Memorial Funeral Book of Hattie F. Stoneman.

54. Patsy Stoneman, telephone interview, August 1, 1989. For background on Eddie Mueller, see M. E. Vogel and N. E. Nondrik, "Eddie and the Mueller Brothers," *Bluegrass Unlimited* 10:1 (July 1975), pp. 40–44.

55. P. Stoneman, autobiography, pp. 94–95.

56. Ibid. p. 95; Work Contracts, 1977–78 (Stoneman Papers). Neil Rosenberg discussed the significance of the Canadian Cultural Preservation Act at a conference in Meridian, Miss., on May 26, 1989.

57. P. Stoneman, autobiography, p. 95.

58. Weintraub, "A Musical Circle Unbroken," p. G1; quoted in Randall Armstrong, "The Stonemans," *Bluegrass Unlimited* 14:12 (June 1980), p. 70.

59. Armstrong, "The Stonemans," pp. 70–72; Waterford, Ontario, Lions Club to President of the United States, July 16, 1980 (copy in Stoneman Papers).

60. *Congressional Record,* July 30, 1980, p. E3677; Bill Boner to Patsy Stoneman, July 29, 1980; Howard H. Baker, Jr., to Patsy Stoneman, August 8, 1980; Lamar Alexander to the Stoneman Family, August 1, 1980 (all in Stoneman Papers).

61. Patsy Stoneman to Paul Wells, July 18, 1981 (copy in Stoneman Papers). See also *The First Family of Country Music* (C M H 2LP 9029, 1982).

62. David Freeman, "County Sales Newsletter # 120," August–September 1983, p. 3.

63. *Bluegrass Unlimited* 17:4 (October 1982), p. 23.

64. John Morefield, "Stonemans and Cardinals on C M H," *Appalachian Journal* 10:3 (Spring 1983), pp. 307–9.

65. Donna Stoneman, autobiographical tape.

66. Ibid.

67. Ibid.

68. R. Stoneman, autobiography, pp. 32–33. Roni and Richard Adams separated in the spring of 1984 and initiated divorce proceedings.

69. R. Stoneman, autobiography, pp. 30–32.

70. P. Stoneman, autobiography, p. 95; "The Stonemans: First Family in Music, Their Story," Slide-Sound Presentation, narrated by Dr. Nat Winston, ca. 1981.

71. Marvin Kaye, *The Grand Ole Opry Murders* (New York: E. P. Dutton and Co., 1974).

72. Donna Stoneman, autobiographical tape; story related by the Reverend Howard Shively to Ivan M. Tribe, McArthur, Ohio, May 2, 1987.

73. Dougherty, interview, August 2, 1989; Lifetime Achievement Commendation, Shenandoah College, September 7, 1984 (Stoneman Papers).

74. Unidentified Stoneman Family fan, interview, Cana, Va., July 29, 1989.

75. Many of the formative discussions that led to the writing of this book took place during the initial weeks the Stonemans spent in Cherokee during the summer of 1985.

Conclusion: An Update and a Retrospect

1. Since most of the events described in this chapter took place while the text was in preparation, documentation has been minimal.

2. Doug Stoneman, interview, Owingsville, Ky., September 3, 1989. Doug also provided most of the updated information concerning Billy Stoneman and family (except his death and funeral).

3. Grace Stoneman, interview, Owingsville, Ky., September 3, 1989.

4. J. M. Stoneman, autobiography, pp. 34–35.

5. Patsy quoted in "Letter to Editor," *Bluegrass Unlimited* 23:10 (April 1989), p. 16; Gene Stoneman quoted in one of Donna's evangelistic newsletters (Stoneman Papers).

6. Sandra Stoneman Humphreys, telephone interview, Lusby, Md., August 13, 1988.

7. *Precious Memories* 2:3 (September–October 1989), p. 37; *Bluegrass Unlimited* (October 1989), p. 61.

8. Van H. Stoneman, interview, Owingsville, Ky., September 3, 1989.

9. In the winter of 1989–90, Roni and Larry had financial reversals that put the future of their park in doubt; see the Associated Press release "Bath County Residents Left in Dark over 'Hee Haw' Star's Theme Park," *Huntington-Herald Dispatch*, January 15, 1990, for a typical story. In spite of the headline, no theme park was ever contemplated, only a country-music park-festival site. By the spring of 1991, since the marriage was all but over, the park had become a dead issue. However, by January 1992, Roni expected to open a country-music theater in Flagler Beach, Florida, called Roni Stoneman's Stompin' Grounds and Opry House (Veronica Stoneman, telephone interview, Daytona Beach, Florida, January 1, 1992), but by March she had returned to Nashville.

10. Norm Cohen, "Review of Ivan Tribe's THE STONEMANS" (unpublished 1991 typescript copy in Tribe possession), p. 5.

11. For a reflection on Ernest Stoneman's ability to do covers, see Charles K. Wolfe, "The Birth of an Industry," in Patrick Carr, ed., *The Illustrated History of Country Music* (Garden City, N.Y.: Doubleday & Co., 1980), pp. 38–39.

12. For brief sketches of those selected for the Country Music Hall of Fame, see Hagan, *Country Music Legends in the Hall of Fame*.

13. Chubby and Rossi Wise, interview, July 10, 1976. Nashville publisher John Denny in a recent conversation at an IBMA meeting (Owensboro, Ky., July 12, 1991) credited Scott's death to "frustration, not alcohol."

14. Loretta Lynn with George Vecsey, *Coal Miner's Daughter* (New York: Warner Books, 1976), pp. 51–59; Charles K. Wolfe, *George Jones* (New York: Time-Life Books, 1982), pp. 5–6.

15. Patsy Stoneman, "Prayers and Pinto Beans," copyright assigned in 1981 to Silverhill Music, BMI; recorded on C M H 9029 and Rutabaga 3012.

16. Calvin Scott Stoneman, "Heartaches Keep On Coming," copyright ca. 1957 by Chris Music, BMI; recorded on Bakersfield 45-121.

Bibliographical Note

Since the notations cover specific materials in some detail, comments here will be of a general nature. Ten Stonemans—Eddie, Grace, Patsy, Jack, Dean, Gene, Donna, Jim, Roni, and Van—contributed manuscript autobiographies. All were typed except Jack's and Eddie's, which were handwritten, and part of Donna's, which remained in oral form (on cassette). Those of the girls tended to be more useful because the male Stonemans were more laconic by nature, while the girls provided more depth and detail. Patsy's was the most detailed, while Roni's contained both the expected humor and some unexpected bittersweet tragedy. Grace's and Donna's understanding ways also gave insight into those who were more reserved. Patsy and Donna supplied hundreds of answers to telephone inquiries, sometimes on an almost daily basis during my more productive moments.

Several Stoneman associates from earlier days granted interviews, but the most helpful tended to be those of Jack Clement and Zeke Dawson. The latter contributed several insightful comments on various incidents and family members over a pair of festival seasons. David Dougherty recalled several incidents from the mid-seventies. Bob Bean and Cecile Howard proved helpful in reconstructing certain events from the fifties.

Earlier historians who provided a starting place for further Stoneman research include Archie Green, "Hillbilly Music: Source and Symbol," *Journal of American Folklore* 78 (1965), pp. 204–28; Norm Cohen, "Ernest Stoneman," in *Stars of Country Music* (Urbana: University of Illinois Press, 1975), pp. 21–23, and his liner notes to *The Stonemans: The First Family of Country Music*, CMH 9029; and Tony Russell, inside liner to *Ernest V. Stoneman and the Blue Ridge Cornshuckers*, Rounder 1008. Another indispensable item is Charles K. Wolfe, "Ralph Peer at Work: The Victor 1927 Bristol Sessions," *Old Time Music* 5 (Summer 1972), pp. 10–16. *Bluegrass Unlimited* has carried several pieces on the Stonemans, including a short article on Scott by Bill Bassin (December 1969), a brief one on the group by Randall Armstrong (June 1980), and two on Roni by Don Rhodes (May 1977) and Wayne Daniel (June 1990). During the course of my own Stoneman research, the periodical carried pieces on Donna (June 1983) and Patsy (March 1989). Two papers were delivered at conferences in 1988. The first was published as "Thar's Gold in Them Hillbillies? The Six Decade Experience of the Stoneman Family as Commercial Appalachian Musicians," *Mid-America Folklore* 16:2 (1988), pp. 80–89; the second, "The Stoneman Family of Virginia," is unpublished as of this writing. *Bluegrass Unlimited* articles on musicians closely connected to the Stonemans include Rhonda Strickland's excellent piece on Buzz Busby (November 1986), Fred Geiger's on Porter Church (January 1986), and H. Conway Gandy's on Don Owens (November 1987).

When the Stonemans received major attention on the Nashville scene in the late sixties, *Billboard, Record World, Music City News,* and *Country Song Roundup* reported frequently on their activities. So, too, did other fan magazines of a more ephemeral nature. Since that time, however, coverage has been increasingly sparse.

Six oral interviews with Ernest Stoneman were at my disposal in doing this study. The most useful included a 1962 one by Archie Green, Doyle Moore, and Richard Spottswood; that of 1964 by Eugene Earle; and that of 1967 by Bob Jennings (in the CMF Oral History Collection). The sessions conducted with Willard Johnson dealt extensively with the sources of older recorded songs. Another interview conducted by Don Owens on radio lacked sufficient length to contain much of a profound nature, while still another by Bill Littleton, conducted jointly with Pop and Maybelle Carter, concentrated so heavily on events connected with the recordings of Jimmie Rodgers and the Carters as to limit its value for a study of Stoneman's career. Library of Congress interviews with Emmett Lundy and Burton and George Stoneman proved quite helpful for establishing the place of music in the Grayson-Carroll social milieu at the turn of the century. Unfortunately, none of these deceased individuals was the subject of an interview suitable for use by a book-length biographer. Nonetheless, one can be thankful for their existence.

In addition to the above oral material, virtually every Stoneman recording, old and new, was listened to several times, as were several unissued recordings, tapes of sound portions of several TV shows (including three of Pop's appearances on "The Big Surprise" and the family on "The Steve Allen Show"), thirty-six videotapes of the syndicated Stoneman show from the late sixties, and the 1956 "Arthur Godfrey's Talent Scouts" show won by the Blue Grass Champs.

A final major source that merits discussion is the collection of family papers amassed by Patsy Stoneman. Although they are uneven in quality and not all that one would hope for, it is in another sense remarkable that some things have survived the years of poverty and residential changes. Items belonging to Ernest Stoneman include a large number of song sheets—typed, handwritten, and clipped from print—that cover his musical repertoire. A few lists of songs for particular shows and programs survive, as well as a few scripts of "Irma and Izary" and "The Big Surprise," royalty sheets, tax returns, and business correspondence. Most of this material was lost over the years. As for more recent material, it tends to be quite thorough for the years 1969–72, when John Murphy kept very good records, and from 1977, when Patsy took over the management. For the other time periods, some contracts have been preserved but other material is incomplete. Nonetheless, much useful information has been gleaned from what exists. Ernest Stoneman apparently had a good sense of what should be saved, and one only regrets that circumstances did not always permit him to do as he wished. Patsy reports one incident when a suitcase full of family papers either bounced out of his "covered wagon" en route home from a show date or was stolen from it in the parking lot. He searched along the roadway and even ran a classified ad in the papers offering a reward for its return, but to no avail. In retrospect, it seems nearly miraculous that Patsy managed to retain anything from the earlier era.

Stoneman Discography

The following represents a nearly complete discography of Ernest V. Stoneman prior to World War II. Also included are sides by his associates when they appeared with him at recording sessions. Although it may be less than perfect, it is as close to definitive as possible and serves as a guide to his musical repertoire. The discography is arranged in chronological order of recording, with headnotes for each session indicating company, location, and date. For each "side" or selection, the information is divided into three columns. The first column gives matrix, or master number, followed by a hyphen and then issued take number(s). In most cases, the take numbers listed have actually been seen on discs. In the case of OKeh and Edison, takes are indicated by letters. On Gennett masters, all takes recorded as indicated in the company ledgers are listed. Issued takes are underlined. The second column gives the title as given on the record label (or in company files if unissued). If composer credits are given on the label, they are given in the second column in parentheses. Composer credits are occasionally abbreviated after first use if no ambiguity results. The third column lists record release numbers. The label names are abbreviated according to the key that follows. Supplementary information, including personnel, label credits, and pseudonyms, is given at the end of an entire session.

The preliminary form of this discography first appeared in *J E M F Newsletter* (No. 7–9, 1967–68), and was compiled by Norman Cohen, Eugene W. Earle, and Graham Wickham. A more complete version by the same authors appeared in *The Early Recording Career of Ernest V. "Pop" Stoneman: A Bio-Discography*, J E M F Special Series, No. 1 (Los Angeles: John Edwards Memorial Foundation, 1968). A revision appeared in Thurston Moore, ed., *Country Music Who's Who* (Denver: Heather Enterprises, Inc., 1970), pt. 7, pp. 43sff. The most recent Stoneman discography is found in Kip Lornell, *Virginia's Blues, Country, & Gospel Records, 1902–1943* (Lexington: University Press of Kentucky, 1989), pp. 182–99. This discography owes some debt to all of these, but especially to that in the J E M F Special Series.

Label Abbreviations Used in Discography

Ba	Banner	Cty	County
Bdy	Broadway	Do	Domino
BRI	Blue Ridge Institute	Ed	Edison

Ca	Cameo	FSSM	Folksong Society
Chal	Challenge		of Minnesota
Champ	Champion	Fw	Folkways
Co	Columbia	Ge	Gennett
Cq	Conqueror	Her	Herwin
CMF	Country Music Foundation	Hist	Historical
Ho	Homestead	RCA	RCA Victor
LBC	Library of Congress	Re	Regal
Li	Lincoln	Ro	Romeo
MW	Montgomery Ward	Rou	Rounder
NWR	New World Records	Sm	Smithsonian
O H	Old Homestead	Spt	Supertone
OK	OKeh	Svt	Silvertone
Para	Paramount	Vi	Victor
Pat	Pathé	Vo	Vocalion

Ernest V. Stoneman Discography

Matrix No.	Title (Composer Credit)	Release No.

OKEH   New York, ca. September 5, 1924

S 72787-A	The Face That Never Returned	unissued
S 72788-A	The Titanic	unissued

Ernest V. Stoneman, vocal with Autoharp and harmonica.

OKEH   New York, ca. January 8, 1925

S 72787-B	The Face That Never Returned	OK 40288
S 72788-B	The Titanic	OK 40288
		Sm P8 15640
S 73089-A	Freckled Face Mary Jane	OK 40312
S 73090-A	Me and My Wife	OK 40312

Ernest V. Stoneman, vocal with Autoharp and harmonica.

OKEH   New York, May 27, 1925

S 73371-C	Uncle Sam and the Kaiser	OK 40430
S 73372-A	Jack and Joe	OK 40408
S 73373-A	Sinful to Flirt	OK 40384
S 73374-A	Dixie Parody	OK 40430
S 73375-A	Dying Girl's Farewell	OK 40384
S 73376-A	The Lightning Express	OK 40408
S 73377-A	Piney Woods Girl (1)	OK 40405
		Cty 535
S73378-A	The Long Eared Mule (1)	OK 40405

Ernest V. Stoneman, vocal with Autoharp and harmonica; (1) add Emmett Lundy, fiddle (OKeh 40405 issued as by Ernest V. Stoneman and Emmett Lundy).

OKEH   *Asheville, N.C., August 27, 1925*

9284	The Sailor's Song	OK 45015
9285-A	Blue Ridge Mountain Blues (Carson)	OK 45009
9286-A	All I've Got's Gone	OK 45009
9287	The Fancy Ball	OK 45015
9288	The Kicking Mule	OK 45036
9289-A	Wreck on the C. & O.	OK 7011
9290-A	John Hardy	OK 7011

Ernest V. Stoneman, vocal with Autoharp and harmonica (except no harmonica on 9284). OKeh 7011 is a twelve-inch disc.

OKEH   *Asheville, N.C., ca. April 1926*

S 74102-B	The Religious Critic	OK 45051
S 74103-A	When My Wife Will Return to Me	OK 45051
S 74104-A	Asleep at the Switch	OK 45044
S 74105-A	The Orphan Girl	OK 45044
S 74108-B	Kitty Wells (1)	OK 45048
S 74109-A	The Texas Ranger (1)	OK 45054
S 74110-B	In the Shadow of the Pine	OK 45048
S 74111-A	Don't Let Your Deal Go Down (1)	OK 45054
		O H 199

Ernest V. Stoneman, vocal with Autoharp and harmonica; on (1) guitar replaces Autoharp.

EDISON   *New York, June 21, 1926*

11053-B	Bad Companions	Ed 51788
		Ed 5201
11054-A	When the Work's All Done This Fall	Ed 51788
		Ed 5188
11055-A	Wreck of the C. & O.	Ed 51823
		Ed 5198
11056-A	Wild Bill Jones	Ed 51869
		Ed 5196
		O H 199
11057-A	John Henry	Ed 51869
		Ed 5194

EDISON   *New York, June 22, 1926*

11058-A	Sinking of the Titanic (Stoneman)	Ed 51823
		Ed 5200
		O H 199
11059-A	Watermelon Hanging on the Vine	Ed 51864
		Ed 5191
11060-C	The Old Hickory Cane	Ed 51864
		Ed 5241

EDISON   *New York, June 23, 1926*
11063   My Little German Home across   Ed 51909
                     the Sea
11064   Bury Me beneath the Willow   ED 51909
                                                                        Ed 5187

Ernest Stoneman, vocal with guitar and harmonica; label credits from this session usually read Ernest V. Stoneman, the Blue Ridge Mountaineer. Four-digit Edison release numbers refer to cylinders, which had different master numbers that are not included in this discography.

OKEH   *New York, ca. August 1926*
S 74300-A   Silver Bell (1)   OK 45060
                                                                        O H 199
S 74301-A   May I Sleep in Your Barn Tonight   OK 45059
                     Mister? (1)
S 74302-A   My Pretty Snow Dear (1)   OK 45060
S 74303-   Are You Angry with Me, Darling (1)   OK 45065
S 74304-A   The Old Hickory Cane (Carper)   OK 45059
S 74305   He's Going to Have a Hot Time By   OK 45062
                     and By
S 74306   The Old Go Hungry Hash House   OK 45062
S 74307   Katie Kline   OK 45065

Ernest V. Stoneman, vocal with guitar and harmonica; (1) add Joe Samuels, fiddle. Label credit reads Ernest V. Stoneman and Fiddler Joe on those cuts.

GENNETT   *New York, August 28, 1926*
X 233-A̲   May I Sleep in Your Barn Tonight   Ge 3368
                     Mister?   Chal 153,
                                                                        Chal 312
                                                                        Her 75530
                                                                        O H 173

X 234̲-A, -B   The Girl I Left Behind in Sunny   Ge 3368
                     Tennessee   Chal 151
                                                                        Her 75529
                                                                        O H 173

X 235̲-A   Silver Bell   Ge 3369
                                                                        Chal 153
                                                                        Her 75529

X 236-A̲   Pretty Snow Dear   Ge 3369
                                                                        Chal 152
                                                                        Her 75530

X 237-A̲   Katy Cline   Ge 3381
                                                                        Chal 151
                                                                        Her 75528

X238-A	Barney McCoy	Ge 3381
		Chal 152
		Chal 309
		Her 75528
		O H 199

Ernest Stoneman, vocal with guitar and harmonica; Hattie Stoneman, fiddle (except X 237, which is Hattie Stoneman, banjo).

VICTOR   Camden, N.J. September 21, 1926

BVE-36198-2	Going Down the Valley (Jessie Brown	Vi 20531
	Pounds–J. H. Fillmore)	Cty 508
		NWR 236
		O H 199
BVE-36199-2	The Sinless Summer (Millard H.	Vi 20531
	Smith–J. L. Heath)	Rou 1008
BVE-36500-2	In the Golden Bye and Bye (Smith-	Vi 20223
	Heath)	O H 173
BVE-36501-2	I Will Meet You In the Morning (J. B.	Vi 20223
	Vaughn)	O H 173
BVE-36502-1	The Great Reaping Day (R. E.	Vi 20532
	Winesett)	
BVE-36503-1	I Love to Walk With Jesus (C. F.	Vi 20224
	Weigell)	O H 173
BVE-36504-2	Hallelujah Side (Rev. Johnson	Vi 20224
	Oatman–J. Howard Entwisle)	Rou 1008

All sides credited to Ernest V. Stoneman and His Dixie Mountaineers, which consisted of Ernest V. Stoneman, vocal with guitar and harmonica; Lee Kahle Brewer, vocal and fiddle; Irma Frost, vocal and organ; Hattie Stoneman, vocals; Walter Mooney, vocals; and Tom Leonard, vocals.

VICTOR   Camden, N.J., September 24, 1926

BVE-36507-1	I'll Be Satisfied (J. H. & T. N. Pannell)	Vi 20533
		O H 173
BVE-36508-1	West Virginia Highway	Vi 20237
		Rou 1008
BVE-36509-2	Peek-a-boo Waltz	Vi 20540
		O H 172
BVE-36510-2	When the Redeemed Are Gathered In	Vi 20532
	(Oatman–W. H. Dutton)	O H 172
BVE-36511-1	I Would Not Be Denied	Vi 20532
BVE-36512-2	Going Up Cripple Creek	Vi 20294
		Rou 1008
BVE-36513-2	Sourwood Mountain	Vi 20235
		Rou 1008
		RCA 6015

BVE-36514-2	Little Old Log Cabin in the Lane	Vi 20235
		MW 8305
		Rou 1008
BVE-36515-2	Ida Red	Vi 20302
		Rou 1008
BVE-36516-2	Sugar in the Gourd	Vi 20294
		Cty 507
		O H 199
BVE-36517-2	Old Joe Clark	Vi 20302
		Rou 1008

Personnel: as above, but add Bolen Frost, banjo. BVE 36508 and BVE 36509 by Ernest V. Stoneman and Kahle Brewer. All of these persons are not present on all sides.

VICTOR Camden, N.J., September 25, 1926

| BVE-36518-2 | All Go Hungry Hash House | Vi 20237 |
| | | Rou 1008 |

Personnel: As above. All sides issued with credit Ernest V. Stoneman and His Dixie Mountaineers, except for those credited only to Stoneman and Brewer.

EDISON New York, January 24, 1927

11460-A,C	Bright Sherman Valley	Ed 51951
		Ed 5383
11461-A,C	Once I Had a Fortune	Ed 51935
		Ed 5357
		Hist 8004

Both sides credited to Ernest V. Stoneman and the Dixie Mountaineers, which are Ernest V. Stoneman, vocal (on 11460) with guitar and harmonica; Kahle Brewer, fiddle; Bolen Frost, banjo.

EDISON New York, January 25, 1927

11462-B	The Long Eared Mule	Ed 52056
11463-C	Hop Light Ladies	Ed 52056
		Hist 8004
11464-B,C	Two Little Orphans—Our Mama's in Heaven	Ed 51935
		Ed 5338
11465-A,C	Kitty Wells	Ed 51994
		Ed 5341
		Hist 8004

Personnel: As above. Edison 52056 credited the Dixie Mountaineers; others to Ernest V. Stoneman and the Dixie Mountaineers.

OKEH New York January 27, 1927

| W 80344 | The Wreck of the 97 | LBC 9 |

W 80345	Little Old Log Cabin in the Lane	O H 173
W 80346-A	Flop Eared Mule [as "Untitled"]	Co 47911/
		47912
W 80347-A	Lonesome Road Blues	OK 45094
		Cty 533
W 80348-A	Round Town Gal	OK 45094
W 80349	Old Joe Clark	unissued

Personnel: As above. All OKeh label credits to the Ernest V. Stoneman Trio.

EDISON	*New York January 28, 1927*	
11481-C	Hand Me Down My Walking Cane	Ed 51938
		Ed 5297
		O H 172
11482-B	Tell Mother I Will Meet Her	Ed 51938
		Ed 5382

Personnel: As above. Releases credited to Ernest V. Stoneman and the Dixie Mountaineers.

EDISON	*New York January 29, 1927*	
11483-A	We Courted in the Rain	Ed 51994
		Ed 5297
11484-C	The Bully of the Town	Ed 51951
		Ed 5314

Personnel: As above except fiddle deleted on 11483, which is credited to Ernest V. Stoneman, the Blue Ridge Mountaineer; 11484 credited to Ernest V. Stoneman and the Dixie Mountaineers.

OKEH	*New York January 29, 1927*	
W 80360-B	The Fatal Wedding	OK 45084
W 80361-A	The Fate of Talmadge Osborne	OK 45084
		BRI 004

Personnel: As above. Label credit to Ernest V. Stoneman.

GENNETT	*New York February 5, 1927*	
GEX 493-A	The Poor Tramp Has to Live	Ge 6044
		Champ 15233
		Chal 324
		Chal 398
		Chal 244
		Svt 5001
		Svt 8155
		Svt 25001
		Spt 9255
		Her 75535

GEX 494	Sweet Bunch of Violets	Ge 6065
		Her 75541
		Champ 15233
		Svt 5004
		Svt 25004
		Cty 533
GEX 495	Kenny Wagner's Surrender	Ge 6044
		Champ 15222
		Her 75535
		Svt 5004
		Svt 25004
		Hist 8003
		O H 173
GEX 496-A	When the Roses Bloom Again	Ge 6065
		Ch 15222
		Chal 244
		Spt 9255
		Svt 5001
		Svt 8155
		Svt 25001
		Her 75441
		O H 173
GEX 497	Long Eared Mule [Flop Eared Mule]	Ge 6052
		Svt 5003
		Svt 25003
		Cty 533
GEX 498-A	Round Town Gal [Buffalo Gals]	Ge 6052
		Svt 5003
		Svt 25003
		Champ 15248
		Cty 533

Personnel: Ernest Stoneman, vocal with guitar and harmonica; Kahle Brewer, fiddle; Bolen Frost, banjo. Gennett and Herwin label credits to Ernest Stoneman, except Ge 6052, which is to Ernest Stoneman and his Graysen [*sic*] County Boys; Champion label credits to Uncle Jim Seaney; Challenge and Silvertone to Jim Seaney or Uncle Ben Hawkins (sometimes with his Boys or Gang added GEX 497 on Silvertone 25003 credited to Logan County Trio. County 533 uses the alternate titles shown in brackets.

EDISON	*New York, May 10, 1927*	
11690-C	Fate of Talmadge Osborne	Ed 52056
		Ed 5369
11691-A	The Orphan Girl	Ed 5367
11692	Pass Around the Bottle	unissued
11693	The Fatal Wedding	Ed 52026
		Ed 5355

Personnel: Ernest V. Stoneman, vocal with guitar and harmonica; Hattie Stoneman, fiddle. Label credit on 11691 and 11692 to the Dixie Mountaineers; on 11693 to Ernest V. Stoneman and Mrs. Stoneman.

PLAZA	*New York, May 1927*	
7222-1	Hand Me Down My Walking Cane	Ba 1933
		Do 3964
		Re 8324
		Ho 16490
		Or 916
7223-1	Pass Around the Bottle	Ba 2157
		Do 3985
		Re 8346
		Ho 16490
		Or 916
		Chal 665
		Cq 7064
		Cq 7755
		Para 3021
		Bdy 8054
7224-1	When the Roses Bloom Again	Ba 1993
		Do 3964
		Re 8324
		Ho 16498
		Or 946
7225-1	Bully of the Town	Ba 2157
		Do 3984
		Re 8347
		Ho 16500
		Or 947
		Chal 665
		Cq 7755
		Pat 32279
		Pe 12358
		Spt 32279
		Ca 8217
		Ro 597
		Li 2822

Personnel: Ernest Stoneman, vocal with guitar and harmonica; Hattie Stoneman, fiddle on 7222, banjo on 7224. Label credits to Ernest Stoneman, except Oriole releases credited to Sim Harris.

PATHÉ	*New York ca. late May 1927*	
?????	The Old Hickory Cane	Pat 32271
		Pe 12350
		Do 0187
		Re 8369

107554-a	The Fatal Wedding	Ca 8220
		Ro 600
		Li 2825
107554-b	The Fatal Wedding	Pat 32278
		Pe 12357
		Chal 666
		Ba 2158
		Do 3984
		Re 8347
		Ho 16498
		Or 946
107555-a	Pass Around the Bottle	Pat 32278
		Pe 12357
		Ca 8217
		Ro 597
		Li 2822
107556-a	Sinful to Flirt	Pat 32271
		Pe 12350
		Chal 666
		Cq 7064
		Ca 8220
		Ro 600
		Li 2825
		Ba 2158
		Do 3985
		Re 8346
		Ho 16500
		Or 947

Personnel: Ernest Stoneman, vocal with guitar and harmonica; all label credits to Ernest Stoneman except Oriole, which is Sim Harris.

OKEH   New York, May 12, 1927

W 81075-B	When the Silvery Colorado Wends Its Way	unissued
W 81078	Two Little Orphans [Two Little Children]	O H 173
W 81079	The Road to Washington	OK 45125
		O H 173
W 81080	The Mountaineer's Courtship	OK 45125
		Fw 2953

Personnel: Ernest Stoneman, vocal with guitar and harmonia; Hattie Stoneman, fiddle and solo vocal part on W 81080. OKeh label credits to Mr. and Mrs. Ernest V. Stoneman.

VICTOR   New York, May 19, 1927

| BVE-38763-2 | The Poor Tramp | Vi 20672 |

		Rou 1008
BVE-38764-2	The Fate of Talmadge Osborne	Vi 20672
		O H 173
BVE-38765-2	The Old Hickory Cane (Stoneman-Carper)	Vi 20799
		Cty 533
BVE-38766-2	Till the Snowflakes Fall Again (Stoneman)	Vi 20799
		O H 172

Personnel: Ernest V. Stoneman, vocal with guitar and harmonica; all label credits to Ernest V. Stoneman.

VICTOR   *New York, May 21, 1927*

BVE-38918-1	The Story of the Mighty Mississippi (Kelly Harrell)	Vi 20671 O H 173
BVE-38919	Joe Hoover's Mississippi Flood Song	unissued

Personnel: Ernest V. Stoneman, vocal with guitar and harmonica; all label credits to Ernest V. Stoneman.

VICTOR   *Bristol, Tenn., July 25, 1927*

BVE-39700-1	The Dying Girl's Farewell (J. D. Patton)	Vi 21129
		Rou 1008
BVE-39701-3	Tell Mother I Will Meet Her (R. S. Tinsman)	Vi 21129
		Cty 533
		CMF 011
BVE-39702-1	Mountaineer's Courtship	CMF 011
BVE-39702-2	Mountaineer's Courtship	Vi 20880
		O H 173
BVE-39703-3	Midnight on the Stormy Deep	CMF 011
BVE-39704-3	Sweeping through the Gates	Vi 20844
		Rou 1008
BVE-39705-2	I Know My Name Is There (D. S. Warner)	Vi 21186
		Rou 1008
		LBC 1
BVE-39706-2	Are You Washed in the Blood	Vi 20844
		MW 8136
		Rou 1008
		CMF 011
BVE-39707-2	No More Goodbyes (R. R. Latter)	Vi 21186
		Cty 533
BVE-39708-2	The Resurrection (G. R. Street)	Vi 21071
		O H 172
BVE-39708-1	The Resurrection (G. R. Street)	CMF 011
BVE-39709-2	I Am Resolved (Palmer Hartsough–J. H. Fillmore)	Vi 21071 Cty 533

Personnel: Ernest V. Stoneman, vocal with guitar and harmonica; Kahle Brewer, vocal and fiddle; Hattie Stoneman, vocal and fiddle; Irma Frost, vocal and organ; Eck Dunford, vocal and fiddle; Walter Mooney, vocals; Edna Brewer, vocals. Label credits on Victor 21129 to Stoneman, Brewer, and Mooney; credits on BVE-39702 to Stoneman, Frost, and Dunford; credits on BVE-39703 to Stoneman and Frost; others to Ernest V. Stoneman and His Dixie Mountaineers. Other than Stoneman, all persons may not be present on every cut.

VICTOR	*Bristol, Tenn., July 27, 1927*	
BVE-39716-1	The Whip-poor-will Song (Eck Dunford)	Vi 20880
		O H 173
BVE-39717-2	What Will I Do, for My Money's All Gone	Vi 21578
BVE-39718-2	Skip to My Lou, My Darling	Vi 20938
		O H 172
		CMF 011
BVE-39719-1	Barney McCoy	Vi 20938
		Cty 533
BVE-39720-2	Old Time Corn Shuckin' Party, Part 1	Vi 20835
		CMF 011
BVE-39721-4	Old Time Corn Shuckin' Party, Part 2	Vi 20835
		CMF 011

Personnel: Ernest Stoneman, vocal with guitar and harmonica; Uncle Eck Dunford, vocal and fiddle or guitar; Hattie Stoneman, fiddle and vocal; Kahle Brewer, fiddle and vocal; Iver Edwards, harmonica and ukelele. On label credits BVE-39716, BVE-39718m and BVE-39719 to Uncle Eck Dunford; BVE-39717 to Dunford and Hattie Stoneman; BVE-39720 and BVE 39721 to Ernest V. Stoneman and The Blue Ridge Corn Shuckers. All persons may not be present on every cut.

EDISON	*New York, September 12, 1927*	
11882	The Little Black Moustache	unissued
11883	Puttin' On the Style	unissued
11884	All Go Hungry Hash House	unissued
11885	Sally Goodwin	unissued

Personnel: Ernest Stoneman, vocal with guitar; others unknown.

EDISON	*New York, September 13, 1927*	
11886	When the Redeemed Are Gathered In (Oatman-Dutton)	unissued
11887	He Was Nailed to the Cross for Me	unissued

Personnel: As above.

VICTOR   *Atlanta, Ga., October 22, 1927*

BVE-40334-1	Sleeping Late (E. Dunford)	Vi 21224
BVE-40335-1	My First Bicycle Ride	Vi 21131
		O H 172
BVE-40336-1	The Taffy Pulling Party (E. Dunford)	Vi 21224
BVE-40337-2	The Savingest Man on Earth	Vi 21131
		Rou 1008

Personnel: Uncle Eck Dunford, narrative vocal; Ernest Stoneman, banjo. Label credit, Uncle Eck Dunford.

VICTOR   *Atlanta, Ga., February 22, 1928*

BVE-41932-2	Possum Trot School Exhibition, Part 1	Vi 21264
		Cty 512
BVE-41933-2	Possum Trot School Exhibition, Part 2	Vi 21264
		Cty 512
BVE-41934-2	A Serenade in the Mountains, Part 1	Vi 21518
		Cty 512
BVE-41935-1	A Serenade in the Mountains, Part 2	Vi 21518
		Cty 512
BVE-41936	Claude Allen	unissued
BVE-41937-1	The Two Little Orphans	Vi 21648
		Rou 1008
		LBC 13
BVE-41938	Once I Had a Fortune	unissued
BVE-41939-1	The Raging Sea, How It Roars	Vi 21648
		BRI 002
		Rou 1008
		FSSM 3796
BVE-41940	Uncle Joe	unissued
BVE-41941-1	Sweet Summer Has Gone Away	Vi 21578
		O H 173
BVE-41942	Tell Me Where My Eva's Gone	unissued
BVE-41943	Old Uncle Jessie	unissued
BVE-41944	Stonewall Jackson	unissued

Personnel: Ernest V. Stoneman, vocal with guitar and harmonica; Uncle Eck Dunford, fiddle and vocal; George Stoneman, banjo; Irma Frost, vocal; Sam Patton, vocal on BVE-41932 and BVE 41933 only. Label credits to Ernest V. Stoneman and His Blue Ridge Corn Shuckers, except for BVE-41941 to Uncle Eck Dunford and Ernest Stoneman. Of the unissued sides, BVE-41936 and BVE 41938 to Stoneman and Frost, BVE-41940 and BVE-41943 to Uncle Eck Dunford, BVE-41942 to Stoneman and Dunford, and BVE-41944 to George Stoneman (a guitar solo).

EDISON   *New York, April 24, 1928*

18433-A	He Was Nailed to the Cross for Me	Ed 52290
		O H 199

18434-B	When the Redeemed Are Gathered In	Ed 52290
	(Oatman-Dutton)	Ed 5527
18435-A	All Go Hungry Hash House	Ed 52350
		Ed 5528
18436-	There'll Come a Time	Ed 52369
		Ed 5636
		Hist 8004
18437-A	Sally Goodwin	Ed 52350
		Ed 5529
		Ed 0000
		Hist 8004
18438-	Careless Love	Ed 52386
		Ed 5530
		Hist 8004

Personnel: Ernest Stoneman, vocal with guitar and harmonica; Kahle Brewer, fiddle; George Stoneman, banjo. All label credits to the Dixie Mountaineers.

EDISON	*New York, April 25, 1928*	
18440-B	The East Bound Train	Ed 52299
		Ed 5548
		Hist 8004
18441-B	The Unlucky Road to Washington	Ed 52299
		Ed 5545
		Hist 8004
18442-B	The Old Maid and the Burglar	Ed 52369
		Ed 5531
		Hist 8004
18443-A	Down on the Banks of the Ohio	Ed 52312
		O H 172
18444-B	We Parted at the River	Ed 52312
		Ed 5635
18445-A	It's Sinful to Flirt	Ed 52386
		Ed 5547
		Hist 8004

Personnel and Credits: As above.

PATHÉ	*New York, late April or early May 1928*	
108203	In the Shadow of the Pine	Pat 32380
		Pe 12459

Personnel: Ernest Stoneman, vocal with guitar and harmonica.

GENNETT	*Richmond, Ind., July 5, 1928*	
GE-14005-A	Katy Lee	Ge 6565
		Champ 15565

GE-14006-A	My Mother and My Sweetheart	Ge 6655
GE-14007-A	Prisoner's Lament	Ge 6567
		Champ 15565
		Spt 9185
		Spt 9305
GE-14008	Once I Knew a Little Girl	unissued
GE-14009-B	Somebody's Waiting for Me	Ge 6620
		Spt 9323
		Champ 15586
GE-14010-A	Falling by the Wayside	Ge 6655
		Spt 9185
		Champ 15586
GE-14011-A	Sugar Hill	Ge 6687

Personnel: Ernest Stoneman, vocal with guitar and harmonica; George Stoneman, banjo; Willie Stoneman, guitar and vocal; Earl Sweet, vocal and banjo; Herbert Sweet, vocal and fiddle. Not all of these individuals are present on every cut. By this time, Ernest Stoneman's contract with Ralph Peer prevented him from using his own name on Gennett recordings, hence the pseudonyms proliferate. Label credit on GE-14005 is to Willie Stoneman (Dave Hunt on Champion); the Sweet Brothers on GE-14006 and GE 14009 (Clark Brothers on Champion and Caldwell Brothers on Supertone); to Herbert Sweet on GE-14007 and Ge-14010 (John Clark on Supertone and Sam Caldwell on Champion); and to the Virginia Mountain Boomers on GE-14011.

GENNETT	*Richmond, Ind., July 6, 1928*	
GE-14012-A	Wake Up in the Morning	Ge 6565
		Champ 15610
		Spt 9083

Personnel: As above. Credit on GE 14012 is to Willie Stoneman. Note: Recording machine breaks down here.

GENNETT	*Richmond, Ind., July 9, 1928*	
GE-14015-A	New River Train	Ge 6619
		Spt 9400
		Hist 8001
		Cty 533
GE-14016-A	John Hardy	Ge 6619
		Hist 8001
		Cty 533
GE-14017-A	Say, Darling Say	Ge 6733
		Spt 9400
		Hist 8001
		Cty 535
GE-14018-A	I'm Gonna Marry That Pretty Little Girl	Hist 8001
		Cty 535

Personnel: As above. Credit on GE-14015, GE 14016, and GE 14017 is to Justin Winfield (a collective pseudonym for Ernest Stoneman and the Sweet Brothers); on GE 14018 to the Virginia Mountain Boomers.

GENNETT	*Richmond, Ind., July 10, 1928*	
GE-14019-A	Cousin Sally Brown	Ge 6687
GE-14020-A	Bluff Hollow Sobs	unissued
GE-14021-A	I Got a Bulldog	Ge 6620
		Hist 8001
		Cty 535
GE-14022-A	East Tennessee Polka	Spt 9406
GE-14023-A	Rambling Reckless Hobo	Ge 6567
		Spt 9305
		Champ 15610
		O H 199

Personnel: As above. All label credits except GE-14021 to the Virginia Mountain Boomers (Pine Mountain Ramblers on Champion); label credit on GE-14021 is to the Sweet Brothers.

VICTOR	*Bristol, Tenn., October 30, 1928*	
BVE-47248-	Beautiful Isle o'er the Sea	unissued
BVE-47249-	Willie, We Have Missed You	unissued
BVE-47252-	The Fate of Shelly and Smith	unissued
BVE-47253-2	The Broken Hearted Lover	Vi 40030
		O H 172
BVE-47254-2	Angeline the Baker	Vi 40060
		O H 199

Personnel: Ernest Stoneman, vocal with guitar and harmonica; George Stoneman, banjo; Uncle Eck Dunford, vocal and fiddle; Hattie Stoneman, vocal and mandolin or fiddle. All label credits to the Stoneman Family except BVE-47254, which is to Uncle Eck Dunford.

VICTOR	*Bristol, Tenn., October 31, 1928*	
BVE-47255-1	Old Shoes and Leggins	Vi 40060
		Fw 2951
BVE-47256	Minnie Brown	unissued
BVE-47257-1	We Parted by the Riverside	Vi 40030
		O H 172
BVE-47258-2	Down to Jordan and Be Saved (Dunford)	Vi 40078
BVE-47259-2	There's a Light Lit Up in Galilee (Stoneman)	Vi 40078
		Cty 533
BVE-47260-2	Going Up the Mountain After Liquor, Pt. 1	Vi 40116
		O H 199

BVE-47261-2	Going Up the Mountain After Liquor, Pt. 2	Vi 40116 O H 199
BVE-47262-2	The Spanish Merchant's Daughter	Vi 40206 Fw 2953
BVE-47263	Twilight Is Stealing over the Sea	unissued

Personnel: As above. All label credits to the Stoneman Family except BVE-47255, credited to Uncle Eck Dunford, and BVE-47258 and BVE-47259, to Ernest Stoneman's Dixie Mountaineers.

VICTOR   *Bristol, Tenn., November 1, 1928*

| BVE-47264-2 | Too Late | Vi 40206 Cty 533 |
| BVE-47265 | I Should Like to Marry | unissued |

Personnel: As above. Label credit to the Stoneman Family.

EDISON   *New York, November 21, 1928*

18881-B	Goodbye Dear Old Stepstone	Ed 52489 O H 172
18882-B	Fallen by the Wayside	Ed 52461 Ed 5686 O H 172
18883-B	All I've Got's Gone	Ed 52489 LBC 7 Rou 1026
18884	My Mother and My Sweetheart	unissued
18885	Remember the Poor Tramp Has to Live	unissued
18886-B	The Prisoner's Lament	Ed 52461 Ed 5673 O H 199

Personnel: Ernest Stoneman, vocal with guitar and harmonica; Uncle Eck Dunford, fiddle; George Stoneman, banjo. All label credits to Ernest V. Stoneman and His Dixie Mountaineers.

EDISON   *New York, November 22, 1928*

18887	Midnight on the Stormy Deep	unissued*
18888	The Pretty Mohea (Indian Maid)	unissued
18891-A	I Remember Calvary (Lemons-Winesett)	Ed 52479 Ed 5676 Ed N-20004 O H 172
18892-A	He Is Coming After me (Hacker-Winesett)	Ed 52479 Ed N-20004 O H 172

Personnel and Credits: As above.

*According to previous Stoneman discographies, this title was issued on Edison cylinder 5536. However, according to Bob Pinson, the Edison cylinder bearing this release number is in the Country Music Foundation Library's collection. It is neither Stoneman nor the Dixie Mountaineers.

GENNETT	*Richmond, Ind., March 5, 1929*	
GE-14861-B	Way Down in North Carolina (Fields Ward)	Hist 8001 Cty 534
GE-14862-A	Ain't That Trouble in Mind (Fields Ward)	Hist 8001
GE-14863-A	You Must Be a Lover of the Lord	Hist 8001
GE-14864-A	Watch and Pray	Hist 8001 Cty 534
GE-14865-A	Goodbye Little Bonnie	Hist 8001
GE-14866-A	Alas My Darling	unissued
GE-14867-A	My Old Sweetheart	unissued
GE-14868-A	The Place Where Ella Sleeps	unissued
GE-14869-A	In Those Cruel Slavery Days (Fields Ward)	Hist 8001
GE-14870-A	The Sweetest Way Home	Hist 8001

Personnel: Fields Ward, vocal and guitar; Ernest Stoneman, vocal with Autoharp and harmonica; Uncle Eck Dunford, fiddle; Sampson Ward, banjo. Primary label credit was to Fields Ward and Justin Winfield [Ernest Stoneman] with the Grayson County Railsplitters (some credits omitted Winfield and some omitted both Ward and Winfield). As released on Historical LP 8001, the artist credit was Fields Ward and his Buck Mountain Band.

GENNETT	*Richmond, Ind., March 7, 1929*	
GE-14876-B	My Only Sweetheart	Hist 8001
GE-14877-A	Tie Up Those Broken Cords	Hist 8001
GE-14878-A	The Birds Are Returning	Hist 8001
GE-14879-A	No One Loves You as I Do	Hist 8001
GE-14880-A	I Don't See Why I Love Her	unissued

Personnel and Credits: As above.

PARAMOUNT	*Chicago, August 1929*	
21381-2	Burial of Wild Bill	Para 3240 Bdy 8249 Cty 522
21382-1	The Railway Flagman's Sweetheart	Para 3240 Bdy 8249

Personnel: Ernest Stoneman, vocal with guitar and harmonica; Frank Jenkins, fiddle; Oscar Jenkins, banjo. Label credit to Oscar Jenkins' Mountaineers.

Note: Frank and Oscar Jenkins were equally adept on fiddle and banjo; it is possible that they may switch instruments.

GENNETT	*Richmond, Ind., September 12, 1929*	
GE-15589-A	The Railroad Flagman's Sweetheart	Cq 7269
	(Jenkins-Stoneman)	O H 199
GE-15590-A	The Murder of Nellie Brown	unissued
GE-15591-A	When the Snowflakes Fall Again	Cq 7270
GE-15592-A	The Burial of Wild Bill	Cq 7270
GE-15593-A	I Will Be All Smiles Tonight	O H 199
GE-15594-A	In the Year of Jubilo	unissued
GE-15595-A	A Message From Home Sweet Home	Cq 7269
GE-15596-A	Sunny Home in Dixie	Ge 7034
		Spt 9677
		Cty 507
GE-15597-A	Old Dad	Ge 7034
		Spt 9677

Personnel: As above. Primary label credit is to Frank Jenkins' Pilot Mountaineers (Alex Gordon on Conqueror and Riley's Mountaineers on Supertone).

VOCALION	*New York, January 8, 1934*	
14545	Good-bye, Dear Old Stepstone	unissued
14546	The Railroad Flagman's Sweetheart	unissued
14547	After the Roses Have Faded Away	unissued
14548	Meet Me by the Seaside	unissued
14549	Six Months Is a Long Time	unissued
14550	My Only Sweetheart	Vo 02901
		O H 172
14551	I'm Alone, All Alone	unissued
14552	There's Somebody Waiting for Me	Vo 02632
14553-1	Nine Pound Hammer	Vo 02665
		O H 199

Personnel: Ernest Stoneman, vocal with guitar and harmonica; Eddie Stoneman, vocal on chorus with banjo (possibly Autoharp on some unissued cuts). All label credits are to Ernest and Eddie Stoneman.

VOCALION	*New York, January 9, 1934*	
14554-1	Broke Down Section Hand	Vo 02655
14555	Texas Ranger	Vo 02632
14556	Prisoner's Advice	unissued
14557-2	All I Got's Gone	Vo 02901
		O H 172
14560	Golden Bye and Bye	unissued
14561	Hallelujah Side	unissued

Personnel: As above, except Ernest Stoneman only on 14554, 14555, 14556, and 14557; label credit, Ernest Stoneman.

VOCALION	*New York, January 10, 1934*	
14562	I'll Live On	unissued
14563	Reaping Days	unissued
14564	The Sweetest Way Home	unissued

Personnel: As above.

The following long-play albums are reissues of the early recordings of Ernest Stoneman and his close associates:

County 533	*Round the Heart of Old Galax, Volume 1, Featuring Ernest Stoneman*
Historical 8001	*Early Country Music: Fields Ward and His Buck Mountain Band, featuring Fields Ward and Ernest Stoneman*
Historical 8004	*Ernest V. Stoneman and His Dixie Mountaineers, 1927–1928*
Old Homestead 172	*Ernest V. Stoneman with Family and Friends, No. 1*
Old Homestead 173	*Ernest V. Stoneman with Family and Friends, No. 2*
Old Homestead 199	*Ernest V. Stoneman: The Sinking of the Titanic, No. 3*
Rounder 1008	*Ernest V. Stoneman and the Blue Ridge Corn Shuckers*

The following long-play albums feature at least one selection by Ernest V. Stoneman:

BRI 002	*Ballads from British Tradition*
BRI 004	*Virginia Traditions: Native Virginia Ballads and Songs*
Country Music Foundation 011	*The Bristol Sessions* (note: contains eight masters)
County 507	*Old Time Fiddle Classics* (contains two cuts featuring Stoneman fiddlers)
County 508	*Mountain Sacred Songs*
County 512	*A Day in the Mountains: 1928* (contains four masters or two complete skits)
County 522	*Old Time Ballads from the Southern Mountains*
County 534	*Round the Heart of Old Galax, Volume 2* (contains three cuts featuring Stoneman associates)

County 535	*Round the Heart of Old Galax, Volume 3* (contains four cuts featuring Stoneman associates)
FSSM LP 3976	[no title, but various old-time numbers] (one Stoneman cut)
Folkways FA 2951	*American Folk Music, Volume 1* (selection by Eck Dunford)
Folkways FA 2953	*American Folk Music, Volume 3* (two cuts)
Historical 8003	*Traditional Country Classics, 1927–1929*
LBC 1	*Religious Music: Congregational and Ceremonial*
LBC 7	*Songs of Complaint and Protest*
LBC 9	*Songs of Death and Tragedy*
LBC 13	*Songs of Childhood*
New World NWR 236	*Going Down the Valley*
RCA LPM 6015	*Stars of the Grand Ole Opry*
Rounder 1026	*Rich Man, Poor Man*
Sm P8-15640	*Smithsonian Collection of Classic Country Music*

Stoneman Family Discography

This portion of the discography follows the same pattern as the preceding section, with record company, location, and date (when known), given in headnotes. The columns give matrix number (when known), song title with composer credits (when given, even if incorrectly, in parentheses, or musical credits in brackets), and release numbers. Information in footnotes includes personnel and label credits.

Label Abbreviations Used in Discography

ACE	ACE	MGM	M-G-M
Bak	Bakersfield	NAL	NAL (England)
B R	Blue Ridge	NLP	Nashville
Cap	Capitol	O H	Old Homestead
CMH	CMH	RCA	RCA Victor
Dis	Disneyland	RPA	RPA
Fk F	Folk Festival	Ruta	Rutabaga
Fw	Folkways	SLP	Starday
G C	Golden Classics	Ston	Stonehouse
G R	Gulf Reef	Sun	Sunset
Heri	Heritage	W P	World-Pacific
Million	Million	Wyn	Wyncote

Matrix No.	Title (Composer Credit and/or Musical Credit)	Release No.

WARL   *Radio Arlington, Va., ca. 1947–52*

	The Golden Bye and Bye [Pop, lead vocal]	unissued
	Will You Be Loving Another Man? [Pop, lead vocal]	unissued
	Remember Me [Eddie, lead vocal]	unissued
	Blue Eyes Crying in the Rain [Eddie, lead vocal]	unissued
	Log Cabin in the Lane [Pop, lead vocal]	unissued
	Somebody's Waiting for Me [Pop, lead vocal]	unissued
	Molly and Tenbrooks [instrumental]	unissued
	John Henry [instrumental]	unissued
	Foggy Mountain Breakdown [instrumental]	unissued
	Bile 'em Cabbage Down [Eddie, lead vocal]	

All of the above were acetate demo discs made at WARL Radio between 1947 and 1952. Beyond Pop's lead vocals and Eddie's lead vocals and electric guitar on certain cuts, the other Stonemans on the sessions are uncertain but are believed to have included some combination of Hattie, Billy, Jack, Gene, Dean, Scott, Donna, Jimmy, and perhaps John. Not all were necessarily made at the same time.

FOLKWAYS   *Carmody Hills, Md., ca. 1956–early 1957*

	Say, Darling Say [Pop, vocal and banjo]	Fw FA 2315
	The Black Dog Blues [Pop, vocal and guitar; Hattie, fiddle]	Fw FA 2315
	When the Springtime Comes Again [Pop, vocal, guitar, and harmonica]	Fw FA 2315
	Stoney's Waltz [Pop, Autoharp]	Fw FA 2315
	New River Train [Pop, vocal and guitar; Hattie, banjo]	Fw FA 2315
	Hallelujah Side [Pop, vocal and Autoharp]	Fw FA 2315
	Cumberland Gap [Hattie, banjo]	Fw FA 2315
	Hang John Brown [Pop, vocal and Autoharp]	Fw FA 2315
	Bile Them Cabbage Down [Pop, vocal, harmonica, and Autoharp]	Fw FA 2315

Personnel: Ernest and Hattie Stoneman as indicated above; Van Stoneman, bass on "The Black Dog Blues." All credits to the Stoneman Family.

FOLKWAYS   *Washington, D.C., ca. 1956–early 1957*

| | Wreck of the Old Ninety-seven | Fw FA 2315 |

Personnel: Ernest Stoneman, vocal and guitar; Hattie Stoneman, fiddle; Gene Stoneman, guitar; Eugene Cox, banjo; Van Stoneman, bass (recorded live at a dance hall). All credits to the Stoneman Family.

BAKERSFIELD   Washington, D.C., ca. 1957

121-A	Heartaches Keep on Coming (Scotty Stoneman)	Bak 121
121-B	The Haunted House (Scotty Stoneman)	Bak 121

Personnel: Scott Stoneman, vocal and fiddle; Donna Stoneman, mandolin; Peggy Brain Stoneman, Dobro; Jimmy Case, guitar; Jimmy Stoneman, bass. Label credit to Scotty Stoneman with the Blue Grass Champs.

WYNCOTE   Washington, D.C., 1958

Bill Bailey, Won't You Please Come Home [Roni, vocal]	Wyn 9032
Wine Bottom Blues [Billy, vocal]	Wyn 9032
Daddy Stay Home [Billy, vocal]	Wyn 9032
Little Tim (Guilty) [Scott, vocal]	Wyn 9032
Bluegrass Breakdown [instrumental]	Wyn 9032

Personnel: Scott Stoneman, vocal and fiddle; Donna Stoneman, mandolin and vocal on chorus; Billy Stoneman, vocal and guitar; Roni Stoneman, vocal and banjo; Jimmy Stoneman, bass and vocal on chorus. Label credit to the Stoneman Family.

Note: This material was issued as the B side of a Jimmy Dean album on a budget label.

BLUE RIDGE   Washington, D.C., ca. 1960

45-6005	Hand Me Down My Walking Cane (Arr: Dixon-Stewart)	B R 504
45-6006	Jubilee March (Childree)	B R 504

Personnel: Ernest Stoneman, vocal and Autoharp; Donna Stoneman, mandolin and vocal on chorus; Lew "Childre" Houston, Dobro; Perry Westland, guitar; Jimmy Stoneman, bass and vocal on chorus. Credit on 6005 to Pop Stoneman with the Blue Grass Champs; on 6006 to Blue Grass Champs [it featured Houston on a Dobro instrumental].

FOLKWAYS   Carmody Hill, Md., December 10, 1961

Stoney's Waltz [instrumental]	Fw FA 2365
Bile 'em Cabbage Down (x)	Fw FA 2365
All I Got's Gone	Fw FA 2365
Wreck of Number Nine	Fw FA 2365
The Great Reaping Day	Fw FA 2365
I'm Alone, All Alone (x)	Fw FA 2365

Personnel: Ernest Stoneman, vocal and Autoharp; Mike Seeger, banjo
on cuts marked (x). Label credit to Ernest V. Stoneman.

GULF REEF   Nashville, Tenn., ca. March 1962

1009-A	Guilty (Scott Stoneman)	G R 1009
1009-AA	My Greatest Friend (Billy Barton)	G R 1009
1010-A	Sadness (Billy Barton)	G R 1010
1010-AA	White Lightning, No. 2 (J. P. Richardson)	G R 1010

Personnel: Scotty Stoneman, fiddle and vocal on chorus; Van Stoneman, guitar and lead vocal on 1010-AA; Donna Stoneman, mandolin
and vocal on chorus; Jimmy Stoneman, bass and lead vocal on 1010-A;
Roni Stoneman, banjo; Ernest Stoneman, Autoharp and vocal part on
1010-AA; Grant Turner, recitation on 1009-A and 1009-AA. Label credit
on 1009 to Grant Turner with the Stonemans, on 1010 to the Stonemans.
Note: there were other recordings on this label, but the masters were
destroyed in a fire; see also the section on Scott Stoneman recordings
for other material recorded either by Gulf Reef or its subsidiary label,
Fire.

STARDAY   Nashville, Tenn., ca. midsummer 1962

5514	Out of School (Van and Scott Stoneman)	SLP 200
		SLP 393
5515	Guilty (Scott Stoneman)	SLP 200
		SLP 393
		NLP 2063
5516	Talking Fiddle Blues (S. Stoneman)	SLP 200
		SLP 393
		SLP 468
		SLP 45-599
5517	That Pal of Mine (E. Stoneman)	SLP 200
		SLP 393
		SLP 45-599
5518	The Girl from Galax (D. Stoneman)	SLP 200
		SLP 221
		SLP 393
5519	Springtime in the Mountains (York)	SLP 200
5520	In the Sweet Bye and Bye (York)	SLP 200
5521	The Sinking of the Titanic (York)	SLP 190
		SLP 200
		SLP 393
5522	The Heroes of Bataan (E. Stoneman)	SLP 200
5523	Somebody's Waiting for Me (York)	SLP 200
5524	The Wreck of Number Nine (York)	SLP 200
		NLP 2063

5525	Going Home (Busby–S. Stoneman)	SLP 200
		SLP 393
5526	White Lightning, No. 2 (Richardson)	SLP 200
		SLP 393
5527	Nobody's Darling But Mine (Davis)	SLP 200
		SLP 393
5528	Lonesome Banjo (V. Stoneman)	SLP 201
		SLP 283
		NLP 2037
		NLP 2063
5529	It's Rain (V. Stoneman)	SLP 232
		NLP 2063

Personnel: Ernest Stoneman, vocal and Autoharp; Scott Stoneman, vocal and fiddle; Donna Stoneman, vocal and mandolin; Roni Stoneman, vocal and banjo; Van Stoneman, vocal and guitar; Jimmy Stoneman, vocal and bass. Label credit to the Stoneman Family.

STARDAY   *Nashville, Tenn., ca. Fall 1963*

6714	Turn Me Loose (Donna and Calvin Stoneman)	SLP 275
		SLP 393
		SLP 430
		SLP 1010
		NLP 2002
		NLP 2063
		G C 1011
6715	Family Life (Van Stoneman)	SLP 275
		NLP 2063
6716	Little Susie (Calvin Stoneman)	SLP 275
		NLP 2063
6717	Orange Blosson Breakdown (York)	SLP 275
		SLP 393
		SLP 430
		NLP 2002
		NLP 2058
		NLP 2063
6718	Life's Railway to Heaven (York)	SLP 275
		SLP 303
6719	I Want to Wander Down Yonder (York)	SLP 275
6720	Snow Deer (York)	SLP 275
		NLP 2063
6721	When Snowflakes Fall Again (Ernest Stoneman)	SLP 275
6722	One Hundred Years Ago (York)	SLP 275
		NLP 2063
6723	On the Banks of the Wabash (York)	SLP 275

6724	When the Roses Bloom Again (York)	SLP 275
6725	Wild Bill Hickok (York)	SLP 275
6726	Ellen Smith (York)	unissued
6727	Out Running Around (Van Stoneman)	unissued

Personnel and Credit: As on previous Starday records.
Note: some releases of "Talking Fiddle Blues" and "Orange Blossom Breakdown" may be to Scotty Stoneman only.

FOLK FESTIVAL   Beaumont, Tex., ca. January 1964

892-a	Big Ball in Houston	Fk F 1140
892-b	Little Maggie	Fk F 1140

Personnel and Credit: As on previous Starday records.
WORLD-PACIFIC   Hollywood, Calif., ca. May 1964

A 972	Big Ball in Monterey	W P 1828
		W P 45-413
		Sun 5203
	Little Maggie	W P 1828
		Sun 5203
	I Wonder How the Old Folks Are at Home (Vandersloot-Lambert)	W P 1828
	Domininque (Soeur Soirire)	W P 1828
		Sun 5203
	Sunny Tennessee	W P 1828
		Sun 5203
	Lost Ball in the High Weeds (A. and S. Johnson)	W P 1828
		Sun 5203
B 972	Ground Hog	W P 1828
		W P 45-413
		Sun 5203
	Busted (Harlan Howard)	W P 1828
	Take Me Home (Clement-Reynolds)	W P 1828
		Sun 5203
	Darling Corey	W P 1828
		Sun 5203
	Dark as a Dungeon (Merle Travis)	W P 1828
		Sun 5203
	Fire on the Mountain	W P 1828
		Sun 5203

Personnel and Credits: As on Starday and Folk Festival except that on "Dominique" Scott plays banjo and Van plays Dobro.
Note: Songs that are listed as traditional on World Pacific are credited to [Jack] Clement on Sunset.

M-G-M   Nashville, Tenn., ca. November 1965

65-XY-846	Tupelo County Jail (Tillis-Pierce)	MGM 13466
		MGM 4363

65-XY-847	Spell of the Freight Train (Clement)	MGM 13466
		MGM 4363
65-XY-848	Blue Ridge Mountain Blues (Clement)	MGM 4363
		MGM 4588
		MGM GAS124
65-XY-849	Mule Skinner Blues (Rodgers-Vaughn)	MGM 4363
		MGM GAS124

Personnel: Ernest Stoneman, Autoharp and lead vocal on 65-XY-848; Van Stoneman, guitar and lead vocal; Donna Stoneman, mandolin and harmony vocal; Roni Stoneman, banjo and harmony vocal; Jimmy Stoneman, bass and harmony vocal; other session musicians and vocalists, unknown. Label credits to the Stonemans.

M-G-M   *Nashville, Tenn., ca. December 1965*

65-XY-907	A Message from Home (E. Stoneman)	MGM 4363
		MGM 4588
		MGM GAS124
65-XY-908	Old Slew-Foot (H. Hausey)	MGM 4511
?	Cripple Creek (Stoneman)	MGM 4363
?	That's the Chance I'll Have to Take (King)	MGM 4363
?	Ashes of Love (Anglin-Anglin-Wright)	MGM 4363
?	Girl from the North Country (Dylan)	MGM 4363
?	He's My Friend (Meredith Willson)	MGM 4363
?	It Ain't Me Babe (Bob Dylan)	MGM 4363
?	My Dirty Lowdown, Rotten, Cotton Pickin' Little Darlin' (Clement)	MGM 4363
?	I Still Miss Someone (J Cash–R Cash, Jr.)	unissued

Personnel and Credits: As on above M-G-M session.

STONEHOUSE   *Nashville, Tenn., ca. spring 1966*

	Are You Washed in the Blood	Ston 10817
	Bring Back to Me My Wandering Boy	Ston 10817
	Endless Day	Ston 10817
	The Great Reaping Day	Ston 10817
	He's Calling for Me	Ston 10817
	How Will It Be with Your Soul	Ston 10817
	I'll Live On	Ston 10817
	In the Golden Bye and Bye	Ston 10817
	The Royal Telephone	Ston 10817
	The Uncloudy Day	Ston 10817
	When the Roll Is Called Up Yonder	Ston 10817
	Where the Soul of Man Never Dies	Ston 10817
	Where We'll Never Grow Old	Ston 10817
	In the Land Beyond the Blue	Ston 10817

Personnel and Credit: Ernest V. Stoneman, vocal and Autoharp.
Note: This material was recorded by Jack Clement to satisfy an over-due contractual obligation to Starday. Don Pierce chose to reject the material and release the Stonemans from their contract. Patsy Stoneman later recovered the tapes and released the material on her own label in a limited edition. Old Homestead Records intends to release these cuts in the future with a lightly overdubbed bass and rhythm guitar.

STONEHOUSE	Nashville, Tenn., ca. 1966–68	
	Rawhide (Bill Monroe)	Ston cas.*
	It Ain't Me Babe (Dylan)	Ston cas.*
	Nine Pound Hammer	Ston cas.*
	Busted (H. Howard)	Ston cas.*
	May I Sleep in Your Barn Tonight, Mister	Ston cas.*
	Ruby (Cousin Emmy Carver)	Ston cas.*
	I Am the Grass (?)	Ston cas.*
	Blues, Stay Away from Me (Delmore B)	Ston cas.*
	Roving Gambler	Ston cas.*
	Everybody Loves a Nut (J. Clement)	Ston cas.*
	Weeping Willow	Ston cas.*
	Roll in My Sweet Baby's Arms (Carter-Young)	Ston cas.*
	Under the Double Eagle (Wagner)	Ston cas.*

Personnel: Ernest Stoneman, vocal and Autoharp; Donna Stoneman, vocal and mandolin; Van Stoneman, vocal and guitar; Roni Stoneman, vocal and banjo; Jerry Monday, vocal and Dobro or drum; Jimmy Stoneman, vocal and bass; Hattie Stoneman, fiddle on "May I Sleep in Your Barn Tonight, Mister"; Bob Jennings, announcer.
*Note: In 1985, Patsy Stoneman assembled material from sound tracks of the Stoneman syndicated television shows, issuing it on an unnumbered cassette entitled *The Stoneman Family: Best of Their TV Shows, Volume I.*

M-G-M	Nashville, Tenn., ca. June–July 1966	
50052	The Five Little Johnson Girls (Clement)	MGM 13557
		MGM 4453
50053	Going Back to Bowling Green (Clement)	MGM 13557
		MGM 4453
50054	Back to Nashville, Tennessee (Clement)	MGM 13667
		MGM 4453

Personnel: As above, but add Jerry Monday, vocal and Dobro; Scott Stoneman, bowed banjo. Credit as above.

M-G-M	Nashville, Tenn., ca. late 1966	
50188	Queen Bee (Jack Clement)	unissued

| 50189 | Bottle of Wine (Tom Paxton) | MGM 13667 |
| | | MGM 4453 |

Personnel: As above, but delete Scott Stoneman. Credit as above.

M-G-M	*Nashville, Tenn., ca. February 1967*	
50264	Shady Grove (Clement)	MGM 4453
50265	There Goes My Everything (D. Frazier)	MGM 4453
50266	Winchester Cathedral (G. Stephens)	MGM 4453
59267	Early Morning Rain (G. Lightfoot)	MGM 4511
		MGM GAS124

Personnel and Credits: As above.

MM-G-M	*Nashville, Tenn., ca. February 1967 (slightly later)*	
50274	Cimarron (Johnny Bond)	MGM 13896
		MGM 4511
50275	Colorado Bound (Jerry Monday)	MGM 4453
		MGM GAS124
50276	Dirty Old Egg Suckin' Dog (Clement)	MGM 4511
50277	Ride, Ride, Ride (Liz Anderson)	MGM 4453
50278	Remember the Poor Tramp Has to Live (E. Stoneman)	MGM 4453
50279	Katie Klein (Ernest Stoneman)	MGM 4511
		MGM 4588
		MGM GAS124
50280	Got Leavin' on Her Mind (Clement)	MGM 4453

Personnel and credits: As above.

M-G-M	*Nashville, Tenn., ca. May–June 1967*	
50320	West Canterbury Subdivision Blues (Clement)	MGM 13755
		MGM 4511
50321	The Three Cent Opera (Jim Malloy)	MGM 13755
		MGM 4511

Personnel and credits: As above.

M-G-M	*Nashville, Tenn., ca. late 1967*	
50448	It's a New World Everyday (John Fitz-morris)	MGM 4511
50449	Rita, Put Your Black Shoes On (D. Kershaw)	MGM 4511
50450	??????????????????????????????	
50451	Tell It to My Heart Sometime (Clement)	MGM 13896
		MGM 4511
50452	The World Is Waiting for the Sunrise (Lockhart-Seitz)	MGM GAS124
		MGM 4511

Personnel and credits: As above.

M-G-M   Nashville, Tenn., ca. late 1967
50497   You're Gonna Be Sorry (Parton)   MGM 4578
50498   The Love I Left Behind (Van Stoneman)   MGM 13945
                                                    MGM 4578

Personnel and credits: As above.

M-G-M   Nashville, Tenn., ca. February 1968
50581   Wrinkled, Crinkled, Wadded Dollar Bill   MGM 4578
          (Vince Matthews)
50582   Christopher Robin (V. Matthews)   MGM 13945
                                                    MGM 4578
50583   Rolling in My Sweet Baby's Arms   MGM 4578
          (Clement)
50584   Bluegrass Ramble (Stoneman)   MGM 4578
                                                    MGM GAS124

Personnel and Credits: As above.

M-G-M   Nashville, Tenn., ca. April 11 and 12, 1968
50628   Baby Is Gone (Clement)   MGM4578
50629   Don't Think Twice (Bob Dylan)   MGM 4578
50630   Hello Dolly (Herman)   MGM 4578
50631   The Baby-O (Stoneman)   MGM 4578
                                                    MGM 4588
50632   Nine Pound Hammer (Merle Travis)   MGM 4578
                                                    MGM 4588
                                                    MGM GAS124

Personnel and Credits: As above.
Note: These are Ernest Stoneman's last live recordings.

M-G-M   Nashville, Tenn., ca. late August 1968
50735   Christmas Time's a-Comin' (B. F. Logan)   MGM 4613
50736   Blue Christmas (Hayes-Johnson)   MGM 4613
50737   A Welcome Stranger (Van and Grace Stone- MGM 4613
          man)
50738   Jingle Bells (Arr: Clement)   MGM 4613
Personnel and Credits: As above, except that Ernest Stoneman and
Jerry Monday deleted. Add Patsy Stoneman, vocal and Autoharp.

M-G-M   Nashville, Tenn., ca. early September 1968
50739   Little Jesus Loves Me (Anita McCune)   MGM 4613
50740   A Stoneman Christmas (Cy Coben)   MGM 4613
50741   Tell It Again (Jerry Foster–Bill Rice)   MGM 4613
50742   Let's Put Christ Back into Christmas (Vince MGM 4613
          Matthews–Kent Westbury)
50743   Santa Played the Autoharp (Cy Coben)   MGM 4613
50744   (I Won't Be) Present This Year (Foster-Rice) MGM 4613
50745   Christmas without Dad (George Hemrick)   MGM 4613
Personnel and Credits: As above.

Note: A time lapse of one or more days occurred in this session as the Stonemans took time out to fill a personal-appearance commitment.

M-G-M	*Nashville, Tenn., ca. November 1968*	
50821	God Is Alive and Well (V. Matthews–Eddie Rabbitt)	MGM 14018
50822	Travelin' Man (Donna Stoneman)	MGM 14018
		MGM GAS124

Personnel and Credits: As above.

M-G-M	*Nashville, Tenn., February 4 and 5, 1969*	
50900	I Love Corrina (Clement)	MGM 4588
50901	Stoney's Waltz (E. Stoneman)	MGM 4588
50902	Hallelujah Side (Clement)	MGM 4588
50903	Where the Soul Never Dies (Clement)	MGM 4588
50904	No Name for It Yet (E. Stoneman)	MGM 4588
50905	The Birds Are Returning (Clement)	MGM 4588
50906	The Mountaineer's Courtship (E. Stoneman)	MGM 4588

Note: This session consisted of overdubbing the above tracks taken from TV-show sound tracks for the *Pop Stoneman Memorial Album.*

RCA Victor   Nashville, Tenn., ca. July 1969 (note: independently produced master purchased by RCA Victor on September 25, 1969).

XWKS-2437	Two Kids from Duluth, Minnesota (Jack Clement–Alex Zanetis)	RCA 74-0266 RCA LP 4264
XWKS-2438	But You Know I Love You (Mike Settle)	RCA LP 4264
XWKS-2439	Bad Moon Rising (John Fogerty)	RCA LP 4264
XWKS-2440	In the Plan (Dillard-Clark-Leadon)	RCA LP 4264
XWKS-2441	Wildwood Flower	RCA LP 4264
XWKS-2442	Me and Bobby McGee (Kris Kristoffer-son–Fred Foster)	RCA LP 4264
XWKS-2443	Weed Out My Badness (Van Stoneman)	RCA LP 4264
XWKS-2444	All the Guys That Turn Me On Turn Me Down (Stoneman-Plott-Powell)	RCA LP 4264
XWKS-2445	Banjo Signal (Reno-Smiley)	RCA LP 4264
XWKS-2446	Tecumseh Valley (Townes–Van Zandt)	RCA 74-0266 RCA LP 4264
XWKS-2447	What Am I Doin' Hangin' 'Round (T. Lewis–B. Clarke)	RCA LP 4264
XWKS-2448	We Live in Two Different Worlds (Fred Rose)	unissued

Personnel: Van Stoneman, vocal and guitar; Donna Stoneman, vocal and mandolin; Roni Stoneman, vocal and banjo; Patsy Stoneman, vocal and Autoharp; Jimmy Stoneman, vocal and bass. Other musicians and vocalists, unknown. Label credits to the Stonemans.

RCA Victor   Nashville, Tenn., November 25, 1969

| XWKM-2623 | Let's Get Together (Chet Powers) | RCA 47-9793 |
| | | RCA LP 4343 |

XWKM-2624	Doesn't Anybody Know My Name	RCA 47-9793
	(R. McKuen)	RCA LP 4431
XWKM-2625	Looks Like Baby's Gone (M. Newbury)	unissued
XWKM 2626	Classical Vibrations (D. Stoneman)	unissued

Personnel and Credits: As above, but all additional session musicians deleted.

RCA Victor	*Nashville, Tenn., March 5, 1970*	
ZWKM-1039	I'll Be Here in the Morning (Townes–	RCA LP 4343
	Van Zandt)	
ZWKM-1040	Six White Horses (Clyde Moody)	RCA LP 4343
ZWKM-1041	According to the Plan (Roni Stone-	RCA LP 4343
	man–George Hemrick)	

Personnel and Credits: As above.

RCA Victor	*Nashville, Tenn., March 6, 1970*	
ZWKM-1042	Colossus (Donna Stoneman)	RCA LP 4343
ZWKM-1043	Who'll Stop the Rain (John Fogerty)	RCA LP 4343
ZWKM-1044	Somebody's Waiting for Me (Arr:	RCA LP 4343
	W. York)	
ZWKM-1045	Hang Them All (Tom T. Hall)	RCA LP 4343

Personnel and Credits: As above.

RCA Victor	*Nashville, Tenn., March 26, 1970*	
ZWKM-1046	Proud to Be Together (Donna Stone-	RCA LP 4343
	man–Cathy Manzer)	
ZWKM-1047	Don't Look Now (John Fogerty)	RCA LP 4343

Personnel and Credits: As above.

RCA Victor	*Nashville, Tenn., May 20, 1970*	
ZWKM-1543	Looks Like Baby's Gone (Mickey New-	RCA 47-9882
	bury)	RCA LP 4431
ZWKM-1544	Shades of Yesterday (Red Lane)	RCA LP 4431
ZWKM-1545	Jimmy's Thing (Jimmy Stoneman)	unissued

Personnel and Credits: As above.

RCA Victor	*Nashville, Tenn., June 10, 1970*	
ZWKM-1629	California Blues (Jimmie Rodgers)	RCA 47-9882
		RCA LP 4431
ZWKM-1630	Little Old Log Cabin in the Lane	RCA LP 4431
	(Hays)	
ZWKM-1631	Turner's Turnpike (Arr: Stonemans)	RCA LP 4431
ZWKM-1632	The Other World You Live In (Hem-	unissued
	rick)	

Personnel and Credits: As above.

RCA Victor   *Nashville, Tenn., July 16, 1970*

ZWKM-1703	I Take a Lot of Pride in What I Am (Merle Haggard)	RCA LP 4431
ZWKM-1704	Best Guitar Picker (Jack Clement)	RCA LP 4431
ZWKM-1705	Jimmy's Thing (Jimmy Stoneman)	RCA LP 4431
ZWKM-1706	Railroad Bill (Arr: Stonemans)	RCA LP 4431

Personnel and Credits: As above.

DISNEYLAND   *Burbank, Calif., ca. August 31, 1970*

    Country Bear Jamboree [Sound track]   Dis LP 3994

Personnel and Credits: As above.

CAPITOL   *Nashville, Tenn., May 4, 1971*

    Who Really Cares?   unissued
    ?????????   unissued
    ?????????   unissued
    ?????????   unissued

Personnel: As above with Larry Butler, keyboards, added; Roni Stoneman, deleted. According to Bob Bean, these tracks were probably uncompleted when George Richey departed from Capitol and the Stonemans' contract was terminated.

MILLION   *Nashville, Tenn., ca. September 1972*

1067	The Touch of the Master's Hand (US)	Million 32
1068	Blue Ridge Mountains (Dan Moose)	Million 32
????	?????????	unissued
????	?????????	unissued

Personnel: Van Stoneman, vocal and guitar; Donna Stoneman, vocal and mandolin; David Dougherty, vocal and banjo; Cathy Manzer, vocal and electric organ; Jimmy Stoneman, vocal and bass. Others unknown. Label credit to The Stonemans.

N A L   *Wembley and Other Locales in England, April 1, 1972; October–November 1972*

    Heartbreak Mountain   NAL LP 5005
    Bringing Mary Home   NAL LP 5005
    Sinking of the Titanic   NAL LP 5005
    Wreck of the Old 97   NAL LP 5005
    Trick or Treat   NAL LP 5005
    Doin' My Time   NAL LP 5005
    Sourwood Mountain   NAL LP 5005
    White Lightning, No. 2.   NAL LP 5005

Personnel: (April) Van Stoneman, guitar and vocal; Donna Stoneman, mandolin and vocal; Patsy Stoneman, Autoharp and vocal; Cathy Manzer, electric organ and vocal; Jimmy Stoneman, bass and vocal.

(October–November), delete Patsy Stoneman; David Dougherty, banjo and vocal. Although this album was advertised on the cover as recorded "live at Wembley," much of it was actually done that fall when the Stonemans returned to England. None of the material was ever released in the U.S.A. Label credit to the Stonemans.

CMH	*Charlotte, N.C., ca. mid-1976*	
	Ruby, Don't Take Your Love to Town (Mel Tillis)	CMH 6210
	What Am I Doin' Hangin' 'Round (M. Murphy)	CMH 6210
	The Prisoner's Song (Guy Massey)	CMH 6210
	Praise the Lord (Arthur Smith)	CMH 6210
	Let's All Go Down to the River (E. Montgomery–S. Richards)	CMH 6210
	Cuttin' the Grass (L. Flatt–B. Graves)	CMH 6210
	I Washed My Face in the Morning Dew (Tom T. Hall)	CMH 6210
	Heartbreak Mountain (Buck Owens)	CMH 6210
	Gypsy Woman (McDill-Reynolds)	CMH 6210
	Little Maggie (Arr: M. Christian)	CMH 6210
	Watermelon on the Vine (Arr: Christian)	CMH 6210
		CMH 5900

Personnel: Van Stoneman, guitar and vocal; Patsy Stoneman, guitar, Autoharp, Jew's harp, tambourine, and vocal; David Dougherty, banjo and vocal; Johnny Bellar, Dobro and vocal; Jimmy Stoneman, bass and vocal. Credit to the Stonemans.

R P A	*Nashville, Tenn., ca. late summer 1976*	
	Country Hospitality (Dallas Corey)	RPA 1019
	Caleb Johnson (D. Corey)	RPA 1019
	That's the Way the Old Ball Bounces (Corey)	RPA 1019
	Coon Hunt (Corey)	RPA 1019
	Send Old Grandpa Off in Style (Corey)	RPA 1019
	If God Is Dead, Who's Living in My Heart (Corey–Grace Pye)	RPA 1019 / ACE 0001
	Iney-Iney It-Zi Iney (Corey)	RPA 1019
	West Virginia Robin Hood (Corey)	RPA 1019
	Music City Yo-Yo (Corey)	RPA 1019
	That's How It Is in the Mountains (Corey)	RPA 1019
	Head to Toe I'm Country (Corey)	RPA 1019
	Touch My Heart Sweet Jesus (Corey)	RPA 1019

Personnel and Credits: As above.

CMH	*Albuquerque, N. M., ca. late March 1977*	
	Mama Don't Allow (M. Christian)	CMH 6219
	Tecumseh Valley (Christian)	CMH 6219
	Soldier's Joy (Christian)	CMH 6219
		CMH 5900

You Better Listen (P. Stoneman)	CMH 6219
Dream of the Miner's Child (Christian)	CMH 6219
Wreck of the Old 97 (Christian)	CMH 6219
City of New Orleans (Steve Goodman)	CMH 6219
Beans and Make Believe (R. D. McCormack)	CMH 6219
Sand Mountain (John Bellar)	CMH 6219
	CMH ????
Lucille (R. Bowling–H. Bynum)	CMH 6219
Steel Guitar Rag (L. McAuliffe)	CMH 6219
White Lightning, No. 2 (Richardson)	CMH 6219

Personnel and Credits: As above, except Eddie Mueller replaces David Dougherty on banjo.

Note: This album was recorded before a live studio audience.

STONEHOUSE   *McKinney, Tx., ca. midsummer 1980*

Steel Guitar Rag [J. Bellar, Dobro]	Ston 001
Red Bandanna [J. Stoneman, solo vocal]	Ston 001
Mama Don't Allow [V. Stoneman, solo vocal]	Ston 001
The Poor Tramp [J. Stoneman, solo vocal]	Ston 001
Soldier's Joy [P. Stoneman, Jew's harp]	Ston 001
But You Know I Love You [V. Stoneman, vocal]	Ston 001
Sand Mountain [J. Bellar, Dobro]	Ston 001
Jimmy's Thing [J. Stoneman, bass]	Ston 001
Dobro Chimes [J. Bellar, Dobro]	Ston 001
Heartbreak Mountain [E. Mueller, banjo]	Ston 001
That's What You Get For Loving Me [Van, vocal]	Ston 001
Beyond the Sunset [J. Bellar, Dobro]	Ston 001
Don't Think Twice [Van, solo vocal]	Ston 001
Truck Drivin' Man [Van, solo vocal]	Ston 001
Tennessee Walker [Eddie Mueller, banjo]	Ston 001
Wreck of the Old 97 [P. Stoneman, vocal and Autoharp]	Ston 001
Stoney's Waltz [P. Stoneman, Autoharp]	Ston 001
John Henry [P. Stoneman, clawhammer banjo]	Ston 001
Soldier's Joy [P. Stoneman, Jew's harp]	Ston 001

Personnel: Van Stoneman, guitar and vocal; Patsy Stoneman, guitar, Autoharp, Jew's harp, and vocal; Johnny Bellar, Dobro; Eddie Mueller, banjo; Jimmy Stoneman, bass and vocal. Credit to the Stoneman Family.

Note: this material recorded live at a bluegrass festival in Texas, released on cassette only.

CMH   *Nashville, Tenn., January–February 1981*

Under the Double Eagle (M. Christian) [Donna Stoneman, mandolin]	CMH 9029
Blue Ridge Mountain Blues (E. Stoneman) [P. Stoneman, vocal]	CMH 9029

Caribbean (M. Torok) [J. Stoneman, vocal]	CMH 9029
Muleskinner Blues (Rodgers) [Dean Stoneman, mandolin and vocal]	CMH 9029
Tupelo County Jail (Tillis-Pierce) [V. Stoneman, vocal]	CMH 9029
Peaceful Easy Feeling (J. Tempchin) [V. Stoneman, Jr., vocal]	CMH 9029
The Poor Tramp Has to Live (Christian) [J. Stoneman, vocal]	CMH 9029
Honeymoon on a Rocket Ship (J. Masters) [G. Stoneman, vocal]	CMH 9029
Old Joe Clark (Christian) [Eddie Stoneman, fiddle]	CMH 9029
When the Snowflakes Fall Again (E. Stoneman) [Grace and Donna K. Jewell, vocals]	CMH 9029
I'm Thinking Tonight of My Blue Eyes (Christian) [Dean Stoneman, vocal]	CMH 9029
Life's Railway to Heaven (Christian) [Donna Stoneman, vocal and mandolin]	CMH 9029 Ruta 3012
Fire on the Mountain (G. McCorkle) [V. Stoneman, Jr., vocal]	CMH 9029
Whippoorwill Song (Christian) [P. Stoneman, vocal and Autoharp]	CMH 9029
I Left My Gal in the Mountains (Carson Robison) [Eddie Stoneman, vocal]	CMH 9029
I Take A Lot of Pride in What I Am (Merle Haggard) [Ron Stoneman, vocal]	CMH 9029
Old Shep (Clyde Foley) [Jack Stoneman, guitar and vocal]	CMH 9029
Orange Blossom Special (Christian) [Donna Stoneman, mandolin]	CMH 9029
Little Old Log Cabin in the Lane (Christian) [V. Stoneman, vocal and clawhammer banjo]	CMH 9029
Guitar Boogie (Arthur Smith) [Eddie Stoneman, electric lead guitar]	CMH 9029
Lonesome Road Blues (Christian) [Roni Stoneman with Barbara Cox and Georgia Hemrick, vocals]	CMH 9029
Cripple Creek (Christian) [V. Stoneman and group, vocals]	CMH 9029
Amie (C. Fuller) [Randy Stoneman, vocals and electric bass]	CMH 9029
Prayers and Pinto Beans (Patsy Stoneman) [P. Stoneman and group, vocals]	CMH 9029 Ruta 3012

Personnel: Van Stoneman, guitar; Patsy Stoneman, guitar, Autoharp, maracas, tambourine, Jew's harp; Eddie Mueller, banjo; Johnny Bellar, Dobro; Jimmy Stoneman, bass; others as indicated above.

Note: Roni, Barbara, and Georgia were not in the studio; their tracks were recorded in Mansfield, Ohio, and overdubbed in Nashville.

STONEHOUSE   Nashville, Tenn., October 31, 1981

Old Joe Clark	Ston cas*
Stoney's Waltz	Ston cas*
Muleskinner Blues	Ston cas*
Tupelo County Jail	Ston cas*
Jimmy's Thing	Ston cas*
Fire on the Mountain	Ston cas*
[All I Have to Do Is] Dream	Ston cas*
[Mr.] Bojangles	Ston cas*
Old Chunk of Coal	Ston cas*
Gospel Medley	Ston cas*
Orange Blossom Special	Ston cas*

Personnel: Van Stoneman, vocal and guitar; Donna Stoneman, vocal and mandolin; Patsy Stoneman, vocal and guitar, Autoharp, maracas; Johnny Bellar, Dobro; Charles Holcomb, banjo; Jimmy Stoneman, vocal and bass.
*Note: This was recorded at a live concert in the Roy Acuff Theater at Opryland and issued on an un-numbered cassette only.

HERITAGE   Galax, Va., August 7 and 8, 1985

The Poor Tramp Has to Live	Heri LP 701
Theme for Roni [comedy routine]	Heri LP 701
Foggy Mountain Breakdown	Heri LP 701
Somebody's Waiting for Me	Heri LP 701
Stoney's Waltz	Heri LP 701
Sinking of the Titanic	Heri LP 701
The Girl from Galax	Heri LP 701

Personnel: Van Stoneman, guitar and vocal; Donna Stoneman, mandolin and vocal; Roni Stoneman, banjo and vocal; Patsy Stoneman, guitar, Autoharp, and vocal; Jimmy Stoneman, bass and vocal. Credit to the Stoneman Family. This material was recorded live at the 1985 Galax Old Fiddler's Convention and released as part of a commemorative double album.

RUTABAGA   Nashville, Tenn., ca. 1986 (two or three sessions)

Family Bible (Gray-Buskirk-Breeland)	Ruta 3012
If God Is Dead, Who's Living in My Heart (Corey-Pye)	Ruta 3012
Written on the Rainbow [Benny Martin, vocal]	unissued
What a Friend We Have in Jesus [instrumental]	unissued
Sinner Man (Arr: Stonemans)	Ruta 3012
Can the Circle Be Unbroken (Arr: Stonemans)	Ruta 3012
I'll Fly Away [instrumental] (Brumley)	Ruta 3012

God Has Made a Little Corner for Me [Benny Martin, vocal]	unissued
He Was There All the Time (Paxton)	Ruta 3012
In the Garden (Miles)	Ruta 3012
The Old Rugged Cross [instrumental]	unissued
Where the Soul of Man Never Dies (Golden)	Ruta 3012
When They Ring the Golden Bells	unissued
Somebody Touched Me	Ruta 3012

Personnel: Van Stoneman, vocal and guitar; Donna Stoneman, vocal and mandolin; Roni Stoneman, vocal and banjo; Patsy Stoneman, vocal, guitar, and Autoharp; Benny Martin, fiddle (and vocal on unissued cuts as indicated); Jack Linneman, Dobro (primarily on unissued cuts); Jimmy Stoneman, bass. Label credit to the Stonemans.

OLD HOMESTEAD   *Lebanon, Tenn., ca. late 1989 (two or three sessions)*

I Saw the Light (Hank Williams)	O H 90200
He Shall Lift You Up (Richard Burt)	O H 90200
Turn to Jesus (D. Stoneman–B. Wilkinson)	O H 90200
White Wings (D. Stoneman)	O H 90200
A Light Lit Up in Galilee (P. Stoneman)	O H 90200
The Great Speckled Bird (Guy Smith)	O H 90200
Old Glory (Cread Holland–D. Stoneman)	O H 90200
Sinner Man (Arr: Stonemans)	O H 90200
Grand Old Flag (Arr: Stonemans)	O H 90200
U. S. A. Forever (Arr: Stonemans)	O H 90200
The Star-Spangled Banner (Francis S. Key)	O H 90200

Personnel: Van Stoneman, vocal and banjo; Donna Stoneman, vocal and mandolin; Patsy Stoneman, vocal and guitar, Autoharp; Randy Stoneman, vocal harmony; Van Stoneman, Jr., vocal harmony and solo lead on "The Star-Spangled Banner"; Jimmy Stoneman, vocal and bass.

The following long-play albums are credited to either the Stoneman Family or the Stonemans:

Starday SLP 200	*Bluegrass Champs*
Starday SLP 275	*The Great Old Timer at the Capitol*
Starday SLP 393	*White Lightning* (reissue of above material)
Nashville NLP 2063	*The Stonemans* (reissue of above material)
World-Pacific 1828	*Big Ball in Monterey*
Sunset 5203	*The Stoneman Family "Live"* (budget label of World-Pacific album)
M-G-M E/SE 4363	*Those Singin', Swingin', Stompin', Sensational Stonemans*
M-G-M E/SE 4453	*Stonemans' Country*
M-G-M E/SE 4511	*All in the Family*
M-G-M E/SE 4578	*The Great Stonemans*
M-G-M E/SE 4588	*Pop Stoneman Memorial Album*

M-G-M E/SE 4613	*A Stoneman Christmas*
M-G-M GAS 124	*The Stonemans* (reissue of previously released material)
RCA LSP 4264	*Dawn of the Stonemans' Age*
RCA LSP 4343	*In All Honesty*
RCA LSP 4431	*California Blues*
NAL 5005	*Live at Wembley* (released only in U.K.)
CMH 6210	*Cuttin' the Grass*
CMH 6219	*On the Road*
CMH 9029	*The First Family of Country Music* (two album set)
RPA LP 1019	*Country Hospitality*
Stonehouse 10817	*A Rare Find!* (solo cuts by Ernest Stoneman, previously recorded by Jack Clement for Starday but rejected).
Rutabaga RR 3012	*Family Bible*
Old Homestead OHS 90200	*For God and Country*

A substantial number of the following albums devote a substantial portion of space to either the Stonemans or the Stoneman Family:

Folkways FA 2315	*Old Time Tunes of the South* (Side A)
Folkways FA 2365	*Mountain Music Played on the Autoharp* (six cuts)
Wyncote W-9032	*Country Favorites: Jimmy Dean/The Stoneman Family* (Side B)
Disneyland LP 3994	*Country Bear Jamboree* (Most of Side A)
Heritage HRC 701	*50th Annual Galax Fiddlers Convention* (seven cuts of a two-album set)

The following items featuring the Stonemans have been released on cassette only:

Stonehouse 001	*Hot and Gettin' Hotter*
Stonehouse No #	*Live! at the Roy Acuff Theater*
Stonehouse No #	*The Stoneman Family, Volume I: "Live" from Their T.V. Shows*

Recordings by Individual Stoneman Family Members

This portion of the discography includes those Stonemans who have recorded under their individual names. These include Ernest Stoneman's children, Roni, Scott, and Donna, as well as those of his first cousins, Burton and George. It does not include those of the Stonemans who may have been merely sidepersons or session musicians on recordings credited to others, nor does it include those of more distant relatives, such as Brian Bowers, Ted Lundy, Emmet Lundy, or Rosa Landreth Cox.

Label Abbreviations Used in Discography

Bri	Briar	[D S]	Donna Stoneman cassette
Cht	Chart	JED	J.E.D.
CML	Country Music Legend	L of C	Library of Congress
CMT	Country Music Time	O H	Old Homestead
Cty	County	Sp Ck	Spin Chek
Dsgn	Design	St Ra	Stone Ray
Dot	Dot	Tem	Temple

Matrix No.   Title (compose credit and/or musical credit)   Release No.

Burton Stoneman

LIBRARY OF CONGRESS   *Galax, Va., August 1941*

AFS 4936 A	[John and Elizabeth Lomax talk with Burton Stoneman]	unissued
	Wagon Tightener	unissued
	Waves on the Ocean	unissued
AFS 4936 B	I'm Gonna Marry that Pretty Little Girl	unissued
	[Unidentified Favorite of Green Leonard]	unissued
	Fiddler's Dram	unissued
	[Small Fragments in Four Keys]	unissued
AFS 4937 B	Cindy (1)	unissued

Personnel: Burton Stoneman, fiddle and talking; (1) add George Stoneman, banjo.

George Stoneman

LIBRARY OF CONGRESS   *Galax, Va., August 1941*

AFS 4937 B	[Elizabeth Lomax talks with George Stoneman]	unissued
	Sally Ann	unissued
	Say Darling Say	unissued
	Cripple Creek	unissued
AFS 4938 A	[unidentified tune]	unissued
	Shady Grove	unissued
	John Hardy	unissued

Personnel: George Stoneman, talking and banjo.
Note: Remainder of AFS 4938 is by Emmet Lundy.

FOLKWAYS   *Galax, Va., August 1961, 1962, or 1963*

	Sally Ann	Fw FA 2935

Personnel: George Stoneman, banjo.
Note: Recorded at Galax Old Fiddler's Convention.

COUNTY   *Galax, Va., October 1964*
          Sweet Boys Tune   Cty 701
          Richmond   Cty 701
          Sandy River Belle   Cty 701
          Stoneman's Tune   Cty 701
          Jimmy Sutton   Cty 757
Personnel: George Stoneman, banjo.

Veronica (Roni) Stoneman

FOLKWAYS   *Washington, D.C. (?), ca. 1956*
          Lonesome Road Blues (1)   Fw FA 2314
          Wildwood Flower (2)   Fw FA 2314
Personnel: Roni Stoneman, banjo; Eugene Cox, guitar (1); Eugene Cox, banjo; Roni Stoneman, guitar (2).

DOT   *Nashville, Tenn., ca. 1972 (two sessions)*
26273   Southbound U. S. A. (Billy Sherill)   Dot 17403
26274   Don't You Kinda Get the Feeling   Dot 17403
          (Hemrick-Plott)
26601   I'm Gonna Keep On Loving Him (Ann   Dot 17431
          Wilson–C. Taylor)
26602   ?????????????????
26603   You Make Me Feel Like Singing (Ann Wil-   Dot 17431
          son–D. Walls)
Personnel: Roni Stoneman, vocal; Donna Stoneman, mandolin; others unknown. Label credit to Roni Stoneman.

CHART   *Nashville, Tenn., ca. 1974*
5226 A   Roy (Ann Morton) (1)   Cht 5226
5226 B   You Can't Take Country from Me (Morton)   Cht 5226
Personnel: Roni Stoneman, vocal; others unknown; (1) add Roy Clark, vocals.

COUNTRY MUSIC TIME   *Nashville, Tenn., ca. late 1974*
73640   Dirty Old Egg Suckin' Dog   C M T #391
          Ruby, Are You Mad at Your Man (1)   C M T #391
Personnel: Roni Stoneman, talking, vocal, and banjo; others unknown; (1) add Harold Morrison, banjo; remainder of #391 by Harold Morrison. Note: This is a program for radio airplay made by the U.S. Air Force to promote recruitment.

SPIN CHEK   *Nashville, Tenn., ca. 1975*
UR 1464   Tomorrow's Child (Geo. Hemrick)   Sp Ck 10305

Personnel: Roni Stoneman, vocal; others unknown.
Note: This 45 *rpm* disc was issued in deejay format only, with the same cut on both sides.

STONE RAY   *Mount Juliet, Tenn., ca. October 1989*

Foggy Mountain Breakdown	St Ra cas.
Cripple Creek	St Ra cas.
Lonesome Road Blues	St Ra cas.
Grandfather's Clock	St Ra cas.
Deliverance [Dueling Banjos]	St Ra cas.
Shuckin' the Corn	St Ra cas.
Spinning Wheel	St Ra cas.
Dear Old Dixie	St Ra cas.
Home Sweet Home	St Ra cas.
Foggy Mountain Special	St Ra cas.
Banjo Signal	St Ra cas.
Lady of Spain	St Ra cas.

Personnel: Roni Stoneman, banjo; Donna Stoneman, mandolin; Bobby Stoneman [Robert Cox], guitar; Jimmy Stoneman, bass. Above issued on *Roni Stoneman: First Lady of Banjo,* Stone Ray cassette (no number).

STONE RAY   *Mount Juliet, Tenn., ca, October 1989*

Watermelon Wine	St Ra cas.
Walkin' after Midnight	St Ra cas.
Wreck of the Ole 97	St Ra cas.
I'm So Lonesome I Could Cry	St Ra cas.
Your Cheatin' Heart	St Ra cas.
Wabash Cannonball	St Ra cas.
Cowboy's Sweetheart	St Ra cas.
Lone Star Two Step [instrumental]	St Ra cas.
Honky Tonk Angel	St Ra cas.
Mama Don't Allow	St Ra cas.

Personnel: Roni Stoneman: vocal and banjo; Donna Stoneman, mandolin; Cliff Parker, electric guitar; Bobby Stoneman [Robert Cox], acoustical guitar; Martin Parker, drums; Lee Southerland, piano; David Owens, bass; Jennifer O'Brien, Sandy Posey, Mary Fielder, background vocals. All material issued as *Roni Stoneman: Pure and Country,* Stone Ray cassette (no number).

Scott Stoneman

OLD HOMESTEAD   *Nashville, Tenn., ca. Spring 1962**

The Eighth of January	O H 90202
Scott's Hoedown [Gray Eagle]	O H 90202
Arkansas Traveler	O H 90202

Boil Them Cabbage Down	O H 90202
Scott's Breakdown	O H 90202
Fire on the Mountain	O H 90202
Once I Had a Fortune	O H 90202
Cotton-Eyed Joe	O H 90202
Cherokee Waltz	O H 90202
Mocking Bird	O H 90202
Turkey in the Straw	O H 90202

Personnel: Scott Stoneman, fiddle; Van Stoneman, guitar; Donna Stoneman, mandolin; Roni Stoneman, banjo; Jimmy Stoneman, bass.
Note: these recordings were made by Billy Barton for release on either his Gulf Reef or his Fire label. They were believed lost for about twenty-five years until Billy Barton's daughter returned the master tapes to Patsy Stoneman. Patsy initially released them on an unlabeled cassette simply titled *Scotty Stoneman; The Lost Master*.
*Patsy Stoneman believes this material dates from 1959. It is my belief that it was recorded in roughly the same time period as the other masters cut by Billy Barton for Gulf Reef.

BRIAR	*Los Angeles, Calif., March 27 and August 1965*	
	Oklahoma Stomp [instrumental]	Bri 4206
	Once a Day	Bri 4206
	Eighth of January [instrumental]	Bri 4206
	Any Damn Thing	Bri 4206
	Down Yonder [instrumental]	Bri 4206
	Sally Goodin' [instrumental]	Bri 4206
	A Wound Time Can't Erase	Bri 4206
	Cherokee Waltz [instrumental]	Bri 4206
	Cacklin' Hen [instrumental]	Bri 4206
	Goodnight Irene	Bri 4206

Personnel: Scott Stoneman, vocal and fiddle; Clarence White, guitar; Roland White, mandolin; Billy Ray Latham, banjo; Roger Bush, bass.
Label credit to Scotty Stoneman with the Kentucky Colonels.
Note: this material remastered from tapes of live shows made at the Ash Grove and at the Cobblestone Club.

DESIGN	*Washington, D.C., ca. early 1967*	
	Low Down Billy	Dsgn 636
		CML 4
	Talkin' Fiddle Blues	Dsgn 636
		CML 4
	Ole Joe Clark	Dsgn 636
		CML 4
	Fire in the Mountain	Dsgn 636
		CML 4
	Billy Low Ground [sic]	Dsgn 636
		CML 4

Eighth of January	Dsgn 636
	CML 4
The Cacklin' Hen	Dsgn 636
	CML 4
Wildwood Flower	Dsgn 636
	CML 4
Orange Blossom Hoedown	Dsgn 636
	CML 4
The Mocking Bird	Dsgn 636
	CML 4

Personnel: Scott Stoneman, fiddle; Charlie Waller, guitar; Bill Emerson, banjo; Tom Grey, bass; others unknown. Label credit to Scotty Stoneman.

J. E. D.   *Nashville, Tenn., April 1, 1967*

8442 BW	You're Gonna Wonder about Me (Mel Tillis)	JED 10012
8443 BW	Big Wheel in Nashville (B. Wilder–Paula Brogan–K. Riley)	JED 10012
??	Orange Blossom Special	unissued
??	Suzie	unissued
??	Scotty's Tune	unissued

Personnel: Scott Stoneman, vocal and fiddle; Patsy Stoneman, guitar; Jack Stoneman, bass; others unknown. Label credit to Scottie Stoneman.

J. E. D.   *Nashville, Tenn., March 4, 1968*

8797	The Martian Band (Paul Brogan Stoneman)	JED 10019
8798	May I Sleep in Your Barn Tonight, Mister (Arr: John Denny–Scott Stoneman)	JED 10019
????	Tie Me to Your Aporn Strings Again	JED ?????
????	Grandfather's Clock	JED ?????
????	John Henry	unissued

Personnel and credit: As above, but add Hattie Stoneman, fiddle, on 8798.

Donna Stoneman

TEMPLE   *Nashville, Tenn., ca. 1976*

I'll Fly Away (Arr: D. Stoneman)	Tem 7706
Leaning on the Arms of Jesus (Phil Johnson)	Tem 7706
There Is Hope (D. Stoneman–Cathy Manzer)	Tem 7706
Psalm 92 (D. Stoneman–C. Manzer)	Tem 7706
Don't Get into Jesus (C. Manzer–Skeeter Davis)	Tem 7706
Is It Too Much to Ask (C. Manzer)	Tem 7706
David's Song (D. Stoneman)	Tem 7706
	[D S]*

Oh! That Joy (D. Stoneman)   Tem 7706
                                              [D S]*#
Jesus Loves Me (Arr: C. Manzer)   Tem 7706
Sanctified Orange Blossom Special (Arr: Tem 7706
   D. Stoneman)   [D S]*

Personnel: Donna Stoneman, vocal and mandolin; Cathy Manzer, vocal and guitar (piano on "David's Song"); Donnie Marrs, drums; Ray Edwards, banjo; Mike Hartgrove, fiddle-viola; Jimmy Murrell, electric guitar (harmonica on "Is It Too Much to Ask"); Jody Wence, piano-flute; Buck Evans, bass; Terry McMillan (harmonica on "Sanctified Orange Blossom Special"); Clayton Head (rhythm guitar on "Sanctified Orange Blosson Special"); Steve Davis (recitation on "Is It Too Much to Ask"). Label credit to Donna Stoneman and Cathy Manzer.

[*DONNA STONEMAN*]   *Nashville, Tenn., ca. Summer 1981*
   Power in the Blood   [D S]*#
   Were You There   [D S]*#
   Jehosophat   [D S]*
   Life's Railway to Heaven   [D S]*
   A New Name in Glory   [D S]*#
   The Hallelujah Side   [D S]*#
   Jesus Set Me Free ["Rocky Top" parody] [D S]*
   I'll Fly Away   [D S]#
   He Was There All the Time   [D S]#
   Old Rugged Cross   [D S]#

Personnel: Donna Stoneman, vocal and mandolin; Van Stoneman; guitar; Patsy Stoneman, guitar; Eddie Mueller, banjo; Johnny Bellar, Dobro; Mitch Fuston, fiddle; Jimmy Stoneman, bass.

Note: This material has been issued on cassette only in two formats.

*Donna Stoneman and Family—Gospel—
#Donna Stoneman and the Stoneman Family: "Old Rugged Cross"

The titles on each unlabeled cassette vary somewhat. Some cuts are taken from the album Temple TLS 7706

The following long-play albums are credited to an individual Stoneman:

Design LP 636	*Scotty Stoneman: Mr. Country Fiddler*
CML 4	*Bluegrass Fiddlin' Banjo Hits* (reissue of above LP with additional material by Bill Emerson)
Briar 4206	*Scotty Stoneman with the Kentucky Colonels*
Old Homestead 90202	*Scotty Stoneman: The Lost Masters* (LP is still unreleased; cassette has been released)
Temple TLS 7706	*Donna Stoneman and Cathy Manzer: I'll Fly Away*

The following albums contain cuts credited to an individual Stoneman:

Folkways FA 2365	*The Galax Old Time Fiddler's Convention* (one cut by George Stoneman)

| County 701 | *Clawhammer Banjo* (four cuts by George Stoneman) |
| County 757 | *Clawhammer Banjo #3* (one cut by George Stoneman) |

The following items featuring an individual Stoneman have been released on cassette only:

Stone Ray no #	*Roni Stoneman: First Lady of Banjo*
Stone Ray no #	*Roni Stoneman: Pure and Country*
No label, no #	*Donna Stoneman and Family—Gospel—*
No label, no #	*Dona Stoneman and the Stoneman Family: "Old Rugged Cross"*

Videocassettes Featuring The Stonemans

OPRYLAND U. S. A. HOME VIDEO

Greats of the Grand Ole Opry, Volume 1: Train Songs Hosted by Boxcar Willie (released 1987). This VCR tape contains one cut by the Stonemans on which they sing "The Atlantic Coastal Line," a number not otherwise recorded by them. The source of this has not yet been identified, but it is not from their syndicated TV shows; it dates from 1966–68 because those pictured are Van, Donna, Roni, Jimmy, and Jerry Monday. Ernest Stoneman is in his rocking chair but is neither playing nor singing.

None of the Stoneman syndicated TV shows has yet appeared on home videocassette, although they may at some future time.

The Stonemans appeared in the following motion pictures:
The Road to Nashville (Robert Patrick Productions, 1967)
Hell on Wheels (Robert Patrick Productions, 1967)
Neither has been released on home video at this time (1991).

Index

Ivan M. Tribe is a professor of history at the University of Rio Grande in Rio Grande, Ohio. He is the author of *Mountaineer Jamboree: Country Music in West Virginia* (1984); numerous articles in *Bluegrass Unlimited, Old Time Music,* and other publications; and liner notes for many country music LPs, including four Stoneman Family LPs. He also serves as record review editor for the *Appalachian Journal.*

Books in the Series Music in American Life

Only a Miner: Studies in Recorded Coal-Mining Songs
Archie Green

Great Day Coming: Folk Music and the American Left
R. Serge Denisoff

John Philip Sousa: A Descriptive Catalog of His Works
Paul E. Bierley

The Hell-Bound Train: A Cowboy Songbook
Glenn Ohrlin

Oh, Didn't He Ramble: The Life Story of Lee Collins,
as Told to Mary Collins
Edited by Frank J. Gillis and John W. Miner

American Labor Songs of the Nineteenth Century
Philip S. Foner

Stars of Country Music: Uncle Dave Macon to Johnny Rodriguez
Edited by Bill C. Malone and Judith McCulloh

Git Along, Little Dogies: Songs and Songmakers of the American West
John I. White

A Texas-Mexican Cancionero: Folksongs of the Lower Border
Americo Paredes

San Antonio Rose: The Life and Music of Bob Wills
Charles R. Townsend

Early Downhome Blues: A Musical and Cultural Analysis
Jeff Todd Titon

An Ives Celebration: Papers and Panels of the Charles Ives
Centennial Festival-Conference
Edited by H. Wiley Hitchcock and Vivian Perlis

Sinful Tunes and Spirituals: Black Folk Music to the Civil War
Dena J. Epstein

Joe Scott, the Woodsman-Songmaker
Edward D. Ives

Jimmie Rodgers: The Life and Times of America's Blue Yodeler
Nolan Porterfield

Goin' to Kansas City
Nathan W. Pearson, Jr.

"Susanna," "Jeanie," and "The Old Folks at Home": The Songs of
Stephen C. Foster from His Time to Ours
Second Edition
William W. Austin

Songprints: The Musical Experience of Five Shoshone Women
Judith Vander

"Happy in the Service of the Lord": Afro-American Gospel
Quartets in Memphis
Kip Lornell

Paul Hindemith in the United States
Luther Noss

"My Song Is My Weapon": People's Songs, American Communism,
and the Politics of Culture
Robbie Lieberman

Chosen Voices: The Story of the American Cantorate
Mark Slobin

Theodore Thomas: America's Conductor and Builder
of Orchestras, 1835-1905
Ezra Schabas

"The Whorehouse Bells Were Ringing" and
Other Songs Cowboys Sing
Guy Logsdon

Crazeology: The Autobiography of a Chicago Jazzman
Bud Freeman, as Told to Robert Wolf

Discoursing Sweet Music: Brass Bands and Community Life
in Turn-of-the-Century Pennsylvania
Kenneth Kreitner

Mormonism and Music: A History
Michael Hicks

Voices of the Jazz Age: Profiles of Eight Vintage Jazzmen
Chip Deffaa

Pickin' on Peachtree: A History of Country Music in Atlanta, Georgia
Wayne W. Daniel

Bitter Music: Collected Journals, Essays, Introductions, and Librettos
Harry Partch; edited by Thomas McGeary

Ethnic Music on Records: A Discography of Ethnic Recordings
Produced in the United States, 1893 to 1942
Richard K. Spottswood

Downhome Blues Lyrics: An Anthology from
the Post-World War II Era
Jeff Todd Titon

Ellington: The Early Years
Mark Tucker

Chicago Soul
Robert Pruter

That Half-Barbaric Twang: The Banjo in American Popular Culture
Karen Linn

Hot Man: The Life of Art Hodes
Art Hodes and Chadwick Hansen

The Erotic Muse: American Bawdy Songs
Second Edition
Ed Cray

Barrio Rhythm: Mexican American Music in Los Angeles
Steven Loza

The Creation of Jazz: Music, Race, and Culture in Urban America
Burton W. Peretti

Charles Martin Loeffler: A Life Apart in Music
Ellen Knight

Club Date Musicians: Playing the New York Party Circuit
Bruce A. MacLeod

Opera on the Road: Traveling Opera Troupes in the United States, 1825-60
Katherine K. Preston

The Stonemans: An Appalachian Family and the Music That
Shaped Their Lives
Ivan M. Tribe